THIS DATE IN

St. Louis Cardinals

HISTORY

THIS DATE IN

St. Louis Cardinals

HISTORY

**John Leptich
and Dave Baranowski**

5B

A SCARBOROUGH BOOK

STEIN AND DAY/*Publishers*/New York

The material on the St. Louis Cardinals-St. Louis Browns City Series, 1903-1923 is incorporated with the permission of Paul Fauks, Cardinal director of minor league operations.

Photographs are reprinted with the permission of the St. Louis National Baseball Club, Inc., and those attributed to *The Sporting News* are reprinted with the permission of that periodical.

Material includes pertinent information to up and including October 11, 1982.

First published in 1983
Copyright © 1983 by John Leptich and Dave Baranowski
All rights reserved, Stein and Day, Inc.
Designed by Louis A. Ditizio
Printed in the United States of America
Stein and Day/*Publishers*
Scarborough House
Briarcliff Manor, N.Y. 10510

Library of Congress Cataloging in Publication Data

Leptich, John, 1949–
    This date in St. Louis Cardinals history.

    "A Scarborough book."
    1. St. Louis Cardinals (Baseball team)—
History. I. Baranowski, Dave, 1954–
II. Title.
GV875.S3L45   1983   796.357′64′0977866   81-40803
ISBN 0-8128-6133-7 (pbk.)   AACR2

To Florence and John V. Leptich, and
Rosa and Amanda Leptich.
He would have been proud, they can
share in the accomplishment.

JAL

To Mr. and Mrs. John Baranowski, for
more than I could ever repay.

DJB

ACKNOWLEDGMENTS

To the St. Louis Cardinals public relations director Jim Toomey, assistant public relations director Robin Monsky, traveling secretary C.J. Cherre, and player development director Paul Fauks. Fauk's six-volume *Cardinal Chronology* is a masterpiece, filling in many holes, especially in the early days.

To *The Sporting News,* especially editor Dick Kaegel, associate editor Ben Henkey, and historian-archivist Paul Mac Farlane. Their fine series of publications, including *The Baseball Register, Baseball Guide,* and *Baseball Dope Book* provided many statistical entries.

To the public relations people of both Chicago baseball teams—Chuck Shriver and Ken Valdiserri of the White Sox; Peter Mead and Bob Ibach. Also Tom Skibosh of the Milwaukee Brewers.

To the staffs of the Chicago and St. Louis Public Libraries who must have found humor in two grown men looking through so much microfilm in so little time.

To the *St. Louis Globe-Democrat* and the *St. Louis Post-Dispatch* for their fine coverage throughout the years and to the *Chicago Tribune* and its library staff for use of its microfilm back to the 1870s. Carol Bebb of the *Tribune* helped with the microfilm.

To Larry Croghan for his expertise with trade analysis.

To Stein and Day editor Benton Arnovitz for his patience and assistance, and Art Ballant for having enough faith in us.

And to: Norm Cohen and Bernie Colbeck of the *Chicago Tribune*; statistician Bob Rosenberg; and more-than-rabid fan helpers Paul Brizzolara, Harold Hammersteadt, Joe Kovecsi, Paul Ladewski, and John Sullivan. Sullivan's two-volume history of the St. Louis Browns aided with the city Series.

Special thanks to Lou Brock for generously consenting to write the foreword for this book and to Bob Colvin of the Carey-Phelps–Colvin Agency, Inc., of Los Angeles for serving as Lou's representative in this matter.

And a special thanks to Enos "Country" Slaughter, who consented to do an introduction after seeing a proof set of this book. Slaughter typifies what baseball is all about. His name on the cover of this book completes it.

CONTENTS

Photo Section between pages 286 and 287

INTRODUCTION BY ENOS SLAUGHTER

The day they told me I was traded from the Cardinals, I broke down and cried. I guess St. Louis meant a lot to me. There were so many wonderful people, so many wonderful moments, so many wonderful memories.

I can still close my eyes and see the last game of the 1946 World Series. There's Leon Culberson throwing the ball to Johnny Pesky, and Pesky hesitating before he threw to the plate. I ran as hard and as fast as I could and I scored from first base. They called it The Mad Dash. I call it a moment of great personal satisfaction.

There were many such moments I spent while in a Cardinal uniform. I guess I always was a Redbird at heart and always will be.

When I got a look at *This Date in St. Louis Cardinals History,* there I was, making that dash again, getting those base hits, catching a few here and there.

Old Cardinal fans will be able to go back in time as I did to remember their heroes. Younger fans can see the way it was and their favorites of today.

This book has more facts and happenings than I thought were possible. I'm just happy that John Leptich and Dave Baranowski asked me to be a part of it.

Enos "Country" Slaughter

FOREWORD BY LOU BROCK

Do you remember when I played my first major league game, or the day I was traded to the Cardinals, or when I played my first game for them? I remember. In St. Louis, baseball was a war of foot soldiers, scrambling and scratching in a nose-to-nose assault. The opponent was challenged head-up. He was forced to perform, forced to throw to you, forced to strike you out. The home run was fine, but the battle was to be won where "eye met eye" and sweat and dirt were partners of performance.

Attitude was the distinction: the Cardinal players viewed themselves as agents of action rather than actors effected by events. Limitations were not defined by others. They were not controlled, they were controlling. They were not passengers, they were the drivers.

The Cardinal game, under which I prospered, was one of confrontation and constant challenge. Now do you remember my 105th stolen base, or number 893, both record breakers? Or how about my 3,000th hit (the only time this feat ever occurred in St. Louis), or how about my last game, or my retirement day?

I remember these days and you can, too, with *This Date in St. Louis Cardinals History*.

If you're a St. Louis Cardinal fan, this book is a must for you. I know it will have an important place in your baseball library, just as it does in mine.

CALENDAR

The following chronological table lists Cardinals of the past and present by their birthdates. Following each name is a symbol indicating the position each played with this team: P = pitcher, C = catcher, 1B = first base, 2B = second base, 3B = third base, SS = shortstop, IF = infield, OF = outfield, PH = pinch-hitter. The years after the names are those in which the individual played for the Cardinals.

Just as important, highlights of Cardinals history are also recorded by date.

JANUARY

January 1

1868 — Dave Zearfoss (C, 1904-05)

1889 — Howie Jones (OF, 1921)

1901 — Joe Benes (IF, 1931)

1904 — Ethan Allen (OF, 1933)

1921 — Royce Lintz (P, 1954)

1927 — Carl Scheib (P, 1954)

January 2

1836 — Dickey Pearce (SS, 1876-77)

1891 — Joe Lotz (P, 1916)

1904 — Sell outfielder-second baseman Jesse Burkett to the Boston Red Sox.

January 3

1883 — John Hopkins (OF, 1907)

1892 — Roland Howell (P, 1912)

1912 — Stanley Bordagaray (3B-OF, 1937-38)

1920 — Ed Sauer (OF, 1949)

1922 — Virgil Stallcup (SS, 1952-53)

1950 — Jim Dwyer (OF 1973-75, 1978-79)

January 4

1883 — Eddie Zimmerman (3B, 1906)

1914 — Herman Franks (C, 1939)

1947 — Ken Reynolds (P, 1975)

January 5

1864 — Bob Caruthers (OF-IF-P, 1892)

1897 — Art Delaney (P, 1924)

1928 — Transfer catcher Bubber Jonnard to Houston of the Texas League.

1935 — Ed Bauta (P, 1960-63)

1

January 5 (continued)

1937 — Clyde Bloomfield (3B, 1963)

1946 — Sell infielder Jimmy Brown to Pittsburgh for $30,000.

1946 — Sell catcher Walker Cooper to the Giants for $175,000.

1950 — John Littlefield (P, 1980)

January 6

1870 — Joe Sullivan (OF–IF, 1896)

1877 — Jack Slattery (C, 1906)

1903 — Howard Holland (P, 1929)

1928 — Dan Lewandowski (P, 1951)

1936 — Ruben Amaro (SS-2B, 1958)

January 7

1913 — Johnny Mize (1B-OF, 1936-41)

1922 — Alvin Dark (IF, 1956-58)

1928 — Transfer pitcher Herman Bell and outfielder Johnny Mokan to Houston of the Texas League.

Transfer pitchers Vic Keen and Tony Kaufmann to Syracuse of the International League.

1935 — Dick Schofield (SS, 1953-58, 68, 71)

1938 — Fred Whitfield (1B, 1962)

January 8

1872 — Chauncey Fisher (P, 1901)

1915 — Walker Cooper (C, 1940-45, 56-57)

1922 — Ralph LaPointe (IF, 1948)

1927 — Rogers Hornsby signs two-year contract with the Giants.

1934 — Gene Freese (IF, 1958)

1950 — Helen Britton Bigsby, Cardinal president in 1916, and former wife of Schuyler P. Britton, president from 1913 until his death in 1916, dies in Philadelphia.

1953 — Bruce Sutter (P, 1981-82)

January 9

1882 — John Bliss (C–SS, 1908-12)

1917 — Johnny Echols (PH, 1939)

1918 — Ferrell Anderson (C, 1953)

1935 — Bob Duliba (P, 1959-60, 62)

1974 — Purchase outfielder Jay Johnstone from Oakland's Tucson affiliate.

1975 — Purchase infielder Terry Hughes from Rhode Island Red Sox affiliate and assign him to Tulsa.

January 10

1870 — John Houseman (IF-OF, 1897)

1873 — Jack O'Neil (C, 1902-03)

1888 — George Pearce (P, 1917)

1922 — Cliff Chambers (P, 1910)

1943 — Jim Campbell (PH, 1970)

January 11

1862 — George Pinckney (3B, 1892)

1888 — Clarence Roberts (C, 1913)

1901 — Bill Magee (P, 1901)

1955 — Trade pitcher Ben Wade to the Pirates for pitcher Paul LaPalme.

1967 — Trade outfielder Alex Johnson to the Reds for outfielder Dick Simpson.

January 12

1866 — Tom Kinslow (C, 1898)

1895 — Elmer Knight (P, 1922)

1940 — George Kernek (1B, 1965-66)

1946 — Outfielder Terry Moore is discharged from the U.S. Army after nearly three years of service.

1976 — Trade outfielder Dick Sharon, on Tucson roster, to the Angels for pitcher Bill Rothan.

January 13

1865 — John Kirby (P, 1885-86)

1869 — Jud Smith (IF-OF, 1893)

1905 — Charlie Wilson (SS-3B, 1932-33, 35)

1914 — Schuyler P. Britton is reelected president of Cards, Mrs. Britton, vice-president, H. D. Seekamp, treasurer, and W. D. Schofield, secretary.

1918 — Steve Mesner (3B, 1941)

1920 — Sam Breadon elected president of the Cardinals.

1944 — Larry Jaster (P, 1965-68)

1950 — Mike Tyson (2B-SS, 1972-79)

Bob Forsch (P, 1974-82)

1958 — Gene Roof (OF, 1981-82)

January 14

1880 — Pat Livingston (C, 1917)

1882 — Fred Alberts (P, 1910)

1911 — Hank Gornicki (P, 1941)

1923 — Ken Johnson (P, 1947-50)

1937 — Sonny Siebert (P, 1974)

1942 — Dave Campbell (IF, 1973)

1970 — First of three layers of asphalt is laid in outfield of the new Busch Memorial Stadium.

January 15

1885 — Grover Lowdermilk (P, 1909)

1937 — Bob Sadowski (2B, 1960)

1949 — Luis Alvarado (2B, 1974, 76)

January 16

1891 — Ferdie Schup (P, 1919-21)

1893 — Marv Goodwin (P, 1917, 22)

1899 — George Fisher (OF, 1930)

4

1911 — Dizzy Dean (P, 1930, 1932-37)

1970 — Outfielder Curt Flood, who was traded to Philadelphia in October 1969, but refused to report, files suit in New York Federal Court to have baseball's reserve clause abolished. Flood sat out the entire 1970 season.

1979 — Sign pitcher Darold Knowles, formerly of the Montreal Expos, as their first reentry signing. He was released May 5, 1980.

January 17

1908 — Ray Cunningham (3B-2B, 1931-32)

1933 — J. W. Porter (C, 1959)

1952 — Darrell Porter (C, 1981-82)

1953 — Mark Littell (P, 1978-82)

January 18

1895 — Danny Clark (OF, 1927)

1904 — Name Kid Nichols manager, replacing Patsy Donovan.

1938 — Curt Flood (OF-IF, 1958-69)

January 19

1917 — Obtain pitcher George Pierce from the Cubs.

January 20

1944 — Carl Taylor (OF-1B-3B, 1970)

January 21

1914 — Sylvester Donnelly (P, 1944-46)

1919 — Trade infielders Doug Baird and Stuffy Stewart, pitcher Gene Packard, and cash to the Phillies for catcher Pickles Dillhoefer, pitcher Frank "Dixie" Davis, and infielder Milt Stock.

1928 — Purchase Rochester franchise for the International League, and move all Syracuse players there.

1947 — Bill Stein (OF-3B-1B, 1972-73)

Bob Reynolds (P, 1971)

1969 — Stan Musial is elected to the Hall of Fame.

January 22

1877 — Ed Murphy (P, 1901-03)

January 22 (continued)

1919 — Diomedes Olivo (P, 1963)

1925 — Johnny Bucha (C, 1948)

Bobby Young (3B, 1948)

1945 — Recall infielder Red Schoendienst from Rochester.

Outfielder Stan Musial enlists in the U.S. Army.

January 23

1855 — Art Croft (IF-OF, 1877)

1861 — Jack McGeachy (OF, 1886)

1873 — Francis Donahue (P, 1895-97)

1901 — Joe Walker (1B, 1923)

1923 — Ellis Deal (P, 1950)

1932 — Trade outfielder Hack Wilson to the Dodgers for outfielder Bob Packham and $45,000.

1934 — Wally Shannon (SS-2B, 1959-60)

1946 — Outfielder Enos Slaughter is discharged from the U.S. Army Air Force after nearly four years of service; pitcher Howie Krist is discharged from the U.S. Army after two years of service.

1967 — General Manager Bob Howsman submits his resignation to take a similar job with the Reds; Stan Musial is named the new general manager.

January 24

1879 — Dave Brain (OF, 1903-05)

1898 — Jim Lindsey (P, 1929-34)

Cliff Heathcote (OF-1B, 1918-22)

1901 — Flint Rhem (P, 1924-28, 1930-32, 34)

1952 — Sell infielder Stan Rojek to the Browns on waviers.

1973 — Trade player to be named later to the Red Sox for pitcher Mike Nagy. Lance Clemons, pitcher, was assigned to the Red Sox Pawtucket affiliate March 29 to complete the deal.

January 25

1890 — Phil Redding (P, 1912-13)

1891 — George Lyons (P, 1920)

1916 — Glenn Gardner (P, 1945)

1922 — Sam Breadon reelected president of the Cardinals.

1943 — Outfielder Enos Slaughter is called for active duty in the U.S. Army Air Force.

1946 — Option outfielder Art Rebel to Rochester.

January 26

1906 — Charley Gelbert (SS-3B, 1929-32, 35-36)

1927 — Bob Nieman (OF, 1960-61)

1932 — Purchase infielder Hod Ford from Cincinnati.

1935 — Bob Uecker (C, 1964-65)

1953 — Tom Bruno (P, 1978-79)

January 27

1877 — John Burke (2B, 1899)

1947 — Tim Plodinec (P, 1972)

1949 — Fred M. Saigh, new owner of the Cardinals, squelches rumors that star outfielder Enos Slaughter will be traded to the New York Giants. He emphasized that Eddie Dyer would continue as manager.

January 28

1869 — James Holmes (OF, 1906)

1891 — Bill Doak (P, 1913-24, 29)

1902 — Pat Crawford (IF, 1933-34)

1906 — Lyn Lary (IF, 1939)

1934 — Bill White (1B-OF, 1959-65, 69)

1952 — Owner Fred Saigh is sentenced to 15 months in prison and fined $15,000 for income tax evasion after he pleads no contest.

January 29

1880 — Ed Conwell (3B, 1911)

1949 — Sell pitcher Murry Dickson to the Phillies for $125,000.

1958 — Stan Musial signs a $100,000-contract, largest in National League history at the time.

January 29 (continued)

1963 — Pitcher Lee Meadows (1915-19) dies at Daytona Beach, Fla. He was the first modern major leaguer to wear glasses on the field.

1971 — Trade pitcher Nelson Briles and outfielder Vic Davalillo to the Pirates for outfielder Matty Alou and pitcher George Brunet.

January 30

1893 — Red Smyth (OF-2B, 1917-18)

1925 — Brooks Lawrence (P, 1954-55)

January 31

1881 — Walter Morris (SS, 1908)

1892 — Rees Williams (P, 1914)

1894 — Stuffy Stewart (2B-OF, 1916-17)

1931 — Tom Alston (1B, 1954-57)

FEBRUARY

February 1

1957 — Bob Smith (P, 1957)

1973 — Trade pitcher Charlie Hudson to Texas for a player to be named. The Ranger obligation was satisfied March 31, in a deal sending pitcher Mike Nagy to the Rangers for pitcher Mike Thompson.

February 2

1879 — Harry Arndt (IF-OF, 1905-07)

1893 — Cy Warmoth (P, 1916)

1923 — Red Schoendienst (OF-IF, 1945-56, 61-63)

1954 — Rob Dressler (P, 1978)

February 3

1885 — Harry Sallee (P, 1908-16)

1903 — Joe Stripp (3B, 1938)

1949 — Bake McBride (OF, 1973-77)

1951 — Mike Wallace (P, 1975-76)

1976 — Purchase pitcher Tom Walker from the Tigers' Evansville roster and assign him to Tulsa.

February 4

1890 — Eddie Ainsmith (C, 1921–23)

George Whitted (OF–IF, 1912–14)

1951 — Stan Papi (SS–2B, 1974)

February 5

1867 — Ed Haigh (OF, 1892)

1890 — Max Flack (OF, 1922–25)

1923 — Chuck Diering (OF, 1947–51)

1938 — Sign pitcher Guy Bush, who was released by the Boston Bees.

1946 — Sell outfielder-first baseman Johnny Hopp to the Braves for reported $40,000 and the transfer of infielder Eddie Joost to Rochester.

Sell outfielder Johnny Wyrostek to the Phillies.

Sell pitcher Al Jurisich to the Phillies.

February 6

1872 — Lou Criger (C–3B, 1899–1900)

1899 — Walter Huntzinger (P, 1926)

1934 — Sell pitcher Dazzy Vance to the Cincinnati Reds.

1940 — Recall catcher Herman Franks from Columbus of the American Association and sell him to the Brooklyn Dodgers.

1948 — Doug Howard (1B, 1975)

February 7

1878 — William Shannon (OF, 1904–06)

1951 — Benny Ayala (OF, 1977)

February 8

1920 — Robert Blattner (SS–2B, 1942)

1923 — Branch Rickey signs a five-year contract to manage the Cardinals.

1939 — Harvey Branch (P, 1962)

1966 — Pitcher Gene Paulette (1917–19) dies at Little Rock, Ark. He had been barred from professional baseball for life for taking active part in thrown games March 21, 1921.

February 8 (continued)

1968 — Trade infielder Jimmy Williams and catcher Pat Corrales to Cincinnati for catcher Johnny Edwards. The Reds assigned Corrales to Indianapolis.

February 9

1899 — George Toporcer (IF-OF, 1921–28)

1916 — Fred Schmidt (P, 1944, 1946–47)

1933 — Trade infielder Jake Flowers and pitcher Owen Carroll to Brooklyn for pitcher Dazzy Vance and shortstop Gordon Slade.

1942 — Hal Gilson (P, 1968)

1949 — John Andrews (P, 1973)

1952 — Eddie Solomon (P, 1976)

1955 — John Urrea (P, 1977–80)

February 10

1920 — Obtain first baseman Jacques Fournier from Los Angeles.

1982 — Cards trade shortstop Garry Templeton to San Diego for shortstop Ozzie Smith to complete deal of December 10, 1981.

February 11

1924 — Hal Rice (OF, 1948–53)

1934 — Purchase pitcher Flint Rhem from the Phillies.

February 12

1902 — George Davis (OF, 1934)

1903 — Charles Hafey (OF, 1924–31)

1921 — Don Bollweg (1B, 1950–51)

1922 — Mike Clark (P, 1952–53)

1926 — Joe Garagiola (C, 1946–51)

February 13

1861 — Emmett Seery (OF, 1885–86)

1868 — Biff Sheehan (OF-1B, 1895–96)

1876 — Frederick Buelow (C-OF, 1899–1900)

1921 — Pete Castiglione (3B, 1953-54)

1926 — Bob Habenicht (P, 1951)

1938 — Dick Hughes (P, 1966-68)

1954 — Donnie Moore (P, 1980)

February 14

1864 — Charlie Getzein (P, 1892)

1867 — Morgan Murphy (C-1B, 1896-97)

1897 — Earl Smith (C, 1928-30)

1915 — Charles Barrett (P, 1945-46)

1918 — Augie Bergamo (OF-1B, 1944-45)

1919 — Del Wilber (C, 1946-49)

1952 — Will McEnaney (P, 1979)

February 15

1888 — Frank Betcher (IF-OF, 1910)

1895 — Jimmy Ring (P, 1927)

1900 — George Earnshaw (P, 1936)

1923 — Trade first baseman Jacques Fournier to Brooklyn for outfielder Harry Myers and first baseman Ray Schmandt. The next day, Fournier said that he would quit baseball rather than play with another club. He finally agreed to play for the Dodgers April 27.

1951 — Cirilio Cruz (OF, 1973)

1979 — Release infielder Jose Baez.

February 16

1912 — Ray Harrell (P, 1935, 37-38)

1918 — Frank Crespi (IF, 1938-42)

1929 — Fred Hahn (P, 1952)

1930 — Judge Kenesaw Mountain Landis, Commissioner of Baseball, forbids the transfer of catcher Gus Mancuso from the Cards to Rochester of the International League.

11

1936 — Don Landrum (OF-2B, 1960-62)

1981 — Conditionally purchase shortstop Rafael Santana from the Yankees.

February 17

1885 — Steve Evans (OF-1B, 1909-13)

1912 — Brusie Ogrodowski (C, 1936-37)

1917 — St. Louis Stock Co. announces its intention to buy the ball club.

1926 — Jack Crimian (P, 1951-52)

1931 — Roger Craig (P, 1964)

1964 — Trade outfielder Jim Beauchamp and pitcher Chuck Taylor, the latter on the Tulsa roster, to Houston for outfielder Carl Warwick.

1966 — Outfielder Finners Quinlan (1913) dies at Scranton, Pa. He lost his right arm and left eye at Argonne Wood, France, September 9, 1918, in World War I battle.

February 18

1878 — Sandy McDougal (P, 1905)

1909 — Transfer pitcher Ulysses S. Grant McGlynn to Milwaukee club.

1927 — Herman Wehmeier (P, 1956-58)

Luis Arroyo (P, 1955)

1939 — Dal Maxvill (IF-OF, 1962-72)

Bob Miller (P, 1957, 59-61)

1949 — Jerry Morales (OF, 1978)

1952 — Marc Hill (C, 1973-74)

February 19

1932 — Don Taussig (OF, 1961)

1943 — Jim Cosman (P, 1966-67)

1944 — Chris Zachary (P, 1971)

1979 — Sign pitcher Will McEnaney as free agent and assign him to Arkansas.

February 20

1874 — Justin Bennett (2B-3B, 1906-07)

1876 — Ike Samuels (3B-SS, 1895)

1922 — Bill Reeder (P, 1949)

1924 — Sal Yvars (C, 1953-54)

1943 — Infielder Frank "Creepy" Crespi is inducted into the U.S. Army.

1953 — The Board of Directors of Anheuser-Busch Inc. approves the purchase of the Cardinals by an overwhelming margin. The company bought 1,665 of 1,676 shares from Fred Saigh for $1,491.65 per share or $2,483,597.25. In addition, the new owners assumed $1,250,000 in indebtedness. Saigh revealed that a group from Milwaukee had offered $4,100,000, but that he had rejected the offer so that the Cards could stay in St. Louis.

February 21

1937 — Ted Savage (OF, 1965-67)

February 22

1868 — Llewellyn Camp (3B-OF, 1892)

1878 — Charley Moran (C–SS-P, 1903)

1884 — Roy Radebaugh (P, 1911)

1891 — Clarence Mitchell (P, 1928-30)

1898 — Tony DeFate (IF, 1917)

1911 — Bill Baker (C, 1948-49)

1922 — Catcher William "Pickles" Dillhoefer dies of typhoid fever in St. Louis.

1931 — Charlie Peete (OF, 1956)

1970 — Pitching coach Billy Muffett is quoted with a newspaper headline: "Cardinals No. 1 problem: Filling bullpen roster." For his efforts, Muffett was fired following the season.

February 23

1877 — Rudy Hulswitt (SS-2B, 1909-10)

1887 — Lou Lowdermilk (P, 1911-12)

1914 — Lynn Myers (IF, 1938-39)

1937 — Acquire first baseman Dick Siebert from the Chicago Cubs.

1941 — Ron Hunt (IF, 1974)

1954 — Purchase pitcher Vic Raschi from the Yankees for a reported $85,000.

February 24

1869 — Con Lucid (P, 1897)

1877 — Champ Osteen (IF, 1908-09)

1882 — Bugs Raymond (P, 1907-08)

1884 — Mike Mowrey (3B-SS, 1909-13)

February 25

1884 — Bob Bescher (OF, 1915-17)

1889 — Elmer Rieger (P, 1910)

1897 — Bob Vines (P, 1924)

1940 — Danny Cater (1B, 1975)

1972 — Trade pitcher Steve Carlton to the Phillies for pitcher Rick Wise.

February 26

1887 — Grover Cleveland Alexander (P, 1926-29)

1915 — Preacher Roe (P, 1938)

1917 — Johnny Grodzicki (P, 1941, 46-47)

1920 — Danny Gardella (PH, 1950)

1942 — Purchase infielder-outfielder Debs Garms from Sacramento of the Pacific Coast League.

1957 — Trade first baseman Whitey Lockman to the Giants for pitcher Hoyt Wilhelm.

February 27

1879 — Miller Huggins (2B, 1910-16)

1896 — Willis Koeningsmark (P, 1919)

1904 — Charles Fullis (OF, 1934)

Art Teachout (P, 1932)

1937 — Carl Warwick (OF, 1961-62, 64-65)

February 28

1875 — George Gilpatrick (P, 1898)

14

1916 — Howie Krist (P, 1937-38, 41-43, 46)

1977 — Trade pitcher Mark Covert to the Chicago Cubs for pitcher Buddy Schultz. Schultz was assigned to New Orleans and Covert to Wichita by their new clubs.

February 29

1904 — Pepper Martin (OF-3B-P, 1928, 30-40, 44)

MARCH

March 1

1881 — Al Shaw (OF-SS-3B, 1907-09)

March 2

1913 — Mort Cooper (P, 1938-45)

1917 — Jim Konstanty (P, 1956)

March 3

1867 — Jack O'Connor (C-1B, 1899-1900)

1879 — Ed Phelps (C, 1909-10)

1934 — Bobby Locke (P, 1962)

1942 — Don Dennis (P, 1965-66)

1943 — Pitcher John Beazley is commissioned a second lieutenant in the U.S. Army Air Force.

1959 — Release pitcher Chuck Stobbs, who is claimed by the Washington Senators.

1981 — Sign outfielder Steve Braun, a free agent, and assign him to Springfield.

March 4

1884 — John Murray (3B, 1902)

1888 — Jeff Pfeffer (P, 1921-24)

1891 — Dazzy Vance (P, 1933-34)

1915 — Art Rebel (OF, 1945)

1936 — Bob Johnson (IF, 1969)

1946 — Dan Frisella (P, 1976)

1948 — Tom Grieve (OF, 1979)

Leron Lee (OF, 1969-71)

March 5

1945 — Dave Bakenhaster (P, 1964)

1956 — Brusie Ogrodowski (C, 1936-37) is found dead in his San Francisco home. Brusie had a penchant for keeping a Persian cat with him at all times during the season.

1959 — Andy Rincon (P, 1980-82)

March 6

1917 — Ben S. Brinkman is elected president of the ball club.

1923 — The Cardinals announce that players will wear uniform numbers for the first time during the 1923 season.

1924 — Ed Mierkowicz (PH, 1950)

1933 — Ted Abernathy (P, 1970)

1939 — Cookie Rojas (IF, 1970)

1962 — St. Louis voters pass a $6,000,000 bond issue for streets, lights, water mains, and other public improvements in a proposed stadium area. Civic Center Redevelopment Corp., backed entirely by private capital, planned to build the park and the supporting facilities as part of an $83,000,000 civic-improvement project. Anheuser-Busch Inc., owner of the Cardinals, subscribed the largest single amount of equity capital, $5,000,000.

March 7

1888 — Dan Griner (P, 1912-16)

1921 — Les Fusselman (C, 1952-53)

1931 — Dick Rand (C, 1953)

March 8

1869 — Jim Hughey (P, 1898)

1879 — Josh Clarke (OF-IF, 1905)

1930 — Bob Grim (P, 1960)

1942 — Richie Allen (IF-OF, 1970)

March 9

1877 — Alex Pearson (P, 1902)

1893 — Billy Southworth (OF, 1926-27, '29)

1932 — Ron Kline (P, 1960)

1944 — Release outfielder Frank Demaree.

1948 — John Curtis (P, 1974-76)

March 10

1868 — Lew Whistler (1B-OF, 1893)

1869 — Frank Bird (C, 1892)

1921 — Johnny Blatnik (OF, 1950)

1934 — Ken MacKenzie (P, 1963)

1942 — Tom Hilgendorf (P, 1969-70)

1953 — Stockholders of Anheuser-Busch Inc. approve the purchase of the Cardinals by an overwhelming vote.

1970 — Start gluing Astroturf to the padding of the new Busch Memorial Stadium.

March 11

1911 — Jim Bucher (2B-3B, 1938)

1933 — Jack Spring (P, 1964)

1953 — Anheuser-Busch Inc. takes over active operation of the Cardinal organization.

Fred Toney (P, 1923) dies of heart attack at his Nashville, Tenn., home. He was best remembered for a 10-inning no-hitter against the Chicago Cubs, while a Cincinnati Red, May 2, 1917. His opponent, Jim "Hippo" Vaughn, pitched 9⅓ hitless innings in the same contest, a feat never equalled by two pitchers. He was also indicted as a draft dodger in World War I, and was tried on Mann Act charges, but was acquitted.

March 12

1866 — Denny Lyons (3B, 1895)

1882 — Johnny Beall (OF, 1918)

1884 — Pat Hynes (P, 1903)

1887 — Wally Mattick (OF, 1918)

1906 — Bud Tinning (P, 1935)

1963 — A model of Civic Center Busch Memorial Stadium is unveiled.

March 13

1877 — Tim Flood (2B, 1899)

1879 — John Kelly (OF, 1907)

1889 — Wally Smith (IF-OF, 1911-12)

1940 — Gary Kolb (OF-3B-C, 1960, 62-63)

1980 — Sign reentry free-agent pitcher Don Hood, who was formerly of the Yankees.

March 14

1898 — Bruce Hitt (P, 1917)

1905 — Jack Rothrock (OF-2B, 1934-35)
1957 — Ty Waller (IF, 1980)

March 15

1859 — Arlie Latham (3B, 1896)

1899 — Hal Kime (P, 1920)

1915 — Don Lang (3B-2B, 1948)

1944 — Wayne Granger (P, 1968, '73)

1946 — Bobby Bonds (OF, 1980)

1959 — Trade pitcher Nelson Chittum to the Boston Red Sox for pitcher Dean Stone.

1961 — Sign veteran infielder Red Schoendienst as free agent.

1978 — Sell outfielder Rick Bosetti to the Toronto Blue Jays.

March 16

1859 — Jerry Denny (3B, 1886)

1865 — Patrick Donovan (OF, 1900-03)

1899 — Vick Keen (P, 1926-27)

1902 — Jake Flowers (IF, 1923, 26, 1931-32)

1913 — Ken O'Dea (C, 1942-46)

1930 — Hobie Landrith (C, 1957-58)

1932 — Don Blasingame (IF, 1955-59)

1938 — Cal Browning (P, 1960)

March 17

1886 — The first copy of the St. Louis-based *The Sporting News*, billed as "Baseball's Bible," appears.

1919 — Hank Sauer (OF, 1956)

1946 — Pitcher John Beazley is discharged from the U.S. Army Air Force.

1969 — Trade first baseman-outfielder Orlando Cepeda to the Braves for catcher-first baseman Joe Torre.

March 18

1910 — Alan Storke (P, 1909) dies at Newton, Mass., at age 36 of grippe followed by complications.

1916 — Eddie Lake (IF, 1934-41)

1919 — Hal White (P, 1953-54)

1926 — Dick Littlefield (P, 1956)

1932 — Lee Tate (IF, 1958-59)

1957 — Al Olmstead (P, 1980)

March 19

1874 — LeRoy Evans (P, 1897)

1965 — The Astros claim catcher Ed Pacheo on first-year waivers.

March 20

1879 — Jake Thielman (P, 1905-06)

1887 — Walter Schmidt (C, 1925)

1888 — Les Backman (P, 1909-10)

1894 — Johnny Butler (3B-SS, 1929)

1912 — Clyde Shoun (P, 1938-42)

1928 — Trade shortstop Les Bell to the Boston Braves for infielder Andy High.

1933 — George Altman (OF, 1963)

1941 — Pat Corrales (C, 1966)

1945 — Outfielder Danny Litwhiler enters the U.S. Army.

1952 — Greg Terlecky (P, 1975)

March 20 (continued)

1972 — Trade outfielder-first baseman Bob Burda to the Red Sox for first baseman Mike Fiore, who is assigned to Tulsa.

Curt Flood's antitrust suit reaches the Supreme Court.

March 21

1921 — Recall infielder George " Specs" Toporcer.

1927 — Bernie Creger (SS, 1947)

1949 — Don Durham (P, 1972)

1980 — Sign pitcher Don Hood in the reentry, free-agent draft.

March 22

1885 — Rube Geyer (P, 1910–13)

1923 — George Crowe (1B, 1959–61)

1929 — Pitcher Bill Doak rejoins the team following his release from the Brooklyn Dodgers.

1936 — Gene Oliver (OF–C–1B, 1959, 61–63)

1952 — Eric Rasmussen (P, 1975–78)

1965 — Claim catcher Mike Buist from the Mets on first-year waivers.

March 23

1863 — Joe Gunson (C, 1893)

1875 — Rudy Kling (SS, 1902)

1878 — Homer Smoot (OF, 1902–06)

1913 — Bill Cox (P, 1936)

1926 — Chuck Harmon (OF–IF, 1956–57)

1974 — Trade pitcher Scipio Spinks to the Chicago Cubs for first baseman-outfielder Jim Hickman. The Cubs assigned Spinks to Wichita.

1977 — Trade pitcher Lerrin LaGrow to the White Sox for pitcher Clay Carroll.

March 24

1884 — Mike Mowrey (3B–SS, 1909–13)

1911 — Matthew Stanley Robison, president of the St. Louis National League ball club, dies unexpectedly in the Cleveland home of his sister-in-law.

1917 — Dave Bartosch (OF, 1945)

1956 — Garry Templeton (SS, 1976-81)

1972 — Trade second baseman Julian Javier to the Reds for pitcher Tony Cloninger.

1977 — Release pitcher Tom Walker.

March 25

1868 — Frank Dwyer (P, 1892)

1933 — Nelson Chittum (P, 1958)

1945 — Jim Ellis (P, 1969)

1948 — Mike Nagy (P, 1973)

1959 — Trade pitchers Sam Jones and Don Choate to the Giants for outfielder-first baseman Bill White and third baseman Ray Jablonski.

1969 — Trade catcher Dave Adlesh to the Braves for infielder Bob W. Johnson.

1974 — Release catcher Jeff Torborg.

1977 — Purchase infielder Tommy Sandt from the A's and assign him to New Orleans.

March 26

1914 — Hal Epps (OF, 1938)

1952 — Purchase infielder Gene Mauch on waivers from the Yankees. They released him to Milwaukee May 21.

1972 — Trade pitcher Frank Linzy to the Brewers for pitcher Rich Stonum, who is assigned from Evansville to Arkansas.

1974 — Release outfielder Jay Johnstone.

Sell catcher Larry Haney to the Oakland A's.

March 27

1879 — Miller Huggins (2B, 1910-16)

1893 — Charlie Boardman (P, 1915)

1899 — Employ grounds keeper Murphy from Baltimore. Manager Patsy Tebeau said that with Murphy in charge, St. Louis would have the smoothest and cleanest playing field in the big leagues by May 1.

Ed Hock (OF, 1920)

March 27 (continued)

1915 — Newt Kimball (P, 1940)

1933 — Don Lassetter (OF, 1957)

1946 — Mike Jackson (P, 1971)

1950 — Vic Harris (IF-OF, 1976)

   Lynn McGlothen (P, 1974-76)

1975 — Release infielder Ron Hunt.

March 28

1909 — Lon Warneke (P, 1937-42)

1911 — The will of team-president Matthew Stanley Robison, who died March 24, is read. He left the St. Louis National League ball club to his sister-in-law, Mrs. Frank de hass Robison, and his niece, Mrs. Schuyler Britton.

1919 — Vic Raschi (P, 1954-55)

1977 — Trade pitcher Bill Caudill to the Reds for outfielder-third baseman Joel Youngblood.

1978 — Release pitcher Larry Dierker.

March 29

1867 — Cy Young (P, 1899-1900)

1873 — Duff Cooley (OF-IF-C, 1893-96)

1894 — Bob Steele (P, 1916-17)

1954 — Mike Ramsey (SS, 1978, 1980-82)

1973 — Assign pitcher Lance Clemons to the Red Sox Pawtucket affiliate to complete a Jan. 24 deal for pitcher Mike Nagy.

1974 — Purchase infielder Ed Crosby from the Phillies and assign him to Tulsa.

1975 — Trade outfielder Danny Godby to the Red Sox for first baseman Danny Cater. Godby was assigned to Pawtucket.

1977 — Release pitcher Roric Harrison.

   Trade pitcher Mike Caldwell to the Reds for pitcher Pat Darcy, who is assigned to New Orleans.

March 30

1867 — Bill Hallman (IF, 1897)

1885 — Herman Bronkie (IF, 1918)

1904 — Rip Collins (1B-OF, 1931-36)

1946 — Release pitcher Stan Partenheimer.

1956 — Trade outfielder Pete Whisenant and an undisclosed amount of cash to the Chicago Cubs for outfielder Hank Sauer.

1962 — Sell first baseman Frank Leja to the Los Angeles Angels.

1977 — Trade infielder Doug Clarey to the Mets for Outfielder Benny Ayala. Ayala was assigned to New Orleans and Clarey to Tidewater by their new teams.

1979 — Release pitcher Jim Willoughby.

March 31

1897 — Jim Brown (OF, 1915)

1918 — Marv Grissom (P, 1959)

1970 — Release pitcher Ramon Hernandez.

1973 — Trade pitcher Mike Nagy to the Rangers for pitcher Mike Thompson, completing a Feb. 1 trade in which the Cards sent pitcher Charlie Hudson to Texas for a player to be named. The Rangers assigned Nagy to Spokane; the Cards sent Thompson to Tulsa.

1977 — The New Orleans farm club sells catcher Ken Rudolph to the Giants.

1980 — Release pitchers Will McEnaney and Tom Bruno.

APRIL

April 1

1967 — Trade infielder Jerry Buchek, pitcher Art Mahaffey, and shortstop Tony Martinez to the Mets for shortstop Ed Bressoud and outfielder Dan Napoleon. Mahaffey and Martinez were transferred from Tulsa to Jacksonville, Napoleon from Jacksonville to Tulsa.

1968 — Sign free-agent infielder Dick Schofield.

April 2

1878 — Jack Harper (P, 1900-01)

1910 — Henry Pippen (P, 1936)

1930 — Gordon Jones (P, 1954-56)

1945 — Reggie Smith (OF-IF, 1974-76)

1950 — Milt Ramirez (SS-3B, 1970-71)

1953 — Hector Cruz (OF–3B, 1975–77)

1958 — Trade outfielder Jim King to the Giants for catcher Ray Katt.

1963 — Sell outfielder Minnie Minoso to the Senators for cash and a player to be named.

1970 — Trade shortstop Steve Huntz to the Padres for pitcher Bill McCool, who is assigned to Tulsa.

1976 — Purchase pitcher Lerrin LaGrow from the Tigers and assign him to Tulsa.

1980 — Release first baseman-outfielder Roger Freed.

April 3

1927 — Alex Grammas (IF–OF, 1954–56, 59–62)

1930 — Wally Moon (OF–1B, 1954–58)

1950 — Claim shortstop Eddie Miller from the Phillies.

1969 — Trade infielder Jim Hutto, assigned to Eugene, and infielder Jerry Buchek, assigned from Tulsa to Eugene, to the Phillies for first baseman Bill White.

1973 — Purchase pitcher Alan Foster from the Angels.

1981 — Sign free agent second baseman Julio Gonzalez.

Mexico City Tigers reclaim outfielder Carlos Lopez from the Cards, who had selected him in the 1980 major league draft.

April 4

1916 — Mickey Owen (C, 1937–40)

1918 — Trade infielder Bert Niehoff and $50,000 to the Phillies for pitcher Mule Watson.

1927 — Sign pitcher Flint Rhem to a one-year contract.

1928 — Frank Smith (P, 1955)

1946 — Catcher Walker Cooper is discharged from the U.S. Navy after less than a year of service.

1950 — Sell pitcher Bill Reeder to Rochester.

1956 — Tom Herr (IF, 1979–82)

1975 — Purchase shortstop Mario Guerrero from the Red Sox and send him to the Tulsa farm. The Red Sox acquire pitcher Jim Willoughby from Tulsa July 4 to complete the deal.

Sell pitcher Ray Bare to the Detroit Tigers.

April 5

1922 — Gene Crumling (C, 1945)

1936 — Jimmy Schaffer (C, 1961-62)

1942 — Sell pitcher Bill Lohrman to Giants.

1976 — Assign shortstop Bob Hrapmann from Arkansas to the Cubs' Midland affiliate to complete the Oct. 28, 1975 deal which sent pitcher Mike Garman to Chicago for shortstop Don Kessinger.

1978 — Sell pitcher Butch Metzger to the Giants.

1979 — Release pitcher Paul Siebert.

April 6

1906 — Benny Frey (P, 1932)

1942 — Sell pitcher Clyde Shoun to the Cincinnati Reds.

1948 — Option outfielder Hal Rice to Rochester.

1952 — Steve Waterbury (P, 1976)

April 7

1873 — John McGraw (3B, 1900)

1886 — Sell second baseman Fred Dunlap to Detroit for $4,700 and outfielder J. C. McGeachy.

1879 — Art Weaver (C, 1902-03)

1911 — The St. Louis Board of Directors elects E. A. Steininger as president.

1933 — Bobby Del Greco (OF, 1956)

1947 — Trade outfielder-first baseman Dick Sisler to the Phillies for infielder Ralph LaPointe and a reported $20,000.

1962 — Trade outfielder Al Herring, transferred from Tulsa to San Antonio, and cash to the Cubs for pitcher Bobby Locke.

1965 — Trade pitcher Bob Humphreys to the Cubs for pitcher Hal Gilson and infielder Bobby Pfeil, both assigned from Salt Lake City to Tulsa.

1966 — Sell pitcher Bob Purkey to the Reds.

1971 — Three judges of the U.S. Circuit Court of Appeals uphold the dismissal of Curt Flood's antitrust suit.

April 7 (continued)

1976 — Trade pitcher Harry Parker to the Indians for pitcher Roric Harrison. Parker was sent to Toledo, Harrison to Tulsa.

1981 — Reclaim catcher George Bjorkman from Giants, who selected him from Springfield in the 1980 major league draft.

April 8

1864 — Pete Daniels (P, 1898)

1885 — Fred Gaiser (P, 1908)

1920 — Release pitcher Red Ames.

1933 — Lloyd Merritt (P, 1957)

1970 — Send first baseman Willie Montanez to the Phillies as partial compensation for the loss of outfielder Curt Flood, who was traded to the Phillies Oct. 7, 1969, but decided to remain out of baseball for the entire 1970 season. Montanez was assigned to Eugene.

1976 — Trade pitchers Ken Reynolds and Bob Stewart, at Arkansas, to San Diego for pitcher Dan Frisella. Reynolds was assigned to Hawaii by the Padres.

April 9

1890 — Joe Willis (P, 1911-13)

1904 — Fred Frankhouse (P, 1927-30)

1926 — Rogers Hornsby, traded to the Giants January 8, obeys Commissioner Landis' Jan. 31 ruling that he cannot play with another team unless he sells his stock in the Cards. He got $100,000 for the stock.

1953 — August A. Busch Jr. purchases Sportsman's Park from Bill Veeck of the Browns for $800,000.

1964 — Trade catcher Jim Coker and outfielder Gary Kolb to the Braves for catcher Bob Uecker.

1972 — Release pitchers Jim Maloney and Stan Williams.

April 10

1868 — Tom Parrott (P, 1896)

1895 — Bob McGraw (P, 1927)

1953 — The name of Sportsman's Park is changed to Busch Stadium.

1956 — Sell pitcher Frank Smith to the Cincinnati Reds.

1959 — Release pitcher Sal Maglie.

1961 — Sell pitcher Ron Kline to the Los Angeles Angels.

Sign pitcher Mickey McDermott as a free agent.

1967 — Sell first baseman Tito Francona to the Phillies.

April 11

1875 — Ossee Schreckengast (C-IF, 1899)

1876 — Win Kellum (P, 1905)

1921 — Jim Hearn (P, 1947-50)

1927 — Jack Faszholz (P, 1953)

1932 — Trade outfielder Chick Hafey to the Reds for pitchers Harvey Hendrick and Benny Frey and cash.

1954 — Trade outfielder Enos Slaughter to the Yankees for pitcher Mel Wright and outfielders Bill Virdon and Emil Tellinger, both transferred to Card farm clubs, and catcher Hal Smith.

1956 — John Martin (P, 1980-82)

1962 — The Cards romp over the Mets 11-4 at St. Louis, marking New York's historic return to the National League. Larry Jackson allowed eight hits in gaining the victory. Taking the field for the first time as a team were Richie Ashburn (cf), Felix Mantilla (ss), Charlie Neal (2b), Frank Thomas (lf), Gus Bell (rf), Gil Hodges (1b), Don Zimmer (3b), Hobie Landrith (c), and Roger Craig (p). Before the dismal evening's toll ended for the Mets—only 2 hours, 53 minutes after it had begun—Bob Moorhead, Herb Moford, and Clem Labine had been used as relief pitchers. Ed Bouchee and Jim Marshall had been summoned to pinch-hit. Two of the Mets scores were the result of homers by Neal and Hodges.

1975 — Release pitcher Claude Osteen, who is signed by the White Sox.

1981 — The Cards pull their first triple play since 1977. With the bases loaded against Philadelphia in the eighth, Gary Matthews hit a low line drive to shortstop Garry Templeton for the first out. Templeton, thinking the ball was trapped, threw to catcher Darrell Porter, who threw to first baseman Keith Hernandez to double Mike Schmidt for the second out. The Cards completed the triple play when Hernandez threw the ball to third baseman Ken Oberkfell, who tagged out Bake McBride.

April 12

1876 — Vic Willis (P, 1910)

1888 — Harry Sullivan (P, 1909)

1889 — Bill Bailey (P, 1921-22)

1922 — Bill Wight (P, 1958)

April 12 (continued)

1926 — Walt Moryn (OF, 1960–61)

1960 — The Giants inaugurate $15-million Candlestick Park with a 3–1 victory over the Cards before 42,269 paid admissions. Winning pitcher Sam Jones allowed only three hits, one of them a 400-foot homer over the right-field fence by Leon Wagner.

1965 — Left-handed pitcher Steve Carlton makes his major-league debut, walking a man in the 11th inning at Wrigley Field. The Cards and the Cubs played to a 10–10 standoff in 11 innings before the game was called because of darkness.

April 13

1863 — Charles Sweeney (P, 1885–86)

1881 — Joseph O'Rourke (SS, 1908)

1945 — Option pitcher Bill Trotter to Rochester.

1954 — St. Louis rookie Wally Moon joins a select group of players by hitting a home run in his major-league debut. Batting second in the lineup, Moon tagged southpaw Paul Minner of the Cubs for a round-tripper in the season inaugural at Busch Stadium. Moon, who proceeded to become N.L. Rookie of the Year, wound up his freshman season the same way he started it— with a home run. This time he connected with a mate aboard against Ernie Johnson at Milwaukee Sept. 26 to give the Cards an 11-inning, 2–0 victory.

Two other Cardinal rookies also homered for their initial hits in 1954, although both had been previously retired. Tom Alston, hitless in his first game, broke the ice with a home run April 17. Joe Cunningham, called up from Rochester as a first baseman replacement for Alston, socked a three-run homer on his third appearance as a Card June 30.

1962 — Stan Musial scores the 1,860th run of his career against the Cubs at Chicago, breaking Mel Ott's National League record.

1968 — Curt Flood slams five straight singles as the Cards rally to rap the Cubs 8–5 before a record opening day crowd of 33,875 at Wrigley Field. The Redbirds, sweeping to their third straight victory, trailed 4–0 after the Cub first, in which Ron Santo belted a three-run homer.

1981 — Anheuser-Busch offers $33.5 million for remaining 75.4 percent interest in the Civic Center Redevelopment Corp.

April 14

1870 — Tom Niland (OF-SS, 1896)

1893 — Roy Walker (P, 1921–22)

1936 — Pinch-hitter Eddie Morgan hits a grand-slam homer in his first major-league at-bat, but the Cubs blast Dizzy Dean 12–7 on opening day behind

Frank Demaree's two home runs. Cubs infielder Billy Herman sets a major-league opening-day record with a single, three doubles and a homer.

1944 — Frank Bertaina (P, 1970)

1959 — Los Angeles plays host to the Cards before 61,552 fans at the Coliseum. The Cards defeat the Dodgers 6–2 for the first victory under new manager Solly Hemus. Hemus, making the shift from utility infielder to skipper, put Stan Musial back at first base after the Cards had lost their first three games at home. Stan the Man (1-for-15) was hitless, but his replacement in left field, Chuck Essegian, paid off with a run-scoring double.

1964 — The Cards open the season at Los Angeles, losing to Sandy Koufax and the Dodgers 4–0. Koufax allowed only six hits while Ernie Broglio yielded nine hits in seven innings on the mound for St. Louis.

1969 — Major-league baseball comes to Canada with the Expos defeating the Cardinals 8–7 before a standing-room crowd of 29,184 at Montreal. The Expos had blown a 6–0 lead as the Cards came back with a seven-run fourth inning. The Expos contributed five errors and light-hitting Dal Maxvill sliced a grand slam to right field in the inning.

1972 — Release first baseman-outfielder Art Shamsky, who is signed by the Cubs later in the day.

April 15

1885 — Sign second baseman Fred Dunlap.

1896 — George Distel (IF–OF, 1918)

1940 — Willie Davis (OF, 1975)

1941 — Ernie Koy, Enos "Country" Slaughter, and Johnny Mize clout homers as the Cards triumph 7–3 over the Reds, 1940 world champions.

1946 — Ted Sizemore (IF–OF, 1971–75)

1949 — Ray Bare (P, 1972, 74)

1954 — Hank Aaron gets the first of his 3,771 major-league hits. He goes two-for-five as the Braves defeat the Cards 7–6 at Milwaukee.

April 16

1898 — With some 4,000 people in the stands during the second inning of a game against the Chicago Cubs, fire destroys the entire grandstands and left-field bleachers at old Sportsman's Park. In the ensuing panic, many people were trampled and burned. It took many hours for city firemen, with horse-drawn apparatus, to extinguish the flames.

1900 — Walt Schulz (P, 1920)

1938 — Trade pitcher Dizzy Dean to the Chicago Cubs for pitchers Curt Davis and Clyde Shoun, outfielder Tuck Stainback, and $185,000.

April 16 (continued)

1946 — Sell first baseman Ray Sanders to the Boston Braves.

1953 — The Cards defeat the Cubs 3–0 at St. Louis in their first game under the ownership of August A. Busch Jr.

1957 — Stan Musial gets four hits in the opener at Cincinnati as the Cards win 13–4.

1959 — The Cards use 25 players to set a major-league record for a nine-inning game as they lose to the Dodgers 7–6.

1966 — The Pirates gain their first home victory over the Cardinals after 18 defeats dating back to May 6, 1964. Pinch-hitter Manny Mota's two-run, tie-breaking triple in the seventh led to a 5–3 victory. The streak established a big-league mark for most consecutive victories over one club on the road.

1978 — Bob Forsch authors the first no-hitter in St. Louis in 54 years as the Cardinals defeat the Phillies 5–0. However, the no-hitter was tainted a bit because of a controversial error which official scorer Neal Russo of the *St. Louis Post-Dispatch* charged to third baseman Ken Reitz in the eighth inning. Garry Maddox of the Phillies led off the eighth with a hard smash to third which skipped under the glove of the usually sure-handed Reitz. After deliberating for about 10 seconds, Russo ruled it an error and the crowd of 11,495 cheered wildly.

April 17

1869 — John Grimes (P, 1897)

1892 — Cincinnati defeats the Redbirds 5–1 in the first Sunday game at St. Louis.

1900 — Sign pitcher Gus Weyhing on a trial basis. He plays in seven games, posting a 3–2 record.

1907 — Eddie Delker (IF, 1929, 31–32)

1923 — Solly Hemus (IF, 1949–56, 59)

1945 — Chicago Cubs beat Cards 3–2 on Don Johnson's 9th inning single in the season opener at Wrigley Field. On the play, Bill Nicholson beat rookie left fielder Red Schoendienst's throw to the plate. The game marks Schoendienst's first of 2,216 major-league contests.

1954 — The Cubs outlast the Cards 23–13 in one of the longest nine-inning games in N.L. history. During the 3-hour, 43-minute marathon, the Redbirds used 19 players, including six pitchers: Starter Gerry Staley, Hal White, Royce Lint, Mel Wright, Al Brazle, and Ellis Deal.

1958 — Stan Musial's home run against the Cubs gives him 5,045 total bases in the National League, breaking Mel Ott's record.

1975 — Ted Simmons connects for a first-inning homer batting right-handed, then belts a fifth-inning homer from the left side. The first homer, a three-run shot, came off veteran New York left-hander Jerry Koosman. Simmons led off the fifth with a home run off Rick Baldwin. Despite Simmons' heroics, the Mets won 14–7 as ex-Cardinal Jack Heidemann drove in four runs.

April 18

1925 — A 22-hit, 20–5 victory by the Cards over the Cubs features Les Bell getting two home runs and two doubles at Chicago. Jim Bottomley, Ray Blades, and Taylor Douthit hit homers for the Cubs and Rogers Hornsby scored five runs.

1938 — Release outfielder Johnny Cooney. Although the Cards obtained him in a deal Oct. 10, 1937, Cooney never played a game with them.

1939 — Von McDaniel (P, 1957–58)

1942 — Chuck Taylor (P, 1969–71)

1947 — Sell pitcher Johnny Beazley to the Boston Braves.

1950 — A total of 20,871 fans pay to see the first season opener under the lights at St. Louis. The Redbirds posted a 4–2 triumph over Pittsburgh behind the six-hit hurling of Gerry Staley; Stan Musial and Red Schoendienst homered and Joe Garagiola's run-scoring single broke a 2–2 tie in the sixth.

April 19

1918 — George Kurowski (IF-OF, 1941–49)

1926 — Sell outfielder Jack Smith to the Boston Braves.

1958 — Purchase pitcher Phil Paine from the Braves.

April 20

1869 — Tommy Dowd (OF-IF, 1893–98)

1876 — Charlie Hemphill (OF, 1899)

1938 — Tim "Voiceless" O'Rourke (IF, 1894) dies in Seattle. He was known as voiceless because an injury to his throat inflicted by a batted ball made it difficult for him to speak above a whisper.

1946 — The Cubs raise their 1945 pennant before 40,887 fans at Wrigley Field, but the Cards promptly hand the champs their first setback in four starts 2–0 as Harry Brecheen scatters six hits.

1953 — The Cards defeat the Braves 9–4 at St. Louis in the first night game played by a Milwaukee team. Big Steve Bilko hammered across four runs in the victory with a homer and a single.

1954 — Doug Clarey (2B, 1976)

1957 — Trade outfielder Bobby Del Greco and pitcher Ed Mayer to the Cubs for outfielder Jim King.

April 21

1863 — George Smith (SS, 1898)

1890 — John Raleigh (P, 1909-10)

1919 — Stan Rojek (SS, 1951)

1948 — The Cards win 5-2 as Cincinnati pitcher Johnny Vander Meer issues 12 walks. George Munger allowed only five hits in gaining the victory.

1957 — Sign coach Walker Cooper to a playing contract.

1959 — Stan Musial's double in seventh inning at Chicago ruins Cub pitcher Glenn Hobbie's no-hitter. The Cards lost the contest 1-0.

April 22

1887 — Charles Burk (P, 1912-13)

1892 — Pittsburgh scores 12 runs in the first inning and routs the Cards 14-3. St. Louis starter Ted Breitenstein failed to last through the first inning.

1901 — Taylor Douthit (OF, 1923-31)

1910 — Lew Riggs (PH, 1934)

1931 — Gabby Street's Cardinals, playing their first game of the season in St. Louis, score once in the seventh inning and once in the eighth to defeat Cincinnati 3-2. Before the game, the N.L. pennant won the previous year by St. Louis was hoisted with ceremonies attended by 7,500 fans, including Gov. Henry S. Caulfield of Missouri.

1954 — Dan O'Brien (P, 1978-79)

1964 — An opening-day crowd of 31,410 at St. Louis sees the Cards hand the world champion Dodgers their seventh consecutive defeat 7-6. The Dodgers suffered an additional blow by losing the services of ace left-hander Sandy Koufax. Koufax, the National League's Most Valuable Player and a 25-game winner in 1963, was forced out of the game with an elbow injury. Charlie James hit a three-run home run in the first inning for the Cards. Carl Warwick and Bill White also homered. Card starter Curt Simmons opened with three hitless innings, but left in the seventh after a home run by Willie Davis. In the sixth inning, Simmons had thrown a fast ball that Frank Howard hit 460 feet into the center-field bleachers.

1968 — Trade pitchers Jack Lamabe and Ron Riche, both on the Tulsa roster, to the Cubs for pitchers Pete Mikkelsen and Dave Dowling, the latter on the Tacoma roster. Mikkelsen and Dowling were assigned to Tulsa.

April 23

1900 — James Bottomley (1B-2B, 1922-32)

1906 — Ray Starr (P, 1932)

1916 — Jack Creel (P, 1945)

1926 — Chuck Harmon (OF-IF, 1956-57)

1937 — Leon Carmel (OF-1B, 1959-60, 63)

1954 — Hank Aaron of the Braves, in his seventh major-league game, hits the first
of his record 755 career home runs, off Cardinal pitcher Vic Raschi with
none on in the fourth inning at St. Louis.

1963 — Ernie Broglio pitches a masterful two-hit shutout as the Cards pound four
pitchers for 17 hits and blast the Houston Colts 15-0 before 2,551 busi-
nessman's special fans at a noonday game in Houston. Bill White batted in
three runs and scored three with four singles and Ken Boyer had four RBI
with two singles, an infield out, and a walk with the bases loaded.

April 24

1873 — Bob Ewing (P, 1912)

1892 — The Cincinnati Reds play their first Sunday game in Cincinnati and defeat
the Cardinals 10-2.

1906 — Robert Worthington (OF, 1934)

1920 — Announce that the club will move from Robison Field to Sportsman's Park
later in the season.

1936 — Glen Hobbie (P, 1964)

April 25

1868 — Fred Hartman (IF, 1897)

1876 — St. Louis loses to Cincinnati 2-1 in the first game in National League
history.

1891 — Pete Standridge (P, 1911)

1898 — Fred Haney (3B, 1929)

1907 — Roy Parmelee (P, 1936)

1910 — Jimmy Brown (IF, 1937-43)

1940 — Release pitcher Nate Andrews.

1942 — Release outfielder Estel Crabtree to serve as Rochester manager.

1943 — Lew Krausse (P, 1973)

1944 — Joe Hague (OF-1B, 1968-72)

April 25 (continued)

1950 — Bill Grief (P, 1976)

1954 — Rookie Hank Aaron hits his second home run of the season off Stu Miller as the Milwaukee Braves beat the Cards 7-5 in 14 innings at St. Louis. Aaron would hit 753 more homers in his career.

April 26

1882 — Irv Higginbotham (P, 1906, 08-09)

1897 — Epp Sell (P, 1922-23)

1917 — Sal Maglie (P, 1958)

1920 — Ron Northey (OF, 1947-49)

1941 — Chicago Cubs become the first major-league team to install an organ. Organist Roy Nelson entertains the crowd with a pre-game medley. Cards defeat Cubs 6-2 at Wrigley Field.

1944 — Pitcher Denny Galehouse enters the U.S. Navy.

1970 — Bob Gibson, knocked out in his first two starts, throttles Cincinnati on five hits, striking out 15, in a 4-1 St. Louis victory. He fanned six batters in order during one stretch.

April 27

1889 — Henry Myers (OF-2B-3B, 1923-25)

1896 — Rogers Hornsby (IF, 1915-26, 33)

1901 — Johnny Stuart (P, 1922-25)

1916 — Enos Slaughter (OF, 1938-42, 46-53)

1950 — Trade pitcher Ken Johnson to the Phillies for outfielder Johnny Blatnik.

1974 — Trade pitcher Ken Tatum to the White Sox for infielder Luis Alvarado.

1977 — Garry Templeton scores five runs as the Cards rout the Cubs 21-3 at Chicago. Ted Simmons and Hector Cruz each batted in four runs as the Cards snapped a three-game losing streak.

April 28

1870 — Bill Hawke (P, 1892-93)

1932 — Release infielder Hod Ford.

1934 — Jackie Brandt (OF, 1956)

1950 — Jorge Roque (OF, 1970-72)

1955 — Release pitcher Vic Raschi.

1961 — Red Schoendienst, recently signed as a free agent, delivers a two-run, pinch-hit homer in the 11th inning to give the Cards a 10-9 victory over Philadelphia. Schoendienst was the 24th Cardinal to play in the 4-hour, 23-minute marathon. Four players—Don Landrum, Joe Cunningham, Charlie James, and Walt Moryn—saw action in right field for the Cards.

1962 — Trade pitcher Bobby Locke and cash to the Phillies for pitcher Don Ferrarese.

April 29

1893 — Allen Sothoron (P, 1924-26)

1931 — Adam Comorosky slashes a single to left field to break up Jesse Haines' no-hitter in the seventh inning, but the Cards still defeat Pittsburgh 7-1.

1947 — Sign free agent Joe Medwick.

1948 — Ted Wilks' string of 77 consecutive mound appearances without a loss ends as Cincinnati defeats the Cards 5-4 in 14 innings. Wilks, whose previous loss was to Pittsburgh 6-5 on Sept. 3, 1945, won 12 games while performing in the 77, all but four in relief. Cincinnati rookie Hank Sauer, who had tied the score with a home run in the eighth, broke up the game with a run-scoring single.

April 30

1892 — Tony Brottem (C-OF-1B, 1916)

1885 — The Cards defeat Chicago 3-2 in the first National League game played at Union Grounds in St. Louis.

1948 — Mike Barlow (P, 1975)

1949 — A disputed inside-the-park home run by Rocky Nelson salvages a 4-3 victory for the Cardinals over the Cubs at Wrigley Field. Cub center fielder Andy Pafko claimed to have caught Nelson's blow, but it was ruled no-catch by Umpire Al Barlick. With the Cards trailing 3-1, Enos Slaughter doubled in the ninth inning and scored on Eddie Kazak's single with two out. Chuck Diering ran for Kazak. Nelson then lined the ball to left center and Pafko made somewhat of a somersault dive and came up with the ball. Barlick did not make any decision until Pafko started running to the infield with the ball. Pafko, unwilling to believe the no-catch ruling, did not throw the ball until Nelson was crossing the plate with the winning run.

1954 — Sell first baseman Steve Bilko to the Chicago Cubs.

1980 — Sign pitcher Pedro Borbon.

MAY

May 1

1905 — Catcher Jack Warner comes to blows with outfielder Otis Clymer of Pittsburgh at St. Louis.

May 1 (continued)

1909 — Obtain infielder Rudy Hulswitt from Cincinnati.

1932 — "Wild Bill" Hallahan fires a three-hitter as the Cards win 7-1 over Chicago, stopping the Cubs' winning streak at seven. He tantalized the Cubs with 10 walks.

1946 — Trade second baseman Emil Verban to the Phillies for catcher Clyde Kluttz.

1956 — Trade pitcher Paul LaPalme to the Reds for third baseman Milt Smith.

May 2

1932 — Ed Bressoud (SS-3B, 1967)

1941 — Clay Carroll (P, 1977)

1945 — Catcher Walker Cooper enters the U.S. Navy.

1948 — Sell shortstop Jeff Cross to the Cubs.

1954 — Stan Musial crashes five home runs in a doubleheader as the Cards defeat the Giants, 10-6, then lose, 9-7. Musial drilled three home runs and a single in the first game and added two more homers in the second. He thereby amassed the most total bases, 21, in a doubleheader.

May 3

1852 — George Gore (OF, 1892)

1897 — Ray Shepherdson (C, 1924)

1938 — Chris Cannizzaro (C, 1960-61)

1941 — Henry Gornicki makes his big-league pitching debut for the Cards by hurling a one-hit, 6-0 victory over the Phillies. The lone Philadelphia hit was a single by Stanley Benjamin, rookie outfielder.

1947 — Trade outfielder Ron Northey and cash to the Phillies for outfielder Harry Walker and pitcher Fred Schmidt.

1952 — Trade pitcher George Munger to the Pirates for pitcher Bill Werle.

1953 — Keith Smith (OF, 1979-80)

May 4

1948 — Option first baseman Rocky Nelson to Rochester.

1949 — Release pitcher Al Papi to the Browns on waivers.

1951 — Option outfielder Hal Rice to Rochester.

1954 — The Cards use eight pitchers and the Phillies seven to set a league record for most pitchers by both teams in an extra-inning game. The Phillies won 14-10 in the 11th inning after Rip Repulski and Sal Yvars had doubled in succession in the ninth for St. Louis to send the game into extra frames.

1956 — Ken Oberkfell (IF, 1977–82)

1964 — The Cards survive a beanball rhubarb and unleash a 14-hit attack that sinks the Phillies 9–2. The Cards built a 5–1 lead before starter Bob Gibson was knocked out of the game in the beanball dispute. He received a warning and automatic $50 fine in the third inning for throwing two straight pitches too close to Phillie pitcher Dennis Bennett. When reliever Jack Baldschun hit Gibson with a pitch in the last half of the fourth inning, Gibson, with an underhand motion, tossed his bat toward the mound and plate umpire Doug Harvey ejected him.

May 5

1871 — Jimmy Bannon (OF–IF–P, 1893)

1876 — St. Louis and George Bradley defeat Chicago 1–0 in St. Louis. It was the first National League game ever played at old Sportsman's Park in St. Louis, and the league's initial 1–0 contest.

1917 — George Dockins (P, 1945)

1918 — Oliver "Patsy" Tebeau (IF, 1899–1900, manager 1900), who retired following the 1900 season to open a saloon in St. Louis, commits suicide at age 54.

1933 — Pepper Martin, having an afternoon reminiscent of his 1931 World Series exploits, gets two doubles, a triple, and a home run as the Cards beat the Phillies 5–3.

1940 — A major-league mark for players used in a single game—39—is set when the Dodgers use 22 players and the Cards 17 in a game at St. Louis. The former mark of 37 was set in 1928 by the Cards-Phillies and tied in 1937 by the Cards-Cubs. A four-run burst in the ninth inning won the game for Brooklyn 9–6.

May 6

1878 — John Lovett (P, 1903)

1883 — Ed Karger (P, 1906–08)

1890 — Walton Cruise (OF, 1914, 16–19)

1926 — Dick Cole (IF, 1951)

1934 — Leo Burke (OF–IF, 1963)

1942 — Sell pitcher Clyde Shoun to Cincinnati.

1956 — Trade pitcher Luis Arroyo and an undisclosed amount of cash to the Pirates for pitcher Max Surkont.

1957 — Kim Seaman (P, 1979–80)

1962 — Trade outfielder Carl Warwick and pitcher John Anderson to the Houston Colt .45s for pitcher Bobby Shantz.

1969 — Bob Gibson records 150th career win, a 3–0, five-hitter over San Francisco at St. Louis.

May 7

1909 — Ed Heusser (P, 1935–36)

1919 — Al Papai (P, 1948)

1930 — Chick Hafey drives in five runs with a home run and a triple to highlight a nine-run fifth inning and the Cards defeat the Phillies 16–11. The game featured 35 hits, including home runs by George Watkins and Hafey. Hafey also scored five runs.

1931 — John A. Heydler, president of the National League, denies an appeal by the St. Louis club to replay a game of April 19 won by the Cubs 4–1. The appeal was based on a protest against the alleged misinterpretation of the rules by Umpire Moran. Moran had ruled that someone in the overflow crowd at St. Louis had ruined Cub left fielder Riggs Stephenson's morale by shouting raucously as Jim Bottomley drove a ball to the edge of the crowd. Stephenson muffed the ball and it caromed into the crowd. The umpire called Bottomley out and further ruled that Ernie Orsatti could go to third and no farther on the same interference penalty.

1933 — Trade pitchers Paul Derringer and Allyn Stout and infielder Earl Adams to Cincinnati for shortstop Leo Durocher and pitchers John Ogden and Frank Henry.

Pepper Martin hits for the cycle, including a home run with two men on base in the ninth inning, as the Cards beat Brooklyn 12–5 in the opening game of a doubleheader. Brooklyn won the second game, however, 4–3.

1940 — The Cards smash seven homers—a club record—as they thrash the Brooklyn Dodgers 18–2. Johnny Mize and Eddie Lake each hit two homers. Stu Martin, Joe Medwick, and Don Padgett also hit roundtrippers.

1950 — Howie Pollett allows just four hits as the Cards humiliate Boston 15–0. Enos Slaughter led the 21-hit attack against Johnny Sain and three relievers with four hits in five times at-bat.

1954 — Conditionally purchase pitcher Carl Scheib from the A's. He was returned and released June 1.

May 8

1910 — Claim outfielder Elmer Zacher from the New York Giants.

1922 — Sam Breadon obtains controlling interest in the Cards by purchasing the stock of J. C. Jones.

1925 — Glenn Wright of Pittsburgh makes unassisted triple play vs. Cards. Bottomley hit a line drive to Wright, with Cooney and Hornsby on base. Wright touched second base, retiring Cooney, who had started for third, and tagged out Hornsby, who was headed for second.

1937 — Mike Cuellar (P, 1964)

1948 — Steve Braun (OF, 1981-82)

1963 — Stan Musial's home run against the Dodgers at St. Louis is his 1,357th extra-base hit, breaking Babe Ruth's major-league record.

1966 — Trade pitcher Ray Sadecki to the Giants for first baseman Orlando Cepeda.

The Cardinals play their final game at old Busch Stadium, defeating the Giants 10-5.

1973 — Trade pitcher Al Santorini to the Royals for pitcher Tom Murphy. The Royals assigned Santorini to Omaha.

May 9

1893 — Bill Bolden (P, 1919)

1909 — Announce that the life of Manager Roger Bresnahan has been insured for $50,000, payable to Owner M. S. Robison.

1927 — Ray Katt (C, 1956, 58-59)

1942 — Jerry Buchek (IF, 1961, 63-66)

1953 — Sam Mejias (OF, 1976)

1958 — Sell pitcher Herman Wehmeier to the Tigers.

1967 — Cardinal outfielder Roger Maris, uniform No. 9, hits his first National League home run at Pittsburgh. The ball was caught by a spectator in row nine, seat nine. (Maris broke into major-league baseball in 1957 with Cleveland with a nine-game hitting streak.)

1975 — Trade outfielder Larry Herndon and pitcher Luis Gonzalez to the Giants, who assign them to Phoenix, for pitcher Ron Bryant.

1979 — Release outfielder Tom Grieve.

1980 — Release pitcher Darold Knowles.

May 10

1872 — Harry Berte (2B-SS, 1903)

William Douglas (OF-C-IF, 1896-97)

1881 — Forrest Crawford (SS-3B, 1906-07)

1894 — Frank Shugart, Doggie Miller, and Joe Peitz successively drive homers in the sixth inning, but St. Louis loses to Cincinnati 18-9.

1928 — Trade catcher Bob O'Farrell to the Giants for outfielder George Harper.

1937 — Jim Hickman (1B-3B, 1974)

1947 — John Cumberland (P, 1972)

1949 — Sam Breadon, former owner of the Cardinals, dies of cancer at age 72. He was president of the Cards from 1920 to 1947, when he sold the club to Bob Hannegan and Fred Saigh. He had run his original investment of $200 into a property he sold for $3,000,000.

1950 — Waive pitcher Jim Hearn.

1952 — Option catcher Bill Sarni to Columbus.

1959 — An oddity takes place in a St. Louis doubleheader against Chicago. Lindy McDaniel of the Cards lost the first game and won the second, both in relief. It was the same story for Chicago's Elmer Singleton, who came from the bull pen to win the first game and then lost the second in relief.

1961 — Trade outfielder Bob Nieman to the Indians for infielder Joe Morgan, who was assigned to San Juan, and a player to be named. The Indians sent pitcher Mike Lee to the Cards Sept. 25, completing the deal.

Cincinnati's Bill Henry—relieving in the ninth inning—strikes out three Cardinal pinch-hitters, Charlie James, Don Taussig, and Alex Grammas, as the Reds run their winning streak to nine games with a 3-2 victory.

1970 — Pitcher Hoyt Wilhelm of the Atlanta Braves becomes the first pitcher to appear in 1,000 games in relief at Atlanta. The Cards won 6-5.

1971 — Release pitcher George Brunet after his last stop among eight major-league clubs. Brunet's biggest claim to fame, other than a constantly ready suitcase, was that he reputedly never wore underwear.

May 11

1867 — Lave Cross (3B-SS, 1898-1900)

1928 — Trade outfielder Homer Peel, catcher Spud Davis, and first baseman Don Hurst to the Phillies for catcher Jimmy Wilson.

Mel Wright (P, 1954-55)

1932 — "Wild" Bill Hallahan earns his nickname with three wild pitches in the 12th inning of a game against the Dodgers. The feat tied Jacob Weimer's record with the Cubs in 1903.

1940 — Harry Fanok (P, 1963-64)

1950 — Dane Iorg (OF, 1977–82)

1956 — Trade pitchers Harvey Haddix, Stu Miller, and Ben Flowers to the Phillies for pitchers Herman Wehmeier and Murry Dickson and a player to be named. The deal was completed May 14 as infielder Solly Hemus was traded to the Phillies for infielder Bobby Morgan.

Purchase third baseman Grady Hatton from the Red Sox.

1957 — Trade infielder-outfielder Chuck Harmon to the Phillies for outfielder Glen Gorbous.

1958 — The Cards tie a major-league record by using 10 pinch-hitters as they sweep a doubleheader from the Chicago Cubs 8–7, 6–5.

1962 — Outfielder Minnie Minoso runs into a wall at St. Louis against the Dodgers, breaking his wrist and fracturing his skull. He returned to the active list July 19, then suffered a cracked bone in his left forearm after being hit by a Craig Anderson pitch at New York Aug. 18.

1965 — The Cubs claim pitcher Dave Dowling on first-year waivers.

1966 — Send pitcher Larry Jaster to Tulsa.

1977 — Release infielder Jerry DaVanon.

May 12

1862 — William Wolf (OF, 1892)

1887 — Kurt Hageman (P, 1914)

1937 — Joe "Ducky" Medwick homers twice and adds two doubles as the Cards go on a 20-hit spree and wallop the Phillies 15–3 before only 2,500 fans at Philadelphia. Pepper Martin had four safeties and Brusie Ogrodowski hit a home run.

1942 — Ted Kubiak (IF, 1971)

1947 — Bob Heise (IF, 1974)

1951 — Stan Musial, out of action because of the flu, enters the second game of a doubleheader in weakened condition and plasters a pitch deep into the right-center seats at Cincinnati for a three-run homer in the eighth inning. Stan's homer gave the Cards an 8–6 victory after they dropped the opener 7–2. Earlier, another Card pinch-hitter, Bill Howerton, had hit a two-run circuit clout.

1953 — Taylor Duncan (3B, 1977)

1964 — Curt Simmons, who has made a practice of beating the Phillies since they released him in 1960, does it again 4–2 with relief help from Roger Craig in the eighth inning. Since the Phillies dropped him, Simmons had beaten them 13 of 15 times.

May 12 (continued)

1966 — The Cards thrill a crowd of 46,048 in their new park by rallying for a 4–3 victory over the Atlanta Braves. The Cards tied the game in the ninth inning and then won it in the 12th with Lou Brock's bases-loaded single driving in the winning run.

1969 — Bob Gibson strikes out three Dodger batters on nine pitches in seventh inning of 6-2 Cardinal win in St. Louis.

May 13

1876 — Third baseman Joe Battin of St. Louis becomes the first National League player to get five hits in a nine-inning game.

1884 — Bert Niehoff (2B, 1918)

1918 — Carden Gillenwater (OF, 1940)

1934 — Leon Wagner (OF, 1960)

1940 — The Cards and Cincinnati play to an 8-8, 14-inning tie in a phantom baseball game, as far as the National League is concerned. According to an account by Associated Press writer Judson Bailey, the story of the "baseball game that wasn't" began April 23 when a flood washed out a contest St. Louis had scheduled at Cincinnati. It was the first time a flood had ever caused postponement of a National League game. Later someone thought of playing the game May 13, when both teams would be heading east together after playing a series in St. Louis. The newspapers were notified. Fans were told. It was a special Ladies Day and 9,370 women thronged Crosley Field.
   However, the National League office in New York didn't know anything about it. President Ford Frick didn't assign any umpires. Larry Goetz, one of the league's staff of arbiters, was located on his day off at his home in Cincinnati and summoned to duty. Coach Jim Wilson of the Reds and pitcher Lon Warneke of the Cards were pressed into service and the game got started a half hour late. Johnny Mize of the Redbirds hit three home runs before Umpire Goetz called the game because of darkness.

1949 — Terry Hughes (3B-1B, 1973)

1950 — Ship first baseman Rocky Nelson to Columbus.

1952 — Trade outfielder Wally Westlake and third baseman Ed Kazak to the Reds for first baseman Dick Sisler and shortstop Virgil Stallcup.

1958 — Stan Musial reaches the 3,000-hit plateau with a pinch-hit double off Moe Drabowsky in the sixth inning at Wrigley Field. Musial was only the eighth player in history to reach the mark. He reached the mark sooner than Ty Cobb, Tris Speaker, Honus Wagner, Eddie Collins, Nap Lajoie, Paul Waner, and Cap Anson.

1959 — Pitcher Warren Spahn of the Milwaukee Braves defeats the Cards 3-2 at St. Louis for his 250th major-league victory.

May 14

1941 — Trade pitcher Bill McGee to the Giants for pitchers Harry Gumbert, Paul Dean, and cash.

Sell outfielder Ernie Koy to Cincinnati.

1946 — Sell pitcher Ernie White to the Boston Braves.

1951 — Trade first baseman Don Bollweg and estimated $15,000 cash to the Yankees for third baseman Billy Johnson.

1956 — Send infielder Solly Hemus to the Phils for infielder Bobby Morgan, completing the deal of May 11 which sent pitchers Harvey Haddix, Stu Miller, and Ben Flowers to the Phils for pitchers Herman Wehmeier and Murry Dickson.

1957 — Sell pitcher Robert G. Smith to the Pirates.

1967 — Sell outfielder Ted Savage to the Cubs.

May 15

1910 — The Cards defeat the Giants for the third straight time 8-3. The victories were the first for St. Louis over New York since 1908. St. Louis' Frank Corridon scattered four hits while gaining the victory. Roger Bresnahan was badly spiked in the hand by Cy Seymour and forced to retire from the game.

1923 — Jim Bottomley's three triples lead the Cards over Boston 10-5.

1946 — Howie Pollet pitches the Cards into undisputed possession of first place by blanking the Brooklyn Dodgers 1-0 on five hits. The Cards scored their only run in the second inning, when Dick Sisler tripled home George Kurowski, who had doubled.

1950 — Purchase infielder Johnny Lindell from the Yankees.

1960 — Don Cardwell, in his first game for the Chicago Cubs, comes through with a no-hit, no-run game en route to a 4-0 victory over the Cards. Cardwell retired the first batter, walked Alex Grammas on a 3-2 pitch, then mowed down 26 Cards in the nightcap of a doubleheader. The Cards' 6-1 decision in the opener, with the help of two home runs by Ken Boyer, snapped a 12-game losing streak on the road.

1968 — St. Louis second baseman Julian Javier, borrowing a page from the Babe Ruth legend after a hospital visit to a six-year-old youngster whose legs were crushed in a recent automobile accident, slams his first home run of the season to back Steve Carlton's four-hit pitching and give the Redbirds a 1-0 victory over Pittsburgh. The boy, who wasn't expected to walk again, asked Javier to hit a home run for him in the Cards' game at Pittsburgh.

1970 — The Cards sell pitcher Rich Nye to the Montreal Expos, who assign him to Buffalo.

May 15 (continued)

1972 — Trade pitcher Jerry Reuss to the Astros for pitchers Scipio Spinks and Lance Clemons.

Trade pitcher Don Shaw to the A's for infielder Dwaine Anderson.

May 16

1875 — George Barclay (OF, 1902-04)

1906 — Abe White (P, 1937)

1946 — Pinch-runner Jeff Cross steals home in the 10th inning as the Cards pull out a 9-8 victory over the Boston Braves, giving the Redbirds nine victories in 10 games on the road for the season so far.

1951 — Mike Potter (OF, 1976-78)

1956 — Trade shortstop Alex Grammas and outfielder Joe Frazier to Cincinnati for outfielder Chuck Harmon.

1970 — The Cards and Chicago tie a major-league record by using seven pitchers in the ninth inning of a game won by the Cubs 3-2. The Redbirds used Jerry Johnson, Sal Campisi, Billy McCool, and Chuck Taylor and the Cubs Ken Holtzman, Ted Abernathy, and Phil Regan.

May 17

1894 — Frank Woodward (P, 1919)

1906 — Al Eckert (P, 1935)

1910 — Transfer infielder Jap Barbeau to Kansas City.

1951 — Trade outfielder Erv Dusak and first baseman Rocky Nelson to Pittsburgh for shortstop Stan Rojek.

1956 — Trade outfielder Bill Virdon to Pittsburgh for pitcher Dick Littlefield and outfielder Bobby Del Greco.

1977 — Trade pitcher John D'Acquisto and infielder Pat Scanlon, the latter transferred from New Orleans to Hawaii, to the Padres for pitcher Butch Metzger.

May 18

1882 — Charles Adams (P, 1906)

1893 — Sam Fishburn (2B-1B, 1919)

1894 — Tim O'Rourke (IF-OF, 1894)

1918 — Sell second baseman Bert Niehoff to the Giants.

1940 — Jim Hicks (OF, 1969)

1965 — Claim catcher Bob Lanning from Houston on first-year waivers.

1972 — Trade infielder Marty Martinez to the A's for outfielder Brant Alyea.

1975 — Trade infielder Ted Martinez to the A's for pitcher Steve Stainland, assigned from Modesto to St. Petersburg, and a player to be named. Pitcher Mike Barlow was assigned to Tulsa from Tucson May 23, completing the deal.

After banging out 17 runs and 23 hits the previous day, the Cards lose to San Francisco 2-0 as Jim Barr allows just two hits, both of them belonging to Lou Brock.

May 19

1859 — Sam Barkley (IF, 1885)

1912 — Norbert Kleinke (P, 1935)

1929 — Curt Simmons (P, 1960–66)

1948 — Al Santorini (P, 1971–73)

1959 — Trade outfielder Irv Noren to the Cubs for outfielder Chick King.

1960 — Sell pitcher Frank Barnes to the White Sox, who option him to San Diego.

1962 — The 41-year-old Stan Musial eclipses Honus Wagner's N.L. record when he collects hit No. 3,431 off Los Angeles' Ron Perranoski in the ninth inning at Dodger Stadium. Musial attained several other milestones that year, surpassing Ty Cobb as the game's all-time total base leader by hiking his total to 5,864 and breaking Mel Ott's N.L. mark for runs batted in when he increased his total to 1,862.

1964 — A record-tying three wild pitches in one inning by Ernie Broglio and errors in the seventh and eighth innings help the Cubs score four runs in a 7-4 victory over the Cards.

1970 — Trade pitcher Jerry Johnson to the Giants for pitcher Frank Linzy.

Curt Flood's antitrust suit goes to trial in U.S. District Court in New York. The onetime $90,000-a-year outfielder appeared ill-at-ease on the witness stand, was admonished by Judge Irving Ben Cooper for not answering questions properly, and needed a baseball bubblegum card to refresh his memory on his own batting averages.

1972 — Trade first baseman Joe Hague to the Reds for outfielder Bernie Carbo.

1976 — Trade outfielder Luis Melendez to the Padres for pitcher Bill Greif.

May 20

1889 — Ted Cather (OF, 1912-14)

45

1900 — Announce that catcher Jack O'Connor is on the trading block.

1912 — A court decision in St. Louis gives Mrs. Schuyler F. Britton complete control of the St. Louis National League ball club.

1913 — Lou Scoffic (OF, 1936)

1931 — Ken Boyer (IF–OF, 1955–65)

1948 — Stan Musial continues his hitting spree against the Dodgers with four hits, including a homer and two doubles, as the Cards slug their way to a 13–4 slaughter. The previous day he led St. Louis to a 14–7 victory, combing Dodger pitching for a triple, a double, and three singles in five official at-bats.

1953 — Red Schoendienst, with a two-run homer and a three-run double among his four hits, leads a 17-hit Cardinal attack in an 11–6 rout of Pittsburgh. Solly Hemus scored five times in the victory.

1958 — Trade third baseman Al Dark to the Cubs for pitcher Jim Brosnan.

1960 — Sign pitcher Curt Simmons, released by the Phillies.

May 21

1859 — Fred Dunlap (IF, 1885–86)

1891 — Bunny Hearn (P, 1910–11)

1909 — Dick Ward (P, 1935)

1930 — Chick Hafey hits for the cycle as the Cards rout the Phils 16–6 before only 2,000 fans at Sportsman's Park. Hafey hit his 23rd home run of the season into the left-field seats in the first inning. In the third he tripled when left fielder Lefty O'Doul collided with shortstop Tommy Thevenow after he caught Hafey's pop fly and the ball bounced out of Thevenow's hands. He followed with a single in the fourth and a double in the seventh.

1934 — Moe Thacker (C, 1963)

1958 — Sign pitcher Bill Wight.

1970 — Card starter Steve Carlton strikes out 16 batters before giving way to a pinch-hitter in the ninth inning as the Phillies nip the Cards 4–3 at Philadelphia. Richie Allen's homecoming was greeted loudly by a mixed reaction in the city of brotherly love. Allen, making his debut at Connie Mack Stadium since being traded away by the Phillies the previous fall, slammed a two-run homer in the ninth.

1974 — Bob Boone of the Phillies throws out Lou Brock attempting to steal second base in the fifth inning at St. Louis. The play ended Brock's longest string without being caught stealing, 28, three short of Max Carey's record 31.

1975 — Sign outfielder Don Hahn, released by the Phillies.

May 22

1901 — Jesse Burkett hits a lead-off homer in the first inning as the Cards defeat the Phillies.

1913 — Bill Lohrman (P, 1942)

1935 — Ron Piche (P, 1966)

1944 — Infielder Red Schoendienst enters the U.S. Army.

1954 — Birdie Tebbetts, rookie manager of Cincinnati, tries a four-man outfield against Stan Musial in a game at Busch Stadium. As a result, the box score for that contest and official N.L. averages for that year showed a left-handed shortstop, Nino Escalera, in the Reds' lineup. At the time, Cincinnati owned a 4-2 lead, two were out, and Red Schoendienst was on first base for the Cards. With Musial coming to bat, the Redleg pilot removed shortstop Roy McMillan from the game and called Escalera off the bench, stationing him in right center between outfielders Wally Post and Gus Bell. Tebbetts explained later that he would rather risk a single through the vacated shortstop spot than an extra-base hit. The shift, however, wasn't needed, because pitcher Art Fowler struck out Musial and emerged with a 4-2 victory.

1969 — Trade shortstop John Sipin and catcher Sonny Ruberto, the latter on the Tulsa roster, to the Padres for shortstop Jerry DaVanon and first baseman Bill Davis, who are both assigned to Tulsa.

1976 — Reggie Smith slams three home runs, accounting for five runs, to give the Cardinals a 7-6 over Philadelphia. Smith laced his third home run with two out in the ninth to break a 6-6 tie and earn reliever Al Hrabosky his first victory of the season. Tug McGraw was the loser.

May 23

1885 — Ralph McLaurin (OF, 1908)

1899 — Charlie Niebergall (C, 1921, 23-24)

1925 — Trade catcher Mike Gonzalez and infielder Howard Freigau to the Cubs for catcher Bob O'Farrell.

1945 — Trade pitcher Mort Cooper to the Boston Braves for pitcher Red Barrett and cash.

1946 — Pitchers Max Macon and Fred Martin and infielder Lou Klein jump to the Mexican League, while the Cards are in New York.

1948 — Reggie Cleveland (P, 1969-73)

1952 — Clarence Metzger (P, 1977-78)

1953 — Trade pitcher Jackie Collum to the Reds for pitcher Eddie Erautt.

May 23 (continued)

1970 — Bob Gibson strikes out 16 batters two days after Steve Carlton does it and Richie Allen drives in all the runs with a pair of homers as the Cards beat the Phillies 3-1.

1975 — Pitcher Mike Barlow is assigned from Tucson to Tulsa, completing the May 18 deal in which the Cards sent infielder Ted Martinez to the A's for pitcher Steve Stainland.

May 24

1887 — Harry Jasper (P, 1916)

1903 — Jack Berly (P, 1924)

1941 — Option pitcher Preacher Roe to Columbus.

1967 — Lou Brock singles in the third inning off a slider, but that is the only hit the Redbirds get off Atlanta fireballer Denny Lemaster as the Braves beat the Cards 2-0.

1970 — The Cards' Richie Allen strikes out five times in regulation play, tying the N.L. record as the Redbirds lose in 10 innings to the Phillies 6-5.

May 25

1845 — Lipman Pike (OF, 1876)

1878 — Bob Wicker (P, 1901-03)

1917 — Willie Sudhoff (P, 1897-1901) dies in a St. Louis insane asylum at age 32.

1918 — Johnny Beazley (P, 1941-42, 46)

1925 — Don Liddle (P, 1956)

1946 — Manager Eddie Dyer of the Cardinals said the team's three leading outfielders have received "fabulous offers" from the Mexican League, but have turned them down. Dyer made the revelation in a long-distance telephone conversation with Sid Keener, *St. Louis Star-Times* sports editor. The offers were made to Terry Moore, Enos Slaughter, and Stan Musial.

1947 — Signed as a free agent shortly before game time, pinch-hitter Joe Medwick, a member of the old Gas House Gang, doubles off Fritz Ostermueller in the second game of a doubleheader with Pittsburgh, producing the only run in a 2-1 Cardinal defeat. His redebut marked the end of a seven-year absence.

1964 — Ground is broken for a new St. Louis stadium. The park, which would seat 50,000 for baseball and 55,000 for football, was scheduled for completion in time for the opening of the 1966 season. The cost of the stadium and the adjoining parking garage was pegged at $25 million.

1978 — Fire Manager Vern Rapp, replacing him with Jack Krol on an interim basis. Ken Boyer took over four days later.

May 26

1872 — Ulysses McGlynn (P, 1906-08)

1891 — Gene Paulette (IF-OF-P, 1917-19)

1942 — Chuck Hartenstein (P, 1970)

1949 — Ed Crosby (IF, 1970, 72-73)

1978 — Trade pitcher Eric Rasmussen to the Padres for outfielder George Hendrick.

Release infielder Gary Sutherland.

May 27

1873 — Jack Taylor (P, 1898)

1882 — Bill Ludwig (C, 1908)

1893 — Frank Snyder (C-1B-SS, 1912-19)

1912 — Terry Moore (OF-3B-P, 1935-42, 46-48)

1956 — Four strikeouts in one inning enable Jim Davis, Chicago relief pitcher, to crash the record books during the first game of a doubleheader against the Cards in St. Louis. The southpaw performed the odd feat in the sixth inning. After Wally Moon led off with a double and stole third base, Davis whiffed Hal Smith and Jackie Brandt with his baffling knuckler. The butterfly pitch also gave battery-mate Hobie Landrith trouble, however. When Lindy McDaniel also fanned, the third strike got away from Landrith and McDaniel reached first base while Moon scored. Davis then got K No. 4 of the inning when Don Blasingame watched another knuckler float by. It was only the fourth time in major-league history that a pitcher had fanned four batters in one frame. The last pitcher to turn the trick was Guy Morton of Cleveland in 1916.

1960 — Trade infielder Jim McKnight to the Cubs, who assign him from Memphis to Houston, for outfielder Walt Moryn.

1980 — Release pitcher Pedro Borbon and outfielder Bernie Carbo.

May 28

1920 — Art Lopatka (P, 1945)

1923 — Bob Kuzava (P, 1957)

May 28 (continued)

1934 — Bobby Gene Smith (OF, 1957-59, 62)

1946 — Skip Jutze (C, 1972)

1953 — Steve Bilko of the Cards fans five times as the Redbirds and Reds play to a 10-10 standoff in Cincinnati. The game was called after the 10th inning to allow St. Louis to catch a train.

1955 — Dissatisfied with the play of his club, Owner August A. Busch Jr. dismisses Eddie Stanky as manager of the Cards and appoints Harry Walker to the helm. Walker was brought up from Rochester. His brother, Dixie, a Card coach, was sent to Rochester to replace him as pilot of the International League club. Stanky, a choice of former Redbird owner Fred Saigh, had managed the club since 1952. After sitting out the remainder of the season, he signed in October to pilot Minneapolis of the American Association in 1956.

1975 — Trade pitchers Elias Sosa and Ray Sadecki to the Braves, for pitcher Ron Reed and a player to be named. Braves assigned outfielder Wayne Nordhagen from Richmond to Tulsa June 2, completing the deal.

1976 — Sell pitcher Cardell Camper to the Indians, who assign him to Toledo.

1978 — Sell pitcher Dave Hamilton to the Pirates.

May 29

1899 — Art Reinhart (P, 1919, 25-28)

1928 — Willard Schmidt (P, 1952-53, 55-57)

1941 — The Cardinals defeat the Reds 10-9 for their 10th straight victory, including their last five by one run. The Reds rallied for three runs in the ninth inning, but shortstop Marty Marion leaped high to catch Ernie Lombardi's liner and threw to second base, doubling off Ernie Koy.

1970 — Trade infielder Phil Gagliano to the Cubs for pitcher Ted Abernathy.

1976 — Trade infielder Mario Guerrero, on Tulsa's roster, to the Angels for catcher Ed Jordan, who is assigned from El Paso to Arkansas, and a player to be named. The Angels assigned first baseman-outfielder Ed Kurpiel from Salt Lake City to Tulsa July 30, completing the deal.

1978 — Ken Boyer replaces Jack Krol as manager, who was serving on an interim basis since the May 25 firing of Vern Rapp.

May 30

1870 — Charlie Frank (OF-1B-P, 1893-94)

1878 — Mike Donlin (OF-IF-P, 1899-1900)

1885 — St. Louis defeats Chicago 3-2 in the first National League game played at Robison Field in St. Louis.

1897 — Wally Kimmick (SS, 1919)

1922 — Trade outfielder Cliff Heathcote to the Cubs for outfielder Max Flack between games of a morning-afternoon doubleheader at St. Louis. Both players went hitless against their old teams in the nightcap.

1925 — Name Rogers Hornsby manager, replacing Branch Rickey. The Cards, in eighth place at the time, finished the season in fourth.

1936 — Mel Nelson (P, 1960, 68-69)

1961 — Trade infielder Daryl Spencer to the Dodgers for infielder Bob Lillis and outfielder Carl Warwick.

1969 — The Cards trade outfielder Jim Hicks to the Angels for outfielder Vic Davalillo.

1978 — Silvio Martinez makes his N.L. debut a memorable one by beating the Mets 8-2 on a one-hitter. Martinez, making his first major-league start after a minor-league no-hitter the previous week, allowed only a home run by Steve Henderson opening up the seventh inning. George Hendrick smashed a three-run homer and Garry Templeton, Jerry Morales, and Ken Reitz all smashed three hits as the Cards scored more than two runs for the first time in 12 games.

May 31

1923 — Transfer pitcher Bill Pertica to Memphis.

1936 — Sell pitcher Bill Hallahan to the Reds.

1938 — Ray Washburn (P, 1961-69)

1944 — Acquire pitcher Mike Naymick from Cleveland.

JUNE

June 1

1869 — George Decker (1B-OF, 1898)

Ted Breitenstein (P, 1892-96, 1901)

1890 — Tommy Long (OF, 1915-17)

1895 — Roger Connor collects six hits in six at-bats as St. Louis drubs the New York Giants 23-2.

1920 — National League baseball will return to Sportsman's Park as Cards Owner Sam Breadon persuades Phil Bell of the St. Louis Browns to lease his park.

1931 — Hal Smith (C, 1956-61)

1943 — The Cards trade outfielders Coaker Triplett, Elvin Adams, and Dain Clay to the Phillies for outfielder Danny Litwhiler and outfielder-pitcher Earl Naylor.

June 1 (continued)

1950 — Cardinal catcher Joe Garagiola suffers a shoulder separation when he tumbles over first base against Brooklyn at St. Louis. A 5-2 victory hoisted the Cards into a first-place tie with the Dodgers.

1957 — Warren Spahn and Gene Conley of Milwaukee stop Wally Moon's hitting streak, which began May 5, at 24 games. But Murry Dickson, 40, gets his first victory of the season and the Cards throttle the Braves 7-1.

1968 — Cardinal reliever Joe Hoerner strikes out the last six batters he faces in a 6-5 victory over the Mets. His consecutive strikeouts equaled a N.L. record for relief pitchers first set by Johnny Meyer of Philadelphia in 1958 and tied later by Pete Richert of Los Angeles in 1962 and Ron Perranoski of the Dodgers in 1966. Mike Shannon's home run in the 10th inning provided Hoerner with the victory.

1974 — The Cards trade infielders Luis Alvarado and Ed Crosby, the latter on the Tulsa roster, to the Indians for shortstop Jack Heidemann.

June 2

1863 — Wilbert Robinson (C, 1900)

1869 — Tom Leahy (C, 1905)

1891 — Oscar Horstman (P, 1917-19)

1930 — Bob Lillis (IF, 1961)

1931 — Marshall Bridges (P, 1959-60)

      Larry Jackson (P, 1955-62)

1933 — Benny Valenzuela (3B, 1958)

1946 — Roger Freed (IF, 1977-79)

1953 — Acquire pitcher Hal White on waivers from the Browns.

1958 — Sell pitcher Morrie Martin to the Indians.

1964 — Trade pitcher Lou Burdette to the Cubs for pitcher Glenn Hobbie.

1980 — Trade outfielder Jim Lentine, on the Springfield roster, to Detroit for pitcher John Martin and outfielder Al Greene, who are both assigned from Evansville to Springfield.

June 3

1902 — St. Louis outfielder Mike O'Neill becomes the first player in the National League to hit a pinch grand-slam homer.

1918 — A game between St. Louis and Brooklyn, which the Cardinals win 15-12, is played under protest. In the sixth inning, with St. Louis' Doug Baird on second base, Walton Cruise hit a liner to center, which Brooklyn's Dave Hickman stopped, but could not hold. Baird reached third and thinking the ball was caught started back for second. After going back about 20 feet, he cut across the diamond to the plate and scored. Umpire Rigler ruled that after a runner once touched third base, he was not compelled to retouch it on the way home.

1939 — Doug Clemens (OF, 1960-64)

1955 — Stan Musial reaches a milestone with the 300th homer of his major-league career in a night game at Brooklyn. The round-tripper, his eighth of the season, came off Johnny Podres with two aboard in the fifth inning of a 12-5 loss to the Dodgers. Musial was the 13th player to achieve the 300 figure in home runs.

1969 — Trade pitcher Gary Waslewski to the Expos for pitcher Jim Grant.

June 4

1889 — Lee Magee (IF-OF, 1911-14)

1902 — George Watkins (OF-1B-2B, 1930-33)

1928 — Sign pitcher Clarence Mitchell.

1934 — Art Mahaffey (P, 1966)

1940 — A crowd of 23,500 sees the Cards lose to Brooklyn 10-1 in the first night game at St. Louis. The Dodgers made three errors, but put the game on ice as early as the first when five runs crossed the plate, three on Pete Coscarart's homer. Joe Medwick went five-for-five for the Cards.

1943 — Mort Cooper pitches his second consecutive one-hit game as he beats the Phillies 5-0. He didn't allow a hit until Jim Wasdell singled in the eighth inning. Just four days earlier he pitched a one-hitter against Brooklyn.

1956 — Terry Kennedy (C, 1978-80)

Sign pitcher Jim Konstanty.

1957 — Sell pitcher Jim Davis to the Giants.

1975 — Trade shortstop Ed Brinkman and pitcher Tommy Moore, the latter assigned to Spokane, to the Rangers for outfielder Willie Davis.

June 5

1874 — Frank Huelsman (OF, 1897)

1928 — Sign pitcher Clarence Mitchell.

1937 — Sign then pitcher Stan Musial to his first contract.

53

1945 — Chip Coulter (2B, 1969)

1946 — Local boy Joe Garagiola gets his first home-park hit in St. Louis, a run-producing double in the seventh, as the Cards beat the Braves 2-1. Pinch-hitter Elvin Adams's single drove in the decisive run in the ninth.

1949 — Baseball Commissioner A. B. (Happy) Chandler lifts the ban on all major-league players who jumped to Mexico in 1946. However, former St. Louis pitchers Max Lanier and Fred Martin announced they would continue to seek redress for damages they suffered as a result of Chandler's suspension in suits pending in New York's federal district court. The suits were kicked around in the courts, but never went to trial.

1962 — Shelled for five quick runs in a relief stint against Cincinnati, southpaw Ray Sadecki receives a dressing down and a $250 fine by Manager Johnny Keane after the game. The next night, Sadecki failed to report and announced he wanted to be traded, but peace was restored the following day.

Trade infielder Alex Grammas and outfielder Don Landrum to the Cubs for outfielder Bobby Gene Smith and infielder Daryl Robertson, the latter assigned to Tulsa.

1968 — St. Louis' Julian Javier falls for the old hidden-ball-trick and is tagged out at second base with the Astros and Cards deadlocked at 1-1 in the seventh inning. But the Cardinals wiped the egg off their faces and unloaded consecutive hits by Curt Flood, Roger Maris, and Orlando Cepeda in the eighth for a run that sent them to a 3-1 victory, their eighth straight.

June 6

1864 — Ed McKean (IF, 1899)

1911 — Transfer pitcher Emil Zmich to the Louisville club.

1920 — The Cards play their last game at Robison Field, beating the Cubs 5-2.

1937 — Umpire Ziggy Sears forfeits the second game of a doubleheader between the Cards and Phillies to the Cards 8-0 for alleged dilatory tactics in what appeared to be a direct attempt by the Phillies to prolong the game so that the Sunday curfew would halt the contest before it became legal. St. Louis was ahead at the time 8-2. The Phillies dropped the first game 7-2 with Lon Warneke pitching for St. Louis.

1948 — Red Schoendienst leads the attack with five doubles and a home run as the Cards defeat the Phillies twice 11-1, 2-0. Red clouted three doubles the previous day. The Cards clubbed four homers—by Enos Slaughter, Erv Dusak, Schoendienst, and Nippy Jones—in the sixth inning of the opener. Al Brazle allowed five hits while gaining the victory in the second game.

1973 — Trade pitcher Jim Bibby to the Texas Rangers for Mike Nagy and catcher John B. Wockenfuss, both assigned from Spokane to Tulsa.

1981 — Trade outfielder Tony Scott to Houston for pitcher Joaquin Andujar.

Sell pitcher George Frazier, on Springfield roster, to New York Yankees, who assign him to Columbus.

June 7

1863 — Frederick Ely (SS, 1893-95)

1877 — Bill Popp (P, 1902)

1882 — Hub Perdue (P, 1914-15)

1885 — Dan McGeehan (2B, 1911)

1893 — John Vann (PH, 1913)

1934 — Long Jim Weaver, recently released by the Browns, pitches the Cubs to a 1-0 victory over the Cards, shading Bill Hallahan in a spirited pitching duel.

1940 — The Cards fire manager Ray Blades and name Billy Southworth as his replacement. Cards stood at 15-29, 15½ games out of first place at the time of Blades' dismissal. After Southworth took over June 14, they went 69-40 for a .633 winning clip.

1966 — Pitcher Bob Gibson ends Willie Stargell's bid for a record-tying 10th straight hit in the first inning. The Pittsburgh slugger bounced to short-stop Jerry Buchek, who cut down Gene Alley trying to score from third.
   Gibson struck out four batters in the fourth inning, but the Cards lost to the Pirates 9-1. He had to whiff four men in the fourth because the third strike to one of them was a wild pitch.

1970 — Trailing 7-1, the Cards rally to beat San Diego 10-7. The Cards got two runs in the sixth inning on Ted Simmons's first major-league home run. Vic Davalillo began a six-run seventh with a single and ended the scoring with a run-scoring single.

1972 — Purchase pitcher Diego Segui from the A's.

1973 — Trade infielder Dwain Anderson to the Padres for second baseman Dave Campbell.

1976 — Trade pitcher Danny Frisella to the Brewers for a player to be named. Sam Mejias was assigned to Tulsa June 23 to complete the deal.

June 8

1859 — John Stricker (2B, 1892)

1913 — The Cubs purchase Roger Bresnahan from the Cards after a prolonged contract hassle and the Cards attempt to release him in October 1912 without asking waivers on him.

1924 — Sell outfielder German Schultz to the Phillies.

55

1925 — Del Ennis (OF, 1957-58)

1930 — Phil Pane (P, 1958)

1934 — Bill Smith (P, 1958-59)

1935 — George Brunet (P, 1971)

1937 — Joe Grzenda (P, 1972)

1946 — Delmar Ennis's eighth-inning single breaks up Red Barrett's chance for a perfect no-hit game, but the Card right-hander goes on after retiring 22 batters to shut out the Phillies 7-0 for his first victory of the season.

1959 — Trade pitcher Jim Brosnan to the Reds for pitcher Hal Jeffcoat.

1970 — Release catcher Bart Zeller as a player and sign him as a coach.

1973 — Trade shortstop Ray Busse to the Astros for infielder Stan Papi, who is assigned to Tulsa.

1978 — Trade pitcher Frank Riccelli to the Astros for outfielder Bob Coluccio. Riccelli was assigned to Charleston.

June 9

1890 — Harry Glenn (C, 1915)

1903 — Mike Ryba (P, 1935-38)

1931 — Bill Virdon (OF, 1955-56)

1939 — Julio Gotay (IF-OF, 1960-62)

1946 — Sell outfielder Danny Litwhiler to the Boston Braves.

1947 — Red Schoendienst suffers an 0-for-12 day as St. Louis splits a doubleheader with Philadelphia, the Cards winning the opener 4-2 and losing the night-cap in 15 innings 2-1. Schoendienst's dismal day set a N.L. record for most at-bats in a doubleheader (more than 18 innings) without a hit. Philadelphia pitcher Lynn Rowe had a shutout brewing in the second game when he went out after being struck by a broken bat in the sixth.

1956 — John Fulgham (P, 1979-80)

1964 — Ray Sadecki posts his sixth straight victory as a starter, besting Juan Marichal and the Giants 1-0, when Charlie James singles in the only run in the ninth inning.

1980 — Whitey Herzog is named manager.

June 10

1870 — Pat McCauley (C, 1893)

1882 — William Barbeau (3B-2B, 1909-10)

1892 — Frank Gilhooley (OF, 1911-12)

1910 — Frank Demaree (OF, 1943)

1912 — Whitey Moore (P, 1942)

1938 — Johnny Edwards (C, 1968)

1941 — Lon Warneke yields a single to Emmett Mueller, the first man to face him, then holds the Phillies hitless the rest of the route in a 3-0 St. Louis victory.

1944 — The Cards give the Cincinnati Reds their lumps by pounding out the most lopsided shutout victory in the National League in 38 years. When the firing was done, the Cards won 18-0. A mark went into the record books when the Reds inserted 15-year-old high school pitcher Joe Nuxhall into the game. Nuxhall, the youngest pitcher to ever work in the majors, pitched two-thirds of the ninth inning, giving up five runs on five passes, two singles, and a wild pitch. Mort Cooper spaced five hits in gaining the shutout. The Cards tied a major-league record by leaving 18 men on base.

1950 — Elias Sosa (P, 1975)

1966 — During batting practice at Philadelphia, a smash by the Phillies' outfielder Johnny Callison hits Orlando Cepeda in the right eye. He was out of the Cardinal lineup for 15 days.

June 11

1866 — William Schriver (C-1B, 1901)

1879 — Roger Bresnahan (C-IF-OF-P, 1909-12)

1887 — William Dell (P, 1912)

1971 — Trade outfielder Leron Lee and pitcher Fred Norman, the latter on Tulsa roster, to the Padres for pitcher Al Santorini.

June 12

1874 — Pat Dillard (OF-IF, 1900)

1922 — Cardinal pinch-hitter George Toporcer pulls a boner and loses credit for a home run during the sixth inning of a game against the Phillies. The Cards had two runs over and runners on first and second bases when Toporcer, batting for pitcher Dixie Walker, slammed the ball over the short right-field fence at National League Park in Philadelphia. But, alas, poor George was deprived of a homer in the official record books when he passed teammate Doc Lavan between first and second and was promptly declared out by Umpire Hart. He was given credit for a single. However, the

Cards tied their own league record with 10 consecutive hits in the inning and scored seven runs to roll to a 14–7 victory.

1940 — Trade outfielder Joe Medwick and pitcher Curt Davis to Brooklyn for pitcher Carl Doyle, outfielder Ernie Koy, pitcher Sam Nahem, infielder-outfielder Bert Haas, and cash.

1945 — Option pitcher Stan Partenheimer to Columbus.

1957 — Stan Musial plays his 823rd consecutive game, breaking Gus Suhr's National League record.

June 13

1891 — Marty Kavanagh (IF–OF, 1918)

1918 — Cliff Heathcote hits for the cycle in nine at-bats as the Cards and Phillies battle to an 8–8 tie in 19 innings. The umpires called the game after 4 hours, 35 minutes because of darkness.

1938 — Trade catcher Spud Davis, pitcher Al Hollingsworth, and $55,000 to the Phillies for pitcher Bill Walters.

1940 — Buy pitcher Ira Hutchinson from Brooklyn.

1949 — Trade catcher Walker Cooper to the Reds for catcher Ray Mueller.

1954 — Eldon (Rip) Repulski, Cardinal outfielder, begins a hitting splurge in a Sunday doubleheader against the Pittsburgh Pirates at Busch Stadium. He set what was believed to be a major-league record when he ran up a streak of ten consecutive games in which he had two or more hits. He went three-for-four at-bat in the opener and then made two hits in five trips in the nightcap. The Cards went on an Eastern road trip the next day and Repulski's spree of two or more hits continued through June 24. In 10 contests he made 22 safeties in 44 appearances, including three doubles, three triples, and five home runs. He was limited to one hit against Brooklyn June 25, but extended his batting streak to 16 games before being halted. Repulski averaged .429 and hit 8 homers in 16 contests.

1964 — Trade catcher Jim Saul and cash to the Reds for outfielder Bob Skinner. Saul was transferred from Jacksonville to San Diego.

1970 — Trade pitcher George Culver to the Astros for outfielder-first baseman Jim Beauchamp and shortstop Leon McFadden, the latter assigned from Oklahoma City to Tulsa.

Trade second baseman Cookie Rojas to the Royals for outfielder Fred Rico, who is assigned from Omaha to Tulsa.

1973 — Rick Wise comes within two outs of pitching a no-hitter as the Cards shut out Cincinnati 8–0. Joe Morgan's single up the middle in the ninth inning was Cincinnati's offense for the evening. Louis Melendez' grand slam led the way as the Cards racked up Jack Billingham early, scoring seven times in the third.

1975 — Purchase pitcher Mike Wallace from the Yankees and assign him to Tulsa.

June 14

1890 — Jack Reis (P, 1911)

1926 — Trade outfielder Heinie Mueller to the Giants for outfielder Billy Southworth.

1953 — Trade outfielder Hal Rice to the Pirates for infielder Pete Castiglione.

1956 — Trade second baseman Red Schoendienst, catcher Bill Sarni, outfielder Jackie Brandt, and pitcher Dick Littlefield to the Giants for shortstop Al Dark, outfielder-first baseman Whitey Lockman, catcher Ray Katt, and pitcher Don Liddle. The Cards also transferred Bob Stephenson from Omaha to Minneapolis as part of the deal.

1958 — Obtain pitcher Sal Maglie from the Yankees for cash and the assignment of pitcher Joe McClain from Rochester to Denver for the balance of the season.

1964 — Houston's Dick Farrell becomes the season's first 10-game winner in the majors by defeating the slumping Cards 4-1. It was their fourth consecutive loss and their 18th in 24 games.

June 15

1891 — Lou North (P, 1917, 20-24)

1927 — Ben Flowers (P, 1955-56)

1931 — Trade outfielder Taylor Douthit to the Reds for outfielder Walter Roettger.

1948 — Release outfielder Ed Sauer to Pittsburgh.

1951 — Trade pitchers Howie Pollet and Ted Wilks, outfielder Bill Howerton, catcher Joe Garagiola, and infielder Dick Cole to Pittsburgh for outfielder Wally Westlake and pitcher Cliff Chambers.

1952 — The Giants build up a seemingly insurmountable 11-0 lead in the first game of a doubleheader at New York, then watched in dismay as the Cardinals make up the deficit in three innings and win 14-12. Solly Hemus tied the game in the eighth with a home run and sewed it up in the ninth with another four-bagger. "Country" Slaughter paced the Cards' 18-hit attack with a home run, a double, and a single, and drove in five runs. His homer came with two on to climax the Redbirds' seven-run outburst in the fifth inning, which shelled Sal Maglie, ace Giant right-hander. The Giants rebounded from the humiliation to defeat the Cards 3-0 in the second game.

1953 — Purchase catcher Sal Yvars from the Giants.

June 15 (continued)

1958 — Trade shortstop Dick Schofield and cash to the Pirates for infielders Gene Freese and Johnny O'Brien.

1959 — Purchase third baseman Dick Gray from the Dodgers.

1960 — Trade infielder Jim McKnight to the Cubs with cash for outfielder Walt Moryn. McKnight was assigned from Memphis to Houston.

Trade pitcher Jim Donohue to the Dodgers for outfielder John Glenn, on the St. Paul roster. Donohue was transferred from Rochester to St. Paul.

1961 — Sell outfielder Walt Moryn to the Pirates.

1963 — Trade catcher-first baseman Gene Oliver and pitcher Bob Sadowski, the latter on the Atlanta roster, to the Milwaukee Braves for pitcher Lou Burdette.

1964 — Trade pitchers Ernie Broglio and Bobby Shantz and outfielder Doug Clemens to the Chicago Cubs for outfielder Lou Brock and pitcher Paul Toth, who is assigned to Jacksonville.

1965 — Trade pitchers Ron Taylor and Mike Cuellar to the Astros for pitcher Hal Woodeshick. The Astros assigned pitcher Chuck Taylor from Oklahoma City to Jacksonville to complete the deal.

1966 — Bob Gibson shuts out the Pirates 1-0 on three hits at St. Louis for career victory No. 100.

1968 — Trade outfielder Dick Simpson and pitcher Hal Gilson to the Astros for outfielder Ron Davis.

1971 — Trade pitcher Mike Torrez to the Expos' Winnipeg affiliate for pitcher Bob Reynolds.

1973 — Purchase pitcher Orlando Pena from the Orioles.

1976 — Trade outfielder Reggie Smith to the Dodgers for catcher-outfielder Joe Ferguson.

1977 — Trade pitcher Doug Capilla to the Reds for pitcher Rawly Eastwick.

Trade outfielder Bake McBride and pitcher Steve Waterbury to the Phillies for pitcher Tom Underwood, first baseman Dane Iorg, and outfielder Rick Bosetti.

Trade third baseman Joel Youngblood to the Mets for infielder Mike Phillips.

1978 — Assign outfielder Jim Dwyer to the Giants, completing an Oct. 25, 1977 deal in which the Cards acquired pitcher Frank Riccelli.

1980 — St. Louis and Cincinnati use 10 relievers, who combine for 11 innings, 14 hits, 10 earned runs, and an ERA of 8.18 before Terry Kennedy mercifully doubles in two runs in the 13th inning to give the Cards a 10–9 victory. The teams used seven pitchers in the ninth inning to tie a major-league record.

June 16

1874 — Harry Blake (OF–IF–C, 1899)

1881 — Aloysius Egan (P, 1905–06)

1889 — Gene Dale (P, 1911–12)

1890 — Fritz Mollwitz (1B, 1919)

1894 — Bob Glenn (P, 1920)

1922 — Max Surkont (P, 1956)

1930 — Trade pitchers Bill Sherdel and Fred Frankhouse to the Braves for pitcher Burleigh Grimes.

1942 — Recall catcher Sam Narron from Rochester.

1964 — Lou Brock steals his first base in a St. Louis uniform and Ken Boyer hits for the cycle as the Cardinals defeat Houston 7–1 at Houston.

1972 — Purchase pitcher John Cumberland from the Giants.

1978 — Cincinnati's Tom Seaver pitches a 4–0, no-hit victory over the Cards. Only three times did the Redbirds come close to getting a hit. In the fourth inning second baseman Joe Morgan made a diving, one-handed stop of Keith Hernandez' grounder far to his left and tossed to first for the out. In the seventh, Hernandez' smash bounced off Seaver's glove and was fielded by shortstop Dave Concepcion who threw to first for the putout. In the top of the eighth Jerry Morales hit a high hopper to Ray Knight at third base. Knight played his position perfectly and his strong throw to first beat Morales by a whisker.

June 17

1917 — The Giants, playing their first game at the Polo Grounds in New York, defeat the Cards 2–1.

1963 — Ernie Broglio hurls the Cards into first place with a five-hit, 8–1 victory over the Mets. The Cards held first place until July 2, when they lost to Los Angeles 1–0, sending the Dodgers into a lead they never relinquished.

1965 — St. Louis second baseman Julian Javier goes on the disabled list for seven weeks after breaking a finger on his right hand when hit by a pitch from Pittsburgh's Vern Law at St. Louis. The Cardinals lost the game 4–1.

June 18

1910 — Obtain catcher Ivy Wingo from Greensville, S.C.

June 18 (continued)

1921 — Trade pitcher Ferdinand Schupp and infielder Hal Janvrin to the Dodgers for pitcher Jeff Pfeffer.

1939 — Lou Brock (OF, 1964–79)

1941 — Max Lanier defeats the Phillies 7–3 but has his scoreless streak stopped at 21 innings.

1968 — Bobby Tolan's first homer of the season and Nelson Briles's eight-hit pitching carry the Cards past the Cubs 1–0. The league-leading Cards increased their lead to 5½ games over second-place Atlanta, winning for the 17th time in 21 games.

June 19

1912 — Don Gutteridge (3B–SS, 1936–40)

1929 — Don Ferrarese (P, 1962)

1949 — Jerry Reuss (P, 1969–71)

1950 — Rudy Arroyo (P, 1971)

1968 — Steve Carlton, 23, allowing only a fourth-inning single to Glenn Beckert, hurls a one-hitter in a 4–0 victory over the Cubs. Orlando Cepeda supplied all the offense Carlton needed, hammering a three-run homer in the bottom of the third off loser Rich Nye at St. Louis.

June 20

1845 — Ned Cuthbert (1B–OF, 1876)

1961 — A medical examination discloses that catcher Hal Smith has a heart condition, putting an end to his major-league career.

1972 — Trade first baseman Mike Fiore and pitcher Bob Chlupsa, the latter transferred from Tulsa to Hawaii, to the Padres for infielder Rafael Robles, who is assigned to Tulsa.

June 21

1876 — Billy Gilbert (2B, 1908–09)

1905 — Randy Moore (C, 1937)

1918 — Cliff Heathcote gets a home run and a double as the Cards score eight runs in the first inning. They went on to beat Cincinnati 12–6.

1927 — The Cards sweep a doubleheader from Chicago 6–5, 12–3, but their pennant chances receive a jolt when able shortstop Tom Thevenow fractures his ankle in the fourth inning of the second game. The ankle healed slowly and poorly and Thevenow was never the same after the accident.

Jackie Collum (P, 1951-53, 56)

1950 — Ralph Beard (P, 1954)

1957 — Rookie Von McDaniel, signed less than a month earlier out of Hollis (Okla.) High School, hurls a two-hit masterpiece in a 2-0 victory over the Dodgers at Busch Stadium. He held the Dodgers hitless until the sixth inning, when Jim Gilliam led off with a looping single, which second baseman Don Blasingame couldn't hold. After an error put runners on first and second, Duke Snider beat out an attempted sacrifice bunt for Brooklyn's other hit, filling the bases. However, McDaniel retired the side without a score.

1959 — Stan Musial hits his 652nd and 653rd career doubles, breaking Honus Wagner's National League mark, in the first game of a doubleheader against Pittsburgh at St. Louis.

1974 — Sell pitcher Pete Richert to the Phillies.

June 22

1877 — Gus Thompson (P, 1906)

1890 — John Mercer (1B, 1912)

1906 — George Puccinelli (OF, 1930)

1925 — In a game featuring nine home runs, Pittsburgh defeats the Cards 24-6. Kiki Cuyler's home run in the first inning and Pie Traynor's in the eighth were with the bases filled for Pittsburgh. George Grantham twice hit for the circuit for the Pirates. Rogers Hornsby, the major leagues' leading home run hitter, slammed his 18th circuit clout of the season for the Cards.

1926 — Obtain pitcher Grover Cleveland Alexander on waivers from the Cubs.

1937 — Charlie O'Rourke (PH, 1959)

1951 — Mike Anderson (OF-1B, 1976-78)

1953 — Roy Thomas (P, 1978-80)

1954 — Recall pitcher Brooks Lawrence from Columbus.

1962 — Stan Musial passes Ty Cobb as baseball's total base leader with No. 5,864 against the Phillies at Philadelphia.

1966 — Sell pitcher Curt Simmons to the Cubs.

1970 — Purchase pitcher Chuck Hartenstein from Pittsburgh.

June 23

1895 — Jack Smith (OF, 1915-26)

1919 — Pittsburgh outfielder Casey Stengel's home run defeats Cards 3-2.

1941 — Pitcher Mort Cooper has an operation to remove a growth from his pitching elbow (right). He didn't return to action until August.

1975 — Ron Reed wins the opener with a seven-hitter and John Denny records his first major-league shutout with a five-hitter in the nightcap as the Cards sweep New York 1-0, 4-0. Ron Fairly's first-inning single scored Lou Brock with a run that won the first game. Ted Simmons hit a grand slam in the eighth to win the nightcap at New York.

1976 — Outfielder Sam Mejias is acquired from the Brewers to complete the June 7 trade for Dan Frisella. Mejias was assigned to Tulsa.

1978 — Purchase pitcher Roy Thomas from the Astros.

June 24

1864 — Jack Clements (C, 1898)

1867 — Jake Stenzel (OF, 1898-99)

1892 — George Harper (OF, 1928)

1898 — Georgetown College product Dick Harley manages six hits in six at-bats as St. Louis edges Pittsburgh 7-6. Harley's sixth hit drove in Bud Lally from third with the decisive run in the top of the 12th inning.

1915 — Elvin Adams (OF, 1939, 43, 45-46)

1920 — Obtain infielder George McCarthy from the Giants.

1931 — Three home runs by George Watkins, St. Louis right fielder, one of them a two-run shot, give the Cards a 4-2 victory in the nightcap of a double-header. The Cards, leading second-place New York by 3½ games, also took the opener by the same score.

1944 — The Cards, held to a 5-5 tie by Pittsburgh in 14 innings the previous night, unlimber their heavy artillery to pound the Pirates 16-0. Ray Sanders' home run highlighted a five-run, fifth-inning rally. In addition, Stan Musial had four hits, including a two-base smash. Big Mort Cooper had a one-hitter until the eighth, when Babe Dahlgren and Fran Zak each hit singles at Pittsburgh.

1951 — Ken Reitz (3B-SS, 1972-75, 77-80)

1960 — Stan Musial returns to the lineup after being benched by Manager Solly Hemus at the start of the year in a youth movement. Hemus' ploy failed and The Man regained his spot.

1963 — Trade infielder Leo Burke to the Cubs for pitcher Barney Schultz.

1965 — Sell outfielder Carl Warwick to the Orioles.

1975 — Sell outfielder Dan Hahn to the Padres.

1978 — The Giants assign pitcher Rob Dressler to Springfield to complete the July 18 deal for catcher John Tamargo.

1979 — Catcher Ted Simmons, hitting .321 and enjoying his finest season, suffers a broken bone in his left wrist when he is struck by a foul bunt off the bat of New York pitcher Andy Hassler in the seventh inning at St. Louis. Simmons continued playing until pain forced him to leave the game, which the Cards lost 6-2.

June 25

1875 — Bill Phyle (P, 1906)

1896 — Earl Howard (P, 1918)

1917 — Shortstop Rogers Hornsby has 10 assists as St. Louis defeats Cincinnati 4-2 in the first game of a doubleheader. However, the Reds garnered 25 hits to win the second game 15-4.

1930 — Guillermo Luna (P, 1954)

1931 — Paul Derringer, rookie right-hander of St. Louis, wins a pitching duel from Brooklyn's Dazzy Vance. Vance allowed only three hits, pitching perfect ball until the seventh inning, when George Watkins beat out a bunt for the first hit of the game, Jim Bottomley singled and sent him around to third, and Watkins then sole home with the eventual winning run while Vance was trying to pick Bottomley off first base. Cards win 1-0.

1934 — Obtain pitcher Dazzy Vance from the Reds.

1954 — Bob Shirley (P, 1981)

1959 — Purchase catcher J. W. Porter from the Senators.

1971 — Conditionally purchase pitcher Daryl Patterson from the A's. Return him Oct. 21.

June 26

1908 — Debs Garms (OF-IF, 1943-45)

1921 — Howie Pollett (P, 1941-43, 46-51)

1933 — Gene Green (OF-C, 1957-59)

1959 — Sell pitcher Gary Blaylock to the Yankees.

1968 — Bob Gibson hurls his fifth straight shutout, one shy of the major-league record set earlier in the month by Los Angeles' Don Drysdale, with a 3-0 triumph over the Pirates in the opener of a doubleheader. The Pirates rebounded from their loss to Gibson and trimmed the Cards 3-1 in the second game, although the Cards stopped Maury Wills' hitting streak at 24 games at St. Louis.

1978 — Obtain infielder Jose Baez from Seattle for a player to be named. Baez was assigned to Springfield. The Mariners purchased outfielder Mike Potter Oct. 27 to complete the deal.

June 27

1906 — Dick Terwilliger (P, 1932)

1915 — Fred Martin (P, 1946, 49-50)

1926 — A large crowd in St. Louis sees Grover Cleveland Alexander reap revenge for having been sold down the river. Alexander, on the slab for the first time as a Cardinal player, beat the Cubs, his former teammates, 3-2 in the first game of a doubleheader.

The Cubs won the second game 5-0, but almost won by forfeit when in the ninth inning the crowd showered the field with thousands of pop bottles. The row started when umpire Charlie Moran ruled that Sparky Adams was safe at first after the entire throng had seen him pop to Rogers Hornsby. Moran declared him safe because the catcher had interfered with Adams as he started to run.

1932 — Eddie Kasko (IF, 1957-58)

1962 — The surging Cards roll to their fourth and fifth straight victories by sweeping a double shutout 4-0 and 8-0 from the Chicago Cubs behind the pitching of veteran Larry Jackson and southpaw Ray Sadecki. Jackson yielded just four singles in the first game. Sadecki hurled a five-hitter in the nightcap at Chicago.

1973 — Joe Torre hits for the cycle as the Cards pound 22 hits and blast Pittsburgh 15-4. Torre, who raised his batting average to .338, doubled in the first inning, homered in the third, and tripled in the fourth. Then he hit into a double play, walked in the eighth, and, figuring he wouldn't bat again, asked Manager Red Schoendienst to take him out. But Schoendienst balked at his request and Torre, batting in the ninth, got his single at Pittsburgh.

June 28

1935 — Bob Blaylock (P, 1956)

1977 — Ken Reitz hits two home runs, including his second grand slam of the season, and drives in eight runs in the nightcap as the Cards sweep a doubleheader from Pittsburgh 6-1, 13-3. Keith Hernandez had three hits in the first game to lead the Cards as Buddy Schultz won his first major-league start with five-hit pitching for $7\frac{1}{3}$ innings at St. Louis.

June 29

1873 — Jack Sutthoff (P, 1899)

1877 — Charles Donahue (IF, 1904)

1910 — Francis Healy (C-OF-3B, 1934)

Burgess Whitehead (IF, 1933-35)

1925 — Nippy Jones (2B-OF-1B, 1946-51)

1926 — Bobby Morgan (IF, 1956)

1933 — Don Shaw (P, 1971-72)

1937 — Chicago and St. Louis use 37 players in a wild and wooly battle won by the Cubs 11-9. Manager Charlie Grimm had to commandeer 20 players in the Chicago ranks during the three-hour battle.

1947 — Enos Slaughter drives in 10 runs, seven in the second game, as the Cards and Cincinnati split a doubleheader. The Reds won the opener 9-7 after piling up an 8-1 lead. The Cards came back to bury the Reds 17-2 in the second game.

1958 — Can a relief pitcher be legally replaced before pitching to a batter or retiring a runner, except in the case of injury or illness? In an unusual suspended-game situation, this question resulted in an affirmative answer. The Cards were playing the Phillies when the Pennsylvania Sunday curfew halted the second game of their twin bill in the eighth inning. The Phillies, trailing 4-2, pushed over one run and had runners on second and third with one out when Billy Muffett replaced Morrie Martin as Card hurler. Before Muffet was able to deliver a pitch, the game was stopped by curfew.

The Cards subsequently optioned Muffett to Omaha of the American Association, but recalled him a few days before the game was to be completed July 29. In the meantime, a check of the N.L. rules revealed a pitcher who had been announced before the game is suspended can be substituted for when the game is resumed, even though he failed to pitch to a batter. As a result, Jim Brosnan took the place of Muffett when the contest was resumed, retiring the side without any further damage, and completing a 4-3 victory.

1969 — Cards drop a doubleheader to Cubs at Wrigley Field, 3-1 and 12-1, as Billy Williams of Chicago plays in his 895th and 896th consecutive games, breaking Stan Musial's record. Williams had five hits before the 41,060 gathered for Billy Williams Day ceremonies.

June 30

1933 — Dizzy Dean strikes out 17 Chicago Cubs during 8-2 Card victory in St. Louis.

1935 — Paul Toth (P, 1962)

1950 — Recall first baseman Rocky Nelson from Columbus.

1959 — In most major-league baseball games, only one ball is in play at a time. But spectators in a game between the Cards and Cubs at Wrigley Field were startled to see two balls bounding around the field at the same time. Among those startled was Stan Musial.

67

Musial was walked in the fourth inning on a 3-1 pitch which caromed off Chicago catcher Sammy Taylor and Umpire Vic Delmore and back toward the home plate screen. While Taylor and pitcher Bob Anderson were busy at home plate protesting the umpire's call, Musial took off for second. At the same time, the Cub batboy picked up the ball and tossed it toward the field announcer, who is supposed to receive errant baseballs. But Al Dark, Cub third baseman, intercepted the ball and threw it to Cub shortstop Ernie Banks who tagged Musial.

At that instant, back at home plate catcher Taylor got another ball from the umpire and was handing it to pitcher Anderson, who turned and threw toward second base. But the ball bounced into center field. Musial was declared out after a 10-minute debate. The umpires ruled he was tagged out with the original ball. The Cards withdrew their protest when they won the game 4-1.

1975 — Trade cash and a player to be named to the White Sox for outfielder Buddy Bradford. Pitcher Bill Parsons was assigned from Tulsa to Denver July 7 to complete the deal.

JULY

July 1

1857 — Roger Connor (1B, 1894-97)

1913 — Frank Barrett (P, 1939)

1915 — Norman Young (1B, 1948)

1920 — Pittsburgh defeats the Cards 6-2 in 10 innings in the first National League game of the century at Sportsman's Park in St. Louis.

1934 — The Cards battle for 18 innings against Cincinnati in the first game of a doubleheader, winning 8-6, as they score two runs in the final inning. The game took 4 hours, 26 minutes to play, after which the teams returned to the field for the second game, which ended in a 2-2 tie when it was called because of darkness after the fifth inning.

1938 — Craig Anderson (P, 1961)

1951 — Outfielder Hal Rice is recalled from Rochester.

Jim Otten (P, 1980-81)

1956 — The Cards exhaust their bull pen by using 12 pitchers as they drop a doubleheader to the Reds 19-15, 7-1. Red slugger Ted Kluszewski hit three home runs in the 10-inning opener. The 3-hour, 47-minute marathon was marked by 43 hits and 8 home runs.

1970 — Trade pitcher Ted Abernathy to the Royals for pitcher Chris Zachary, who is assigned from Omaha to Tulsa.

July 2

1900 — Ernie Vick (C, 1922, 1924-26)

1929 — Chuck Stobbs (P, 1958)

1933 — A brilliant pitching performance by Carl Hubbell of the New York Giants turns back the Cardinals 1-0 in 18 innings. With 45,000 fans on hand at the Polo Grounds in the first game of a doubleheader, Hubbell gave up six hits and walked one batter. Tex Carleton of the Cardinals opposed him evenly on the mound before being lifted for a pinch-hitter after 16 innings. The Giants also took the second game 1-0 as Leroy Parmelee struck out 13 Redbird batters, besting Dizzy Dean.

1935 — Joe Medwick homers and Bill Hallahan scatters three hits as the Cards blank Pittsburgh 7-0.

1959 — Cardinal Manager Solly Hemus has a run-in with Umpire Shag Crawford, resulting in a $250 fine and a five-day suspension for the Redbird skipper from Warren Giles, league president. Hemus's freshman year as field boss saw him ejected by umps eight times, with fines totalling $650.

July 3

1869 — George Cuppy (P, 1899)

1888 — Wes Callahan (1B-OF, 1913)

1939 — Johnny Mize smashes two homers, a triple, and a double off Bill Lee as the Cards defeat the Cubs 5-3 at Wrigley Field.

1946 — As a wire service report described it, the Cards "broke out like measles at an orphanage" by scoring 10 runs in the fourth inning and defeating the Reds 16-0 at St. Louis.

1952 — Ryan Kurosaki (P, 1975)

1953 — Keith Smith (OF, 1979-80)

1960 — Hank Aaron of the Milwaukee Braves belts career homer No. 200, a solo shot, off Card hurler Ron Kline in the seventh inning at St. Louis.

1972 — The Padres return first baseman Mike Fiore to the Cards, who assign him to Tulsa.

July 4

1890 — Milt Reed (PH, 1911)

1935 — The Cards climb into second place by sweeping a doubleheader from the Cubs. After three hits off Charlie Root gave the Cards a 5-3 victory in the first game, they went on to win another close one 6-4 for Dizzy Dean, this time with the aid of four Chicago errors.

1939 — Famed Cardinal scout Charles F. Barkett dies of a heart attack at his St.

Louis home. He recommended such Cardinals as Don Gutteridge, Jim Bottomley, and Si Johnson and others as Muddy Ruel, Charlie Grimm, Ray Blades, and Ival Goodman to other clubs.

1945 — Augie Bergamo slugs 10 hits, including two homers, one a grand slam, and bats in nine runs as the Cards sweep a doubleheader from the Giants 8-4, 9-2. Eight of his RBI came in the nightcap, when he hit a pitch into the stands at the Polo Grounds with the bases loaded.

1970 — The Cards call on three pinch-hitters in the eighth inning of a game at Montreal and all three strike out. Steve Renko of the Expos boosted his strikeout total to 10 in the game, which the Cards lost 8-0, by fanning pinch-hitters Jim Beauchamp, Vic Davalillo, and Leron Lee.

July 5

1895 — George Kopshaw (C, 1923)

1955 — The majors' biggest rhubarb of the season takes place between two managers, Harry Walker of St. Louis and Birdie Tebbetts of Cincinnati. The incident took place during the second half of the ninth inning of a game at Cincinnati and resulted from the alleged delaying tactics by Walker and catcher Bill Sarni of St. Louis. When Tebbetts went on the field to protest to Umpire Jocko Conlan, Walker rushed out to his battery's defense. Heated words were followed by an exchange of punches and the two pilots wrestled each other to the ground. Players from both sides joined in the general melee. The only real casualties were a bruised forehead for Walker and a bloody nose and a scraped mouth for Tebbetts. The Reds, scoring twice in the ninth, won 5-4. The next day Warren Giles, league president, a spectator at the free-for-all, fined both managers $100 and Sarni $25 for his repeated refusal to heed Conlan's orders.

1963 — Trade pitcher Ed Bauta to the Mets for pitcher Ken MacKenzie.

July 6

1871 — George Paynter (OF, 1894)

1876 — John Heidrick (OF-IF, P, 1899–1901)

1879 — Ed Holly (SS-2B, 1906–07)

1929 — After losing 11 straight games, the Cards emerge from their slump and set a major-league record by romping over the Phillies 28-6 in the second game of a doubleheader. They amassed 10 runs in both the first and the fifth innings. First baseman Jim Bottomley accounted for seven RBI and outfielder Chick Hafey had four. Each Redbird scored in the first inning with Andy High counting twice. The Cards were beaten 10-6 in the first game.

1933 — St. Louis hurler Bill Hallahan starts for the National League in the first major-league All-Star game at Chicago's Comiskey Park. In that contest, St. Louis' Frankie Frisch belted the first National League homer. Fittingly,

Yankee slugger Babe Ruth hit the game's first four-bagger to lead the Americans to a 4-2 victory.

1934 — Having used 20 of the 22 men on his roster, St. Louis Manager Frankie Frisch lets pitcher Tex Carleton bat for himself with two out in the ninth inning and with the tying run on second base against Cincinnati. Carleton singled, but the runner on second, Leo Durocher, was out trying to score and the Cards lost 16-15. Rip Collins scored five times in the defeat.

1947 — Jim Hearn throws a three-hitter in the first game of a doubleheader against the Reds at Cincinnati, and teammate Murry Dickson hurls a four-hitter in the nightcap as the Cards sweep 3-0, 2-0.

Lance Clemons (P, 1972)

1950 — The Cards capture their 12th straight home victory with 10 runs in the first inning en route to a 13-1 victory over Cincinnati. Bill Howerton scored twice in the first frame.

1961 — Johnny Keane succeeds Solly Hemus as St. Louis manager. Keane got a rude welcome that night at Los Angeles as Don Drysdale held the Cardinals to five hits and the Dodgers won 10-1.

July 7

1886 — Bob James (OF, 1909)

1929 — John Romonosky (P, 1953)

1936 — St. Louis' Dizzy Dean gains the National League's first All-Star victory 4-3 at Braves Field in Boston.

1937 — Earl Averill's line drive in the sixth inning hits Cards' pitcher Dizzy Dean in the toe at the All-Star game at Washington's Griffith Stadium, breaking the bone. Dean never was the same following the accident and remembered it until the day he died.

1946 — Sell first baseman Jeoff Long to the White Sox.

1948 — Tommy Moore (P, 1975)

1975 — Assign pitcher Bill Parsons from the Tulsa affiliate to the White Sox Denver farm team to complete the June 30 deal that sent Buddy Bradford to the Cards.

July 8

1883 — Howard Holmes (C, 1898)

1890 — Ivy Wingo (C-1B-OF, 1911-14)

1891 — Clyde Barfoot (P, 1922-23)

1931 — Ed Phillips (PH, 1953)

1942 — Sell pitcher Lon Warneke to the Cubs.

1943 — George Culver (P, 1970)

1946 — Sell pitcher Blix Donnelly to the Phillies.

1948 — Lerrin LaGrow (P, 1976)

1950 — The Cards lose to Pittsburgh 7–6 after leading 6–3 when they entered the ninth inning at Forbes Field. The Pirates loaded the bases with one out, then Jack Phillips sent a long fly to center field near the 376-foot sign. Stan Musial appeared to make the catch, leaping high against an eight-foot screen. But he slumped to the ground and a Pirate bull pen member picked up the ball that dropped into the enclosure for a game-winning grand slam.

1951 — Red Schoendienst hits a home run from each side of the plate as the Cards and Pittsburgh split a doubleheader. In the sixth inning of the second game he hit a home run left-handed with no one on base. In the next inning he hit one right-handed with one man on base. The Pirates took the opener 6–2 behind rookie pitcher Bob Friend, but the Cards won the nightcap 9–8, belting six Pirate hurlers for 17 hits.

1961 — Release coach Darrell Johnson, who signs with the Phillies as a catcher.

1962 — Stan Musial hits three home runs in consecutive times at bat and four in a row during two games, July 7–8, against the New York Mets at the Polo Grounds. The first was off Craig Anderson in the eighth inning of the second game July 7 to beat the Mets 3–2. The next day he homered off Jay Hook in the first and again in the fourth, and off Willard Hunter in the seventh, all into the right-field stands, to pace a 15–1 victory. In the eighth, with a shot at the major-league record for five in a row, he struck out against right-hander Bob Miller.

July 9

1874 — Jack Powell (P, 1899–1901)

1875 — Pete McBride (P, 1899)

1906 — Johnny Vergez (3B, 1936)

1929 — Chick Hafey runs his streak to 10 consecutive hits, a league record, during a three-game span before Philadelphia pitcher Phil Collins stops him in the eighth inning of a game the Cardinals win 7–4 in 10 innings.

1940 — The National League wins the All-Star game 4–0 at Sportsman's Park in St. Louis.

1944 — The Cards hand the Braves a double blanking with Mort Cooper allowing five hits in the 1–0 opener and Harry Brecheen scattering five hits in the 9–0 nightcap at St. Louis.

1956 — *The Sporting News* presents Stan Musial with its Player of the Decade award for 1946 through 1955.

1957 — The National League loses the All-Star game 6–5 at Busch Stadium.

1958 — Purchase pitcher Chuck Stobbs from the Senators.

July 10

1896 — Bill Schindler (C, 1920)

1923 — Johnny Stuart, a former Ohio State pitcher, hurls St. Louis to victories over Boston 11–1, 6–3 with two complete games.

1928 — John Glenn (OF, 1960)

1950 — Sell pitcher Jim Hearn to the Giants.

1951 — Stan Musial hits two home runs as the National League wins the All-Star game 8–3 at Detroit.

1954 — Bob Rush of the Cubs ends Red Schoendienst's 28-game hitting streak at St. Louis.

1956 — Ken Boyer goes three-for-five in the National League's 7–3 All-Star victory at Washington.

July 11

1872 — Harry Maupin (P, 1898)

1884 — Harry Wolter (OF-P, 1907)

1893 — Milt Stock (IF, 1919-23)

1911 — Manager Roger Bresnahan and about 14 or 15 Cardinal players survive Federal Express train wreck on the New York, New Haven, and Hartford Railroad. Running from Washington to Boston, the train plunged down an 18-foot embankment one-and-one-half miles west of Bridgeport, killing 14 people and leaving 47 others injured. After realizing that none of their own teammates was injured seriously, the Card players labored in the midst of the wreckage until the last body had been pulled out 15 hours later. Ironically, the Pullman car of the St. Louis team was repositioned from near the front of the train shortly before the wreck, as Bresnahan complained that his players couldn't sleep because of the engine noise. The train crashed at high speed into a viaduct, leaving scores of passengers in a mass of splinters and twisted iron. The day coach, which took the place of the Cardinal Pullman, was so badly mangled that it was unrecognizable. Many of the Redbird players later credited Bresnahan's complaint with saving their lives.

1931 — Dick Gray (IF, 1959-60)

1935 — Virgil Davis' double in the ninth inning scores both the tying and the

July 11 (continued)

winning runs as Cards defeat the Phillies 5–4. Dizzy Dean posted his 14th victory of the season.

1949 — Jack Heidemann (IF, 1974)

1950 — Red Schoendienst's 14th-inning home run gives the Nationals a 4–3 All-Star game victory at Comiskey Park, Chicago.

1956 — Sell pitcher Ellis Kinder to the White Sox.

July 12

1888 — Roy Golden (P, 1910-11)

1894 — Lee Meadows (P, 1915-19)

1913 — Sign pitcher John Blade, who was released by Browns.

1928 — Sign catcher Earl Smith.

1931 — In sweltering heat before a sometimes unruly crowd of 45,715 at Sportsman's Park, the Cards and Cubs split one of the most interesting doubleheaders in history. The Cubs took the opener 7–5 behind Hack Wilson's three-run homer. The Cards took the nightcap 17–13. As early as 1:00 P.M., the overflow crowd, some of which was standing in the outfield, developed into a crush that park ushers and attendants couldn't control. The fans began swarming around the dugouts and completely surrounded the infield. Police reserves and firefighters were called in to handle the nearly 8,000 fans on the field. After calm was restored, a ruling was made that every pop fly hit into the crowd in the outfield would be a double. The teams hit 32 pop flies into the crowd on that day. There were 23 doubles, 13 by St. Louis and 10 by the Cubs, as 43 extra base hits were recorded.

1935 — Dave Ricketts (C, 1963, 65, 67–69)

1938 — Ron Fairly (1B-OF, 1975-76)

1943 — Ron Willis (P, 1966-69)

1947 — Scipio Spinks (P, 1972-73)

1955 — Stan Musial's home run on the first pitch in the 12th inning at Milwaukee County Stadium gives the National League a 6–5 All-Star victory.

1966 — Tim McCarver scores the winning run in the National League's 2–1 All-Star game victory at Busch Memorial Stadium.

1969 — Trade infielder Bob W. Johnson to the A's for outfielder Joe Nossek, who is assigned from Des Moines to Tulsa.

July 13

1852 — Joe Bradley (P, 1876)

1885 — Tom O'Hara (OF, 1906-07)

1887 — Gene Packard (P, 1917-18)

1922 — Bill Doak, pitcher of the Cardinals, misses a no-hitter because of his own mental lapse. He held the Phillies hitless except for an infield single by outfielder Curt Walker in the seventh inning. Walker hit a bounding ball to first baseman Jacques Fournier and beat out the hit because Doak was caught off guard and failed to cover first, which he had ample time to do. The Cardinals won 1-0.

1928 — Send catcher Gus Mancuso to Minneapolis of the American Association.

1929 — Daryl Spencer (IF, 1960-61)

1935 — Bill Hallahan two-hits the Phillies as the Cards take their eighth straight 4-0.

1938 — Johnny Mize hits three homers in as many at-bats, but the Cards drop a 10-5 decision to Boston.

1943 — St. Louis' Mort Cooper is the loser 5-3 in the first night All-Star game at Philadelphia.

1944 — Pitcher George Munger and infielder Jimmy Brown enter the U.S. Army.

1948 — The American League bests the National 5-2 in the All-Star game at Sportsman's Park.

1958 — The Cards equal a major-league record they first tied two months earlier by using 10 pinch-hitters in a doubleheader. The Pirates swept both contests 10-8, 8-6 at St. Louis.

1964 — The Cards lash 20 hits and make the most of six Pittsburgh errors while beating the Pirates 12-5 in the second game of a doubleheader at Pittsburgh. The Cards also took the opener in 12 innings on Julian Javier's single. Lou Brock collected seven hits during the two contests.

July 14

1855 — Jack Gleason (3B-OF, 1877)

1871 — Art Nichols (C-OF-1B, 1901-03)

1888 — Ken Nash (IF, 1914)

1899 — Infielder Fred Parent plays the first of two games for St. Louis on loan from New Haven.

1919 — Trade pitcher Lee Meadows and first baseman Gene Paulette to the Phillies for pitcher Elmer Glazner and infielder Jim Tierney.

1929 — Bob Purkey (P, 1965)

1935 — More than 23,000 fans watch the world-champion Cards sweep a twin bill from Philadelphia. Paul Dean hurled his ninth victory in the opener 5-1 and Bill Walker stretched the Cards' victory string to 10 in the nightcap 10-1. In ceremonies before the game, Commissioner K. M. Landis presented the Redbirds with their 1934 World Series rings and the world-championship flag was hoisted on the center-field flagpole.

1936 — Earl Francis (P, 1965)

1944 — Bill McCool (P, 1970)

1946 — James Coulter Jones, 80, former St. Louis owner, dies at his home. Jones, originator of the knothole gang for young fans, had been suffering from heart trouble for some time.

1953 — Enos Slaughter collects two hits, a walk, and one RBI as the National League defeats the American League 5-1 in the All-Star game at Cincinnati's Crosley Field. The catch Slaughter made on Harvey Kuenn's sinking drive down the right-field line was acknowledged as one of the finest catches in midsummer-classic history.

July 15

1872 — Dan McGann (1B-2B, 1900-01)

1874 — Mike Heydon (C-OF, 1901)

1876 — Pitcher George Bradley no-hits Hartford 2-0 at St. Louis. It was the first no-hitter in major-league history.

1901 — Christy Mathewson of New York no-hits the Cards 5-0 at St. Louis.

1915 — John Antonelli (IF, 1944-45)

1935 — Donn Clendenon (1B, 1972)

1939 — Mike Shannon (OF-C-3B, 1962-70)

1943 — Pitcher Howie Pollet enters the U.S. Army Air Force.

1944 — The Cards score 11 runs in the first inning and coast to a 12-1 decision over Cincinnati at St. Louis. The Cards also turned their second triple play of the season in the second inning. After Frank McCormick singled and Ray Mueller walked, Eric Tipton lined to Emil Verban, who threw to Marty Marion at second base, doubling McCormick. Marion threw to Ray Sanders at first, tripling Mueller.

1946 — The Cards defeat the league-leading Dodgers for the third straight time on a 10-4 decision to move within a game and a half of first. A crowd of 26,476 saw the Cards best five Brooklyn hurlers for 13 hits in a game marked by the banishing of Dodger skipper Leo Durocher and outfielder Pete Reiser during a five-minute argument with Umpire Al Barlick. The game was held at Sportsman's Park.

1967 — Bob Gibson, struck in the right leg by a liner off the bat of Pittsburgh's Roberto Clemente in the fourth inning at St. Louis, suffers a fractured fibula above his right ankle. The Cards lost the contest 6-4.

1971 — Purchase pitcher Dennis Higgins from the Indians and assign him to Tulsa.

July 16

1895 — Herman Bell (P, 1924, 26-27, 29-30)

1916 — Transfer pitcher Slim Sallee to the Giants.

1936 — Eddie Fisher (P, 1973)

1938 — Bob Burda (OF, 1962, 71)

1946 — Pinch-hitter Erv Dusak's three-run, ninth-inning homer gives the second-place Redbirds a 5-4 victory and a clean sweep of a four-game series against the Dodgers at St. Louis. A total of 87,027 fans saw the Cards in the three-day series. The sweep moved St. Louis to within one-half game of the league-leading Brooklynites.

1954 — Jim Lentine (OF, 1978-80)

1967 — Obtain pitcher Jack Lamabe from the Mets for a player to be named. The Cards optioned pitcher Jim Cosman to Jacksonville as part of the deal. The Mets got pitcher Al Jackson Oct. 13 to complete the deal.

1973 — Trade pitcher Don Durham to the Rangers for pitcher Jim Kremmel, who is assigned to Tulsa.

1974 — Release outfielder-first baseman Jim Hickman

July 17

1851 — John Clapp (C-OF-1B, 1876-77)

1858 — Pete Browning (OF, 1894)

1917 — Pitcher Jesse Haines no-hits Boston 5-0 at St. Louis.

1942 — Don Kessinger (SS, 1976-77)

1945 — Send pitcher Stan Partenheimer to Rochester.

1957 — The Cards defeat Brooklyn pitcher Don Newcombe 7-3. Newk had beaten the Redbirds 12 times since Aug. 23, 1951.

1974 — Bob Gibson records his 3,000th career strikeout in the second inning against Cincinnati's Cesar Geronimo at St. Louis.

July 18

1881 — Larry McLean (C, 1904)

1916 — George Fallon (IF, 1943–45)

Johnny Hopp (OF–1B, 1939–45)

1920 — Ed Kazak (3B–2B, 1948–52)

1935 — The Cards stretch their winning streak to 14 games, besting the Braves 13–3. St. Louis batters tagged Boston hurlers Danny MacFayden and Bob Smith for 18 hits while Card twirler Paul Dean held the visiting Braves to five. Burgess Whitehead and Rip Collins each had four hits for the Redbirds while Pepper Martin and Bill DeLancey tagged homers. Through 1981, 14 remained the longest winning streak in St. Louis history.

1940 — Joe Torre (C–1B–3B, 1969–74)

1947 — Enos Slaughter's sharp single to right field breaks up Dodger pitcher Ralph Branca's no-hitter in the eighth inning. The Cards lost to Brooklyn 7–0 at Ebbets Field.

1954 — Perhaps the biggest rhubarb of the season takes place in the second game of a twin bill at St. Louis, resulting in a forfeit of the game to the Phillies. Rain had caused a delay of more than one hour in the opener, which went 10 innings before the Phillies won 11–10. As a result, the nightcap didn't start until 6:48 P.M. In the fifth inning, with the Phillies leading 8–1 and darkness setting in, Card skipper Eddie Stanky began stalling tactics. He believed that the lights couldn't be turned on, as it was Sunday. The delaying tactics, coupled with the wild pitching of Cot Deal and a free-for-all precipitated by an argument between the Cards' Sal Yvars and Earl Torgeson of the Phillies, led Umpire Babe Pinelli to forfeit the game to Philadelphia.
Stanky was immediately suspended by N.L. President Warren Giles. Two days later Giles conducted a hearing into the matter at St. Louis. He set Stanky's penalty at a $100 fine and a five-day suspension, starting that day, and suspended Yvars and Torgeson two days each for their part in the melee. The same afternoon Stanky issued a public apology and promised to change his ways. Coach Johnny Riddle piloted the Redbirds for five days, winning five straight contests, before losing his final game.

1961 — First baseman Bill White completes a streak of 14 hits in 18 at-bats against the Cubs. He started the string July 17 in a doubleheader and continued it the next day in another twin bill at St. Louis. This equalled the record of Ty Cobb, which he had held for 49 years. White ironically launched his spree the day Cobb died. White went four-for-five in each game July 17 as the Cards swept 10–6, 8–5. He went three-for-four in each game July 18 with a homer, two triples, and a double in another Redbird twin killing 8–3, 7–5. White drove in six runs within a four-game span.

1978 — Trade catcher John Tamargo to the Giants for a player to be named. The Giants assigned pitcher Rob Dressler from Phoenix to Springfield July 24 to complete the deal.

July 19

1865 — Bill Hart (P, 1896–97)

Jim Donely (3B, 1898)

1888 — John Dunleavy (OF–2B–P, 1903-05)

1910 — Purchase pitcher Ed Zmich from the Marion, Ohio, club.

Purchase pitcher Hennis from the Terre Haute, Ind., club.

1924 — Herman "Hi" Bell pitches and wins both games of a doubleheader over Boston 6-1 and 2-1. Boston managed a mere six hits in the two contests while Bell issued two walks.

1939 — Gordon Richardson (P, 1964)

July 20

1906 — Mal Eason of Brooklyn no-hits the Cards 2-0 at St. Louis.

July 21

1865 — Perry Werden (1B–Of, 1892-93)

1879 — Hugh Hill (OF, 1904)

1930 — Jim Bottomley and George Puccinelli each hit pinch-homers, but the Cards drop the first of a twin bill to Brooklyn. Harvey Hendrick provided a dramatic finish for Brooklyn with a three-run, ninth-inning homer. The Cards came back to win the nightcap 17-10, scoring seven times in the second inning.

1935 — Moe Drabowsky (P, 1971-72)

1936 — Joe Medwick equals a National League record for consecutive hits by getting three to bring his total to 10. The Cards still lost to the Giants on Dick Bartell's 10th-inning homer.

1941 — Gary Waslewski (P, 1969)

1944 — Send pitcher Mike Naymick to Rochester.

1949 — Al Hrabosky (P, 1970-77)

1954 — The Cards use eight pitchers, tying a major-league record, as they defeat Pittsburgh 13-12 at St. Louis.

1961 — Sell pitcher Mickey McDermott to the A's.

1970 — Release pitcher Chuck Hartenstein, who signs with the Red Sox and is assigned to Louisville.

1975 — Harry Rasmussen, a 23-year-old right-hander, tosses a seven-hitter in his major-league debut and singles in a run as the Cards best San Diego 4-0. Ted Simmons hit a homer for the Redbirds, but it was nullified when the umpires ruled that he had used an illegal bat. Lou Brock left the contest early with a minor ankle sprain after stealing his 42nd base of the season.

July 22

1859 — Jack Glasscock (IF-OF, 1885-86, 92-93)

1893 — Jesse Haines (P, 1920-37)

1898 — Joe Bratcher (OF, 1924)

1941 — Bart Zeller (C, 1970)

1947 — Option pitcher Gerry Staley to Columbus.

1948 — Option pitcher Al Papai to Rochester.

1968 — Lou Brock, pinch-hitting for Orlando Cepeda, bounces a single to key a three-run, ninth-inning rally that sweeps the Cards past Philadelphia 5-4 in a nationally televised game. Brock, who had been the Cards' hottest hitter in recent weeks, was given a rest by Manager Red Schoendienst. But he got the call for Cepeda, who was hitting .264.

July 23

1889 — Lee Dressen (1B, 1914)

1897 — Hod Ford (IF, 1932)

1900 — Jimmy Wilson (C-IF, 1928-33)

1915 — Hersh Lyons (P, 1941)

1916 — Sell pitcher Slim Sallee to the Giants for a reported $10,000.

1918 — Walter Sessi (OF, 1941)

1929 — Manager Billy Southworth trades places with Rochester Manager Bill McKechnie.

July 24

1893 — Joe Schultz (OF-1B-3B, 1919-24)

1915 — Purchase pitcher Red Ames from Cincinnati.

1931 — Three homers by right fielder George Watkins give the Cards a 4-2 victory over the Phillies in the second game of a doubleheader. Watkins accounted for all the Card RBI.

1933 — Under the new leadership of Frankie Frisch, who stepped into the shoes of Gabby Street as manager, the Cardinals give the Quincy Warriors of the Mississippi Valley League a 10-1 lacing in an exhibition game at Quincy, Ill.

Dizzy Dean, eccentric pitcher of the Cardinals, receives a half dozen neckties as a gift from one of two bandits who held up a St. Louis drugstore the previous week. Dean walked into the holdup and was lined up with the other victims. According to Dean, the robber called and said he had nothing against him personally and to show it would send a half dozen neckties.

July 25

1900 — Boston scores 13 runs in the first inning and rips the Cards 18-5. Rain mercifully ended the contest after six innings.

1926 — Whitey Lockman (OF, 1956)

1933 — Unconditionally release Rogers Hornsby.

1941 — Johnny Mize's error against the Braves is his first in 61 games.

1944 — Buddy Bradford (OF, 1975)

1947 — Mick Kelleher (SS, 1972-73, 75)

1949 — Santiago Guzman (P, 1969-72)

1958 — Sell outfielder Joe Taylor to the Orioles.

1962 — Stan Musial's two-run homer against the Dodgers at St. Louis gives him 1,862 runs batted in, breaking Mel Ott's National League record.

1968 — Bob Gibson blanks Philadelphia 5-0 to set a club record with 11 straight victories. He struck out six and walked one in posting his 12th complete game in succession. In his last 92 innings, he had allowed only two runs. Gibson tied the club record of 11 wins in a row by Ted Wilks in 1944 and the career record of 33 shutouts set by William Doak.

1975 — Trade outfielder Jim Dwyer, who was on the Tulsa roster, to the Expos for infielder Larry Lintz.

July 26

1879 — Sam Breadon, who would become Cards' president in 1920 and hold the position until 1947, is born in New York's Greenwich Village.

John Butler (C, 1904)

1884 — Otto McIver (OF, 1911)

1914 — Ellis Kinder (P, 1956)

1923 — Hoyt Wilhelm (P, 1957)

1945 — Obtain outfielder Art Rebel from Columbus.

1948 — Waive pitcher Ken Burkhart to the Cincinnati Reds.

1964 — Southpaw Gordon Richardson, making his first major-league start, and lefty Ray Sadecki pitch the Redbirds to a doubleheader sweep over the Phillies 6-1 and 4-1 at Philadelphia.

81

July 26 (continued)

1972 — Release pitcher Tony Cloninger.

1973 — Pitcher Bob Gibson drives in five runs with a grand-slam homer and a single while pitching the Redbirds to a 13-1 rout of the Mets in the opening game of a twin bill at St. Louis. The Cards also took the nightcap 2-1. In that contest, outfielder Bernie Carbo threw out two runners and doubled home the game's first run. Joe Torre's eighth-inning homer was the winning run.

July 27

1849 — Davy Force (SS-3B, 1877)

1885 — Charley Hall (P, 1916)

1905 — Leo Durocher (SS, 1933-37)

1918 — The Cards lose a pitchers' duel to Brooklyn 2-0 in the opening game of a doubleheader, then score a 22-7 victory in the nightcap. Bob Fisher, Gene Paulette, Rogers Hornsby, and Austin McHenry each got four of the 26 hits off Brooklyn pitchers Henry Heitman and Burleigh Grimes. At the time, Heitman had just joined the Navy and was awaiting call.

1944 — The league-leading Redbirds widen their margin to 14½ games over second place Cincinnati as Mort Cooper beats the Phillies 5-0 for his 11th victory in 12 starts since May 28. Harry Brecheen pitched an 8-7 victory in the opener of the doubleheader at Philadelphia.

1946 — Behind the three-hit pitching of Warren Spahn, a purple-heart Army dischargee who rejoined the Braves eight weeks earlier, Boston defeats the Cards 5-2 at Boston. Spahn had a no-hitter going until the sixth inning, when Buster Adams doubled off the left-center field fence and scored on Stan Musial's single

1959 — Joe DeSa (IF, 1980)

1972 — Return outfielder Brandt Alyea to the A's, who assign him to Iowa.

1973 — Trade infielder Ed Crosby and catcher Gene Dusan, the latter assigned to Indianapolis, to the Reds for pitcher Ed Sprague and a player to be named. First baseman-outfielder Roe Skidmore was assigned from Indianapolis to Tulsa Sept. 30 to complete the deal.

July 28

1868 — Charles Esper (P, 1897-98)

1890 — Elmer Miller (OF, 1912)

1928 — Outfielder Chick Hafey hits four doubles and two home runs as the Cardinals (62-35) strengthen their lead in the National League race to 4½ games over Cincinnati by taking both games of a twin bill from Phillies 7-6 and 12-2.

1943 — Dick Simpson (OF, 1968)

1957 — Von McDaniel misses a perfect game while defeating Pittsburgh 4–0 in the opener of a doubleheader at St. Louis. Only one Pirate, Gene Baker, reached base with a double down the left-field line with two out in the second inning. The Card rookie retired the next 22 batters in order, striking out four, en route to his fifth victory. He went on to compile a 7–2 record and a 3.21 ERA in his first season.

1969 — Stan Musial is inducted into the Hall of Fame.

July 29

1891 — Fred Smith (IF, 1917)

1911 — Roy Henshaw (P, 1938)

1920 — Erv Dusak (OF-IF-P, 1941-42, 46-51)

1922 — Ray Yochim (P, 1948-49)

1935 — Outfielder Joe Medwick hits for the cycle in five at-bats, but the Cards lose to the Reds 8–6.

1936 — The Brooklyn Robins belt the Cards' Leroy Parmelee and Ed Heuser for 21 hits in taking the first game of a twin bill 22–7. The Cards gained revenge in the nightcap with a 5–4 victory because of the excellent relief pitching of Jesse Haines.

1944 — The league-leading Redbirds sweep a doubleheader from last place Brooklyn 14–7, 12–7, giving them 26 victories in July, their winningest month ever.

1959 — David LaPoint (P, 1981-82)

1960 — Purchase pitcher Bob Grim from the Reds.

1963 — Trade outfielder-first baseman Duke Carmel to the Mets for cash and outfielder Jacke Davis, who is assigned from Buffalo to Atlanta.

1971 — Trade outfielder Jose Cardenal, infielder Dick Schofield, the latter on the Tulsa roster, and pitcher Bob Reynolds to the Brewers for infielder Ted Kubiak and pitcher Chuck Loseth, who is on the Raleigh-Durham roster. Reynolds was assigned to Evansville, Loseth to St. Petersburg.

1974 — Lou Brock, zeroing in on Maury Wills's fabulous single-season record of 104, steals his 65th base of the season and the 700th of his career in the first inning of an 11–2 victory over the Cubs at Chicago. Only four players had stolen 700 or more bases—Ty Cobb (892), Eddie Collins (743), Max Carey (738), and Honus Wagner (701).

July 30

1912 — Carl Doyle (P, 1940)

July 30 (continued)

1933 — Dizzy Dean strikes out 17 Cubs in the first game of a doubleheader, setting a record that stood for 26 years. The Cards swept the twin bill 8-2, 6-5.

1944 — Brooklyn snaps a nine-game Cardinal winning streak with a 10-4 victory in the first game of a doubleheader at Brooklyn. The Cards came back with a 9-7 victory in 11 innings as Stan Musial stole third base and went home with the winning run on catcher Mickey Owen's throwing error.

1956 — Purchase first baseman Rocky Nelson from the Dodgers.

1959 — Pitcher Bob Gibson gets his first major-league victory, a 1-0, eight-hit shutout over the Reds at Cincinnati.

1973 — Lou Brock walks and steals the 600th base of his career in the first inning against the Cubs at Wrigley Field. Brock came home on a single by Tim McCarver, but Rick Reuschel outdueled Bob Gibson and the Cubs won 3-1.

July 31

1870 — Joe Sugden (C-OF-1B, 1898)

1910 — Leonard Cole of Chicago no-hits the Cards 4-0 in seven innings of the second game of a doubleheader at Chicago. The game was abbreviated, as both teams had to catch a train.

1929 — Bill Hallahan walks 10 in the nightcap as the Cards and Dodgers split a twin bill. The Cards took the opener 5-2, Brooklyn the nightcap 8-2.

1931 — Joe Durham (OF, 1959)

1935 — The Cards play the first night game in their history, losing to the Reds 4-3 in 10 innings before 30,000 fans at Cincinnati.

1939 — Vic Davalillo (OF, 1969-70)

1956 — Sell infielder Grady Hatton to the Orioles.

1957 — Purchase outfielder Irv Noren from the A's.

Leon Durham (OF, 1979-80)

1974 — Trade infielder Bob Heise, on the Tulsa roster, to the Angels for a player to be named. The Angels assign outfielder Doug Howard to Tulsa Oct. 7 to complete the deal.

1975 — Release pitcher Ron Bryant.

AUGUST

August 1

1902 — Howard Freigau (IF-OF, 1922-25)

1938 — Sell infielder Joe Stripp to the Boston Bees.

1951 — Purchase catcher Bob Scheffing on waivers from Cincinnati.

1975 — Purchase pitcher Lloyd Allen from the White Sox and assign him to Tulsa.

August 2

1877 — Warren Sanders (P, 1903-04)

1882 — Leon Ames (P, 1915-19)

1899 — Art Riviere (P, 1921)

1938 — A dandelion-colored baseball is used as Brooklyn defeats the Cards 6-2 at Ebbets Field. The yellow ball was devised by Frederick Rah, who thought its high visibility would lessen the dangers of players being hit by pitched balls. The trial drew mixed reactions from the players.

1960 — Sell pitcher Marshall Bridges to the Reds.

August 3

1874 — Ed McFarland (C-OF, 1896-97)

1884 — Tom Reilly (SS, 1908-09)

1902 — Joe Sprinz (C, 1933)

1937 — Card catcher Mickey Owen has three putouts, including an unassisted double play, in a 5-2 victory over the Boston Bees. The first putout was a pop foul off the bat of Jim Turner. Roy Johnson then hit a triple to left and attempted to score on a squeeze play. Rabbit Warstler popped up to Owen, who ran down and tagged third, doubling Johnson.

1946 — John Beazley limits the Phillies to one hit as the Cards win 3-1 in a game ended by rain after five innings. The lone Philadelphia safety was a homer by Frank McCormick in the fifth.

August 4

1867 — Jake Beckley (1B, 1904-07)

1879 — Patrick O'Connor (C, 1914)

1895 — Sid Benton (P, 1922)

1902 — Bill Hallahan (P, 1925-26, 29-36)

1910 — Tucker Stainback (OF, 1938)

1931 — The Cards halt a 45-inning scoreless streak by Pittsburgh pitchers as they score three runs off Heinie Meine in the sixth inning and win the contest 7-1. The Pirate no-run streak included shutouts over New York and Cincinnati in four consecutive games.

August 4 (continued)

1937 — Outfielder Joe Medwick collects four doubles and the Cards rally for five runs in the ninth inning to edge Boston 7-6 at St. Louis.

1939 — Dennis Higgins (P, 1971-72)

1944 — Rich Nye (P, 1970)

1968 — Stan Musial, the National League's seven-time batting champ before he moved into the Cardinal front office in 1964, dons old No. 6 and joins former 1941 teammates during pre-game ceremonies honoring him at Busch Memorial Stadium. A 10-foot bronze statue of Musial was unveiled after the game at one of the stadium's main entrances. In the game, a capacity crowd of 47,445 saw the Cubs battle Card ace Bob Gibson to a standoff for 12 innings before Lee Elia singled home the winning Cub run in the 13th for a 6-5 victory.

1971 — Pitcher Bob Gibson wins his 200th career game, 7-2 over the Giants at St. Louis.

1975 — Purchase pitcher Harry Parker from the New York Mets.

August 5

1905 — Ray Pepper (OF, 1932-33)

1916 — Milt Watson, who was obtained in June, but didn't report to the Cards until July, pitches his first full game, defeating Grover Cleveland Alexander and the Philadelphia Phillies 2-0.

1924 — Ed Yuhas (P, 1952-53)

1925 — Tony Jacobs (P, 1955)

1931 — The Cards get 23 hits off Pittsburgh pitching, including a six-for-six day by first baseman Jim Bottomley, as the Cards split a doubleheader against the Pirates, losing the first game 5-4, winning the nightcap 16-2. Bottomley also had four hits in the opener, giving him 10 for the day.

1943 — Nelson Briles (P, 1965-70)

1947 — Bernie Carbo (OF, 1972-73, 79-80)

1950 — Recall outfielder Hal Rice from Rochester.

1953 — Rick Bosetti (OF, 1977)

1960 — Sign catcher Darrell Johnson as a coach.

1968 — Cardinal outfielder Roger Maris, saying that he has experienced "probably two of the most enjoyable years" of his career, announces he will retire at the end of the season.

1974 — Purchase outfielder Richie Scheinblum from the Royals and assign him to Tulsa.

August 6

1872 — Sam Mertes (OF, 1906)

1896 — Ray Blades (OF–IF, 1922-28, 30-32)

1908 — John Lush no-hits the Dodgers in a six-inning game at Brooklyn 2-0.

1928 — Herb Moford (P, 1955)

1936 — Trade pitcher Bill Walker to the Reds for pitcher Si Johnson.

1944 — The Cards win a Sunday marathon over the Reds 5-4 after Max Lanier opens the 13th inning with a double and scores on another double by Johnny Hopp. Also in the contest, Card rookie pitcher Ted Wilks suffered a slight concussion when he was hit by a liner off the bat of Steve Mesner and was knocked out. He was carried from the field and sent to Christ Hospital in Cincinnati.

August 7

1907 — Clarence Heise (P, 1934)

1927 — Rocky Bridges (IF, 1960)

1936 — Jerry McNertney (C, 1971-72)

1951 — Charlie Chant (OF, 1976)

1972 — Release first baseman Donn Clendenon.

1973 — Trade pitcher Wayne Granger to the Yankees for two players to be named. The deal was completed Sept. 12 when the Yanks assigned pitcher Ken Crosby from Syracuse to Tulsa and gave the Cards cash in lieu of a second player.

August 8

1917 — Ken Raffensberger (P, 1939)

1927 — Branch Rickey signs a five-year contract as business manager.

1934 — Wilbert Robinson, catcher in 1900 and future Hall of Famer, dies following a brain hemorrhage at Atlanta.

1947 — Jose Cruz (OF–1B, 1970-74)

1954 — Purchase pitcher Ben Wade from the Dodgers on waivers.

1968 — Starters Ray Washburn and Tony Cloninger of Cincinnati lock up in a brilliant pitching duel, matching two-hit shutouts over the first nine innings. Manager Dave Bristol, figuring Cloninger had gone far enough, brought on Clay Carroll. The Cards went down in the 10th, but won it in the next inning when Bobby Tolan singled and raced all the way home on Roger Maris' double. Joe Hoerner, who took over for Washburn in the tough 10th, got credit for the victory.

1969 — Sell pitcher Ron Willis to the Astros. Houston returned him Oct. 15, and the Cards then shipped him to Tulsa.

August 9

1912 — Tom Sunkel (P, 1937)

1931 — Chuck Essegian (OF, 1959)

1932 — The Cards collect 25 hits in beating the Phillies 18-13. Jim Bottomley, Rip Collins, and Frank Frisch got four hits apiece. Bottomley had two homers and drove in six runs.

1936 — Julian Javier (2B-3B, 1960-71)

1939 — Claude Osteen (P, 1974)

1942 — Tommie Agee (OF, 1973)

1949 — Ted Simmons (C-OF-IF, 1968-80)

1951 — Steve Swisher (C, 1978-80)

1952 — Recall pitcher Stu Miller from Columbus.

1972 — Catcher Ted Simmons agrees to sign a contract through the 1973 season at $75,000 per year. Simmons was the last player in major-league baseball to sign a 1972 pact and the first player to play most of a season without having signed a contract.

August 10

1908 — Bill Trotter (P, 1944)

1939 — Johnny Lewis (OF, 1964)

1941 — Card outfielder Enos Slaughter breaks his collarbone after a collision with teammate Terry Moore in front of the right-center-field wall at Sportsman's Park. The injury sidelined Slaughter for the remainder of the year.

1955 — Stan Musial doubles off Braves' pitcher Lou Burdette at Milwaukee to become the ninth player in major-league history to get 1,000 extra-base hits. It was double No. 529 for The Man, who also owned 155 triples and 316 homers among his 2,541 major-league hits up to 1955.

1981 — Philadelphia's Pete Rose strokes career hit No. 3,631 off Cardinal reliever Mark Littell in the sixth inning of a contest at Veterans Stadium, topping Stan Musial's National League hit mark. A 50-day players' strike had forced Rose to wait an extra two months for his historic hit. Despite Rose's heroics, the Cardinals won the game 7-3.

August 11

1904 — Kid Nichols fans 14 batters as the Cards defeat Brooklyn 4-3 in 15 innings.

1907 — Ed Karger throws a perfect game at St. Louis as the Cards defeat Boston 4-0 in a seven-inning contest.

1915 — Bob Scheffing (C, 1951)

1928 — Bobby Stephenson (IF, 1955)

1942 — Sal Campisi (P, 1969-70)

1946 — Stan Musial collects eight hits in nine at-bats as the Cards sweep a doubleheader from the Reds 15-4, 7-3 at Cincinnati.

1949 — Luis Melendez (OF-SS, 1970-76)

1960 — Stan Musial's homer in the 12th inning enables the Cards to defeat the Pirates 3-2 at Pittsburgh. It moved the second-place Cards within four games of the Pirates in the N.L. race.

1974 — Sign pitcher Steve Barber, who was released by the Giants, and assign him to Tulsa.

1980 — Leon Durham's two-run homer and Tony Scott's three-run triple highlight an eight-run first inning that sparks the Cards to a 16-0 victory over the Expos at St. Louis. Bob Sykes allowed four hits and Dane Iorg went four-for-five—three doubles and a triple—and scored three times.

August 12

1867 — Bud Lally (OF-1B, 1897)

1878 — Bob Brashear (IF-OF, 1902)

1934 — After pitching and losing a doubleheader at St. Louis, Dizzy and Paul Dean miss a train for Detroit, where an exhibition game is scheduled. St. Louis Manager Frankie Frisch fined Dizzy $100 and Paul $50. The brothers refused to appear on the field and Frisch suspended them. In the clubhouse Dizzy tore up two uniforms, one in anger and the second one, obligingly, for a photographer.

1936 — Ellis Burton (OF, 1958)

1946 — Stan Musial, the National League's leading hitter, goes four-for-four as the Cards defeat the Cubs 5-0 at Chicago. Al Brazle gains victory No. 4 with a three-hitter. The four safeties gave Musial 12 hits in three consecutive games.

1952 — Rookie right-hander Stu Miller shuts out the Cubs 1-0 at Wrigley Field in his first major-league game. Five days later, he was within one out of a seven-hit, 2-0 victory over the Reds at St. Louis, when shortstop Solly Hemus fumbled a grounder and threw wildly, permitting a Cincinnati runner to score. The Cards won 2-1.

1963 — Stan Musial announces his retirement at the club's annual picnic. Club officials announced he would get a front-office job.

August 12 (continued)

1970 — A district court in St. Louis dismisses Curt Flood's antitrust suit.

1974 — Purchase catcher Rick Billings from the Rangers and assign him to Tulsa.

1977 — Trade pitcher Steve Dunning, who is on the New Orleans roster, to the A's for pitcher Randy Scarberry, who is assigned from San Jose to New Orleans.

August 13

1858 — Charles Briody (C, 1885)

1930 — Wilmer Mizell (P, 1952-53, 56-60)

1935 — Jim Grant (P, 1969)

1940 — Tony Cloninger (P, 1972)

1962 — St. Louis Owner August A. Busch Jr. threatens a shakeup with the Cardinals in sixth place.

1979 — Lou Brock calmly strokes two hits against the Chicago Cubs, the team that traded him away 15 years beforehand, to become the 14th player in the major leagues to reach the 3,000-hit plateau. Brock got his 2,999th hit, a bloop single to left field in the first inning, and reached the milestone when he singled off the hand of Chicago starter Dennis Lamp to open the fourth. His 3,000th hit was instrumental in the Cardinals' 3-2 victory before 46,161 fans at St. Louis.

August 14

1856 — Alex McKinnon (LF, 1885-86)

1868 — Clarence Childs (2B, 1899)

1883 — Bill O'Hara (OF-1B, 1910)

1891 — Fred Lamline (P, 1915)

1913 — Paul Dean (P, 1934-39)

1941 — Purchase pitcher Howie Pollet from Houston.

1970 — Purchase pitcher Frank Bertaina from Rochester in the Baltimore chain.

1971 — Bob Gibson no-hits the Pirates 11-0 at Pittsburgh. Teammates Jose Cruz and Joe Torre made spectacular plays to preserve the gem, Cruz a running catch of Milt May's 400-foot drive to center field in the seventh inning and Torre a leaping stab of Dave Cash's hot grounder to third base in the eighth.

August 15

1865 — Doggie Miler (IF-OF-C, 1894-95)

1871 — Bill Kissinger (P, 1895-97)

1872 — John Warner (C, 1905)

1896 — Bill Sherdel (P, 1918-30, 32)

1926 — Barney Schultz (P, 1955, 63-65)

1941 — Send pitcher Sam Nahem to Columbus.

1968 — Mike Shannon hits the first grand-slam homer of his major-league career and drives in another run with a single as the pennant-bound Cardinals turn back the Cubs 8-0 at Wrigley Field. Nelson Briles allowed seven hits while recording his 16th triumph against seven losses.

1972 — Release pitcher Moe Drabowsky, who is signed by the White Sox and released Oct. 6.

1974 — Trade pitcher Ron Selak, who is assigned from Arkansas to Columbus, and a player to be named to the Astros for pitcher Claude Osteen. The Cards assigned pitcher Dan Larson to Denver Oct. 14 to complete the deal.

August 16

1855 — Warren Carpenter (3B, 1892)

1889 — Hank Robinson (P, 1914-15)

1897 — Jacques Fournier (1B-P, 1920-22)

1925 — Recall shortstop Tommy Thevenow from Syracuse.

1944 — The Cards set a modern record by reaching victory No. 80 at the earliest date in history, shutting out the Giants 5-0 behind Fred Schmidt, who usually sees duty only in relief, at St. Louis.

1964 — Curt Flood tags Dodger pitching for eight consecutive hits as the Cards and Los Angeles split a doubleheader. St. Louis' Curt Simmons threw a 4-0, six-hit shutout in the second game after Sandy Koufax had blanked the Redbirds on seven hits 3-0, in the opener at Los Angeles.

August 17

1874 — Bill Keister (IF, 1900)

1898 — Bill Pertica (P, 1921-23)

1924 — Larry Ciaffone (OF, 1951)

1937 — Diego Segui (P, 1972-73)

1946 — Ed L. (Les) Wilson, 37, baseball scout for the Cardinals, kills himself in a Dallas hotel, where his body is found naked and bloody. Two physicians, after an autopsy, reported he had killed himself with alcoholic gluttony in an all-night wrestle against "whisky-inspired phantoms."

August 17 (continued)

1958 — Curt Flood and Gene Freese open a 12-7 Cardinal victory over the Dodgers with homers off Sandy Koufax, who only lasts an inning and a third. It marked the fourth time in N.L. history that players hit back-to-back leadoff home runs. The Dodgers came back to win the nightcap 9-3.

1964 — Two key St. Louis executives, General Manager Bing Devine and Business Manager Art Routzong, resign. Devine was stepping down because Cardinal President August A. Busch Jr. had become "disappointed and frustrated" over his team's failure to win a pennant.

1976 — Lou Brock steals three bases against the Padres at St. Louis. This was the 19th and final time in his career that he stole three in one game. The Cardinals defeated San Diego 9-4.

August 18

1893 — Burleigh Grimes (P, 1930-31, 33-34)

1898 — Hal Goldsmith (P, 1929)

1915 — Max Lanier (P, 1938-46, 49-51)

The Cards and Braves play the first game at Braves Field, Boston. The Braves won 3-1.

1934 — The Cards hammer 20 hits, while pitcher Bill Hallahan limits the Braves to five, to defeat Boston 15-0. Leo Durocher and Jack Rothrock hit homers for the Redbirds.

1935 — Bob Humphreys (P, 1963-64)

1943 — Harry Walker's 29-game hitting streak, which began July 21, is ended against the Phils at Philadelphia.

1947 — Lowell Palmer (P, 1972)

1949 — Charles Hudson (P, 1972)

1962 — Stan Musial becomes the first visiting player ever given a special night by the New York Mets at the Polo Grounds.

1973 — Trade infielder Dave Campbell and cash to the Astros for outfielder Tommie Agee.

1980 — August A. Busch Jr. fires Senior Executive Vice-President and Chief Operating Officer John W. Claiborne III, who has held the position since Oct. 18, 1978.

August 19

1859 — Charlie Comiskey (1B-OF-P, 1885-86, 91)

1888 — Mike Murphy (C, 1912)

1893 — Ike McAuley (SS, 1917)

1903 — Estell Crabtree (OF-3B, 1933, 40-41)

1906 — Tex Carleton (P, 1932-34)

1909 — Trade third baseman Robert Byrne to the Pirates for infielders Jap Barbeau and Alan Storke.

1949 — Release catcher Bill Baker.

1950 — Mike Phillips (IF, 1977-80)

1958 — Luis DeLeon (P, 1981)

August 20

1869 — Frank Bonner (IF, 1895)

1886 — Gene Woodburn (P, 1911-12)

1910 — Bill Crouch (P, 1941)

1925 — Larry Miggins (OF-1B, 1948)

1941 — St. Louis outfielder Terry Moore is hit on the head by a pitch from Art Johnson of the Boston Braves. He didn't return to the lineup until Sept. 14.

1942 — Fred Norman (P, 1970-71)

1944 — The Cards extend their winning streak to nine games with a 15-5 victory over Boston in the first game of a doubleheader at St. Louis. The Braves snapped the streak in the nightcap 12-3. Pitcher Ted Wilks gained his ninth consecutive victory in the opener.

1959 — Sell third baseman Ray Jablonski to the A's.

1977 — Trade shortstop Don Kessinger to the White Sox for a player to be named. Pitchers Dave Hamilton and Silvio Martinez came to the Cards Nov. 29, completing the deal. Cards also transfer pitcher Steve Staniland to White Sox Iowa farm club.

August 21

1876 — St. Louis wins the first forfeited game in major-league history over Chicago 9-0. The trouble began when St. Louis' Ned Cuthbert hit a grounder to third base in the bottom of the ninth inning and Mike McGeary started home with the winning run. The ball struck McGeary as he ran and was knocked foul, causing the Chicago players to claim interference. Umpire Walker decided that the incident was accidental and McGeary scored the winning run. Chicago captain Albert Spalding couldn't get Walker to reverse the call, so he refused to finish the contest. He and the rest of the Chicago players entered their carriages and drove away, amid the hisses and boos of the St. Louis fans. At the time of the incident, the score was tied at six.

1883 — Owen Wilson (OF, 1914-16)

1907 — Art Garibaldi (3B-2B, 1936)

1908 — Catcher Gabby Street (1931) becomes the second player to catch a baseball dropped from the Washington Monument.

1916 — Murry Dickson (P, 1939-40, 42-43, 46-48, 56-57)

1920 — Gerry Staley (P, 1947-54)

1936 — Jim Beauchamp (1B-OF, 1963, 70-71)

1937 — Jack Damaska (OF-2B, 1963)

1945 — Jerry DaVanon (IF-OF, 1969-70, 74, 77)

1946 — Obtain pitcher Gerry Staley from Sacramento.

1973 — The Cards lose to Atlanta 11-7 at Atlanta, despite pitcher Rick Wise's grand-slam homer off Roric Harrison, which helped give the Redbirds a 7-0 lead in the third inning. Dave Johnson hit his 33rd homer for Atlanta and Hank Aaron doubled.

August 22

1909 — Bob Keely (C, 1944-45)

Trade second baseman Ray Charles to the Reds for third baseman Mike Mowery.

1949 — Doug Bair (P, 1981-82)

1957 — Stan Musial establishes a National League endurance record when he extends his streak of consecutive games played to 895 before an injury forces him to the bench. His streak broke by 73 games the former mark of 822 by Gus Suhr. The mishap which stopped Musial occurred at Philadelphia Aug. 22, when he tore a muscle and chipped a bone in his shoulder blade as he swung at a high, outside pitch. Four nights later at Pittsburgh, Musial entered the St. Louis lineup as a pinch-runner and also played first base in the last half of the ninth inning as the clubs played the last half inning of a game suspended July 21. The appearance officially lengthened his streak to 895, although technically it ended on this date.

1974 — Sign free agent infielder Tommy Herr.

August 23

1874 — Albert Jones (P, 1899-1901)

1894 — Roy Leslie (1B, 1919)

1901 — Guy Bush (P, 1938)

1911 — Nelson Potter (P, 1936)

1928 — Recall pitcher Herman Bell from Rochester.

1931 — League-leading Cards (78-44) swamp the Braves 16-1 in the first game of a
doubleheader, then come back to take the nightcap in 11 innings 1-0. Chick
Hafey led the assault in the opener with five-for-five and eight RBI, including two homers. Jim Bottomley's homer in the bottom of the 11th won the
nightcap.

1934 — John Romano (C, 1967)

1941 — Orlando Martinez (IF, 1972)

1942 — Dave Dowling (P, 1964)

1977 — Purchase pitcher Randy Wiles from the White Sox.

August 24

1894 — Jimmy Cooney (IF-OF, 1924-25)

1902 — Jimmy Hudgens (1B-2B, 1923)

1924 — The Cards supply Eddie Dyer with 25 hits in a 17-0 victory over Brooklyn
in the second game of a doubleheader. The Cards also took the opener 7-6
when Rogers Hornsby hit a homer into the right-field bleachers at Sportsman's Park to start the ninth inning. Leo Dickerman of the Cards had his
left arm broken when hit by Dutch Ruether's pitch just above the wrist in
the second inning of the opener.

1932 — Hal Woodeshick (P, 1965-67)

1954 — Sell second baseman Lou Ortiz to the Phillies.

August 25

1900 — Outfielder Joe Heidrick steals four bases in 2-0 victory over Chicago.

1913 — Sam Narron (C, 1935, 42-43)

1921 — Al Jurisich (P, 1944-45)

1928 — Darrell Johnson (C, 1960)

Floyd Woolridge (P, 1955)

1936 — The Boston Bees, scoring 11 times in the first inning, hit the offerings of
pitchers Si Johnson and Ed Heusser for seven doubles. That broke a
53-year-old record of six doubles in one inning by the Chicago Cubs Sept. 6,
1883. The Cards, meanwhile, lost their National League lead as they
dropped both ends of a doubleheader 20-5 and 5-4. The Bees collected 25
hits in the second gme.

August 26

1890 — Bill Hopper (P, 1913-14)

1894 — Earl Adams (IF, 1930-33)

1909 — Gene Moore (OF, 1933-35)

1914 — The Redbirds, having risen from sixth place since the start of June, split a doubleheader with the New York Giants before a midweek crowd of 27,000 at League Park in St. Louis. The Cards moved to within a fraction of a game of first place as Bill Doak outdueled Al Demaree and Rube Marquard 1-0 in the opener. In the nightcap, the league-leading Giants bounced back to a 4-0 victory behind the pitching of Christy Mathewson.

1924 — Rogers Hornsby belts a homer and three doubles in four times at-bat, but Brooklyn defeats the Cards 7-4. It was Hornsby's 24th homer of the season.

Alex Kellner (P, 1959)

1928 — Frank Barnes (P, 1957-58, 60)

1929 — Obtain pitcher Carmen Hill from Pittsburgh.

Tom Poholsky (P, 1950-51, 54-56)

1964 — Pitcher Mike Cuellar pitches his first complete game in the majors as the Cards complete a three-game sweep with a 4-2 victory over Pittsburgh at St. Louis.

1981 — St. Louis Manager Whitey Herzog fines shortstop Garry Templeton $5,000 and suspends him indefinitely without pay for making obscene gestures at fans during a game at St. Louis. The incident started in the first inning, when Templeton struck out, but San Francisco Giant catcher Milt May dropped the ball. Templeton made a half-hearted jog toward first before veering toward the Card dugout. The small crowd, which waited in the rain for more than an hour before the contest started, began booing and Templeton responded with an upraised arm gesture. After two similar gestures later in the game and animated discussions between Templeton and home plate umpire Bruce Froemming, Templeton was ejected prior to the start of the fourth inning. As he got to the Cardinal dugout, Herzog grabbed him by the shirt and pulled him into the dugout and a brief scuffle ensued. Templeton later agreed to seek psychiatric help and returned to the Cardinal lineup Sept. 15.

August 27

1873 — Ed Beecher (OF, 1897)

1892 — Hal Janvrin (IF-OF, 1919-21)

1899 — Clyde Day (P, 1924-25)

1900 — Phil Collins (P, 1935)

1915 — Emil Verban (2B, 1944-46)

1918 — Peanuts Lowrey (OF-IF, 1950-54)

1931 — Joe Cunningham (1B-OF, 1954, 56-61)

1932 — Jim King (OF, 1957)

1935 — Ernie Broglio (P, 1959-64)

1944 — For the first time the entire season, the Cards fail to win at least one game of a Sunday doubleheader when they drop the opener to Pittsburgh 14-6 and then play to a 1-1, 11-inning tie in the second game, which is called because of darkness at St. Louis.

1946 — Pitcher George Munger is discharged from the U.S. Army.

1963 — Giant great Willie Mays hits career homer No. 400 off Cardinal pitcher Curt Simmons in the third inning with none on base in San Francisco's Candlestick Park.

1972 — Trade outfielder Matty Alou to the A's for outfielder Bill Voss and pitcher Steve Easton, the latter assigned from Birmingham to Arkansas. This was a follow-up to the Cards purchasing Diego Segui June 7.

August 28

1876 — Doc Hazleton (1B, 1901-02)

1898 — Charlie Grimm (IF-OF, 1918)

1902 — Wally Roettger (OF, 1927-29, 31)

1918 — Jeff Cross (IF, 1942, 1946-48)

1919 — Charlie Marshall (C, 1941)

Ferdie Schupp, regaining his old-time form, pitches the Cards to a one-hit, 3-1 victory over Pittsburgh. The Pirates got their run in the first inning on a walk to Carson Bigbee, who went to second on a fly to Joe Schultz in right and scored on Possum Whitted's hit.

1927 — Purchase pitchers Syl Johnson and Fred Frankhouse from Syracuse.

1930 — Andy High's single scoring Taylor Douthit in the 20th inning gives the Cards an 8-7 victory over the league-leading Cubs. High was put out at second just after Douthit reached home, but the score counted, giving the Cards the victory.

1935 — Terry Moore delivers three doubles and a homer as the Cards sweep two from the Phillies 13-5 and 5-1. Pepper Martin's grand-slam homer and Rip Collins's 21st homer of the year spark a nine-run sixth in game two.

August 28 (continued)

1942 — Outfielder Enos Slaughter enlists in the U.S. Army Air Force.

1943 — Vada Pinson (OF, 1969)

1945 — Recall pitcher Stan Partenheimer from Rochester.

1946 — Mike Torrez (P, 1967-71)

1951 — Joel Youngblood (OF-1B, 1977)

August 29

1889 — William "Pop" Schriver (C, 1901) catches the second ball thrown to him from the top of the Washington Monument, being the first person ever to accomplish the feat.

1907 — Lemuel Young (IF, 1941)

1928 — Mickey McDermott (P, 1961)

1944 — Ted Wilks (14-1) boosts his personal win streak to 11 games with a 3-0 shutout over Cincinnati at St. Louis. The streak ended Sept. 2 with a 5-4 defeat at the hands of the Pirates at Pittsburgh.

1948 — The Cards set a major-league record by using 42 players in losing a doubleheader to Brooklyn 12-7 and 6-4. The second game went 10 innings. Harry Brecheen and Red Munger were the losing pitchers.

1973 — Purchase pitcher Eddie Fisher from the White Sox.

1980 — Name Whitey Herzog general manager, Red Schoendienst interim manager.

August 30

1892 — William Perritt (P, 1912-14)

1916 — Johnny Lindell (OF, 1950)

1918 — Billy Johnson (3B, 1951-53)

1941 — Lon Warneke pitches the Cards into first place with a 2-0, no-hitter over the Reds at Cincinnati. All that spoiled his magnificent work was a walk in the seventh inning to Lonnie Frey, a high throw by Creepy Crespi on Frank McCormick's grounder in the fifth, and Jimmy Brown's muff of Jimmy Gleeson's short fly in the eighth.

1952 — Sell infielder Tom Glaviano to the Phillies for the waiver price.

1953 — The Brooklyn Dodgers score 12 runs in the seventh inning to wallop the Cards 20-4 for their ninth consecutive victory over St. Louis that year at Ebbets Field. Dodger catcher Roy Campanella batted in five runs, including two in the first inning with a homer with Jackie Robinson aboard.

1963 — Ken Boyer's three-run homer at Philadelphia paces an 11–6 Card victory with the club in third place. The Cards proceeded to win nine straight, 19-of-20 and bolt from third place to one game behind league-leading Los Angeles.

1970 — Send pitcher Jim Browning to the Phillies as final payment of the Curt Flood deal of Oct. 9, 1969. Browning was assigned from St. Petersburg to the Peninsula club.

1972 — Trade shortstop Dal Maxvill to the A's for infielder Joe Lindsey, who is assigned from Birmingham to Arkansas, and a player to be named. The A's sent catcher Gene Dusan to the Cards Oct. 27 to complete the deal.

August 31

1866 — Art Clarkson (P, 1893–95)

1868 — Phillip Ehret (P, 1895)

1869 — Monte Cross (SS, 1896–97)

1881 — Charlie Brown (P, 1905–07)

1892 — Elmer Jacobs (P, 1919–20)

1893 — Murphy Currie (P, 1916)

1910 — Ira Hutchinson (P, 1940–41)

1913 — Mays Copeland (P, 1935)

1916 — Danny Litwhiler (OF, 1943–44, 46)

1926 — The Cards capture both ends of a doubleheader from Pittsburgh to gain first place. Bill Sherdel won the opener 6–1, followed by Al Sothoron's 2–1 victory on a three-hitter in the finale. No previous St. Louis team had ever led the league going into September.

1937 — Tracy Stallard (P, 1965–66)

1946 — Recall pitcher Al Papai from Lynchburg.

1947 — Boots Day (OF, 1969)

1955 — Silvio Martinez (P, 1978–81)

1977 — Trade pitcher Clay Carroll to the White Sox for a player to be named. This was part of the Aug. 20 deal for Don Kessinger and it was completed with the transfer of outfielder Nyls Nyman to New Orleans Sept. 2, the transfer of pitcher Steve Staniland to Iowa, also Aug. 20, and the transfer of Silvio Martinez and Dave Hamilton, pitchers, to the Cards Nov. 29.

SEPTEMBER

September 1

1874 — Henry Adkinson (C, 1921-23)

1882 — Carl Druhot (P, 1906-07)

1906 — Cardinal catcher Peter Noonan and Cub pitcher Carl Lundgren are chosen to act as umpires. The regularly assigned men in blue are ill, apparent food poisoning victims. Cubs find the change to their liking, defeating the Cards 8-1 at West Side Grounds in Chicago.

1917 — Cardinal pitchers Oscar Horstmann and Milt Watson each hurl 1-0 shutout victories over Pittsburgh in a doubleheader. Jack Miller's single scored Jack Smith with the only run in the opener. Watson allowed a mere one hit in the nightcap.

1918 — Jim Mallory (OF, 1945)

1927 — Tom Burgess (OF, 1954)

1930 — Dean Stone (P, 1959)

1953 — The Cards tie a major-league record with five solo homers. Stan Musial, Harry Elliott, and Rip Repulski each hit one and Steve Bilko belted two. All the shots were off Dodger pitcher Preacher Roe, but Brooklyn got 17 hits to win the game 12-5.

1958 — Vinegar Bend Mizell walks nine Redleg batters, but still pitches a 1-0 shutout over Cincinnati at St. Louis in the first game of a doubleheader. Mizell set a National League record for most base on balls in a shutout. The Reds came back in the nightcap 9-3.

1962 — Trade pitcher Paul Toth to the Cubs for pitcher Harvey Branch, who is on the Cubs' San Antonio roster.

1964 — Bob Uecker, who hit his first home run of the season earlier, singles in the winning run to give St. Louis a 5-4 victory over the Braves at St. Louis. The Cards still trailed the front-running Phillies by 7½ games.

1971 — Receive pitcher Stan Williams from the Twins for a player to be named. The Cards assigned pitcher Dan Ford from Arkansas to Portland and catcher-outfielder Fred Rico from Tulsa to Portland Sept. 14 to complete the deal.

1973 — Purchase pitcher Lew Krausse and catcher Larry Haney from the Oakland A's Tucson affiliate.

1974 — Sell catcher Tim McCarver to the Red Sox.

Lou Brock steals four bases against the Giants at San Francisco as the Cards defeat the Giants 8-1. It was the third and last time of Brock's career that he stole four bases in one contest. They were Nos. 95 through 98 that season.

1975 — Bob Gibson, who will retire at season's end at age 39, is honored by a sellout crowd at St. Louis on "Bob Gibson Day." He heard salutes from Commissioner Bowie Kuhn, Cards Chairman August A. Busch Jr., and a laudatory telegram from President Ford. Lou Brock drilled three singles, stole three bases, and scored three runs to pace a 6-3 victory over the Cubs.

September 2

1879 — Rube DeGroff (OF, 1905-06)

1927 — Trade shortstop Rabbit Maranville to Rochester for cash and Syracuse player Kapl.

1929 — Chicago Cubs defeat Cards 11-7 and 12-10 before 81,000 fans at Wrigley Field. 38,000 attend the morning game, 43,000 the afternoon contest.

1948 — Recall first baseman Rocky Nelson from Rochester.

1960 — Purchase infielder Rocky Bridges from the Indians.

1963 — Shortstop Dick Groat is hit by a Don Cardwell pitch at St. Louis against the Pirates. Groat led the league in hitting until he took the pitch in the ribs. He wound up finishing third in batting with a .319 mark, to tie with Hank Aaron behind Tommy Davis of Los Angeles and Pirate outfielder Roberto Clemente.

1965 — Chicago Cub great Ernie Banks hits career homer No. 400 off Curt Simmons in the third inning with two on at Wrigley Field.

1977 — White Sox transfer outfielder Nyls Nyman to Cardinals' New Orleans farm as part of August 20 trade.

September 3

1883 — Art Fromme (P, 1906-08)

1885 — Ed Konetchy (1B-OF-P, 1907-13)

1916 — Eddie Stanky (2B, 1952-53)

1922 — Morrie Martin (P, 1957-58)

1924 — Bill Greason (P, 1954)

1967 — Sign free-agent pitcher Barney Schultz, enabling him to qualify for a major-league pension. He was released Oct. 20.

1976 — Trade outfielder Mike Easler, on Tulsa roster, to the Angels for infielder Ron Farkas, assigned from El Paso to Tulsa Sept. 7.

1981 — Brewers conditionally purchase pitcher Donnie Moore from Cards Springfield affiliate. They return him November 5.

September 4

1901 — Al Grabowski (P, 1929-30)

1906 — Jim Mooney (P, 1933-34)

1918 — Bill Endicott (OF, 1946)

1952 — Recall catcher Bill Sarni from Columbus.

1968 — Ernie Orsatti (OF, 1927-35) dies at Canoga Park, Cal. In addition to being a consistent outfielder, Ernie was a stunt man in Hollywood movies in the '20s and doubled for comic Buster Keaton.

1973 — Sell pitcher Ed Sprague, at Tulsa, to the Brewers.

September 5

1896 — Ody Abbott (OF, 1910)

1916 — Ernie White (P, 1940-43)

1934 — Terry Moore goes six-for-six against the Boston Braves.

1947 — Recall pitcher Al Papai from Houston.

1962 — Walter Shannon, farm club director, signs a three-year pact with the Cleveland Indians as Midwest director of scouting. Shannon, who was with the Cards for 27 years, was succeeded as director of player procurement by George Silvey, while Eddie Stanky took Silvey's former job as director of player development.

1974 — Release pitcher Orlando Pena, who is signed by the Angels. In a related deal, pitcher Rich Hand was assigned to Tulsa by the Angels Oct. 15.

Purchase infielder Ron Hunt from the Montreal Expos.

September 6

1903 — Tommy Thevenow (IF, 1924-28)

1917 — Mike Naymick (P, 1944)

1924 — Hal Jeffcoat (P, 1959)

1934 — Tom Flanigan (P, 1958)

1948 — The Cards and Pirates set a major league record for fewest strikeouts in a doubleheader, two, by both clubs. The Cards lost both contests 2-1 and 4-1 at Pittsburgh.

1949 — Mike Thompson (P, 1973-74)

1957 — Pirate pinch-hitter Jerry Lynch's homer on the first pitch in the sixth inning of a night game at St. Louis ends Card relief specialist Willard

Schmidt's 10-game winning streak. Lynch's homer with a man on gave Pittsburgh a 5–3 victory.

1963 — Bob Gibson beats the Pirates 5–1 at Pittsburgh for career victory No. 50.

1971 — Lou Brock steals four bases against the Phillies in Philadelphia. It was the second of three times in his career that Brock stole four in one game. The Cards defeated the Phils 2–1.

1973 — Purchase outfielder Matty Alou from the Yankees.

September 7

1862 — Mike McDermott (P, 1897)

1877 — Mike O'Neill (P, 1901–04)

1903 — Curt Davis (P, 1938–40)

1912 — Arthur "Bugs" Raymond (P, 1907–08) is found dead in his room at the Hotel Valley, Chicago, of a cerebral brain hemorrhage. Police took into custody one Fred Cigranz, who admitted having attacked Raymond at a semipro game the Sunday before his death. Raymond was always considered somewhat of a problem, having been suspended from the game by the National Commission in July, 1910 for his activities. He was later reinstated, but never again played in the majors because Manager John McGraw of the Giants, to whom Raymond was traded for Roger Bresnahan in 1909, refused to have anything to do with him because of his drinking.

1944 — Barry Lersch (P, 1974)

1946 — Willie Crawford (OF, 1976)

1956 — Orlando Sanchez (C, 1981–82)

1977 — Purchase third baseman Taylor Duncan from the Orioles.

September 8

1886 — Ray Rolling (2B, 1912)

1891 — Verne Clemons (C, 1919–24)

1896 — Johnny Schulte (C, 1927)

1903 — Ernie Orsatti (OF-1B, 1927–35)

1940 — The Pirates sweep a doubleheader from the Cards, but the big show for St. Louis fans is Johnny Mize's three homers in the opener. Big Jawn thus became the first player ever to hit three round-trippers in one game four times. They were homers No. 38 through 40.

September 9

1871 — John McDougal (P, 1895–96)

1880 — Ambrose Puttman (P, 1906)

1886 — Dots Miller (IF, 1914-17, 19)

1894 — A crowd of more than 8,000, paying 25 cents each at St. Louis, sees Roger Connor go eight-for-ten in a twin bill against Brooklyn. The Cards took the opener 7-5, but lost the nightcap 11-7.

1898 — Frank Frisch (IF, 1927-37)

1926 — Ed Mickelson (1B, 1950)

1929 — Obtain Leland Nelson, a 16-year-old pitcher from a Fargo, N.D., American Legion team. He never played in the majors.

Chick Hafey hits a homer and three doubles, but the Cards lose to Philadelphia.

1941 — Recall outfielder Walter Sessi from Houston.

Option first baseman-outfielder Bert Haas to Columbus, which sells him to the Reds.

1952 — Jerry Mumphrey (OF, 1974-79)

September 10

1868 — Dusty Miller (OF, 1899)

1911 — John Chambers (P, 1937)

1938 — Fire Frank Frisch as manager and replace him him with Mike Gonzalez.

1934 — Roger Maris (OF, 1967-68)

Purchase outfielder Ival Goodman from Rochester and sell him to the Reds.

1941 — Recall first baseman Ray Sanders from Columbus.

Sell pitcher Hank Gornicki to the Cubs. The deal was cancelled by Commissioner K. M. Landis Sept. 22. The Cards in turn sold Gornicki to Pittsburgh Dec. 1.

1953 — Enos Slaughter's home run sparks a three-run eighth inning for the Redbirds, just enough to post a 7-6 victory over the Giants at St. Louis. Rookie New York hurler Al Worthington, who walked 11 batters, suffered his eighth consecutive defeat since pitching shutouts in his first two starts for New York.

1963 — Stan Musial hits a homer on his first at-bat since becoming a grandfather. His daughter-in-law, Mrs. Dick Musial, gave birth to a son at Ft. Riley, Kansas, where 23-year-old Dick was stationed as an Army lieutenant. That night at Busch Stadium against Glen Hobbie, Musial cracked the four-bagger in his first plate appearance.

1974 — Sell pitcher Mike Thompson to the Braves. In a related deal, the Cards buy pitcher Barry Lersch from Richmond Sept. 14.

Lou Brock steals second base in the first inning against Philadelphia at St. Louis, giving him 104 for the season, tying Maury Wills' record and breaking Max Carey's National League mark of 738 career steals. In the seventh inning, Brock stole second again, breaking Wills' record, held since 1962. The Cards lost to the Phillies 8-2.

1981 — Trade second baseman Neil Fiala and pitcher Joe Edelen to Cincinnati for pitcher Doug Bair.

September 11

1926 — Eddie Miksis (OF, 1957)

1974 — The Cardinals win a 4-3 decision over the Mets at New York in 25 innings, the second longest game in major-league history. Bake McBride opened the 25th with an infield single and scored all the way from first on pitcher Hank Webb's errant pickoff throw. It was the longest night game in major-league history, both in terms of innings and in terms of time (7 hours, 13 minutes). And it fell only one inning short of the all-time marathon record, a 26-inning dandy between the Brooklyn Dodgers and the Boston Braves May 1, 1920.

1975 — Eight Card pitchers can't avert a 12-6 defeat at the hands of the Cubs at Chicago. The eight hurlers tied a league record for most pitchers used by one club in a nine-inning contest.

September 12

1867 — John Dolan (P, 1893)

1934 — Joe Medwick's 28-game hitting streak ends versus the team he started it against, New York, Aug. 17. In that time, Medwick batted .358, with 43 hits in 120 at-bats.

1943 — Floyd Wicker (OF, 1968)

1973 — The Yanks assign pitcher Ken Crosby from Syracuse to Tulsa and give the Cards cash in lieu of another player to complete the Aug. 8 deal that sent Wayne Granger to the Yankees.

September 13

1873 — Jack Taylor (P, 1904-06)

1889 — Bill Chambers (P, 1910)

1890 — Walt Marbet (P, 1913)

1893 — John Kelleher (3B, 1912)

1911 — Roger Bresnahan signs a five-year managerial pact.

September 13 (continued)

1927 — Pitcher Tony Kaufmann is awarded to the Cards after a second waiver request by the Phillies.

1931 — Paul Derringer has his scoreless inning streak stopped at 33, but allows a mere six hits as the Cards defeat the Phillies 6-2 in the first game of a doubleheader.

1934 — Paul Dean limits the Giants to five hits in winning a 2-0, 12-inning decision.

Tom Hughes (P, 1959)

1945 — Rick Wise (P, 1972-73)

1949 — Big George Munger delivers his greatest performance of all—a one-hitter against the Giants at New York. He faced only 28 men in a 1-0 triumph. Sid Gordon's single in the second inning kept Munger from a no-hit game.

1959 — Third baseman Ken Boyer's hitting streak ends after 29 games as Chicago righty Glen Hobbie holds him hitless in four tries at Wrigley Field. Hobbie blanked the Cards 8-0 on four hits. The streak was the longest in the majors in nine seasons. It began Aug. 10 and was the best since Stan Musial's 30-gamer in 1950. Boyer also had a 15-game streak earlier in the year.

1964 — Walloping the Cubs 15-2 at Wrigley Field, the Cards become only the second club in modern history to score at least one run in each inning. The Giants turned the trick in 1923 against Philadelphia.

1971 — Purchase pitcher Mike Jackson from the Royals' Omaha affiliate. They returned him Oct. 18.

1977 — Sign outfielder Jim Dwyer, released by the Cubs.

September 14

1869 — Kid Nichols (P, 1904-05)

1903 — Red Ames of the Giants no-hits the Cardinals 5-0 in a five-inning game, which is the nightcap of a doubleheader at St. Louis.

1936 — Stan Williams (P, 1971)

1947 — Harry Parker (P, 1969-71, 75)

1951 — Walter Roettger (OF, 1927-29, 31) is found dying of self-inflicted wounds by his wife, Marjorie, in their Champaign, Ill., home. Roettger suffered from malignant high blood pressure, which was destroying his eyesight.

1952 — It takes the Redbirds nearly two years to catch up with Giant hurler Dave Koslo, but they do so with a vengeance, hitting him with an 11-run barrage in the fifth inning at New York to beat the Giants 14-4. Koslo was charged with the loss, ending a hex the 32-year-old lefty had over St. Louis

106

since June 11, 1950. He had beaten the Cards 13 consecutive times in that period.

1961 — Ken Boyer climaxes a seven-for-eleven night with his 22nd homer leading off the 11th inning to lift the Cards to a 6-5 victory over Chicago at St. Louis and giving them a sweep of their twi-night doubleheader. Boyer had a triple, single, and two RBI as the Cards took the opener 8-7. He also belted two singles, a double, and a triple in game two.

1971 — Assign pitcher Dan Ford from Arkansas to Portland and catcher-outfielder Fred Rico from Tulsa to Portland to complete the Sept. 1 deal in which they received pitcher Stan Williams from the Twins.

1974 — The Cards purchase pitcher Barry Lersch from the Braves' Richmond farm team.

1975 — Sell first baseman-outfielder Ron Fairly to the A's.

The largest crowd in Busch Memorial Stadium history—50,545—sees the Cards defeat the Mets 6-2. New York rookie Mike Vail extended his hitting streak to 22 games in a losing cause.

September 15

1900 — Harry McCurdy (C-1B, 1922-23)

1919 — Sell pitcher Red Ames to the Phillies. They returned him to the Cards a month later.

1924 — Jim Davis (P, 1957)

1928 — The Cards strand 29 runners, including 18 in the second game, but still manage to sweep the Phillies in a doubleheader 3-2, 8-6. The 29 still stands as a record for most men left on base in an 18-inning doubleheader in the majors.

1932 — Right-hander Ray Starr, making his first start in the majors, goes the distance to shut out Brooklyn 3-0 on two hits.

1937 — Charlie Smith (3B-SS, 1966)

1940 — Frank Linzy (P, 1970-71)

1951 — The Cards take advantage of 11 walks, five of them to Solly Hemus, to hand the Boston Braves a 10-1 defeat at St. Louis. Boston pitcher Dave Cole set the trend by walking the first three Cards to face him, then striking Enos Slaughter with a pitch to force Hemus in. Del Rice hit a two-run homer and Vern Benson a two-run double in the victory.

1968 — Roger Maris' 275th and last career homer leads the Cards to a 7-4, pennant-clinching victory over the Astros at Houston. Curt Flood had five hits in the contest.

1969 — Steve Carlton strikes out 19 New York Mets at St. Louis, breaking Bob Feller's single-game record. Even so, the Mets defeat the Cards 4-3.

107

1973 — The Cards rename their clubhouse the Butch Yatkeman Clubhouse, after the man who tended to their needs as clubhouse attendant since 1923.

September 16

1887 — James Galloway (2B-SS, 1912)

1899 — Heinie Mueller (OF-1B, 1920-26)

1908 — Buster Mills (OF, 1934)

1924 — Jim Bottomley goes six-for-six, including two homers and a double, as the Cards wallop Brooklyn 17-3 at Ebbets Field. The Cards pounded five Dodger hurlers for 18 total hits. Bottomley had 12 RBI to establish an all-time, major-league record.

1926 — Kurt Krieger (P, 1949)

1930 — Obtain infielder George Toporcer and pitcher Paul Derringer from Rochester.

1931 — The Reds trim the Giants 7-3 and 4-3 to clinch a second-straight pennant for the Cards. Later that night at St. Louis, Bill Hallahan won his 18th of the campaign, a 6-3 victory over Philadelphia.

1934 — A crowd of 62,573 turns out at the Polo Grounds in New York and sees the Dean brothers work their magic as the Cards sweep a doubleheader 5-3, 3-1. The second game went 11 innings in a struggle between Paul Dean and Carl Hubbell before Pepper Martin's homer started the Redbirds off to the victory. A four-run rally in the seventh won the opener for Dizzy Dean, although he went out for a pinch-hitter in that inning. The Cards thus moved to within 3½ games of the Giants in the pennant race.

1945 — Bob Chlupsa (P, 1970-71)

Ed Sprague (P, 1973)

1949 — Mike Garman (P, 1974-75)

September 17

1853 — Joe Blong (OF-P-2B, 1876-77)

1870 — Dick Padden (2B-SS, 1901)

1874 — Willie Sudhoff (P, 1897-1901)

1876 — Otto Krueger (OF, 1900-02)

1883 — Elmer Zacher (OF, 1910)

1899 — John Blake (P, 1937)

1909 — Ernie Koy (OF, 1940-41)

1920 — The Cards, launching 12 straight hits in the fourth and fifth innings, set a record for most consecutive hits in a 9-4 victory over Boston. With one out in the fourth, the Cards made 10 hits in succession and scored eight runs. The last two men in the inning were thrown out trying to stretch hits (Milt Stock tried to make second on a single and Austin Henry tried to stretch a double into a triple). Doc Lavan opened the fifth with a double to left and Cliff Heathcote followed with a single before a man was out.

1937 — Orlando Cepeda (1B, 1966-68)

1941 — Stan Musial plays his first major-league game against the Boston Braves at St. Louis. He went two-for-four with two RBI in the second game of a doubleheader before 3,585 fans.

1955 — Al Gettel (P, 1955)

1958 — Fire Manager Fred Hutchinson and replace him with Stan Hack on an interim basis. Hack was the only coach retained as Al Hollingsworth and Terry Moore also got the boot.

1968 — Gaylord Perry no-hits the Cards 1-0 at San Francisco. He permitted only two baserunners and retired 18 batters in a row between walks to Mike Shannon in the second inning and Phil Gagliano in the eighth. He threw 101 pitches, getting 12 outs on grounders and striking out nine, including Curt Flood on a called third strike to end the game.

1970 — Purchase pitcher Fred Reahm from the Mets.

September 18

1889 — Charlie Miller (OF, 1913-14)

1897 — Card shortstop Monte Cross and Pirate pitcher Pink Hawley engage in a fierce fistfight in a game at Pittsburgh.

1901 — Tige Stone (OF-P, 1923)

1915 — Boston takes both ends of a doubleheader from the Cards, 20-1 and 6-3.

1917 — Bill Doak adds a couple of hundred dollars to his bankroll with two complete game victories over Brooklyn, 2-0 and 12-4. That spring, Doak and Card management were considerably apart on salary. An agreement was finally reached whereby Doak would get a bonus if he won 15 games and another if he reached 20. The two victories this day gave him 15 in the win column, but he won only one more that year.

1925 — Harvey Haddix (P, 1952-56)

1948 — Lee Richard (IF, 1976)

1951 — Tony Scott (OF, 1977-80)

September 18 (continued)

1967 — Bob Gibson's 3-hit, 5-1 victory over the Phillies at Philadelphia clinches the pennant for the Redbirds. It was Gibby's first game in 52 days, because of a broken right leg sustained July 15 when hit by a liner off Roberto Clemente's bat.

1968 — Ray Washburn no-hits the Giants 2-0 at San Francisco, one day after Gaylord Perry of San Francisco no-hit the Cards 1-0. These were the first back-to-back no-hit performances in baseball history. Washburn walked five and struck out eight en route to his 13th victory, against seven losses.

1972 — Sell pitcher Lowell Palmer to the Indians.

1977 — Keith Hernandez hits his third grand-slam homer of the year, against Warren Brusstar of the Phils, as the Cards defeat Philadelphia 12-5 at Busch Memorial Stadium.

September 19

1858 — Sandy Griffin (OF, 1893)

1924 — Vern Benson (3B, 1951-53)

1926 — The Cards humiliate the Phillies 23-3 in the first game of a doubleheader, then add insult to injury by drubbing them 10-2 in the nightcap. The Redbirds sent 15 batters to the plate to score 12 runs in the third inning of the opener. Taylor Douthit walked, singled, stole two bases, and scored twice; Rogers Hornsby singled, walked, and scored twice; Jim Bottomley walked, doubled, and scored two runs; and Hi Bell singled twice and scored once. The only Cardinal who didn't hit safely in the inning was Billy Southworth, who was robbed of at least a two-base hit by center fielder Fred Leach's fine running catch. The victory moved St. Louis into a first-place tie with Cincinnati.

1927 — Bill Sarni (C, 1951-52, 54-56)

1946 — Joe Ferguson (C-OF, 1976)

1950 — Buddy Schultz (P, 1977-79)

1957 — Sell infielder Eddie Miksis to the Orioles.

1975 — Sign pitcher John Sielicki, released by the Giants, and assign him to Tulsa.

September 20

1860 — Henry Boyle (P-OF, 1885-86)

1922 — Burleigh Grimes holds the Cards to three scratch hits and stops second baseman Rogers Hornsby's hitting streak at 33 games as Brooklyn wins the first game of doubleheader 6-1. Hornsby resumed his slugging with homers in the first and ninth innings in the nightcap. The 33-game record still stands as the Cards' longest hitting streak.

1928 — A crowd of close to 50,000 at the Polo Grounds in New York sees George Harper hit three homers as the Cards bombard the Giants 8-5 in the first game of two. The Cards (89-56) lost the nightcap 7-4, but remained two games ahead of the second-place Giants.

1931 — St. Louis Manager Gabby Street uses himself in the lineup, the first major-league game he has played in since 1912. He failed to get a hit in his only at-bat as the Cards defeated Brooklyn 6-1. But Street showed he still had a good throwing arm from behind the plate, tossing out the only Brooklyn player attempting to steal, Babe Herman.

1941 — Dennis Ribant (P, 1969)

September 21

1858 — Dick Buckley (C, 1892-94)

1860 — Tom Brown (OF, 1895)

1930 — Billy Muffett (P, 1957-58)

1934 — Paul Dean no-hits Brooklyn 3-0 in second game of doubleheader. In the opener, brother Dizzy tosses a three-hitter. Questioned after the second game, Dizzy said: "I'd a done it too, if I'd a knowed Paul was gonna."

1948 — Aurelio Lopez (P, 1978)

1951 — After five years in the minors, Jackie Collum makes his first major-league start against Cubs at St. Louis and shuts out Chicago 6-0 on two hits. Collum, who threw a natural screwball due to the loss of an inch off the middle finger of his left hand and half an inch from the index finger sustained when his left hand was caught in a pulley at his farm near Grinnell, Ia., issued five walks, three in the first five innings and two in the ninth. A stout doubleplay defense helped him avoid serious trouble.

1957 — Sell pitcher Hoyt Wilhelm to Indians.

September 22

1875 — William Marshall (C-OF, 1906-08)

1890 — Denney Wilie (OF, 1911-12)

1895 — Austin McHenry (OF, 1918-22)

1926 — Les Bell leads the Card attack with three triples and a double as St. Louis defeats Brooklyn 15-7. Jim Bottomley and Tommy Thevenow contributed homers in a victory that increased the Redbirds' lead over second-place Cincinnati to 2½ games.

1941 — Commissioner K. M. Landis cancels the deal of Sept. 10 in which the Cards sold pitcher Hank Gornicki to the Cubs.

September 22 (continued)

1948 — Stan Musial gets five hits in a game for the fourth time this season, equalling the major-league record set by Ty Cobb in 1922. His five-for-five day against the Braves at Boston included a homer, a double, and three triples. At the end of his illustrious career, The Man called this his greatest day in baseball.

1979 — Lou Brock steals second base in the fourth inning of the first game of a doubleheader against the Mets in New York. It was career steal No. 937, tying him with Billy Hamilton's all-time mark.

September 23

1879 — Lee DeMontreville (IF–OF, 1903)

1897 — Walt Irwin (PH, 1921)

1941 — Stan Musial belts his first major-league homer as the Cards win the second game of a doubleheader 9–0 over the Pirates at Pittsburgh.

1943 — Recall second baseman Emil Verban from Columbus.

1944 — Recall pitcher Fred Schmidt from Rochester.

1957 — Hank Aaron hits St. Louis pitcher Bill Muffett's first pitch in the bottom of the 11th inning of a 2–2 tie at Milwaukee over the center field wall and wins the game 4–2 to clinch the pennant for the Braves. Following his career, Aaron called this the most memorable of his homers.

1962 — Los Angeles' Maury Wills ties and breaks Ty Cobb's record for stolen bases in a season with Nos. 96 and 97 at St. Louis. But the Cards slowed the Dodgers' pennant drive with a 12–2 victory.

1979 — Lou Brock steals second base in the fifth inning of a 7–4 victory over the Mets at New York, giving him 938 career thefts. It was Brock's last stolen base of his 19-year career.

September 24

1890 — Mike Gonzalez (C–1B–OF, 1915–18, 24–25, 31–32)

1906 — Grant McGlynn no-hits Brooklyn in the second game of a doubleheader at Brooklyn. The game ended in a 1–1 tie after seven innings because of darkness.

1922 — Rogers Hornsby hits his 41st and 42nd homers of the year against the New York Giants' Barnes brothers, Jesse and Virgil.

1926 — Flint Rhem and Bill Sherdel share the pitching chores as the Cardinals turn back the Giants 6–4 at the Polo Grounds to clinch their first pennant.

1934 — The Cards keep up their gallant pennant battle with a 3–1 decision over pitcher Lon Warneke and the Cubs. Veteran pitcher Bill Walker shut out the Cubs until the ninth inning, when Kiki Cuyler hit a homer. Pepper

Martin had hit one into the center-field bleachers at Wrigley Field following a double by Leo Durocher in the third inning. The victory left the Cards in second place, two games behind the Giants with six left.

1947 — Recall outfielder Hal Rice from Rochester.

1948 — Recall outfielder Hal Rice from Rochester, the exact same day as they did one year earlier.

1957 — Hank Aaron belts a Sam Jones offering in the first inning at Milwaukee for the first grand-slam homer of his career. The homer was No. 110 of Aaron's career and his 44th of the season, giving him his first National League home run title.

September 25

1872 — Dick Harley (OF, 1897-98)

1888 — Arnold Hauser (IF, 1910-13)

1908 — Cardinal President Frank DeHaas Robison dies of apoplexy in Cleveland at age 54. Frank and his younger brother, Matthew Stanley Robison, bought the club after the 1898 season. They helped change St. Louis' uniform trimmings to a vivid red and after the 1898 season practically transplanted the entire Cleveland team to St. Louis. Their wheeling and dealing transformed St. Louis from a 39-111 team in 1898 to 84-67 in 1899.

1934 — The Cards move to within one game of the National League-leading Giants with a 3-2 victory over Pittsburgh.

1940 — The Cards manage a mere two hits, both by Enos Slaughter, off Junior Thompson as they lose the first game of a doubleheader to Cincinnati 5-0. In the nightcap, Johnny Mize's 27th homer led the Cards to a 4-3 victory.

1948 — Ray Busse (IF, 1973)

1963 — Cardinal Owner August A. Busch Jr. appoints Stan Musial as the vice-president of the team. He also announced that The Man's uniform No. 6 would be permanently retired.

September 26

1889 — George Anderson (OF, 1918)

1924 — Eddie Erautt (P, 1953)

1925 — Bobby Shantz (P, 1962-64)

1930 — The Cards clinch the National League pennant at Sportsman's Park with a 10-5 victory over Pittsburgh.

1944 — Recall pitcher Stan Partenheimer from Columbus.

September 27

1884 — Alan Storke (IF, 1909)

September 27 (continued)

1891 — Doug Baird (IF-OF, 1917-19)

1936 — Cardinal first baseman Walter Alston strikes out in his first and only major-league at-bat. Alston went on to managerial greatness with the Dodgers, guiding them to seven National League pennants and four World Series titles in 23 seasons.

1944 — Gary Sutherland (IF, 1978)

1968 — For the second time in as many years, the Cards sign free-agent pitcher Barney Schultz to enable him to get pension time. He was let go Oct. 8.

Pitcher Bob Gibson shuts out Houston 1-0 at St. Louis to win his 22nd game of the season and give him an ERA of 1.12, breaking Grover Cleveland Alexander's mark of 1.22, which stood since 1915.

September 28

1865 — Lou Bierbauer (OF, 1897-98)

1876 — John Barry (OF, 1906-08)

1907 — Recall outfielder Al Shaw from Springfield.

1930 — St. Louis fans get their first look at pitching farmhand Jay Hanna Dean. Dizzy pitched a three-hit, 3-1 victory over Pittsburgh, further impressing the partisan crowd by bunting the ball into left field for a hit.

1949 — Mario Guerrero (SS, 1975)

1966 — Larry Jaster shuts out the Los Angeles Dodgers for the fifth time in one season, 2-0 at St. Louis. Grover Cleveland Alexander was the last to do it in 1916 when he pitched five scoreless victories for Philadelphia over Cincinnati. Jaster had beaten the Dodgers by two other 2-0 scores and a pair of 4-0 victories. The Dodgers only managed 24 hits, 8 walks and a .157 batting average in 45 innings that year against Jaster while he struck out 31.

1970 — Purchase pitcher Fred Norman from the Dodgers.

September 29

1866 — Gus Weyhing (P, 1900)

1871 — Russ Hall (IF-OF, 1898)

1928 — The Cards clinch the National League pennant with a 3-1 victory over the Boston Braves. Bill Sherdel notched the victory with relief help from Flint Rhem.

1934 — The Cards move into the undisputed lead in the National League race with a 6-1 victory over the Reds while the Giants lose to Brooklyn 5-1. The Cards took a one-game lead over the Giants with each team having one to

114

play. Although St. Louis pitcher Paul Dean was pounded for 11 Redleg hits, he was effective with men on base.

1943 — Recall pitcher Preacher Roe from Columbus and sell him to the Pittsburgh Pirates.

1952 — Stan Musial turns in his first and only major-league pitching performance as he faces Frank Baumholtz of the Cubs with two out and nobody on in the first inning at Sportsman's Park. Baumholtz reaches first on an error. As it was the final game of the season and the two players were vying for the National League batting title, both managers decided to let them face each other. Musial beats out Baumholtz for the crown, .336 to .325 but the Cubs win 3-0 behind Paul Minner.

1958 — Trade infielder Gene Freese to the Phillies for second baseman Solly Hemus, who is named manager to replace interim boss Stan Hack.

1963 — Stan Musial bows out in a blaze of glory. The final day of the season was designated as Stan Musial Day in St. Louis and a near-capacity crowd of 27,576 turned out for the swan song. In Stan's first appearance at-bat, Cincinnati fireballer Jim Maloney got him on a called third strike. In the fourth inning, Musial smashed a single past second baseman Pete Rose for the Cards' initial hit. Two frames later, Stan smashed another single to right to score the game's first run. It was his 3,630th hit and 1,951st run batted in. Gary Kolb went in as a pinch-runner and Musial received a tumultuous ovation as he trotted off the field for the last time as a player. The Cards appropriately went on to win the game in 14 innings 3-2.

1965 — Pitcher Bob Gibson's grand-slam homer off Gaylord Perry and the Giants at San Francisco lifts the Cards to an 8-6 victory. It was Gibson's fifth round-tripper of the season.

1975 — Release catcher Rick Billings.

September 30

1882 — Gabby Street (C, 1931)

Art Hoelskoetter (IF–OF–P, 1905-08)

1885 — Zinn Beck (IF, 1913-16)

1893 — Forrest More (P, 1909)

The Sporting News of this date honors Cardinal second baseman Joe Quinn as the most popular baseball player in America. Quinn received a gold watch with a diamond setting from the St. Louis-based publication as the first prize in the contest. Quinn responded by getting eight hits in a doubleheader, the first National League player to accomplish the feat.

1897 — Mike Kircher (P, 1920-21)

1913 — Nate Andrews (P, 1937)

1934 — St. Louis hurler Dizzy Dean fans two Cincinnati batters with the bases loaded in the ninth inning and gets the last man to foul out to gain his 30th victory of the season 9-0. It was the first time a National Leaguer turned the trick since Grover Cleveland Alexander won 30 in 1917 for the Phillies. It was also Dean's seventh shutout of the season, the first year he won more than 20 games, and a pennant-clinching final game before 35,274 St. Louis partisans.

1944 — Recall catcher Del Rice from Rochester.

1950 — Gerry Staley and George Munger sweep the Cards to two shutout victories over the Cubs 2-0, 4-0 in a twi-night doubleheader at St. Louis. They were the third and fourth shutouts in five games for the Redbirds. Staley allowed three hits and Munger four.

1956 — Sell pitcher Gordon Jones to the Giants.

1973 — The Reds assign first baseman-outfielder Roe Skidmore from Indianapolis to Tulsa to complete a July 27 trade which had sent Ed Crosby and Gene Dusan to the Reds.

1975 — Trade pitcher Mike Barlow to the Astros for outfielder Mike Easler, who had been loaned to Tulsa June 25.

Assign first baseman Doug Howard to the Indians' Oklahoma City affiliate to complete the deal in which Tulsa acquired shortstop Luis Alvarado from Oklahoma City May 27.

1977 — Lou Brock steals second base in the eighth inning against the Mets at St. Louis for career steal No. 900. The Cards defeated the Mets 7-2.

OCTOBER

October 1

1877 — Jim Hackett (1B–OF–P, 1902-03)

1884 — Ed Zmich (P, 1910-11)

1895 — Carmen HIll (P, 1929-30)

Duster Mails (P, 1925-26)

1904 — Jimmy Reese (2B, 1932)

1946 — The Cards defeat Brooklyn 4-2 before 26,012 at St. Louis to win baseball's first pennant play-off game. Stan Musial's triple helped Howie Pollet to a two-hit victory. Catcher Joe Garagiola's three singles in four at-bats knocked across two Redbird runners.

1952 — Sell first baseman Ed Mickelson and pitcher Bob Habenicht to the Browns on waivers.

116

1953 — Pete Falcone (P, 1976-78)

1963 — Trade pitcher Ken MacKenzie to the Giants for catcher Jim Coker.

October 2

1853 — Mike Morgan (OF-C-3B, 1877)

1878 — Jim McGinley (P, 1904-05)

1931 — Pepper Martin goes two-for-three, including a double, and steals two bases to lead the Cardinals to a 2-0 victory over the Philadelphia A's in the second game of the World Series at St. Louis.

1951 — Bob Coluccio (OF, 1978)

1952 — Sell pitcher Bill Werle to the Red Sox on waivers.

1969 — First baseman Bill White is placed on the voluntarily retired list.

1978 — Trade outfielder Bob Coluccio to the Mets for pitcher Paul Siebert, who is assigned to Springfield.

October 3

1866 — Bill Goodenough (OF, 1893)

1910 — Bob Bowman (P, 1939-40)

1926 — Billy Southworth hits a three-run homer into the right-field bleachers at Yankee Stadium for the Cards' first World Series homer in their second World Series game. Tommy Thevenow added a solo homer as the Cards defeated the Yankees 6-2 for their first World Series victory. Grover Cleveland Alexander allowed four hits in gaining the victory.

1931 — Bob Skinner (OF, 1964-66)

1932 — Phil Clark (P, 1958-59)

1936 — Jack Lamabe (P, 1967)

1946 — The Cards defeat the Dodgers 8-4 to win the pennant play-offs 2-0 and advance into the World Series against the Boston Red Sox. Doubles by Terry Moore and Stan Musial and triples by pitcher Murry Dickson, Erv Dusak, and Enos Slaughter led the Cards. Reliever Harry Brecheen fanned the last two Brooklyn batters, Eddie Stanky and Howie Schultz, to send the 31,437 fans at Ebbets Field home silent.

1958 — Trade outfielder Del Ennis, infielder Eddie Kasko, and pitcher Bob Mabe to the Reds for first baseman George Crowe, pitcher Alex Kellner, and infielder Alex Grammas.

October 4

1879 — Bob Rhoads (P, 1903)

1895 — Ralph Shinners (OF, 1925)

1904 — The Cards close their season by capturing a forfeited game over the Giants 9–0 in the second game of a doubleheader at the Polo Grounds in New York. A crisis arose in the top of the fourth inning, when Umpire Johnson ruled that St. Louis' Danny Shay had stolen second base before Giant Bill Dahlen applied the tag. Dahlen and the entire Giant infield encircled Johnson and argued against the call. Johnson ejected Dahlen for using profane language, but his teammates continued to argue. When Johnson felt he had enough, he forfeited the game to the Cards. He was punched in the ribs by a spectator as he left the field and needed a police escort to the dressing room.

1918 — George Munger (P, 1943–44, 46–52)

1927 — Rip Repulski (OF, 1953–56)

1937 — Trade shortstop Leo Durocher to Brooklyn for infielders Jim Bucher and Joe Stripp, outfielder Johnny Cooney, and pitcher Roy Henshaw.

1943 — Jim Williams (SS–2B, 1966–67)

1944 — The Browns, acting as the visitors, defeat the Cards 2–1 before 33,242 fans in the first game of the first all-St. Louis World Series. George McQuinn led the Brownies with a two-run homer over the right-field stands in the top of the second inning while Denny Galehouse picked up the victory.

1955 — Lary Sorensen (P, 1981)

1964 — The Cards defeat the Mets 11–5 at St. Louis while the Phillies bomb the Reds 10–0, giving the Cards their first pennant in 18 years. Bill White's homer with a man on in the sixth inning drove across the winning runs.

1967 — San Diego selects St. Louis pitcher Dave Giusti in the expansion draft.

1972 — Pittsburgh outfielder Roberto Clemente plays his final regular game against the Cardinals at Pittsburgh. The Cards won 4–3. Clemente, one of baseball's all-time greats, was killed in a plane crash during the off-season.

October 5

1885 — Bill Steele (P, 1910–14)

1906 — Si Johnson (P, 1936–38)

1926 — Pitcher Jesse Haines limits the Yankees to five hits and belts a two-run homer into the right-field bleachers in the bottom of the fourth inning, leading the Cards to a 4–0 victory over the Yankees in game three of the World Series. A total of 37,708 fans attended the first Series game ever played in St. Louis.

1930 — Right-fielder Ray Blades has seven putouts in the fifth game of the World Series at St. Louis. But the A's defeated the Cards 2–0.

1942 — The Cards defeat the Yankees 4-2 before a crowd of 69,052 to take the World Series crown four games to one. Catches by Stan Musial and Enos Slaughter in the outfield each averted Yankee home runs.

1962 — Release second baseman Red Schoendienst as a player and sign him as a coach.

1970 — Trade infielder Richie Allen to the Dodgers for infielder Ted Sizemore and catcher Bob Stinson.

October 6

1872 — Dave Young (1B, 1895)

1887 — Charlie Enwright (SS, 1909)

1901 — Carlisle Littlejohn (P, 1927-28)

1904 — Pitcher Jack Taylor hurls the last of 352 consecutive innings without relief, a streak that began April 15.

1922 — Joe Frazier (OF-1B, 1954-56)

1928 — Fred Marolewski (1B, 1953)

1944 — Robert Cooper, father of pitcher Mort and catcher Walker, dies at his Independence, Mo., home. But both players decided to play in the second game of the World Series, which Mort won 4-3 by holding the Yankees to six hits. Mort went one-for-three on a single in the eighth. Mort went right home after the game; Walker left at Series' end Oct. 11.

1954 — Mike Dimmel (OF, 1979)

1955 — Frank Lane, who submitted his resignation to the Chicago White Sox Sept. 22 after seven years as their general manager, signs a three-year contract as Cards' general manager. He succeeded Richard A. Meyer, who doubled as a Card official while continuing as an executive of Anheuser-Busch Inc., owner of the Redbirds. Meyer was given the title of executive vice-president. The day before Lane was hired, Vice-President Bill Walsingham, who was the nephew of one-time owner Sam Breadon, resigned after 29 years.

1968 — Homers by Lou Brock and Bob Gibson lead the Cards to a 10-1 victory over Detroit in the fourth game of the World Series. It was a short-lived celebration, however, as the Tigers went on to capture the Series in seven games.

October 7

1883 — Al Burch (OF, 1906-07)

1903 — Bill Walker (P, 1933-36)

1916 — Russ Derry (PH, 1949)

1922 — Grady Hatton (IF, 1956)

119

1928 — Joe Presko (P, 1951-54)

1943 — Jose Cardenal (OF, 1970-71)

1958 — Trade catcher Hobie Landrith, pitcher Billy Muffett, and third baseman Benny Valenzuela to the Giants for pitchers Marv Grissom and Ernie Broglio.

1969 — Trade catcher Tim McCarver, outfielders Curt Flood and Byron Browne, and pitcher Joe Hoerner to the Phillies for first baseman Richie Allen, infielder Cookie Rojas, and pitcher Jerry Johnson.

1974 — Receive outfielder Doug Howard from the Angels, who is assigned to Tulsa, as completion of a July 31 trade which sent Bob Heise to the Angels.

October 8

1877 — Bill Richardson (1B, 1901)

1885 — Johnny Lush (P, 1907-10)

1887 — James Crandall (P, 1913)

1896 — Tim Murchison (P, 1917)

1929 — Bob Mabe (P, 1958)

1936 — Trade first baseman Rip Collins and pitcher Leroy Parmelee to the Cubs for pitcher Lon Warneke.

1956 — Release catcher Walker Cooper and sign him as a coach. Release pitcher Jim Konstanty.

1967 — Release pitcher Barney Schultz.

October 9

1904 — Gordon Slade (SS-2B, 1933)

1909 — Jim Winford (P, 1932, 34-37)

1928 — Babe Ruth's three runs lead the Yankees to a 7-3 World Series victory and a four-game sweep of the Cards before 37,331 fans at St. Louis. The Yankees outscored the Redbirds 27-10 in the four games.

1929 — Bob Tiefenauer (P, 1952, 55)

1934 — The Cards defeat Detroit 11-0 before 40,902 angry Tigers fans to capture the seventh game and the World Series title. Cardinal left fielder Joe Medwick had to be removed from the game by Commissioner Kenesaw Mountain Landis in the bottom of the sixth as partisan Detroit fans threw garbage at the Redbird star when he took his position in the field. The incident was precipitated by a near fight Medwick had in the top of the inning with Tiger third baseman Marv Owen following a hard Medwick slide. After a five-minute delay, he again was pelted by fruit and bottles. Landis intervened at that point. Chick Fullis replaced Medwick in left after a delay of nearly 20 minutes.

1938 — Draft outfielder Jimmy Outlaw from Syracuse and trade him to the Dodgers for pitcher Lew Krausse, Sr.

1941 — Jeoff Long (OF, 1963-64)

1944 — The Cardinals, acting as the home team, defeat the Browns 3-1 in the sixth game to capture the World Series crown. Max Lanier limited the Browns to three hits in $5\frac{1}{3}$ innings and Ted Wilks held them hitless the rest of the way before 31,630.

1963 — Release pitcher Sam "Toothpick" Jones.

October 10

1902 — Homer Peel (OF, 1927)

1926 — Grover Cleveland Alexander relieves Jesse Haines in the seventh inning of the seventh game of the World Series at New York before 38,093. The ageless veteran struck out Yankee shortstop Tony Lazzeri on four pitches with the bases loaded and two out and then got the Yanks in the next two innings to earn a save and give the Cards their first world championship in their first World Series.

1930 — Third baseman Andy High goes three-for-four and right fielder George Watkins two-for-three, including a two-run homer over the right-field pavilion in the bottom of the third inning, to lead the Cards to a 4-2 victory and the World Series title before 20,805 Cardinal fans in the seventh game.

1932 — Trade catcher Gus Mancuso and pitcher Ray Starr to the Giants for outfielder Ethan Allen, catcher Bob O'Farrell, and pitchers Jim Mooney and Bill Walker.

1946 — Gene Tenace (C, 1981-82)

1947 — Teddy Martinez (IF-OF, 1975)

Release outfielder Joe Medwick.

1949 — Larry Lintz (IF, 1975)

1952 — The Cards ask waivers on pitcher Harry Brecheen, indicating they want him to stay on as a coach for $10,000. The St. Louis Browns announced Oct. 30 that they had signed Brecheen for $20,000 as a player-coach for 1953, and $14,000 as a coach in 1954. The Cards filed tampering charges, which were overruled by Commissioner Ford Frick.

1958 — The Cards take off for a goodwill tour of Japan. They won 14-of-16 games over the top teams from Japan's Central and Pacific leagues.

1961 — The first National League expansion draft is held. The Houston Colt .45s select infielder Bob Lillis and outfielders Ed Olivares and Don Taussig from St. Louis and the Mets catcher Chris Cannizzaro and outfielder Jim Hickman. The Mets also selected pitcher Bob Miller as the first of their designated "premium players."

1979 — Sign free-agent outfielder Bernie Carbo.

October 11

1900 — Eddie Dyer (OF-P, 1922-27)

1905 — Ed Clough (P, 1924-26)

Joel Hunt (OF, 1931-32)

1931 — Gary Blaylock (P, 1959)

1945 — Bob Stinson (C-OF, 1971)

1968 — Trade catchers Johnny Edwards and Tommie Smith, the latter assigned from Tulsa to Oklahoma City, to the Astros for pitcher Dave Giusti and catcher Dave Adlesh.

Trade outfielder Bobby Tolan and pitcher Wayne Granger to the Reds for outfielder Vada Pinson.

October 12

1874 — Jimmy Burke (IF-OF, 1903-05)

1938 — Release outfielder Frenchy Bordagaray to Rochester.

1950 — Option catcher Bill Sarni to Columbus.

1955 — Frank Lane, who was hired six days earlier as general manager, signs former pitcher Fred Hutchinson to a two-year contract as Cardinal manager.

1967 — Bob Gibson's fifth-inning homer helps him in 7-2, game-seven victory over the Red Sox at Boston. A total of 35,188 saw the Cards capture their eighth World Series title.

October 13

1858 — Fred Lewis (OF, 1885)

1894 — William Dillhoefer (C, 1919-21)

1936 — Trade outfielder Johnny Rizzo to Pittsburgh for catcher Tom Padden and first baseman Bernard Cobb.

1954 — George Frazier (P, 1978-80)

1959 — Release pitcher Hal Jeffcoat.

1962 — Sell pitcher Al Cicotte to the Colt .45s.

1967 — Send pitcher Al Jackson to the Mets, completing the deal of July 16, which sent pitcher Jack Lamabe to the Cards and pitcher Jim Cosman to the Mets' Jacksonville affiliate.

1974 — Trade first baseman-third baseman Joe Torre to the Mets for pitchers Ray Sadecki and Tommy Moore, the latter on the Tidewater roster.

October 14

1914 — Harry Brecheen (P, 1940, 43-52)

1915 — Max Macon (P, 1938)

1934 — Tom Cheney (P, 1957)

1974 — Send pitcher Dan Larson to the Astros' Denver affiliate, completing the trade of Aug. 15, which sent pitcher Claude Osteen to the Cards for pitcher Ron Selak and a player to be named.

Trade catcher Marc Hill to the Giants for pitcher Elias Sosa and catcher Ken Rudolph.

Trade second baseman Tom Heintzelman, on the Tulsa roster, to the Giants for pitcher Jim Willoughby, who is assigned from Phoenix to Tulsa.

1981 — Release pitcher Jim Otten.

October 15

1881 — Charlie O'Leary (SS-2B, 1913)

1887 — Bob Harmon (P, 1909-13)

1904 — Bill Lewis (C, 1933)

1946 — Outfielder Enos Slaughter puts on his now-famous "mad dash" to lead the Cards to a 4-3, game-seven World Series victory over Boston before 36,143 at St. Louis. Ironically, Slaughter's single in the bottom of the eighth, which he turned into a score two plays later as Johnny Pesky hesitated to throw to the plate after Harry Walker's hit, was his only safety of the game.

1964 — Homers by Ken Boyer and Lou Brock pace the Redbirds to a 7-5 victory over the Yankees in game seven of the World Series before 30,346 fans at St. Louis. It was the Redbirds' first Series title since 1946.

October 16

1941 — Tim McCarver (C-1B, 1959-61, 63-69, 73-74)

1949 — Don Hood (P, 1980)

October 16 (continued)

1950 — Manager Eddie Dyer resigns.

1964 — Manager Johnny Keane announces his resignation, one day after Cards capture the World Series title from the Yankees. Keane acknowledged that the firing of General Manager Bing Devine and Business Manager Art Routzong, the subsequent resignation of Eddie Stanky as director of player development, and the rumors of Leo Durocher's hiring prompted his resignation. Ironically, Keane's resignation was dated Sept. 28, but only he and his wife knew about it until he revealed it to August A. Busch Jr. this day.

October 17

1906 — Paul Derringer (P, 1931–33)

1946 — Rich Folkers (P, 1972–74)

1958 — Release pitcher Bill Wight.

1962 — Trade pitchers Larry Jackson and Lindy McDaniel and catcher Jim Schaffer to the Cubs for outfielder George Altman, pitcher Don Cardwell, and catcher Moe Thacker. Thacker was assigned to Atlanta.

1979 — Trade second baseman Mike Tyson to the Cubs for pitcher Donnie Moore.

October 18

1859 — Cliff Carroll (OF, 1892)

1875 — Joe Delahanty (OF-2B, 1907–09)

1884 — Burt Shotton (OF, 1919–23)

1935 — Howie Nunn (P, 1959)

1949 — George Hendrick (OF, 1978–82)

1971 — Return pitcher Mike Jackson to the Royals' Omaha affiliate.

Trade first baseman-outfielder Jim Beauchamp, pitchers Charles G. Taylor and Harry Parker, and infielder Chip Coulter, the latter two assigned to Tidewater by the Mets, to the Mets for outfielder-first baseman Art Shamsky and pitchers Jim Bibby, Rich Folkers, and Charlie Hudson, the latter on the Memphis roster.

1978 — The Cards fire General Manager Bing Devine and name John Claiborne to succeed him with the title of senior executive-vice president and chief operating officer.

October 19

1896 — John Brock (C-OF, 1917–18)

Bob O'Farrell (C, 1925–28, 33)

1914 — Al Brazle (P, 1943, 46-54)

1915 — Sam Nahem (P, 1941)

1945 — Pitcher Denny Galehouse is discharged from the U.S. Navy.

1949 — Bill Steele (P, 1910-14) dies after being hit by a streetcar at Overland, Mo.

1964 — The Cards drop Branch Rickey and his $65,000 consulting fee, while the Yankees announce the signing of Johnny Keane, who quit the Redbirds three days earlier as manager. Not to be outdone, the Cards named Red Schoendienst as their manager the same day. Both Keane and Schoendienst received one-year pacts.

October 20

1953 — Keith Hernandez (1B, 1974-82)

1965 — Trade third baseman Ken Boyer to the Mets for third baseman Charlie Smith and pitcher Al Jackson.

1967 — Release pitcher Barney Schultz, pitcher Hal Woodeshick, and catcher John Romano.

1970 — Trade pitcher Sal Campisi and infielder Jim Kennedy, the latter on the Tulsa roster, to the Twins for outfielders Herman Hill and Charles Wissler, the latter assigned from Evansville to Tulsa. Hill drowned in the Caribbean Sea near Valencia, Venezuela, Dec. 14, 1970.

Trade outfielder-first baseman Carl Taylor and pitcher Jim Ellis, the latter assigned from Arkansas to Portland, to the Brewers for catcher Jerry McNertney and pitchers George Lauzerique, and Jesse Huggins, the latter assigned from Portland to Tulsa.

1975 — Trade outfielder Willie Davis to the Padres for outfielder Dick Sharon, who is assigned to Tulsa.

1976 — Trade outfielder Willie Crawford, infielder-outfielder Vic Harris, and pitcher John Curtis to the Giants for pitchers John D'Acquisto and Mike Caldwell and catcher Dave Rader.

1982 — Take World Series, defeating Milwaukee Brewers 6-3 in seventh game.

October 21

1887 — Roy Corhan (SS, 1916)

Finners Quinlan (OF, 1913)

1922 — Stan Partenheimer (P, 1945)

1934 — Acquire catcher Jim O'Dea from Columbus and trade him to Cubs for pitchers Pat Malone and Bud Tinning.

1941 — Ron Davis (OF, 1968)

October 21 (continued)

1969 — Trade pitcher Dave Giusti and catcher Dave Ricketts to Pittsburgh for first baseman-outfielder Carl Taylor and outfielder Frank Vanzin, the latter assigned from York to Tulsa.

1970 — Trade first baseman Jim Campbell, assigned from Tulsa to Louisville, to the Red Sox for infielder Dick Schofield.

1971 — Return pitcher Daryl Patterson to the A's.

1981 — Trade pitcher Bob Sykes to the Yankees for outfielder Willie McGee.

October 22

1870 — Wilfred Carsey (2B-OF-P, 1897-98)

1896 — Sammy Bohne (SS, 1916)

1912 — After a dispute with Mrs. Robison, St. Louis owner, the Cards fire Roger Bresnahan (catcher-manager). Bresnahan, having four seasons left on his contract, insisted that the Cards live up to their side of the contract. The dispute was not settled until the following season, when the Cubs assumed his five-year contract and St. Louis settled with him for $20,000.

1918 — Lou Klein (IF-OF, 1943, 45-46, 49)

Harry Walker (OF-2B-1B, 1940-43, 46-47, 50-51, 55)

1976 — The Cards trade pitcher Mike Wallace to the Rangers for pitcher Johnny Ike Sutton, who is assigned from Sacramento to New Orleans.

October 23

1894 — Raymond Bressler (OF, 1932)

1973 — Sell shortstop Mick Kelleher to the Astros.

1978 — Trade outfielder John Scott to the White Sox for pitcher Jim Willoughby.

October 24

1858 — Willie Kuehne (IF, 1892)

1892 — Dick Niehaus (P, 1913-15)

1905 — Jack Russell (P, 1940)

1924 — Sign second baseman Rogers Hornsby.

1929 — Jim Brosnan (P, 1958-59)

1950 — Rawly Eastwick (P, 1977)

1961 — Release second baseman Red Schoendienst as a player and sign him to a coaching contract.

1974 — Sell outfielder Jose Cruz to the Astros.

1980 — Sell pitcher Hector Eduardo, on the Springfield roster, to the White Sox on a conditional basis.

October 25

1871 — Marty Hogan (OF, 1894-95)

1913 — Herb Bremer (C, 1937-39)

1917 — Miller Huggins resigns as manager to take a similar job with the New York Yankees.

1920 — Obtain infielder Al LeFevre from the Giants.

1939 — Pete Mikkelsen (P, 1968)

1954 — Tito Landrum (OF, 1980-82)

1973 — Sell outfielder Matty Alou to the Padres.

1977 — Purchase pitcher Frank Riccelli from the Giants' Phoenix affiliate.

1980 — Release pitcher Don Hood.

October 26

1866 — Bill Gleason (OF-P-SS, 1892-94)

1877 — Charlie Swindell (C, 1904)

1884 — Harry Camnitz (P, 1911)

1920 — Bud Byerly (P, 1943-45)

1923 — Tom Glaviano (IF-OF, 1949-52)

1926 — Dick Bokelmann (P, 1951-53)

1956 — Release outfielder Hank Sauer, who is signed by the Giants.

1972 — Trade pitchers Rudy Arroyo and Greg Millikan, the latter assigned from Arkansas to Albuquerque, to the Dodgers for outfielder Larry Hisle, on the Albuquerque roster.

1973 — Trade pitcher Jim Kremmel, on the Tulsa roster, to the White Sox for pitcher Dennis O'Toole, the latter assigned from Iowa to Tulsa.

Release pitchers Eddie Fisher and Lew Krausse.

October 26 (continued)

Trade pitcher Rick Wise and outfielder Bernie Carbo to the Red Sox for outfielder Reggie Smith and pitcher Ken Tatum.

Trade outfielder Cirilio Cruz to the Rangers for pitcher Sonny Siebert.

1977 — Purchase pitcher Aurelio Lopez from the Mexico City Reds.

October 27

1866 — John Healy (P, 1885-86)

1919 — Don Richmond (3B, 1951)

1922 — Del Rice (C, 1945-55, 60)

1952 — Pete Vuckovich (P, 1978-80)

1965 — Trade first baseman Bill White, shortstop Dick Groat, and catcher Bob Uecker to the Phillies for pitcher Art Mahaffey, outfielder Alex Johnson, and catcher Pat Corrales.

1972 — Receive catcher Gene Dusan from the A's in completion of an Aug. 30 deal which sent Dal Maxvill to the A's for infielder Joe Lindsey and a player to be named.

Release catcher Jerry McNertney.

1978 — Sell outfielder Mike Potter to the Mariners, completing the deal of June 26 which sent infielder Jose Baez to the Cards.

October 28

1863 — Tommy Tucker (1B, 1898)

1877 — Joe Adams (P, 1902)

1890 — John Lavan (IF, 1919-24)

1945 — Infielder Jimmy Brown is discharged from the U.S. Army.

1975 — Trade pitcher Mike Garman and a player to be named to the Cubs for shortstop Don Kessinger. Shortstop Bob Hrapmann was sent to Midland from Arkansas April 5, 1976, to complete the deal.

Trade infielder Larry Lintz to the A's for outfielder Charlie Chant.

October 29

1923 — Johnny Mackinson (P, 1955)

1939 — Pete Richert (P, 1974)

1942 — Branch Rickey resigns as vice-president-general manager and accepts a five-year contract as president of the Dodgers.

1944 — Jim Bibby (P, 1972-73)

1962 — Exactly 20 years to the date he left the Cardinal organization, Branch Rickey returns as a special consultant on player personnel. The hiring of the 80-year-old mahatma was another part of August A. Busch Jr.'s wholesale organizational revamping. The changes started Sept. 5 as farm boss Wally Shannon resigned and was replaced by George Silvey and Eddie Stanky took Silvey's job as director of player development. Since stepping down as Pittsburgh Pirate general manager in 1955, Rickey had been in virtual retirement.

October 30

1898 — Jesse Fowler (P, 1924)

1929 — Name Charles "Gabby" Street manager for 1930.

October 31

1884 — Ernie Lush (OF, 1910)

1896 — Leo Dickerman (P, 1924-25)

1887 — Ed Burns (C, 1912)

1904 — Allyn Stout (P, 1931-33)

1941 — Ed Spiezio (3B-OF, 1964-68)

1945 — Bill Voss (OF, 1972)

NOVEMBER

November 1

1884 — Robert Hyatt (1B-OF, 1915)

1906 — Heinie Schuble (SS-3B, 1927, 36)

1927 — Cloyd Boyer (P, 1949-52)

1946 — Jim Kennedy (SS-2B, 1970)

November 2

1860 — Frank Graves (P, 1886)

1866 — Frank Genins (IF-OF, 1892)

1868 — Jim McCormick (2B-3B, 1892)

1877 — Otto Williams (IF, 1902-03)

November 2 (continued)

1914 — Maurice Jones (OF, 1940)

1920 — Dick Sisler (1B-OF, 1946-47, 52-53)

1942 — Ron Reed (P, 1975)

1977 — Relief pitcher Rawly Eastwick is granted free agency. He signed with the Yankees Dec. 11.

November 3

1866 — Harry Staley (P, 1895)

1887 — Bob Fisher (2B, 1918-19)

1943 — Outfielder Harry Walker enters the U.S. Army.

1946 — Tom Heintzelman (IF, 1973-74)

1953 — Larry Herndon (OF, 1974)

1968 — Harry Caray, flamboyant radio voice of the Cardinals since 1944, is struck by a car as he crosses a rain-slicked street in St. Louis. Caray suffers fractures of both legs, a broken and dislocated shoulder, and facial lacerations. Police ticketed the vehicle's driver, Michael Poliquin, 21, for failure to display a driver's license. Caray was ticketed for crossing a street in mid-block.

1971 — Trade catcher Bob Stinson to the Astros for infielder Marty Martinez.

Trade shortstop Ted Kubiak to the Rangers for pitcher Joe Grzenda.

November 4

1873 — Billy Campbell (P, 1905)

Bobby Wallace (IF, 1899-1901, 17-18)

1897 — Ted Menze (OF, 1918)

1909 — Skeeter Webb (SS, 1932)

1912 — Appoint Miller Huggins manager.

1927 — Carl Sawatski (C, 1960-63)

1928 — Jay Van Noy (OF, 1951)

1930 — Dick Groat (SS-3B, 1963-65)

1933 — Tito Francona (OF-1B, 1965-66)

1940 — Trade catcher Mickey Owen to Brooklyn for catcher Gus Mancuso, pitcher John Pinter, and $60,000.

1946 — Danny Godby (OF, 1974)

1963 — Trade outfielder George Altman and pitcher Bill Wakefield to the Mets for pitcher Roger Craig.

November 5

1871 — Pete Childs (IF, 1901)

1909 — Harry Gumbert (P, 1941–44)

1938 — Ed Olivares (2B-OF, 1960–61)

1942 — Richie Scheinblum (OF, 1974)

1945 — Pitcher Murry Dickson is discharged from the U.S. Army.

1969 — Trade pitcher Ray Washburn to the Reds for pitcher George Culver.

1981 — Brewers return pitcher Donnie Moore, whom they had conditionally purchased from Springfield September 3.

November 6

1917 — Bob Repass (2B, 1939)

1938 — Name Ray Blades manager for 1939.

1945 — Billy Southworth resigns as manager to take the same job with the Boston Braves. He was replaced by Eddie Dyer.

1972 — Trade outfielder Jorge Roque to the Expos for catcher Tim McCarver.

1976 — Trade pitchers Bill Greif and Angel Torres and outfielder Sam Mejias to the Expos for pitcher Steve Dunning, infielder Pat Scanlon and outfielder Tony Scott, the latter on the Denver roster.

Release pitcher Lloyd Allen, infielder Bee Bee Richard, and sell infielder Luis Alvarado to the Tigers.

November 7

1898 — Mike Pasquriello (PH, 1919)

1927 — The Cards name head coach Bill McKechnie as manager for 1928.

1938 — Jim Kaat (P, 1980–82)

1945 — Release Billy Southworth as manager.

1948 — Tom Walker (P, 1976)

November 7 (continued)

1951 — John Tamargo (C, 1976-78)

1967 — Orlando Cepeda becomes the National League's first unanimous Most Valuable Player.

November 8

1876 — Danny Shay (SS-2B, 1904-05)

1895 — Mike Knode (OF-IF, 1920)

1920 — Wally Westlake (OF-3B, 1951-52)

1940 — Joe Nossek (OF, 1969-70)

1952 — John Denny (P, 1974-79)

November 9

1866 — John Crooks (IF-OF-C, 1892-93, 98)

1897 — Harvey Hendrick (IF, 1932)

1935 — Bob Gibson (P, 1959-75)

1958 — Release catcher Ray Katt as a player and sign him as a coach.

1979 — Sell pitcher Dan O'Brien to the Mariners.

November 10

1886 — Del Gainor (IF-OF, 1922)

1930 — Chick King (OF, 1959)

1948 — Draft outfielder Ed Sauer from Los Angeles.

November 11

1851 — Joe Battin (IF-P-OF, 1876-77)

1868 — Steve Brodie (IF-OF, 1892-93)

John Ryan (C-P-OF-IF, 1901-03)

1891 — Rabbit Maranville (SS-2B, 1927-28)

1914 — Manager Miller Huggins signs a two-year contract.

1920 — Acquire outfielder Les Mann from the Braves on waivers.

1929 — Trade pitcher Grover Cleveland Alexander and catcher Harry McCurdy to the Phillies for outfielder Homer Peel and pitcher Bob McGraw.

1945 — Pitcher Howie Pollet is discharged from the U.S. Army Air Force.

1946 — Art Reinhart (P, 1919, 25-28) dies of leukemia at Houston at age 47.

November 12

1867 — Harry DeMiller (3B, 1892)

1868 — John Ryan (C-P-OF-IF, 1901-03)

1920 — Obtain outfielder Leslie Mann from the Boston Braves.

1936 — Joe Hoerner (P, 1966-69)

1947 — Ron Bryant (P, 1975)

1957 — Frank Lane resigns as general manager to take the same post with the Indians. Owner August A. Busch Jr. named Bing Devine as Lane's replacement. Lane's decision to leave following the second year of a three-year contract was believed hastened by an ultimatum by August A. Busch Jr. that Lane "... would be out on his rump ..." if the Cards didn't win the 1958 pennant.

November 13

1915 — Ted Wilks (P, 1944-51)

1928 — Steve Bilko (1B, 1949-54)

1952 — Johnny Sutton (P, 1977)

1968 — Pitcher Bob Gibson is named the National League Most Valuable Player. Gibson thus capped an unprecedented sweep of baseball's most coveted prizes, the MVP and National League Cy Young Award. The double conquest by the 33-year-old right-hander after Detroit ace Denny McLain took similar honors in the American League marked the first time two pitchers ever divided the four awards. Gibson earned his with a 1.12 ERA and 22 victories. Gibson narrowly beat out Cincinnati star Pete Rose for the MVP award, but he was a unanimous choice for the Cy Young.

November 14

1902 — Gil Paulsen (P, 1925)

1939 — Rename Ray Blades as manager.

November 15

1856 — Tom Loftus (OF, 1877)

1889 — Rolla Daringer (SS, 1914-15)

1913 — Lyle Judy (2B, 1935)

November 15 (continued)

1933 — Trade catcher Jim Wilson to the Phillies for catcher Spud Davis and infielder Eddie Delker.

1936 — Acquire pitcher Leroy Parmelee from the Chicago Cubs.

November 16

1909 — Bill McGee (P, 1935-41)

1948 — Don Hahn (OF, 1975)

November 17

1885 — George Ellis (OF, 1909-12)

1888 — Lew McCarthy (C, 1920-21)

1896 — George Scott (P, 1920)

1913 — Stu Martin (IF, 1936-40)

1933 — Orlando Pena (P, 1973-74)

1958 — The Cards leave Tokyo after winning 14 games and losing only two before a total of 430,000 fans during a goodwill tour of Japan.

November 18

1892 — Harry Trekell (P, 1913)

1893 — Les Mann (OF, 1921-23)

1900 — Vince Shields (P, 1924)

1916 — Ken Burkhart (P, 1945-48)

1924 — Rocky Nelson (1B, 1949-51, 56)

1925 — Gene Mauch (SS, 1952)

1951 — Tony Scott (OF, 1977-80)

1974 — In a three-team deal, the Padres trade first baseman Nate Colbert to the Tigers for shortstop Ed Brinkman, pitcher Bob Strampe, and outfielder Dick Sharon; the Padres then trade Brinkman and a player to be named to the Cards for pitchers Alan Foster, Rich Folkers, and Sonny Siebert. The deal was completed Dec. 12 when the Padres assigned catcher Dan Breeden from Hawaii to the Cards' Tulsa affiliate.

November 19

1914 — Eddie Morgan (OF, 1936)

1930 — Joe Morgan (PH, 1964)

1940 — Purchase pitcher Forest "Tot" Pressnell from Brooklyn.

1942 — Larry Haney (C, 1973)

1945 — Bobby Tolan (OF-1B, 1965-68)

1962 — Trade pitcher Don Cardwell and infielder Julio Gotay to Pittsburgh for shortstop Dick Groat and pitcher Diomedes Olivo.

November 20

1880 — George McBride (SS, 1905-06)

1956 — Trade outfielder Rip Repulski and infielder Bobby Morgan to the Phillies for outfielder Del Ennis and a minor-league player to be named.

1969 — Trade outfielder Vada Pinson to the Indians for outfielder Jose Cardenal.

1981 — In a three-team deal, the Indians trade catcher Bo Diaz to Philadelphia for outfielder Lonnie Smith and a player to be named. Cleveland then trades Smith to the Cards for pitchers Silvio Martinez and Lary Sorensen.

November 21

1880 — Simmy Murch (IF, 1904-05)

1897 — Andy High (3B-2B, 1928-31)

1920 — Stan Musial (OF-1B-P, 1941-44, 46-63)

1928 — Name Billy Southworth as manager, with Bill McKechnie to manage the Rochester farm club.

1934 — Trade pitcher Tex Carleton to the Cubs for Pitchers Lyle Tinning and Dick Ward and cash.

1943 — Daryl Patterson (P, 1971)

November 22

1890 — Jack Roche (C, 1914-15, 17)

1922 — Transfer pitcher Bill Jacobs to Cincinnati.

1926 — Lou Burdette (P, 1963-64)

1931 — Neal Hertweck (1B, 1952)

1946 — Larry Dierker (P, 1977)

November 23

1878 — Jimmy Sheckard (OF, 1913)

135

November 23 (continued)

1897 — Bubber Jonnard (C, 1929)

1932 — John Anderson (P, 1962)

1947 — Dwain Anderson (IF, 1972-73)

1949 — Send outfielder Hal Rice to Rochester.

1953 — After a request for a two-year contract and other differences with Cardinal owner Fred Saigh, Marty Marion is released as manager.

1954 — Glenn Brummer (C, 1981-82)

1975 — Trade catcher-outfielder Joe Ferguson and outfielder Bobby Detherage, the latter assigned to Memphis, to the Astros for pitcher Larry Dierker and infielder Jerry DaVanon.

November 24

1881 — Pete Noonan (C-1B, 1906-07)

1909 — Tom Winsett (OF, 1935)

1911 — Joe Medwick (OF, 1932-40, 47-48)

1964 — Purchase pitcher Fritz Ackley from the White Sox.

November 25

1875 — Fred Parent (2B, 1899)

1880 — Frank Corridon (P, 1910)

1895 — Jakie May (P, 1917-21)

1930 — Transfer infielder Andy High to Rochester.

1940 — Sell infielder Joe Orengo to the Giants.

Dennis Aust (P, 1965-66)

November 26

1866 — Art Twineham (C, 1893-94)

1897 — Bill Warwick (C, 1925-26)

1916 — Eddie Miller (SS-2B, 1950)

1922 — Ben Wade (P, 1954)

November 27

1922 — Left fielder Austin McHenry dies of a brain tumor at age 27 in Mt. Oreb, Ohio. McHenry stayed at his post until midseason, batting .303 in 64 contests.

1930 — Purchase pitcher Hi Bell from Rochester.

1939 — Dave Giusti (P, 1969)

1943 — Infielder Lou Klein inducted into the U.S. Coast Guard.

1961 — Trade first baseman Joe Cunningham to the White Sox for outfielder Minnie Minoso.

November 28

1870 — Heinie Pietz (C–SS–OF–P, 1892–95, 1913)

1901 — Bill DeLancey (C, 1932, 34–35, 40)

1907 — Lynn King (OF, 1935–36, 39)

1937 — Ray Withrow (OF, 1963)

1953 — Sixto Lezcano (OF, 1981)

1972 — Trade outfielder Bill Voss to the Reds for pitcher Pat Jacquez. Voss was assigned from Tulsa to Indianapolis, Jacquez from Indianapolis to Tulsa.

November 29

1914 — Joe Orengo (IF, 1939–40)

1922 — Saturnino Orestes Arrieta "Minnie" Minoso (Armas) (OF, 1962)

Lynn Lovenguth (P, 1957)

1924 — Irv Noren (OF, 1957–59)

1942 — Bob Bescher (OF, 1915–17) is killed in an auto-train crash.

1950 — Marty Marion signs a one-year managerial contract.

1972 — Trade outfielder Larry Hisle and pitcher John Cumberland, the latter assigned from Arkansas to Tacoma, to the Twins for pitcher Wayne Granger.

1977 — Receive pitchers Silvio Martinez and Dave Hamilton from White Sox to complete trade of August 20.

November 30

1899 — Reuben King (SS, 1921)

1970 — Trade infielder Jerry DaVanon to the Orioles for pitcher Moe Drabowsky.

DECEMBER

December 1

1870 — Tommy Raub (C, 1906)

1908 — Les Munns (P, 1936)

1911 — Walter Alston (1B, 1936)

1917 — Marty Marion (SS, 1940-50)

1927 — Danny Shay (IF, 1904-05) commits suicide in Kansas City, Mo.

1961 — Trade infielder Ron Kabbes to Baltimore for pitcher Johnny Kucks.

December 2

1913 — Glenn Crawford (OF-IF, 1945)

1931 — Sell infielder Andy High to the Reds.

1936 — Sell catcher Virgil Davis and infielder Charlie Gelbert to Cincinnati.

1940 — Sell second baseman Stu Martin to the Pirates.

1946 — Pedro Borbon (P, 1980)

1948 — Stan Musial is named the National League's Most Valuable Player. Batting champ at .376, leader with 135 runs, 230 hits, 131 runs batted in, 46 doubles, and 13 triples, Musial fell short of a perfect score by one home run in a most remarkable season. He hit 39 out of the park, but Ralph Kiner of Pittsburgh and Johnny Mize of New York each smashed 40.

1953 — Trade pitcher Jack Crimian and approximately $75,000 to the Reds for shortstop Alex Grammas.

1959 — Trade catcher-outfielder Gene Green to the Orioles for outfielder Bob Nieman. The Cards also assigned catcher Charlie Staniland from Rochester to Miami as part of the deal.

1974 — Purchase pitcher Bill Parsons from the A's.

December 3

1872 — Cozy Dolan (OF, 1914-15)

1904 — Pitcher Jack Taylor returns to St. Louis from his honeymoon, denounces growing charges of crookedness against him, and threatens to sue the president of the Chicago Cubs, James A. Hart, for slander and damages.

1936 — Receive outfielder Frenchy Bordagaray, infielder Jimmy Jordan, and pitcher Dutch Leonard from Brooklyn as partial payment for outfielder John Winsett.

1943 — Jerry Johnson (P, 1970)

1945 — Steve Huntz (IF, 1967)

1947 — Wayne Garrett (3B, 1978)

1958 — Trade shortstop Ruben Amaro to the Phillies for outfielder Chuck Essegian.

1968 — Trade third baseman Ed Spiezio, outfielder Ron Davis, catcher Dan Breeden, and pitcher Phil Knuckles to the Padres for pitcher Dave Giusti.

Trade infielder Dick Schofield to the Red Sox for pitcher Gary Waslewski.

December 4

1868 — Jesse Burkett (OF-2B, 1899-1901)

1875 — Joe Corbett (P, 1904)

1876 — John Farrell (IF-OF, 1902-05)

1916 — Ray Sanders (1B, 1942-45)

1933 — Dick Ricketts (P, 1959)

1942 — Sign outfielder Frank Demaree.

Dick Billings (PH, 1974-75)

1959 — Trade outfielder Bobby Gene Smith to the Phillies for catcher Carl Sawatski. The Cards later assigned pitcher Bill Smith from Rochester to Buffalo to complete the deal.

1960 — David Green (OF, 1981-82)

1969 — Trade outfielder Boots Day to the Cubs for pitcher Rich Nye.

1978 — Trade outfielder Jerry Morales and pitcher Aurelio Lopez to the Tigers for pitchers Bob Sykes and Jack Murphy.

December 5

1864 — Oliver Tebeau (IF, 1899-1900)

1869 — Bill Moran (C, 1892)

1871 — Tom Smith (P, 1898)

1872 — Emerson Hawley (P, 1892-94)

1873 — Mike Mahoney (1B, 1889)

1901 — Carey Selph (2B, 1929)

December 5 (continued)

1905 — Gus Mancuso (C, 1928, 30–32, 41–42)

1911 — Don Padgett (OF–1B–C, 1937–41)

1928 — Jack Urban (P, 1959)

1940 — Sell pitcher Bob Bowman to the Giants.

Trade pitcher Carl Doyle to Rochester for outfielder Estel Crabtree.

1955 — Purchase pitcher Ellis Kinder from the Red Sox.

1957 — Trade pitchers Willard Schmidt, Ted Wieand, and Marty Kutyna to the Reds for outfielders Curt Flood and Joe Taylor.

1967 — Stan Musial resigns as Card general manager and is replaced by Bing Devine. Musial was the only general manager to direct a team to the World Series in his first year. Musial cited business interests as his reasons for stepping down, but added he would remain a senior vice-president and consultant to Devine.

1969 — Sell pitcher Jim Grant to A's.

Purchase pitcher Bill Dillman from the Orioles.

1973 — Trade outfielder Tommie Agee to the Dodgers for pitcher Pete Richert.

1978 — Trade pitcher Pete Falcone to the Mets for outfielder Tom Grieve and pitcher Kim Seaman.

December 6

1894 — Bruno Betzel (IF–OF, 1914–18)

1896 — Bob Larmore (SS, 1918)

1925 — The National League announces that Rogers Hornsby is the Most Valuable Player for 1925.

1936 — Sell pitcher Dutch Leonard to Atlanta.

1963 — Release catcher Carl Sawatski.

1973 — Trade pitcher John Andrews to the Angels for catcher Jeff Torborg.

1974 — Trade infielder Rudy Kinard and first baseman Ed Kurpiel, the latter assigned from Tulsa to Memphis, to the Expos for first baseman-outfielder Ron Fairly.

1977 — Trade pitchers Tom Underwood and Victor Cruz, the latter on the Arkansas roster, to the Blue Jays for pitcher Pete Vuckovich and a player to be named. Cruz was assigned to Syracuse and John Scott assigned to the Cards Dec. 16 to complete the deal.

December 7

1886 — Bobby Schang (C, 1927)

1942 — Alex Johnson (OF, 1966-67)

1964 — Trade pitcher Gordon Richardson and outfielder Johnny Lewis to the Mets for pitcher Tracy Stallard and a player to be named. Infielder Elio Chacon was transferred from Buffalo to Jacksonville in February, 1965 to complete the deal.

1973 — Trade pitchers Reggie Cleveland and Diego Segui and infielder Terry Hughes to the Red Sox for pitchers Lynn McGlothen, John Curtis, and Mike Garman.

1979 — Trade outfielder Jerry Mumphrey and pitcher John Denny to the Indians for outfielder Bobby Bonds.

1980 — Sign reentry free-agent catcher Darrell Porter, formerly with the Kansas City Royals.

1981 — Purchase pitcher Mike Stanton from Cleveland.

December 8

1907 — Bill Beckman (P, 1942)

1938 — Sell pitcher Ray Harrell to the Chicago Cubs.

1940 — Brant Alyea (OF, 1972)

1941 — Ed Brinkman (IF, 1975)

1946 — Alan Foster (P, 1973-74)

1954 — Trade third baseman Ray Jablonski and pitcher Gerry Staley and a minor-league player to be named to the Reds for pitcher Frank Smith.

1966 — Trade third baseman Charlie Smith to the Yankees for outfielder Roger Maris.

1973 — Trade pitcher Tom Murphy to the Brewers for infielder Bob Heise, who is assigned to Tulsa.

1975 — Trade third baseman Ken Reitz to the Giants for pitcher Pete Falcone.

1977 — Trade catcher Dave Rader and outfielder-third baseman Hector Cruz to the Cubs for outfielder Jerry Morales, catcher Steve Swisher, and player to be named.

Trade pitcher Al Hrabosky to the Royals for pitcher Mark Littell and catcher Buck Martinez. The Cards then traded Martinez to the Brewers for pitcher George Frazier, who was assigned from Spokane to New Orleans.

December 8 (continued)

1980 — Trade catchers Terry Kennedy and Steve Swisher; infielder Mike Phillips; and pitchers John Littlefield, John Urrea, Kim Seaman, and Al Olmsted to the Padres for pitchers Rollie Fingers and Bob Shirley, catcher-first baseman Gene Tenace, and a player to be named. Catcher Bob Green was sent from Waco to Gastonia Dec. 10 to complete the deal.

December 9

1918 — Clarence Beers (P, 1948)

1935 — Trade infielder Burgess Whitehead to the New York Giants for pitcher Leroy Parmelee, first baseman Phil Weintraub, and cash.

1941 — Darold Knowles (P, 1979-80)

1946 — Sell pitcher Red Barrett to the Boston Braves.

1971 — Sign first baseman Donn Clendenon, who was released by the Mets.

1975 — Trade pitcher Ron Reed to the Phillies for outfielder Mike Anderson.

1976 — Trade first baseman-outfielder Ed Kurpiel who was on the New Orleans roster, to the Mets for outfielder Leon Brown and first baseman Brock Pemberton, who were both on the Tidewater roster. Kurpiel was assigned to Tidewater; Brown and Pemberton went to New Orleans.

1977 — Trade pitcher Randy Wiles to the Astros for pitcher Ron Selak. Wiles was assigned from New Orleans to Charleston, Selak to New Orleans.

1980 — Trade first baseman-outfielder Leon Durham, third baseman Ken Reitz, and a player to be named to the Chicago Cubs for pitcher Bruce Sutter. Outfielder Ty Waller was sent to the Cubs Dec. 22 to complete the deal.

1981 — Purchase pitchers Eric Rasmussen from Yucatan and Vicente Romo from Coatzacoal of the Mexican League and assign both to Louisville.

December 10

1879 — Charlie Shields (P, 1907)

1898 — Tim Greisenbeck (C, 1920)

1927 — Billy Southworth accepts the managerial position at Syracuse.

1931 — Trade pitcher Burleigh Grimes to the Cubs for outfielder Hack Wilson and pitcher Art Teachout.

1941 — Sell first baseman-outfielder Don Padgett to Brooklyn.

1946 — Bobby Fenwick (2B, 1973)

1951 — Trade pitcher Max Lanier and outfielder Chuck Diering to the Giants for second baseman Eddie Stanky, who is appointed manager.

1956 — Trade pitchers Tom Poholsky and Jackie Collum, catcher Ray Katt, infielder Wally Lammers, and two minor-league players to be named to the Chicago Cubs for pitchers Sam Jones and Jim Davis, infielder Eddie Miksis, and catcher Hobie Landrith.

1976 — Trade pitcher Lynn McGlothen to the Giants for third baseman Ken Reitz.

1980 — Receive catcher Bob Green as player to be named later in Dec. 8 deal with the Padres. He was sent from Waco to Gastonia. The original deal sent catchers Terry Kennedy and Steve Swisher, infielder Mike Phillips, and pitchers John Littlefield, John Urrea, Kim Seaman, and Al Olmsted to the Padres for pitchers Rollie Fingers and Bob Shirley, catcher-first baseman Gene Tenace, and a player to be named.

1981 — Trade outfielder Sixto Lezcano and a player to be named to the San Diego Padres for pitcher Steve Mura and a player to be named later. The deal is completed February 10, 1982, as Cards send shortstop Garry Templeton to San Diego for shortstop Ozzie Smith.

December 11

1886 — Joe Riggert (OF, 1914)

1887 — Fred Toney (P, 1923)

1925 — Transfer shortstop Jimmy Cooney to the Cubs for pitcher Howard Keen.

1928 — Trade pitcher Grover Cleveland Alexander and catcher Harry McCurdy to the Phillies for pitcher Bob McGraw and outfielder Homer Peel.

1930 — Johnny O'Brien (IF, 1958)

1941 — Trade first baseman Johnny Mize to the Giants for catcher Jim O'Dea, pitcher Bill Lohrman, first baseman John McCarthy, and $50,000.

1944 — Mike Fiore (1B, 1972)

1954 — Bob Sykes (P, 1979-81)

1974 — Trade infielder Jack Heidemann and outfielder Mike Vail, the latter assigned from Tulsa to Tidewater, to the Mets for infielder Teddy Martinez.

December 12

1904 — Trade pitcher Mordecai Brown and catcher John O'Neill to Cubs for pitcher John Taylor and catcher John McLean.

1908 — Trade outfielder Red Murray, catcher George Schlei and pitcher Bugs Raymond to Giants for catcher Roger Bresnahan.

1913 — Trade first baseman Ed Konetchy, infielder Mike Mowrey and pitcher Bob Harmon to Pittsburgh for infielders Art Butler, John Miller and Cozy Dolan, outfielder Owen Wilson and pitcher John Henry Robertson.

Gene Lillard (P, 1940)

1917 — Clyde Kluttz (C, 1946)

1921 — Bill Howerton (OF, 1949-51)

1958 — Trade outfielder Wally Moon and pitcher Phil Pane to Dodgers for outfielder Gino Cimoli.

1974 — Padres assign catcher Dan Breeden from Hawaii to Cards' Tulsa affiliate, completing November 18 deal which sent pitchers Alan Foster, Rich Folkers and Sonny Siebert from Cards to Padres; Nate Colbert, from Padres to Tigers; Bob Strampe and Dick Sharon from Tigers to Padres and Ed Brinkman from Tigers to Padres to Cards.

1975 — Trade outfielder Buddy Bradford and pitcher Greg Terlecky to White Sox for infielder Bee Bee Richard.

1977 — Blue Jays assign outfielder John Scott to Cards, completing December 12 deal that sent Tom Underwood and Victor Cruz to Blue Jays, Pete Vuckovich to Cards.

1980 — Trade pitchers Pete Vuckovich and Rollie Fingers and catcher Ted Simmons to Milwaukee Brewers for outfielders Sixto Lezcano and David Green, latter assigned from Holyoke to Arkansas, and pitchers Lary Sorensen and Dave LaPoint.

December 13

1860 — Leonidas Lee (OF-SS, 1877)

1927 — Trade pitcher Jimmy Ring and catcher Johnny Schulte to the Phillies for outfielder Johnny Mokan, infielder Jimmy Cooney, and catcher Bubber Jonnard.

1935 — Lindy McDaniel (P, 1955-62)

1936 — Acquire catcher Mickey Owen from Columbus.

1937 — Ron Taylor (P, 1963-65)

1938 — Trade outfielder Jimmy Outlaw to Brooklyn for pitcher Lew Krausse, Sr., and cash.

1947 — Dave Hamilton (P, 1978)

1974 — Purchase shortstop Mick Kelleher from the Astros and assign him to Tulsa.

1980 — Sign reentry free-agent catcher Darrell Porter.

December 14

1879 — John Calhoun (1B-OF, 1902)

1901 — Les Bell (SS-3B, 1923-27)

1905 — Bob Weiland (P, 1937-40)

1923 — Paul LaPalme (P, 1955-56)

1925 — Sam Jones (P, 1957-58, 63)

1929 — Pete Whisenant (OF, 1955)

1949 — Trade outfielder Ron Northey and infielder Lou Klein to the Reds for outfielder Harry Walker and an unnamed player.

1964 — Trade pitcher Roger Craig and outfielder Charlie James to the Reds for pitcher Bob Purkey and a player to be named.

1966 — Trade pitcher Don Dennis and outfielder Walt Williams to the White Sox for catcher John Romano and pitcher Lee White, the latter transferred from Indianapolis to Little Rock.

1970 — Outfielder Herman Hill, obtained in a trade with the Minnesota Twins Oct. 20, drowns in the Caribbean Sea near Valencia, Venezuela.

December 15

1863 — Bill Van Dyke (OF, 1892)

1950 — Mike Proly (P, 1976)

1955 — Sign catcher Walker Cooper.

1959 — Trade second baseman Don Blasingame to the Giants for infielder Daryl Spencer and outfielder Leon Wagner.

1962 — Trade first baseman Fred Whitfield to the Indians for pitcher Ron Taylor and infielder Jack Kubiszyn, the latter assigned from Jacksonville to Atlanta.

1965 — Trade cash and a player to be named to the Indians for first baseman-outfielder Tito Francona.

December 16

1897 — Fred Wiginton (P, 1923)

1900 — Tony Kaufmann (P, 1927-28, 30-31, 35)

1909 — Sell outfielder Joe Delahanty to Toronto for $2,000.

1940 — Sell pitcher Forest "Tot" Pressnell to Cincinnati.

1969 — The first day of groundwork for AstroTurf at Busch Memorial Stadium begins.

December 17

1859 — Bill Hutchison (P, 1897)

1886 — Ennis Oakes (OF, 1910-13)

Jack McAdams (P, 1911)

1892 — Oscar Tuero (P, 1918-20)

1926 — Ray Jablonski (3B-1B, 1953-54, 59)

1932 — Trade first baseman Jim Bottomley to the Reds for pitcher Owen Carroll and outfielder Estel Crabtree.

December 18

1911 — Coaker Triplett (OF, 1941-43)

1914 — First baseman-outfielder Robert Hyatt is transferred from Pittsburgh to St. Louis.

1924 — Herb Gorman (PH, 1952)

1929 — Gino Cimoli (OF, 1959)

December 19

1887 — Art Butler (IF-OF, 1914-16)

December 20

1881 — Branch Rickey, who would build the Cards farm system and the parent club into a two-decade dynasty, is born on a farm near Lucasville, Ohio.

1887 — Art Butler (IF-OF, 1914-16)

1904 — Virgil Davis (C-IF, 1928, 34-36)

1923 — Grant Dunlap (OF, 1953)

1926 — Trade second baseman Rogers Hornsby to the Giants for second baseman Frank Frisch and pitcher Jimmy Ring.

1936 — Sell pitcher Al Smith to the Phillies.

1937 — Purchase pitcher Al Smith from the Giants and sell him to the Phillies on waivers.

December 21

1863 — Dell Darling (C, 1891)

1897 — Hal Haid (P, 1928-30)

1920 — Bill Werle (P, 1952)

1952 — Joaquin Andujar (P, 1981-82)

1959 — Trade outfielder Gino Cimoli and pitcher Tom Cheney to the Pirates for pitcher Ron Kline.

December 22

1937 — Charlie James (OF, 1960-64)

1938 — Matty Alou (OF, 1971-73)

1944 — Steve Carlton (P, 1965-71)

1953 — Tom Underwood (P, 1977)

1975 — Trade shortstop Mick Kelleher to the Cubs for second baseman Vic Harris.

1980 — Send outfield Ty Waller to the Cubs, to complete a Dec. 9 trade that sent first baseman-outfielder Leon Durham, third baseman Ken Reitz, and a player to be named to Cubs for pitcher Bruce Sutter.

Release outfielder Bobby Bonds.

December 23

1860 — Mike Grady (C-IF, 1897, 1904-06)

1884 — Palmer Hildebrand (C-OF, 1913)

1904 — Howie Williamson (PH, 1928)

1912 — Pat Ankenman (SS, 1936)

1929 — Al Cicotte (P, 1961)

1943 — Ron Allen (1B, 1972)

December 24

1869 — Zeke Wilson (P, 1899)

1884 — George Zackert (P, 1911-12)

1951 — John D'Acquisto (P, 1977)

1969 — Curt Flood sends his now famous "piece of property" letter to Commissioner Bowie Kuhn, chastising the reserve clause.

147

December 24 (continued)

1974 — Lou Brock is named Sportsman of the Year by *The Sporting News,* besting such sports luminaries as tennis' Jimmy Connors, golf's Johnny Miller, and baseball's Mike Marshall.

December 25

1855 — Pud Galvin (P, 1892)

1864 — Joe Quinn (OF-IF, 1885-86, 93-96, 98)

1895 — Herb Hunter (1B, 1921)

1901 — Joe McCarthy (C, 1906)

1935 — Al Jackson (P, 1966-67)

1953 — Julio Gonzalez (IF, 1981-82)

1954 — Jeff Little (P, 1980-81)

December 26

1887 — Jim Clark (OF, 1911-12)

1901 — Ed Farrell (IF, 1930)

1927 — Stu Miller (P, 1952-54, 56)

1940 — Ray Sadecki (P, 1960-66, 75)

1946 — Sell catcher Clyde Kluttz to Pittsburgh.

1948 — Dave Rader (C, 1977)

December 27

1873 — Tom Thomas (P, 1899-1900)

1939 — Recall pitcher Ken Raffensberger from Rochester and trade him to the Cubs for pitcher-infielder Gene Lillard, infielder Steve Mesner, and cash.

1941 — Phil Gagliano (IF-OF, 1963-70)

1942 — Byron Browne (OF, 1969)

December 28

1901 — Wattie Holm (OF-C-3B, 1924-29, 32)

1921 — Nelson Burbrink (C, 1955)

1926 — The Cards name Bob O'Farrell as manager for 1927 and Bill McKechnie as head coach

December 29

1946 — Ken Rudolph (C, 1975–76)

1981 — Re-sign reentry free-agent pitcher Joaquin Andujar.

December 30

1851 — Ed Caskin (IF, 1885)

1878 — Clarence Currie (P, 1902–03)

1925 — Harry Elliott (OF, 1953)

1929 — Joe Taylor (OF, 1958)

1945 — Tom Murphy (P, 1973)

December 31

1863 — Pete Sweeney (3B, 1889–90)

1880 — Fred Beebe (P, 1906–09)

1884 — Bobby Byrne (3B, 1907–09)

1900 — Syl Johnson (P, 1926–33)

1917 — Jack Hendricks, manager of the Indianapolis club of the American Association, is signed as manager, replacing Miller Huggins.

THE ALL-TIME ST. LOUIS NATIONAL LEAGUE BALLCLUB ROSTER

Fans are frequently curious as to whether a given player ever played for a particular team. The purpose of this section is to list the name of every player who ever wore the uniform for at least one fraction of an inning and made an appearance on the playing field in some capacity during a regular-season game.

The players are listed in alphabetical order under their last names. The year(s) in which the player was on the roster, and his position(s) are shown immediately to the right of the name. The player's date of birth and date of death (if deceased and if available) are also shown.

Code:
INF— Indicates the player played third base (3B), shortstop (SS), and second base (2B) with roughly equal frequency during his Cardinal career.
OF— Indicates the player played one or more outfield positions
C— Indicates the player played as a catcher
1B— First baseman
P— Pitcher
PH — Indicates that the player's only major-league appearance(s) in a Cardinal uniform was (were) as a pinch-hitter.
PR— Indicates that the player's only St. Louis appearance(s) was (were) as a pinch-runner.

149

Note: pitchers are listed separately before all of the other positions. For a complete list of every nickname for every player, see the separate nicknames section.

The St. Louis team competed in the new National League in 1876 and 1877, but withdrew after two years. A National League team returned in 1885, but again lasted only two seasons. A third St. Louis franchise in the league was born in 1892 and has lasted ever since.

THE ALL-TIME ST. LOUIS NATIONAL LEAGUE BALLCLUB ROSTER

Pitchers

Player	Years	Born	Died	Rec.
Abernathy, Ted	1970	3/6/33		1-0
Adams, Charles	1906	5/18/82	7/27/68	0-1
Adams, Joe	1902	10/28/77	10/8/52	0-0
Alberts, Frederick	1910	1/14/82	8/27/17	1-2
Alexander, Grover Cleveland	1926–29	2/26/87	11/4/50	55-34
Ames, Leon	1915–19	8/2/82	10/8/36	47-48
Anderson, Craig	1961	7/1/38		4-3
Anderson, John	1962	11/23/32		0-0
Andrews, John	1973	2/9/49		1-1
Andrews, Nate	1937	9/30/13		1-2
Andujar, Joaquin	1981–82	12/21/52		21-11
Arroyo, Luis	1955	2/18/27		11-8
Arroyo, Rudy	1971	6/19/50		0-1
Aust, Dennis	1965–66	11/25/40		0-1
Backman, Les	1909–10	3/20/88		10-18
Bailey, Bill	1921–22	4/12/89	11/2/26	2-7
Bair, Doug	1981–82	8/22/49		7-3
Bakenhaster, Dave	1964	3/5/45		0-0
Baldwin, O.F.	1908	(unknown)		1-3
Bare, Ray	1972, 74	4/15/49		1-3
Barfoot, Clyde	1922–23	7/8/91	3/11/71	7-8
Barlow, Mike	1975	4/30/48		0-0
Barnes, Frank	1957–58, 60	8/26/28		1-3
Barrett, Charles	1945–46	2/14/15		24-11
Barrett, Frank	1939	7/1/13		0-1
Bates, Frank	1899	(unknown)	(deceased)	0-0
Bauta, Ed	1960–63	1/6/35		6-4
Beard, Ralph	1954	6/21/50		0-4
Beazley, Johnny	1941–42, 46	5/25/18		29-11
Beckman, Bill	1942	12/8/07		1-0
Beebe, Fred	1906–09	12/31/80	10/30/57	36-63
Beers, Clarence	1948	12/9/18		0-0
Bell, Herman	1924, 26–27, 29–30	7/16/95	6/7/49	14-22
Benton, Sid	1922	8/4/95	3/8/77	0-0
Berly, Jack	1924	5/24/03	6/26/77	0-0
Bernard, Joe	1909	(unknown)		0-0
Bertaina, Frank	1970	4/14/44		1-2
Betts, Hal	1903	1888	(unknown)	0-1
Bibby, Jim	1972–73	10/29/44		1-5
Blake, John	1937	9/17/99		0-3

Player	Years	Born	Died	Rec.
Blaylock, Bob	1956	6/28/35		1-7
Blaylock, Gary	1959	10/11/31		4-5
Boardman, Charlie	1915	3/27/93	8/10/68	1-0
Bokelmann, Dick	1951–53	10/26/26		3-4
Bolden, Bill	1919	5/9/93	12/8/66	0-1
Borbon, Pedro	1980	12/2/46		1-0
Bowman, Bob	1939–40	10/3/10	9/4/72	20-10
Boyer, Cloyd	1949–52	11/1/27		15-18
Boyle, Henry	1885–86	9/20/60	(deceased)	25-39
Bradley, Joe	1876	7/13/52	10/2/31	45-19
Branch, Harvey	1962	2/8/39		0-1
Brazle, Al	1943, 46–54	10/19/14	10/24/73	97-64
Brecheen, Harry	1940, 43–52	10/14/14		127-79
Breitenstein, Ted	1892–96, 1901	6/1/69	5/3/35	100-123
Bridges, Marshall	1959–60	6/2/31		8-5
Briles, Nelson	1965–70	8/5/43		61-54
Broglio, Ernie	1959–64	8/27/35		70-55
Brosnan, Jim	1958–59	10/24/29		9-7
Brown, Charlie	1905–07	8/31/81	2/9/14	17-33
Brown, Mordecai	1903	10/19/76	2/14/48	9-13
Browning, Cal	1960	3/16/38		0-0
Brunet, George	1971	6/8/35		0-1
Bruno, Tom	1978–79	1/26/53		4-3
Bryant, Ron	1975	11/12/47		0-1
Burdette, Lew	1963–64	11/22/26		4-8
Burk, Charles	1912–13	4/22/87	10/11/34	1-2
Burkhart, Ken	1945–48	11/18/16		28-17
Burns, James	1901	(unknown)		0-0
Bush, Guy	1938	8/23/01		0-1
Byerly, Bud	1943–45	10/26/20		7-7
Callahan, Jim	1898	(unknown)	(deceased)	0-2
Camnitz, Harry	1911	10/26/84	1/6/51	1-0
Campbell, Billy	1905	11/4/73	10/7/57	1-1
Campisi, Sal	1969–70	8/11/42		3-2
Capilla Doug	1976–77	1/7/52		1-0
Carleton, Tex	1932–34	8/19/06	1/11/76	43-35
Carlton, Steve	1965–71	12/22/44		77-62
Carroll, Clay	1977	5/2/41		4-2
Chambers, Bill	1910	9/13/89	3/27/62	0-0
Chambers, Cliff	1951–53	1/10/22		18-16
Chambers, John	1937	9/10/11	5/11/77	0-0
Cheney, Tom	1957	10/14/34		0-2
Chittum, Nelson	1958	3/25/33		0-1
Chlupsa, Bob	1970–71	9/16/45		0-2
Cicotte, Al	1961	12/23/29		2-6
Clark, Mike	1952–53	2/12/22		3-0
Clark, Phil	1958–59	10/3/32		0-2
Clarkson, Arthur	1893–95	8/31/66	2/6/11	21-32
Clemons, Lance	1972	7/6/47		0-1
Cleveland, Reggie	1969–73	5/23/48		40-41
Cloninger, Tony	1972	8/13/40		0-2
Clough, Ed	1924–26	10/11/05	1/30/44	0-1
Coleman, John	1895	1870	(deceased)	0-1
Coleman, Percy	1897	(unknown)	(deceased)	1-2

Player	Years	Born	Died	Rec.
Collins, Phil	1935	8/27/00	8/14/48	7-6
Collum, Jackie	1951–53, 56	6/21/27		8-3
Cooper, Mort	1938–45	3/2/13	11/17/58	105-50
Copeland, Mays	1935	8/31/13		0-0
Corbett, Joe	1904	12/4/75	5/2/45	5-9
Corridon, Frank	1910	11/25/80	2/21/41	7-15
Cosman, Jim	1966–67	2/19/43		2-0
Cox, Bill	1936	3/23/13		0-0
Craig, Roger	1964	2/17/31		7-9
Crandall, James	1913	10/8/87	8/17/51	0-0
Creel, Jack	1945	4/23/16		5-4
Crimian, Jack	1951–52	2/17/26		1-0
Crouch, Bill	1941	8/20/10	12/25/80	2-2
Cuellar, Mike	1964	5/8/37		5-5
Culver, George	1970	7/8/43		3-3
Cumberland, John	1972	5/10/47		1-1
Cuppy, George	1899	7/3/69	7/27/22	11-8
Currie, Clarence	1902–03	12/30/78	7/15/41	10-17
Currie, Murphy	1916	8/31/93	6/22/39	0-0
Curtis, John	1974–76	3/9/48		24-34
D'Acquisto, John	1977	12/24/51		0-0
Daily, Hugh	1885	1857	(deceased)	3-8
Dale, Gene	1911–12	6/16/89	3/20/58	1-7
Daniels, Pete	1898	4/8/64	2/13/28	1-6
Davis, Curt	1938–40	9/7/03	10/13/65	34-28
Davis, Jim	1957	9/15/24		0-1
Day, Clyde	1924–25	8/27/99	3/21/34	3-5
Deal, Ellis	1950	1/23/23		2-3
Dean, Dizzy	1930, 32–37	1/16/11	7/17/74	134-75
Dean, Paul	1934–39	8/14/13	3/17/81	46-30
Delaney, Art	1924	1/5/97	5/2/70	1-0
DeLeon, Luis	1981	8/19/58		0-1
Dell, William	1912	6/11/87	8/24/66	0-0
Dennis, Don	1965–66	3/3/42		6-5
Denny, John	1974–79	11/8/52		51-46
Derringer, Paul	1931–33	10/17/06		29-24
Dickerman, Leo	1924–25	10/31/96		11-15
Dickson, Murry	1939–40, 42–43, 46–48, 56–57	8/21/16		72-54
Dierker, Larry	1977	11/22/46		2-6
Doak, Bill	1913–24, 29	1/28/91	11/26/54	145-136
Dockins, George	1945	5/5/17		8-6
Dolan, John	1893	9/12/67	5/8/48	0-1
Donahue, Francis	1895–97	1/23/73	8/25/13	18-58
Donnelly, Sylvester	1944–46	1/21/14	6/20/76	11-13
Dowling, Dave	1964	8/23/42		0-0
Doyle, Carl	1940	7/30/12	9/4/51	3-3
Drabowsky, Moe	1971–72	7/21/35		7-2
Dressler, Rob	1978	2/2/54		0-1
Druhot, Carl	1906–07	9/1/82	2/11/18	6-9
Duliba, Bob	1959–60, 62	1/9/35		6-5
Dunham, Wiley	1902	(unknown)		2-3

Player	Years	Born	Died	Rec.
Durham, Don	1972	3/21/49		2-7
Dwyer, Frank	1892	3/25/68	2/4/43	2-8
Earnshaw, George	1936	2/15/00	12/1/76	2-1
Easton, Jack	1892	1867	Nov. 1903	2-0
Eastwick, Rawly	1977	10/24/50		3-7
Eckert, Al	1935	5/17/06		0-0
Egan, Aloysius	1905–06	6/16/81	4/13/51	8-24
Ehret, Phillip	1895	8/31/68	7/28/40	6-19
Ellis, Jim	1969	3/25/45		0-0
Erautt, Eddie	1953	9/26/24	10/6/76	3-1
Esper, Charles	1897–98	7/28/68	8/31/10	4-11
Evans, LeRoy	1897	3/19/74		0-0
Ewing, Bob	1912	4/24/73	6/20/47	0-0
Falcone, Pete	1976–78	10/1/53		18-31
Fanok, Harry	1963–64	5/11/40		2-1
Faszholz, Jack	1953	4/11/27		0-0
Ferrarese, Don	1962	6/19/29		1-4
Fisher, Chauncey	1901	1/8/72	4/27/39	0-0
Fisher, Eddie	1973	7/16/36		2-1
Flanigan, Tom	1958	9/6/34		0-0
Flowers, Ben	1955–56	6/15/27		2-1
Folkers, Rich	1972–74	10/17/46		11-6
Forsch, Bob	1974–82	1/13/50		109-82
Foster, Alan	1973–74	12/8/46		20-19
Fowler, Jesse	1924	10/30/98	9/23/73	1-1
Francis, Earl	1965	7/14/36		0-0
Frankhouse, Fred	1927–30	4/9/04		17-8
Frazier, George	1978–80	10/13/54		1-4
Frey, Benny	1932	4/6/06	11/1/37	0-2
Frisella, Danny	1976	3/4/46	1/1/77	0-0
Fromme, Art	1906–08	9/3/83	8/24/56	11-27
Fulgham, John	1979–80	6/9/56		14-12
Gaiser, Fred	1908	4/8/85	11/14/18	0-0
Galvin, Pud	1892	12/25/55	3/7/02	5-6
Gannon, Bill	1898	(unknown)	April 1927	0-1
Gardner, Glenn	1945	1/25/16	7/7/64	3-1
Garman, Mike	1974–75	9/16/49		10-10
Gettel, Al	1955	9/17/17		1-0
Getzein, Charlie	1892	2/14/64	6/19/32	5-8
Geyer, Rube	1910–13	3/22/85	10/12/62	17-25
Gibson, Bob	1959–75	11/9/35		251-174
Gilpatrick, George	1898	2/28/75	12/15/41	0-2
Gilson, Hal	1968	2/9/42		0-2
Giusti, Dave	1969	11/27/39		3-7
Glenn, Bob	1920	6/16/94		0-0
Golden, Roy	1910–11	7/12/88	10/4/61	6-12
Goldsmith, Hal	1929	8/18/98		0-0
Goodwin, Marv	1917, 19–22	1/16/93	10/22/25	21-23
Gornicki, Hank	1941	1/14/11		1-0
Grabowski, Al	1929–30	9/4/01	10/29/66	9-6
Granger, Wayne	1968, 73	3/15/44		6-6
Grant, Jim	1969	8/13/35		7-5
Graves, Frank	1886	11/2/60	(deceased)	0-0
Greason, Bill	1954	9/3/24		0-1

Player	Years	Born	Died	Rec.
Grief, Bill	1976	4/25/50		1-5
Grim, Bob	1960	3/8/30		1-0
Grimes, Burleigh	1930-31, 33-34	8/18/93		32-17
Grimes, John	1897	4/17/69	1/17/64	0-2
Griner, Dan	1912-16	3/7/88	6/3/50	26-50
Grissom, Marv	1959	3/31/18		0-0
Grodzicki, Johnny	1941, 46-47	2/26/17		2-2
Grzenda, Joe	1972	6/8/37		1-0
Gumbert, Harry	1941-44	11/5/09		34-17
Guzman, Santiago	1969-72	7/25/49		1-2
Habenicht, Bob	1951	2/13/26	12/24/80	0-0
Haddix, Harvey	1952-56	9/18/25		53-40
Hageman, Kurt	1914	5/12/87	4/1/64	1-4
Hahn, Fred	1952	2/16/29		0-0
Haid, Hal	1928-30	12/21/97	8/13/52	14-13
Haines, Jesse	1920-37	7/22/93	8/5/78	210-158
Hall, Charley	1916	7/27/85	12/6/43	0-4
Hallahan, Bill	1925-26, 29-36	8/4/02	7/8/81	93-68
Hamilton, Dave	1978	12/13/47		0-0
Harmon, Bob	1909-13	10/15/87	11/27/61	66-81
Harper, Jack	1900-01	4/2/78	9/30/50	23-13
Harrell, Ray	1935, 37-38	2/16/12		6-11
Hart, Bill	1896-97	7/19/65	9/19/36	21-56
Hartenstein, Chuck	1970	5/26/42		0-0
Hawke, Bill	1892-93	4/28/70	12/12/02	5-6
Hawley Emerson	1892-94	12/5/72	9/19/38	30-58
Healey, John	1885-86	10/27/66	3/6/99	18-30
Hearn, Bunny	1910-11	5/21/91	10/10/59	1-3
Hearn, Jim	1947-50	4/11/21		21-17
Heise, Clarence	1934	8/7/07		0-0
Henshaw, Roy	1938	7/29/11		5-11
Heusser, Ed	1935-36	5/7/09	3/1/56	12-8
Higginbotham, Irv	1906, 08-09	4/26/82	6/12/59	6-12
Higgins, Dennis	1971-72	8/4/39		2-2
Higgins, Festus	1909-10	1893	10/4/24	3-4
Hilgendorf, Tom	1969-70	3/10/42		0-4
Hill, Carmen	1929-30	10/1/95		0-1
Hitt, Bruce	1917	3/14/98	11/10/73	0-0
Hobbie, Glen	1964	4/24/36		1-2
Hoerner, Joe	1966-69	11/12/36		19-10
Holland, Howard	1929	1/6/03	2/16/69	0-1
Hood, Don	1980	10/16/49		4-6
Hopper, Bill	1913-14	8/26/90	1/14/65	0-3
Horstman, Oscar	1917-19	6/2/91		9-7
Howard, Earl	1918	6/25/96	April, 1937	0-0
Howell, Roland	1912	1/3/92		0-0
Hrabosky, Al	1970-77	7/21/49		40-20
Hudson, Charles	1972	8/18/49		1-0
Hughes, Dick	1966-68	2/13/38		20-9
Hughes, Tom	1959	9/13/34		0-2
Hughey, Jim	1898	3/8/69	3/29/45	12-31
Humphreys, Bob	1963-64	8/18/35		2-1
Hunt, Ben	1913	1888		0-1

Player	Years	Born	Died	Rec.
Huntzinger, Walter	1926	2/6/99	8/11/81	0-4
Hutchinson, Ira	1940-41	8/31/10	8/21/73	5-7
Hutchison, Bill	1897	12/17/59	3/19/26	1-4
Hynes, Pat	1903	3/12/84	3/12/07	0-1
Jackson, Al	1966-67	12/25/35		22-19
Jackson, Larry	1955-62	6/2/31		101-86
Jackson, Mike	1971	3/27/46		0-0
Jacobs, Elmer	1919-20	8/10/92	2/10/58	6-14
Jacobs, Tony	1955	8/5/25	12/21/80	0-0
Jasper, Harry	1916	5/24/87	5/22/37	5-6
Jaster, Larry	1965-68	1/13/44		32-25
Jeffcoat, Hal	1959	9/6/24		0-1
Johnson, Adam	1918	2/4/88		1-1
Johnson, Jerry	1970	12/3/43		2-0
Johnson, Ken	1947-50	1/14/23		3-5
Johnson, Si	1936-38	10/5/06		17-18
Johnson, Syl	1926-33	12/31/00		52-50
Jones, Albert	1899-1901	8/23/74	2/8/58	22-30
Jones, Gordon	1954-56	4/2/30		5-10
Jones, Sam	1957-58, 63	12/14/25	11/5/71	26-22
Jurisich, Al	1944-45	8/25/21		10-12
Kaat, Jim	1980-82	11/7/38		19-16
Karger, Ed	1906-08	5/6/83	9/9/57	23-42
Kaufmann, Tony	1927-28, 30-31, 35	12/16/00		1-2
Keen, Vic	1926-27	3/16/99		12-10
Keener, Jeff	1982	1/14/59		1-1
Kellner, Alex	1959	8/26/24		2-1
Kellum, Win	1905	4/11/76	8/10/51	3-3
Kimball, Newt	1940	3/27/15		1-0
Kime, Hal	1920	3/15/99	5/16/39	0-0
Kinder, Ellis	1956	7/26/14	10/16/68	2-0
Kirby, John	1885-86	1/13/65	10/6/31	16-33
Kircher, Mike	1920-21	9/30/97	6/26/72	2-2
Kissinger, Bill	1895-97	8/15/71	4/20/29	6-25
Kleinke, Norbert	1935	5/19/12	3/16/50	1-1
Kline, Ron	1960	3/9/32		4-9
Knight, Elmer	1922	1/12/95		0-0
Knowles, Darold	1979-80	12/9/41		2-6
Koeningsmark, Willis	1919	2/27/96	7/1/72	0-0
Konstanty, Jim	1956	3/2/17	6/11/76	1-1
Krausse, Lew	1973	4/25/43		0-0
Krieger, Kurt	1949	9/16/26	8/16/70	0-0
Krist, Howie	1937-38, 41-43, 46	2/28/16		37-11
Kurosaki, Ryan	1975	7/3/52		0-0
Kuzava, Bob	1957	5/28/23		0-0
LaGrow, Lerrin	1976	7/8/48		0-1
Lahti, Jeff	1982	10/8/56		5-4
Lamabe, Jack	1967	10/3/36		3-4
Lamline, Fred	1915	8/14/91	9/20/70	0-0
Lanier, Max	1938-46, 49-51	8/18/15		101-80
LaPalme, Paul	1955-56	12/14/23		4-3
Lawrence, Brooks	1954-55	1/30/25		18-14
LaPoint, David	1981-82	7/29/59		10-3
Lersch, Barry	1974	9/7/44		0-0
Lewandowski, Dan	1951	1/6/28		0-1

Player	Years	Born	Died	Rec.
Liddle, Don	1956	5/25/25		1-2
Lillard, Gene	1940	11/12/13		0-1
Lindsey, Jim	1929–34	1/24/98	10/25/63	17-14
Lintz, Royce	1954	1/1/21		2-3
Linzy, Frank	1970–71	9/15/40		7-8
Littell, Mark	1978–82	1/17/53		18-18
Little, Jeff	1980–81	12/25/54		2-4
Littlefield, Dick	1956	3/18/26		0-2
Littlefield, John	1980	1/5/54		5-5
Littlejohn, Carlisle	1927–28	10/6/01		5-2
Locke, Bobby	1962	3/3/34		0-0
Lohrman, Bill	1942	5/22/13		1-1
Lopatka, Art	1945	5/28/20		1-0
Lopez, Aurelio	1978	9/21/48		4-2
Lotz, Joe	1916	1/2/91	1/1/71	0-3
Lovenguth, Lynn	1957	11/29/22		0-1
Lovett, John	1903	5/6/78	12/6/37	0-1
Lowdermilk, Grover	1909	1/15/85	3/31/68	0-3
Lowdermilk, Lou	1911–12	2/23/87	12/27/75	4-5
Lucid, Con	1897	2/24/69		1-5
Luna, Guillermo	1954	6/25/30		0-1
Lush, Johnny	1907–10	10/8/85	11/18/46	43-61
Lyons, George	1920	1/25/91	8/12/81	2-1
Lyons, Hersh	1941	7/23/15		0-0
Mabe, Bob	1958	10/8/29		3-9
MacKenzie, Ken	1963	3/10/34		0-0
Mackinson, Johnny	1955	10/29/23		0-1
Macon, Max	1938	10/14/15		4-11
Magee, Bill	1901	1/11/68	(deceased)	0-0
Maglie, Sal	1958	4/26/17		2-6
Mahaffey, Art	1966	6/4/34		1-4
Mails, Duster	1925–26	10/1/95	7/5/74	7-8
Marbet, Walt	1913	9/13/90	9/24/56	0-1
Martin, Freddie	1946, 49–50	6/27/15	6/11/79	12-3
Martin, John	1980–82	4/11/56		14-13
Martin, Morrie	1957–58	9/3/22		3-1
Martinez, Silvio	1978–81	8/31/55		31-31
Mason, Ernie	1894	(unknown)	7/30/04	0-3
Maupin, Harry	1898	7/11/72	8/23/52	0-2
May, Jakie	1917–21	11/25/95	6/3/70	10-25
McAdams, Jack	1911	12/17/86	5/21/37	0-0
McBride, Pete	1899	7/9/75	7/3/44	2-4
McCool, Bill	1970	7/14/44		0-3
McDaniel, Lindy	1955–62	12/13/35		66-54
McDaniel, Von	1957–58	4/18/39		7-5
McDermott, Mickey	1961	8/29/28		1-0
McDermott, Mike	1897	9/7/62	6/30/43	1-2
McDougal, John	1895–96	9/9/71	4/28/36	3-11
McDougal, Sandy	1905	2/18/78	10/4/10	1-4
McEnaney, Will	1979	2/14/52		0-3
McFarland, Charles	1902–06	(unknown)	12/15/24	33-55
McGee, Bill	1935–41	11/16/09		38-29

Player	Years	Born	Died	Rec.
McGinley, Jim	1904–05	10/2/78	9/20/61	2-2
McGlothen, Lynn	1974–76	3/27/50		44-40
McGlynn, Ulysses	1906–08	5/26/72	8/26/41	17-33
McGraw, Bob	1927	4/10/95		4-5
Meadows, Lee	1915–19	7/12/94	1/29/63	52-67
Melter, Steve	1909	(unknown)		2-1
Merritt, Lloyd	1957	4/8/33		1-2
Metzger, Clarence	1977–78	5/23/52		4-2
Mikkelsen, Pete	1968	10/25/39		0-0
Miller, Bob	1957, 59-61	2/18/39		9-9
Miller, Stu	1952-54, 56	12/26/27		15-15
Milton, Larry	1903	(unknown)		0-0
Mitchell, Clarence	1928–30	2/22/91	11/6/63	17-20
Mizell, Wilmer	1952-53, 56-60	8/13/30		69-70
Moford, Herb	1955	8/6/28		1-1
Mooney, Jim	1933–34	9/4/06	4/27/79	4-9
Moore, Donnie	1980	2/13/54		1-1
Moore, Tommy	1975	7/7/48		0-0
Moore, Whitey	1942	6/10/12		0-1
More, Forrest	1909	9/30/83	8/17/68	1-5
Muffett, Billy	1957–58	9/21/30		7-8
Munger, George	1943-44, 46-52	10/4/18		74-49
Munns, Les	1936	12/1/08		0-3
Mura, Steve	1982	2/12/55		12-11
Murchison, Tim	1917	10/8/96	10/20/62	0-1
Murphy, Ed	1901–03	1/22/77	1/29/35	23-24
Murphy, Tom	1973	12/30/45		3-7
Nagy, Mike	1973	3/25/48		0-2
Nahem, Sam	1941	10/19/15		5-2
Naymick, Mike	1944	9/6/17		0-0
Nelson, Mel	1960, 68-69	5/30/36		2-3
Nichols, Charles	1904–05	9/14/69	4/11/53	22-18
Nichols, Tricky	1877	(unknown)	(deceased)	18-23
Niehaus, Dick	1913–15	10/24/92	3/12/57	3-3
Norman, Fred	1970–71	8/20/42		0-0
North, Lou	1917, 20-24	6/15/91	5/16/74	20-13
Nunn, Howie	1959	10/18/35		2-2
Nye, Rich	1970	8/4/44		0-0
O'Brien, Dan	1978–79	4/22/54		0-2
Olivo, Diomedes	1963	1/22/19	2/15/77	5-6
Olmstead, Al	1980	3/18/57		1-1
O'Neill, Mike	1901–04	9/7/77	8/12/59	33-42
Osteen, Claude	1974	8/9/39		0-2
Otten, Jim	1980–81	7/1/51		1-5
Packard, Gene	1917–18	7/13/87	5/19/59	21-18
Paine, Phil	1958	6/8/30	2/19/78	5-1
Palmer, Lowell	1972	8/18/47		0-3
Papai, Al	1948	5/7/19		1-1
Parker, Harry	1969-71, 75	9/14/47		1-2
Parker, Roy	1919	1897		0-0
Parmalee, Roy	1936	4/25/07	8/31/81	11-11
Parrott, Tom	1896	4/10/68	1/1/32	1-1
Partenheimer, Stan	1945	10/21/22		0-0
Patterson, Daryl	1971	11/21/43		0-1
Patton, Harry	1910	(unknown)		0-0

Player	Years	Born	Died	Rec.
Paulsen, Gil	1925	11/14/02		0-0
Pearce, George	1917	1/10/88	10/11/35	1-1
Pears, Frank	1893	1866	(deceased)	0-0
Pearson, Alex	1902	3/9/77	10/30/66	2-6
Pena, Orlando	1973–74	11/17/33		9-6
Perdue, Hub	1914–15	6/7/82	10/31/68	14-20
Perritt, William	1912–14	8/30/92	10/15/47	23-28
Pertica, Bill	1921–23	8/17/98	12/28/67	22-18
Pfeffer, Jeff	1921–24	3/4/88	8/15/72	40-29
Phyle, Bill	1906	6/25/75	8/7/53	0-0
Piche, Ron	1966	5/22/35		1-3
Pickett, Charlie	1910	(unknown)		0-0
Pippen, Henry	1936	4/2/10		0-2
Plodinec, Tim	1972	1/27/47		0-0
Poholsky, Tom	1950–51, 54–56	8/26/29		30-45
Pollett, Howie	1941–43, 46–51	6/26/21	8/8/74	97-65
Popp, Bill	1902	6/7/77	9/7/09	2-6
Potter, Nelson	1936	8/23/11		0-0
Powell, Jack	1899–1901	7/9/74	10/17/44	59-56
Presko, Joe	1951–54	10/7/28		24-36
Proly, Mike	1976	12/15/50		1-0
Purkey, Bob	1965	7/14/29		10-9
Puttman, Ambrose	1906	9/9/80	6/21/36	1-2
Radebaugh, Roy	1911	2/22/84	1/17/45	0-0
Raffensberger, Ken	1939	8/8/17		0-0
Raleigh, John	1909–10	4/21/90	8/24/55	1-9
Raschi, Vic	1954–55	3/28/19		8-10
Rasmussen, Eric	1975–78, 82	3/22/52		25-41
Raymond, Bugs	1907–08	2/24/82	9/7/12	16-29
Redding, Phil	1912–13	1/25/90	3/31/28	2-1
Reed, Ron	1975	11/2/42		9-8
Reeder, Bill	1949	2/20/22		1-1
Reinhart, Art	1919, 25–28	5/29/99	11/11/46	30-18
Reis, Jack	1911	6/14/90	7/20/39	0-0
Reuss, Jerry	1969–71	6/19/49		22-22
Reynolds, Bob	1971	1/21/47		0-0
Reynolds, Ken	1975	1/4/47		0-1
Rhem, Flint	1924–28, 30–32, 34	1/24/01	7/30/69	81-63
Rhoads, Bob	1903	10/4/79	2/12/67	5-8
Rhodes, Charlie	1906, 08–09	(unknown)	(deceased)	6-11
Ribant, Dennis	1969	9/20/41		0-0
Richardson, Gordon	1964	7/19/39		4-2
Richert, Pete	1974	10/29/39		0-0
Ricketts, Dick	1959	12/4/33		1-6
Rieger, Elmer	1910	2/25/89	10/21/59	0-2
Rincon, Andy	1980–82	3/5/59		8-5
Ring, Jimmy	1927	2/15/95	7/6/65	0-4
Riviere, Art	1921	8/2/99	9/27/65	1-0
Robinson, Hank	1914–15	8/16/89	7/2/65	13-16
Roe, Elwin	1938	2/26/15		0-0
Romonosky, John	1953	7/7/29		0-0
Russell, Jack	1940	10/24/05		3-4
Ryba, Mike	1935–38	6/9/03	12/13/71	16-9
Sadecki, Ray	1960–66, 75	12/26/40		68-64

Player	Years	Born	Died	Rec.
Sallee, Harry	1908–16	2/3/85	3/22/50	104-107
Sanders, Warren	1903–04	8/2/77	8/3/62	2-7
Santorini, Al	1971–73	5/19/48		8-13
Scheib, Carl	1954	1/1/27		0-1
Schmidt, Freddy	1944, 46–47	2/9/16		8-3
Schmidt, Willard	1952–53, 55–57	5/29/28		25-22
Schultz, Barney	1955, 63–65	8/15/26		6-7
Schultz, Buddy	1977–79	9/19/50		12-8
Schulz, Walter	1920	4/16/00	2/27/28	0-0
Schupp, Ferdie	1919–21	1/16/91	12/16/71	22-17
Scott, George	1920	11/17/96		0-0
Seaman, Kim	1979–80	5/6/57		3-2
Segui, Diego	1972–73	8/17/37		10-7
Sell, Epp	1922–23	4/26/97	2/19/61	4-3
Shantz, Bobby	1962–64	9/26/25		12-10
Shaw, Don	1971–72	6/29/33		7-3
Sherdel, Bill	1918–30, 32	8/15/96	11/14/68	153-131
Shields, Charlie	1907	12/10/79	8/27/53	0-2
Shields, Vince	1924	11/18/00	10/17/52	1-1
Shirley, Bob	1981	6/25/54		6-4
Shoun, Clyde	1938–42	3/20/12	3/20/68	25-23
Siebert, Sonny	1974	1/14/37		8-8
Simmons, Curt	1960–66	5/19/29		69-58
Smith, Bill	1958–59	6/8/34		0-1
Smith, Bob	1957	2/1/31		0-0
Smith, Frank	1955	4/4/28		3-1
Smith, Tom	1898	12/5/71	3/2/29	0-1
Solomon, Eddie	1976	2/9/52		1-1
Sorensen, Lary	1981	10/4/55		7-7
Sosa, Elias	1975	6/10/50		0-3
Sothoron, Allen	1924–26	4/29/93	6/17/39	23-29
Spinks, Scipio	1972–73	7/12/47		6-10
Sprague, Ed	1973	9/16/45		0-0
Spring, Jack	1964	3/11/33		0-0
Staley, Gerry	1947–54	8/21/20		89-76
Staley, Harry	1895	11/3/66	1/12/10	6-13
Stallard, Tracy	1965–66	8/31/37		12-13
Standridge, Pete	1911	4/25/91	8/2/63	0-0
Starr, Ray	1932	4/23/06	2/9/63	1-1
Steele, Bill	1910–14	10/5/85	10/19/49	36-42
Steele, Bob	1916–17	3/29/94	1/27/62	6-18
Stobbs, Chuck	1958	7/2/29		1-3
Stone, Dean	1959	9/1/30		0-1
Stout, Allyn	1931–33	10/31/04	12/22/74	10-5
Stuart, Johnny	1922–25	4/27/01	5/13/70	20-18
Stuper, John	1982	5/9/57		9-7
Sudhoff, Willie	1897–1901	9/17/74	5/25/17	48-73
Sullivan, Harry	1909	4/12/88	9/22/19	0-0
Sunkel, Tom	1937	8/9/12		4-4
Surkont, Max	1956	6/16/22		0-0
Sutter, Bruce	1981–82	1/8/53		3-5
Sutthoff, Jack	1899	6/29/73	8/3/42	12-13
Sutton, Johnny	1977	11/13/52		2-1
Sweeney, Charlie	1885–86	4/13/63	4/4/02	17-27

Player	Years	Born	Died	Rec.
Sykes, Bob	1979–81	12/11/54		12-13
Taylor, Chuck	1969–71	4/18/42		16-13
Taylor, Ed	1903	(unknown)		0-0
Taylor, Jack	1898	5/27/73	2/7/00	15-29
Taylor, Jack	1904–06	9/13/73	3/4/38	43-49
Taylor, Ron	1963–65	12/13/37		19-12
Teachout, Arthur	1932	2/27/04		0-0
Terlecky, Greg	1975	3/20/52		0-1
Terwilliger, Dick	1932	6/27/06		0-0
Thielman, Jake	1905–06	3/20/79	1/28/28	15-17
Thomas, Roy	1978–80	6/22/53		1-1
Thomas, Tom	1899–1900	12/27/73	9/22/42	3-3
Thompson, Gus	1906	6/22/77	3/28/58	2-10
Thompson, Mike	1973–74	9/6/49		0-3
Tiefenauer, Bobby	1952, 55	10/10/29		1-4
Tinning, Bud	1935	3/12/06	1/17/61	0-0
Toney, Fred	1923	12/11/87	3/11/53	11-12
Torrez, Mike	1967–71	8/28/46		21-18
Toth, Paul	1962	6/30/35		1-0
Trekell, Harry	1913	11/18/92	11/4/65	0-1
Trotter, Bill	1944	8/10/08		0-1
Tuero, Oscar	1918–20	12/17/92		6-9
Underwood, Tom	1977	12/22/53		6-9
Urban, Jack	1959	12/5/28		0-0
Urrea, John	1977–80	2/9/55		15-16
Vance, Dazzy	1933–34	3/4/91	2/16/61	7-3
Vines, Bob	1924	2/25/97		0-0
Vuckovich, Pete	1978–80	10/27/52		39-31
Wade, Ben	1954	11/26/22		0-0
Walker, Bill	1933–36	10/7/03	6/14/66	39-28
Walker, Roy	1921–22	4/13/93	2/10/62	12-14
Walker, Tom	1976	11/7/48		1-2
Wallace, Mike	1975–76	2/3/51		3-2
Ward, Dick	1935	5/21/09	5/31/66	0-0
Warmoth, Cy	1916	2/2/93	6/20/57	0-0
Warneke, Lon	1937–42	3/28/09	6/23/76	83-49
Washburn, Ray	1961–69	5/31/38		68-60
Waslewski, Gary	1969	7/21/41		0-2
Waterbury, Steve	1976	4/6/52		0-0
Watson, Milt	1916–17	1893		14-19
Wehmeier, Herm	1956–58	2/18/27	5/21/73	22-17
Weiland, Bob	1937–40	12/14/05		41-37
Werle, Bill	1952	12/21/20		1-2
Weyhing, Gus	1900	9/29/66	9/3/55	3-2
White, Abe	1937	5/16/06		0-1
White, Ernie	1940–43	9/5/16	5/22/74	30-18
White, Hal	1953–54	3/18/19		6-5
Wicker, Bob	1901–03	5/25/78	1/22/55	5-13
Wight, Bill	1958	4/12/22		3-0
Wigington, Fred	1923	12/16/97		0-0
Wilhelm, Hoyt	1957	7/26/23		1-4
Wilks, Ted	1944–51	11/13/15		51-20
Williams, Rees	1914	1/31/92	6/29/79	6-8

160

Player	Years	Born	Died	Rec.
Williams, Stan	1971	9/14/36		3-0
Willis, Joe	1911–13	4/9/90	12/3/66	4-10
Willis, Ron	1966–69	7/12/43	11/21/77	8-10
Willis, Vic	1910	4/12/76	8/3/47	9-12
Wilson, Zeke	1899	12/24/69	4/26/28	1-1
Winford, Jim	1932, 34–37	10/9/09	12/16/70	14-17
Wise, Rick	1972–73	9/13/45		32-28
Wood, John	1896	(unknown)	(deceased)	0-0
Woodburn, Gene	1911–12	8/20/86	1/18/61	2-10
Woodeshick, Hal	1965–67	8/24/32		7-4
Woodward, Frank	1919	5/17/94	6/11/61	4-5
Wooldridge, Floyd	1955	8/25/28		2-4
Wright, Mel	1954–55	5/11/28		2-2
Yerkes, Stan	1901–03	(unknown)		14-22
Yochim, Ray	1948–49	7/29/22		0-0
Young, Cy	1899–1900	3/29/67	11/4/55	46-33
Young, J. D.	1892	(unknown)	(deceased)	0-0
Yuhas, Eddie	1952–53	8/5/24		12-2
Zachary, Chris	1971	2/19/44		3-10
Zackert, George	1911–12	12/24/84	2/18/77	0-2
Zmich, Ed	1910–11	10/1/84	8/20/50	1-5

THE ALL-TIME ST. LOUIS NATIONAL LEAGUE ROSTER

Non-Pitchers

Name	Pos.	Years	Born	Died	Games
Abbott, Ody	OF	1910	9/5/86	4/13/33	22
Adams, Earl	IF	1930–33	8/26/94		319
Adams, Elvin	OF	1939, 43 45-46	6/24/15		91
Adkinson, Henry	PH	1895	9/1/74	5/1/23	1
Agee, Tommie	OF	1973	8/9/42		26
Ainsmith, Eddie	C	1921–23	2/4/90	9/6/81	228
Allen, Ethan	OF	1933	1/1/04		91
Allen, Richie	IF-OF	1970	3/8/42		122
Allen, Ron	1B	1972	12/23/43		7
Alou, Matty	OF	1971–73	12/22/38		257
Alston, Tom	1B	1954–57	1/31/31		91
Alston, Walter	1B	1936	12/1/11		1
Altman, George	OF	1963	3/20/33		135
Alvarado, Luis	2B	1974, 76	1/15/49		33
Alyea, Brandt	OF	1972	12/8/40		13
Amaro, Ruben	SS-2B	1958	1/6/36		40
Anderson, Dwain	IF	1972–73	11/23/47		75
Anderson, Ferrell	C	1953	1/9/18		12
Anderson, George	OF	1918	9/26/89	5/28/62	35
Anderson, Mike	OF-1B	1976–78	6/22/51		180
Ankenman, Pat	SS	1936	12/23/12		1
Antonelli, John	IF	1944–45	7/15/15		10
Arndt, Harry	IF-OF	1905–07	2/2/79	3/25/21	193
Ayala, Benny	OF	1977	2/7/51		1

Name	Pos.	Years	Born	Died	Games
Baird, Doug	IF-OF	1917–19	9/27/91	6/13/67	202
Baker, Bill	C	1948–49	2/22/11		65
Baker, George	C	1885	1859	(deceased)	38
Ball, Art	2B	1894	(unknown)	12/26/15	1
Bannon, Jimmy	OF-IF-P	1893	5/5/71	3/24/48	26
Barbeau, Jap	3B-2B	1909–10	6/10/82	9/10/69	54
Barclay, George	OF	1902–04	5/16/75	4/2/09	348
Barry, John	OF	1906–08	9/28/76	11/27/36	216
Bartosch, Dave	OF	1945	3/24/17		24
Battin, Joe	IF-OF	1876–77	11/11/51	12/11/37	121
Baxter, John	1B	1907	(unknown)		6
Beall, Johnny	OF	1918	3/12/82	6/13/26	19
Beauchamp, Jim	1B-OF	1963, 70–71	8/21/36		125
Beck, Zinn	IF	1913–16	9/30/85		279
Beckley, Jake	1B	1904–07	8/4/67	6/25/18	395
Beecher, Ed	OF	1897	8/27/73	(deceased)	3
Bell, Les	SS-3B	1923–27	12/14/01		455
Benes, Joe	IF	1931	1/1/01		10
Bennett, Justin	2B-3B	1906–07	2/20/74	9/12/35	240
Benson, Vern	3B	1951–53	9/19/24		46
Bergamo, Augie	OF-1B	1944–45	2/14/18		174
Berte, Harry	2B-SS	1903	5/10/72		4
Bescher, Bob	OF	1915–17	2/25/84	11/29/42	323
Betcher, Frank	IF-OF	1910	2/15/88		35
Betzel, Bruno	IF-OF	1914–18	12/6/94	2/7/65	448
Bierbauer, Lou	IF	1897–98	9/28/65	2/1/26	16
Bilko, Steve	1B	1949–54	11/13/28	3/7/78	219
Billings, Dick	PH	1974–75	12/4/42		4
Bird, Frank	C	1892	3/10/69	5/20/58	17
Blades, Ray	OF-IF	1922–28, 30–32	8/6/96	5/18/79	767
Blake, Harry	OF-IF-C	1899	6/16/74	10/14/19	97
Blank, Coonie	C	1909	(unknown)		11
Blasingame, Don	IF	1955–59	3/16/32		502
Blatnik, Johnny	OF	1950	3/10/21		7
Blattner, Robert	SS-2B	1942	2/8/20		19
Bliss, John	C-SS	1908–12	1/9/82	10/23/68	241
Blong, Joe	OF-2B	1876–77	9/17/53	9/22/92	120
Bloomfield, Clyde	3B	1963	1/5/37		1
Bohne, Sammy	SS	1916	10/22/96	5/23/77	14
Bollweg, Don	1B	1950–51	2/12/21		10
Bonds, Bobby	OF	1980	3/15/46		86
Bonner, Frank	IF	1895	8/20/69	12/31/05	15
Bordagaray, Stanley	3B-OF	1937–38	1/3/12		177
Bosetti, Rick	OF	1977	8/5/53		41
Bottomley, James	1B-2B	1922–32	4/23/00	11/11/59	1392
Boyer, Ken	IF-OF	1955–65	5/20/31	9/7/82	1667
Bradford, Buddy	OF	1975	7/25/44		50
Brain, Dave	OF	1903–05	1/24/79	5/25/59	290
Brandt, Jackie	OF	1956	4/28/34		27
Brashear, Robert	IF-OF	1902	8/12/78	12/23/34	110

Name	Pos.	Years	Born	Died	Games
Bratcher, Joe	OF	1924	7/22/98		4
Braun, Steve	OF	1981–82	5/8/48		102
Bremer, Herb	C	1937–39	10/25/13	11/28/79	70
Bresnahan, Roger	C-IF OF-P	1909–12	6/11/79	12/4/44	289
Bressler, Raymond	OF	1932	10/23/94	11/7/66	10
Bressoud, Ed	SS-3B	1967	5/2/32		52
Bridges, Rocky	IF	1960	8/7/27		3
Briggs, Grant	C-OF	1892	(unknown)	(deceased)	23
Brinkman, Ed	IF	1975	12/8/41		28
Briody, Charles	C	1885	8/3/58	(deceased)	62
Brock, John	C-OF	1917–18	10/19/96	10/27/51	34
Brock, Lou	OF	1964–79	6/18/39		2289
Brodie, Steve	OF-IF	1892–93	11/11/68	10/30/35	261
Bronkie, Herman	IF	1918	3/30/85	5/27/68	18
Brottem, Tony	C-OF-1B	1916	4/30/92	8/5/29	28
Brown, Jim	OF	1915	3/31/97		1
Brown, Jimmy	IF	1937–43	4/25/10		811
Brown, Tom	OF	1895	9/21/60	10/27/27	83
Brown, Willard	1B	1894	1866	12/20/97	3
Browne, Byron	OF	1969	12/27/42		22
Browning, Pete	OF	1894	7/17/58	9/10/05	2
Brummer, Glenn	C	1981–82	11/23/54		56
Bucha, Johnny	C	1948	1/22/25		24
Buchek, Jerry	IF	1961, 63–66	5/9/42		224
Bucher, Jim	2B-3B	1938	3/11/11		17
Buckley, Dick	C	1892–94	9/21/58	12/12/29	159
Buelow, Frederick	C-OF	1899–1900	2/13/76	12/27/33	13
Burbrink, Nelson	C	1955	12/28/21		58
Burch, Al	OF	1906–07	10/7/83	10/5/26	139
Burda, Bob	OF	1962, 71	7/16/38		72
Burgess, Tom	OF	1954	9/1/27		17
Burke, Jimmy	IF-OF	1903–05	10/12/74	3/26/42	355
Burke, John	2B	1899	1/27/77	8/4/50	2
Burke, Leo	OF-IF	1963	5/6/34		30
Burkett, Jesse	OF-2B	1899–1901	12/4/68	5/27/53	425
Burnett, John	OF	1907	(unknown)		59
Burns, Ed	C	1912	10/31/87	6/1/42	1
Burton, Ellis	OF	1958	8/12/36		8
Busse, Ray	IF	1973	9/25/48		24
Butler, Art	IF-OF	1914–16	12/19/87		302
Butler, John	C	1904	7/26/79		12
Butler, Johnny	3B-SS	1929	3/20/94	4/29/67	17
Byers, Bill	C-1B	1904	(unknown)		19
Byrne, Bobby	3B-SS	1907–09	12/31/84	12/31/64	280
Cabrera, Al	SS	1913	1883		1
Cahill, John	OF	1886	(unknown)	11/1/01	125
Calhoun, John	1B-OF	1902	12/14/79	2/27/47	20
Callahan, Wes	1B-OF	1913	7/3/88	9/13/53	7
Camp, Llewellyn	3B-OF	1892	2/22/68	10/1/48	42
Campbell, Dave	IF	1973	1/14/42		13
Campbell, Jim		1970	1/10/43		13

Non-Pitchers (continued)

Name	Pos.	Years	Born	Died	Games
Cannizzaro, Chris	C	1960–61	5/3/38		13
Carbo, Bernie	OF	1972–73, 79–80	8/5/47		210
Cardenal, Jose	OF	1970–71	10/7/43		237
Carmel, Leon "Duke"	OF-1B	1959–60, 63	4/23/37		71
Carpenter, Warren	3B	1892	8/16/55	4/18/37	1
Carroll, Cliff	OF	1892	10/18/59	6/12/23	101
Carsey, Wilfred	2B-OF-P	1897–98	10/22/70	(deceased)	51
Caruthers, Bob	OF-IF-P	1892	1/5/64	8/5/11	143
Caskin, Ed,	IF	1885	12/30/51	(deceased)	71
Castiglione, Pete	3B	1953–54	2/13/21		72
Cater, Danny	1B	1975	2/25/40		22
Cather, Ted	OF	1912–14	5/20/89	4/9/45	111
Cepeda, Orlando	1B	1966–68	9/17/37		431
Chant, Charlie	OF	1976	8/7/51		15
Charles, Raymond	IF	1908–09	1883	8/4/59	220
Childs, Clarence	2B	1899	8/14/68	11/8/12	125
Childs, Pete	IF	1901	11/5/71	2/15/22	29
Ciaffone, Larry	OF	1951	8/17/24		5
Cimoli, Gino	OF	1959	12/18/29		143
Clapp, John	OF-C-1B	1876–77	7/17/51	12/17/04	121
Clarey, Doug	2B	1976	4/20/54		9
Clark, Danny	OF	1927	1/18/95	5/23/37	58
Clark, Jim	OF	1911–12	12/26/87		16
Clarke, Josh	OF-IF	1905	3/8/79	7 /2/62	50
Clemens, Doug	OF	1960–64	6/3/39		93
Clements, Jack	C	1898	6/24/64	5/23/41	99
Clemons, Verne	C	1919–24	9/8/91	5/5/59	470
Clendenon, Donn	1B	1972	7/15/35		61
Cole, Dick	IF	1951	5/6/26		15
Collins, Rip	1B-OF	1931–36	3/30/04	4/16/70	777
Collins, William	OF	1892	1867	6/8/93	1
Coluccio, Bob	OF	1978	10/2/51		5
Connor, Joe	3B	1895	(unknown)	(deceased)	2
Connor, Roger	1B	1894–97	7/1/57	1/4/31	351
Conwell, Ed	3B	1911	1/29/80		1
Cooley, Duff	OF-IF-C	1893–96	3/29/73	8/9/37	250
Cooney, Jimmy	IF-OF	1924–25	8/24/94		264
Cooper, Walker	C	1940–45, 56 –57	1/8/15		525
Corhan, Roy	SS	1916	10/21/87	11/24/58	92
Corrales, Pat	C	1966	3/20/41		28
Coulter, Chip	2B	1969	6/5/45		6
Coveney, John	C	1903	1880		4
Crabtree, Estel	OF-3B	1933, 40–41	8/19/03	1/4/67	110
Crawford, Forrest	SS-3B	1906–07	5/10/81	3/27/08	52
Crawford, Glenn	OF-IF	1945	12/2/13	1/2/72	4
Crawford, Pat	IF	1933–34	1/28/02		152
Crawford, Willie	OF	1976	9/7/46		120
Creger, Bernie	SS	1947	3/21/27		15

Name	Pos.	Years	Born	Died	Games
Crespi, Frank	IF	1938–42	2/16/18		264
Criger, Lou	C-3B	1899–1900	2/6/72	5/14/34	157
Croft, Art	IF-OF	1877	1/23/55	3/16/84	54
Crooks, John	IF-OF-C	1892–93, 98	11/9/66	1/29/18	328
Crosby, Ed	IF	1970, 72–73	5/26/49		261
Cross, Jeff	IF	1942, 46–48	8/28/18		103
Cross, Lave	3B-SS	1898–1900	5/11/67	9/4/27	254
Cross, Monte	SS	1896–97	8/31/69	6/21/34	256
Crowe, George	1B	1959–61	3/22/23		157
Cruise, Walton	OF	1914, 16–19	5/6/90		230
Crumling, Gene	C	1945	4/5/22		6
Cruz, Cirilio	OF	1973	2/15/51		3
Cruz, Hector	OF-3B	1975–77	4/2/53		315
Cruz, Jose	OF-1B	1970–74	8/8/47		545
Cunningham, Joe	1B-OF	1954, 56–61	8/27/31		738
Cunningham, Ray	3B-2B	1931–32	1/17/08		14
Cuthbert, Ned	OF	1876	6/20/45	2/6/05	62
Damaska, Jack	OF-2B	1963	8/21/37		5
Daringer, Rolla	SS	1914–15	11/15/89	5/23/74	12
Dark, Alvin	IF	1956–58	1/7/22		258
Davalillo, Vic	OF	1969–70	7/31/39		174
DaVanon, Jerry	IF-OF	1969–70, 74, 77	8/21/45		36
Davis, George	OF	1934	2/12/02		16
Davis, Ron	OF	1968	10/21/41		33
Davis, Virgil	C-IF	1928, 34–36	12/20/04		323
Davis, Willie	OF	1975	4/15/40		98
Day, Clarence "Boots"	OF	1969	8/31/47		11
Decker, George	1B-OF	1898	6/1/69	6/9/09	76
DeFate, Tony	IF	1917	2/22/98	9/6/63	14
DeGroff, Rube	OF	1905–06	9/2/79	12/17/55	16
Dehlman, Harmon	1B-OF	1876–77	1850	3/13/85	96
Delahanty, Joe	OF-2B	1907–09	10/18/75	1/9/36	269
DeLancey, Bill	C	1932, 34–35, 40	11/28/01	11/28/46	219
Del Greco, Bobby	OF	1956	4/7/33		102
Delker, Eddie	IF	1929, 31–32	4/17/07		43
Demaree, Frank	OF	1943	6/10/10	8/30/58	39
DeMiller, Harry	3B	1892	11/12/67	10/19/28	1
DeMontreville, Lee	IF-OF	1903	9/23/79	3/22/62	26
Denny, Jerry	3B	1886	3/15/59	8/16/27	119
Derry, Russ	PH	1949	10/7/16		2
DeSa, Joe	IF	1980	7/27/59		11
Diering, Chuck	OF	1947–51	2/5/23		396
Dillard, Pat	OF-IF	1900	6/12/74	7/22/07	57

Name	Pos.	Years	Born	Died	Games
Dillhoefer, William	C	1919–21	10/13/94	2/22/22	197
Dimmel, Mike	OF	1979	10/6/54		6
Distel, George	IF-OF	1918	4/15/96	2/12/67	8
Dolan, Cozy	OF	1914–15	12/3/72	3/29/07	237
Donahue, Charles	IF	1904	6/29/77	8/28/47	4
Donely, Jim	3B	1898	7/19/65	3/5/15	1
Donlin, Mike	OF-IF-P	1899–1900	5/30/78	9/24/33	144
Donovan, Patrick	OF	1900–03	3/16/65	12/25/53	487
Dorgan, Mike	OF-C-3B	1877	1850	3/13/85	96
Douglas, William	OF-C-IF	1896–97	5/10/72	12/13/53	206
Douthit, Taylor	OF	1923–31	4/22/01		855
Dowd, Tommy	OF-IF	1893–98	4/20/69	7/2/33	684
Dressen, Lee	1B	1914	7/23/89	6/30/31	46
Duncan, Taylor	3B	1977	5/12/53		8
Dunlap, Fred	IF	1885–86	5/21/59	12/1/02	177
Dunlap, Grant	OF	1953	12/20/23		16
Dunleavy, John	OF-P-2B	1903–05	7/19/88		231
Durham, Joe	OF	1959	7/31/31		6
Durham, Leon	OF	1979–80	7/31/57		96
Durocher, Leo	SS	1933–37	7/27/05		683
Dusak, Erv	OF-IF-P	1941–42, 46–51	7/29/20		372
Dwyer, Jim	OF	1973–75, 77–78	1/3/50		170
Dyer, Eddie	OF-P	1922–27	10/11/00	4/20/64	129
Echols, Johnny	PH	1939	1/9/17	11/13/72	2
Edwards, Johnny	C	1968	6/10/38		54
Elliott, Harry	OF	1953	12/30/25		45
Ellis, George	OF	1909–12	11/17/85	3/13/38	510
Ely, Frederick	SS	1893–95	6/7/63	1/10/52	288
Endicott, Bill	OF	1946	9/4/18		20
Ennis, Del	OF	1957–58	6/8/25		242
Enwright, Charlie	SS	1909	10/6/87	1/19/17	3
Epps, Hal	OF	1938	3/26/14		28
Essegian, Chuck	OF	1959	8/9/31		17
Evans, Steve	OF-1B	1909–13	2/17/85	12/28/43	680
Ewing, Reuben	SS	1921	11/30/99	10/5/70	3
Fagin, Fred	C	1895	(unknown)	(deceased)	1
Fairly, Ron	1B-OF	1975–76	7/12/38		180
Fallon, George	IF	1943–45	7/18/16		129
Farrell, Edward	IF	1930	12/26/01	12/20/66	23
Farrell, John	IF-OF	1902–05	12/4/76	5/14/21	406
Fenwick, Bobby	2B	1973	12/10/46		5
Ferguson, Joe	C-OF	1976	9/19/46		71
Fiore, Mike	1B	1972	12/11/44		17
Fishburn, Sam	2B-1B	1919	5/18/93	4/11/65	9
Fisher, Bob	2B	1918–19	11/3/87	8/4/63	66
Fisher, George	OF	1930	1/16/99		92
Flack, Max	OF	1922–25	2/5/90	7/31/75	340
Flood, Curt	OF-IF	1958–69	1/18/38		1738
Flood, Tim	2B	1899	3/13/77	6/15/29	10

Name	Pos.	Years	Born	Died	Games
Flowers, Jake	IF	1923, 26, 31-32	3/16/02	12/27/62	165
Force, Davy	SS-2B	1877	7/27/49	6/21/18	58
Ford, Hod	IF	1932	7/23/97	1/29/77	1
Fournier, Jacques	1B-P	1920-22	8/16/97	3/20/38	418
Francona, Tito	OF-1B	1965-66	11/4/33		164
Frank, Charlie	OF-1B-P	1893-94	5/30/70		120
Franks, Herman	C	1939	1/4/14		17
Frazier, Joe	OF-1B	1954-56	10/6/22		153
Freed, Roger	IF	1977-79	6/2/46		135
Freese, Gene	IF	1958	1/8/34		62
Freigau, Howard	IF-OF	1922-25	8/1/02	7/18/32	223
Frisch, Frankie	IF	1927-37	9/9/98	3/12/73	1311
Fullis, Charles	OF	1934	2/27/04	3/28/46	116
Fusselman, Les	C	1952-53	3/7/21	5/21/70	43
Gagliano, Phil	IF-OF	1963-70	12/27/41		468
Gainor, Del	1B-OF	1922	11/10/86	1/29/47	43
Galloway, James	2B SS	1912	9/16/87	5/3/50	21
Garagiola, Joe	C	1946-51	2/12/26		317
Gardella, Danny	PH	1950	2/26/20		1
Garibaldi, Art	3B-2B	1936	8/21/07	10/20/67	71
Garms, Debs	OF-IF	1943-45	6/26/08		237
Garrett, Wayne	3B	1978	12/3/47		33
Gelbert, Charley	SS-3B	1929-32, 35-36	1/26/06	1/13/67	693
Genins, Frank	IF-OF	1892	11/2/66	9/30/22	15
Gilbert, Billy	2B	1908-09	6/21/76	8/8/27	100
Gilhooley, Frank	OF	1911-12	6/10/92	7/11/59	74
Gillenwater, Carden	OF	1940	5/13/18		7
Glasscock, Jack	IF-OF	1885-86, 92-93	7/22/59	2/24/47	419
Glaviano, Tommy	IF-OF	1949-52	10/26/23		336
Gleason, Jack	OF	1877	7/14/55	9/4/44	1
Gleason, William	OF-P-SS	1892-94	10/26/66	1/2/33	134
Glenn, Harry	C	1915	6/9/90	10/12/18	6
Glenn, John	OF	1960	7/10/28		32
Godby, Danny	OF	1974	11/4/46		13
Gonzalez, Julio	IF	1981-82	12/25/53		62
Gonzalez, Mike	C-1B-OF	1915-18 24-25, 31-32	9/24/90	2/19/77	566
Goodenough, Bill	OF	1893	10/3/66	2/12/20	10
Gore, George	OF	1892	5/3/52	9/16/33	20
Gorman, Herb	PH	1952	12/18/24	4/5/53	1
Gotay, Julio	IF-OF	1960-62	6/9/39		140
Grady, Mike	C-IF	1897, 1904-06	12/23/69	12/3/43	298
Grammas, Alex	IF-OF	1954-56, 59-62	4/3/27		619
Gray, Dick	IF	1959-60	7/11/31		45
Green, Dave	OF	1981-82	12/4/60		97
Green, Gene	OF-C	1957-59	6/26/33	5/23/81	173
Greisenbeck, Tim	C	1920	12/10/98	3/25/53	5
Grieve, Tom	OF	1979	3/4/48		9

Non-Pitchers (continued)

Name	Pos.	Years	Born	Died	Games
Griffin, Sandy	OF	1893	9/19/58	6/5/26	23
Grimm, Charlie	IF-OF	1918	8/28/98		50
Groat, Dick	SS-3B	1963–65	11/4/30		472
Guerrero, Mario	SS	1975	9/28/49		64
Gunson, Joe	C	1893	3/23/63	11/15/42	40
Gutteridge, Don	3B-SS	1936–40	6/19/12		501
Hackett, Jim	1B-OF-P	1902–03	10/1/77	3/28/61	105
Hafey, Chick	OF	1924–31	2/12/03	7/2/73	812
Hague, Joe	OF-1B	1968–72	4/25/44		342
Hahn, Don	OF	1975	11/16/48		7
Haigh, Ed	OF	1892	2/5/67	2/14/53	1
Hall, Russ	IF-OF	1898	9/29/71	7/1/37	39
Hallman, Bill	IF	1897	3/30/67	9/11/20	79
Haney, Fred	3B	1929	4/25/98	11/9/77	10
Haney, Larry	C	1973	11/19/42		2
Harley, Dick	OF	1897–98	9/25/72	4/3/52	131
Harmon, Chuck	OF-IF	1956–57	4/23/26		29
Harper, George	OF	1928	6/24/92	8/18/78	99
Harris, Vic	IF-OF	1976	3/27/50		97
Hartman, Fred	IF	1897	4/25/68	11/11/38	114
Hatton, Grady	IF	1956	10/7/22		44
Hauser, Arnold	IF	1910–13	9/25/88	5/22/56	410
Hazleton, Doc	1B	1901–02	8/28/76	3/17/41	7
Healy, Francis	C-OF-3B	1934	6/29/10		15
Heathcote, Cliff	OF-1B	1918–22	1/24/98	1/19/39	431
Heidemann, Jack	IF	1974	7/11/49		47
Heidrick, John	OF-IF-P	1899–1901	7/6/76	1/20/16	349
Heintzelman, Tom	IF	1973–74	11/3/46		61
Heise, Bob	IF	1974	5/12/47		3
Hemphill, Charlie	OF	1899	4/20/76	6/22/53	11
Hemus, Solly	IF	1949–56, 59	4/17/23		716
Hendrick, George	OF	1978–82	10/18/49		629
Hendrick, Harvey	IF	1932	11/9/97	10/29/41	28
Hernandez, Keith	1B	1974–82	10/20/53		1110
Herndon, Larry	OF	1974	11/3/53		12
Herr, Tom	IF	1979–82	4/4/56		328
Hertweck, Neal	1B	1952	11/22/31		2
Heydon, Mike	C-OF	1901	7/15/74	10/13/13	16
Hickman, Jim	1B-3B	1974	5/10/37		50
Hicks, Jim	OF	1969	5/18/40		19
High, Andy	3B-2B	1928–31	11/21/97	2/22/81	392
Hildebrand, Palmer	C-OF	1913	12/23/84	1/25/60	26
Hill, Hugh	OF	1904	7/21/79	9/6/58	23
Hill, Marc	C	1973–74	2/18/52		11
Himes, John	OF	1905–06	(unknown)	(deceased)	52
Hock, Ed	OF	1920	3/27/99	11/11/63	1
Hoelskoetter, Art	IF-OF-P	1905–08	9/30/82	8/3/54	299
Hogan, Marty	OF	1894–95	10/25/71	8/16/23	34
Holly, Ed	SS-2B	1906–07	7/6/79	11/27/73	159

Name	Pos.	Years	Born	Died	Games
Holm, Wattie	OF-C-3B	1924–29, 32	12/28/01	5/19/50	436
Holmes, Howard	C	1898	7/8/83	9/18/45	9
Holmes, James	OF	1906	1/28/69	8/6/32	23
Hopkins, John	OF	1907	1/3/83	10/2/29	15
Hopp, Johnny	OF-1B	1939–45	7/18/16		669
Hornsby, Rogers	IF	1915–26, 33	4/27/96	1/5/63	1580
Houseman, John	IF-OF	1897	1/10/70	11/4/22	80
Howard, Doug	1B	1975	2/6/48		17
Howerton, Bill	OF	1949–51	12/12/21		143
Hudgens, Jimmy	1B-2B	1923	8/24/02	8/26/55	6
Huelsman, Frank	OF	1897	6/5/74	6/9/59	2
Huggins, Miller	2B	1910–16	3/27/79	9/25/29	802
Hughes, Terry	3B-1B	1973	5/13/49		11
Hulswitt, Rudy	SS-2B	1909–10	2/23/77	1/16/50	145
Hunt, Joel	OF	1931–32	10/11/05		16
Hunt, Ron	IF	1974	2/23/41		12
Hunter, Herb	1B	1921	12/25/95	7/25/70	9
Huntz, Steve	IF	1967	12/3/45		74
Hyatt, Robert	1B-OF	1915	11/1/84	9/11/63	106
Iorg, Dane	OF	1977–82	5/11/50		526
Irwin, Walt	PH	1921	9/23/97		4
Jablonski, Ray	3B-1B	1953–54, 59	12/17/26		369
James, Bob	OF	1909	7/7/86		6
James, Charlie	OF	1960–64	12/22/37		484
Janvrin, Hal	IF-OF	1919–21	8/27/92	3/2/62	112
Javier, Julian	2B-3B	1960–71	8/9/36		1622
Johnson, Alex	OF	1966–67	12/7/42		106
Johnson, Billy	3B	1951–53	8/30/18		105
Johnson, Bob	IF	1969	3/4/36		19
Johnson, Darrell	C	1960	8/25/28		8
Jones, Howie	OF	1921	1/1/89	7/15/72	3
Jones, Maurice	OF	1940	11/2/14		12
Jones, Nippy	2B-OF-1B	1946–51	6/29/25		374
Jonnard, Bubber	C	1929	11/23/97		18
Judy, Lyle	2B	1935	11/15/13		8
Jutze, Alfred "Skip"	C	1972	5/28/46		21
Kasko, Eddie	IF	1957–58	6/27/32		238
Katt, Ray	C	1956, 58–59	5/9/27		81
Kavanagh, Marty	IF-OF	1918	6/13/91	7/28/60	12
Kazak, Ed	3B-2B	1948–52	7/18/20		205
Keely, Bob	C	1944–45	8/22/09		2
Keister, Bill	IF	1900	8/17/74	8/19/24	126
Kelleher, John	3B	1912	9/13/93	8/21/60	8
Kelleher, Mick	SS	1972–73, 75	7/25/47		73
Kelly, Bill	C	1910	(unknown)		2
Kelly, John	OF	1907	3/13/79	4/19/44	53
Kennedy, Jim	SS-2B	1970	11/1/46		12
Kennedy, Terry	C	1978–80	6/4/56		127

Name	Pos.	Years	Born	Died	Games
Kernek, George	1B	1965–66	1/12/40		30
Kessinger, Don	IF	1976–77	7/17/42		204
Kimmick, Wally	SS	1919	5/30/97		2
King, Chick	OF	1959	11/10/30		5
King, Jim	OF	1957	8/27/32		22
King, Lynn	OF	1935–36, 39	11/28/07	5/11/72	175
Kinlock, Walt	3B	1895	1878	(deceased)	1
Kinslow, Tom	C	1898	1/12/66	2/22/01	14
Klein, Lou	IF-OF	1943, 45–46, 49	10/22/18	6/20/76	254
Kling, Rudy	SS	1902	3/23/75	3/14/37	4
Kluttz, Clyde	C	1946	12/12/17	5/12/79	52
Knode, Mike	OF-IF	1920	11/8/95		42
Kolb, Gary	OF-3B-C	1960, 62–63	3/13/40		90
Konetchy, Ed	1B-OF-P	1907–13	9/3/85	5/27/47	980
Kopshaw, George	C	1923	7/5/95	12/26/34	2
Koy, Ernie	OF	1940–41	9/17/09		106
Krueger, Otto	IF	1900–02	9/17/76	2/20/61	282
Kubiak, Ted	IF	1971	5/12/42		32
Kuehne, Willie	IF	1892	10/24/58	10/27/21	7
Kurowski, George	IF-OF	1941–49	4/19/18		916
Lake, Eddie	IF	1939–41	3/18/16		79
Lally, Bud	OF-1B	1897	8/12/67	4/14/36	87
Landrith, Hobie	C	1957–58	3/16/30		145
Landrum, Don	OF-2B	1960–62	2/16/36		73
Landrum, Tito	OF	1980–82	10/25/54		195
Lang, Don	3B-2B	1948	3/15/15		117
LaPointe, Ralph	IF	1948	1/8/22	9/13/67	87
Larmore, Bob	SS	1918	12/6/96	1/15/64	4
Lary, Lyn	IF	1939	1/28/06	1/9/73	34
Lassetter, Don	OF	1957	3/27/33		4
Latham, Arlie	3B	1896	3/15/59	11/29/52	8
Lavan, John	IF	1919–24	10/28/90	5/30/52	535
Leahy, Tom	C	1905	6/2/69	6/12/51	35
Lee, Leonidas	OF-SS	1877	12/13/60	6/11/12	4
Lee, Leron	OF	1969–71	3/4/48		153
Lentine, Jim	OF	1978–80	7/16/54		28
Leonard	OF	1892	(unknown)	(deceased)	1
Leslie, Roy	1B	1919	8/23/94	4/10/72	12
Lewis, Bill	C	1933	10/15/04	10/24/77	15
Lewis, Fred	OF	1885	10/13/58	6/5/45	45
Lewis, Johnny	OF	1964	8/10/39		40
Lezcano, Sixto	OF	1981	11/28/53		72
Lillis, Bob	IF	1961	6/2/30		86
Lindell, Johnny	OF	1950	8/30/16		36
Lintz, Larry	IF	1975	10/10/49		27
Little, Harry	OF	1877	(unknown)	1/25/92	3
Litwhiler, Danny	OF	1943–44, 46	8/31/16		146
Livingston, Pat	C	1917	1/14/80	9/19/77	7

Name	Pos.	Years	Born	Died	Games
Lockman, Whitey	OF	1956	7/25/26		70
Loftus, Tom	OF	1877	11/15/56	4/16/10	3
Long, Jeoff	OF	1963–64	10/9/41		33
Long, Tommy	OF	1915–17	6/1/90	6/15/72	403
Lowrey, Harry "Peanuts"	OF-IF	1950–54	8/27/18		44
Ludwig, Bill	C	1908	5/27/82	9/5/47	66
Lush, Ernie	OF	1910	10/31/84	2/26/37	1
Lyons, Denny	3B	1895	3/12/66	1/2/29	33
Mack, Denny	SS	1876	1851	4/10/88	48
Magee, Lee	IF-OF	1911–14	6/4/89	3/14/66	452
Mahoney, Mike	1B	1898	12/5/73	1/3/40	2
Mallory, Jim	OF	1945	9/1/18		13
Mancuso, Gus	C	1928, 30–32, 41–42	12/5/05		368
McGeachy, Jack	OF	1886	1/23/61	4/5/30	59
McGeary, Mike	IF	1876–77	1851	(deceased)	117
McGee, Willy	OF	1982	11/2/58		123
McGraw, John	3B	1900	4/7/73	2/25/34	99
McGrillis, Mark	3B	1892	(unknown)	(deceased)	1
McHenry, Austin	OF	1918–22	9/22/95	11/27/22	543
McIver, Otto	OF	1911	7/26/84	5/4/54	30
McKean, Ed	IF	1899	6/6/64	8/16/19	67
McKenna, Ed	OF	1877	(unknown)	(deceased)	1
McKinnon, Alex	IF	1885–86	8/14/56	7/24/87	222
McLaurin Ralph	OF	1908	5/23/85	2/11/43	8
McLean, Larry	C	1904	7/18/81	3/14/21	27
McNertney, Jerry	C	1971–72	8/7/36		95
Medwick, Joe	OF	1932–40, 47–48	11/24/11	3/21/75	1216
Mejias, Sam	OF	1976	5/9/53		18
Melendez, Luis	OF-SS	1970–76	8/11/49		561
Menze, Ted	OF	1918	11/4/97	12/23/69	1
Mercer, John	1B	1912	6/22/90		1
Mertes, Sam	OF	1906	8/6/72	3/11/45	53
Mesner, Steve	3B	1941	1/13/18	4/6/81	24
Meyers, Bert	3B-SS	1896	(unknown)	(deceased)	122
Mickelson, Ed	1B	1950	9/9/26		5
Mierkowicz, Ed	PH	1950	3/6/24		1
Miggins, Larry	OF-1B	1948	8/20/25		43
Miksis, Eddie	OF	1957	9/11/26		49
Miller, Charlie	OF	1913–14	1892	6/16/61	40
Miller, Doggie	IF-OF-C	1894–95	8/15/64	4/6/09	248
Miller, Dots	IF	1914–17, 19	9/9/86	9/5/23	697
Miller, Dusty	OF	1899	9/10/68	9/3/45	10
Miller, Eddie	SS-2B	1950	11/26/16		64
Miller, Elmer	OF	1912	7/28/90	11/28/44	12
Mills, Buster	OF	1934	9/16/08		29
Minoso, Minnie	OF	1962	11/29/22		39
Mize, Johnny	1B-OF	1936–41	1/7/13		854
Mollowitz, Fritz	1B	1919	6/16/90	10/3/67	25
Moon, Wally	OF-1B	1954–58	4/3/30		702
Moore, Gene	OF	1933–35	8/26/09		23
Moore, Randy	C	1937	6/21/05		8

Non-Pitchers (continued)

Name	Pos.	Years	Born	Died	Games
Moore, Terry	OF-3B-P	1935–42, 46–48	5/27/12		1298
Morales, Jerry	OF	1978	2/18/49		126
Moran, Charly	C-SS-P	1903	2/22/78	6/13/49	25
Moran, William	C	1892	12/5/38		24
Morgan, Bobby	IF	1956	6/29/26		61
Morgan, Eddie	OF	1936	11/19/14		8
Morgan, Joe	PH	1964	11/19/30		3
Moriarity, Gene	OF	1892	(unknown)	(deceased)	47
Morris, Walter	SS	1908	1/31/81	8/2/61	23
Morse, Peter	SS-OF	1911	(unknown)	(deceased)	4
Moryn, Walt	OF	1960–61	4/12/26		92
Mowrey, Mike	3B-SS	1909–13	3/24/84	3/20/47	537
Mueller, Heinie	OF-1B	1920–26	9/16/99	1/23/74	420
Mumphrey, Jerry	OF	1974–79	9/9/52		522
Murch, Simmy	IF	1904–05	11/21/80	6/6/39	16
Murdock, Wilbur	OF	1908	(unknown)		27
Murphy, Howard	OF	1909	1882	9/5/26	25
Murphy, John	3B	1902	1879	6/1/14	1
Murphy, Mike	C	1912	8/19/88	10/27/52	1
Murphy, Morgan	C-1B	1896–97	2/14/67	10/3/38	111
Murray, John	OF-C	1906–08	3/4/84	12/4/58	132
Musial, Stan	OF-1B-P	1941–44, 46–63	11/21/20		3026
Myers, George	C	1886	1860	12/1925	79
Myers, Henry	OF-3B-2B	1923–25	4/27/89	5/1/65	140
Myers, Lynn	IF	1938–39	2/23/14		144
Narron, Sam	C	1935, 42–43	8/25/13		24
Nash, Ken	IF	1914	7/14/88	2/16/77	24
Nelson, Rocky	1B	1949–51, 56	11/18/24		205
Newell, T.E.	SS	1877	(unknown)	(deceased)	1
Nichols, Art	C-OF-1B	1901–03	7/14/71	8/9/45	202
Niebergall, Charlie	C	1921, 23–24	5/23/99		54
Niehoff, Bert	2B	1918	5/13/84	12/8/74	22
Nieman, Bob	OF	1960–61	1/26/27		87
Niland, Tom	OF-SS	1896	4/14/70	4/30/50	18
Noonan, Pete	C-1B	1906–07	11/24/81	1/11/65	118
Noren, Irv	OF	1957–59	11/29/24		142
Northey, Ron	OF	1947–49	4/26/20	4/16/71	296
Nossek, Joe	OF	1969–70	11/8/40		10
Oakes, Ennis	OF	1910–13	12/17/86	2/8/48	567
Oberkfell, Ken	IF	1977–82	5/4/56		523
O'Brien, Johnny	IF	1978–79	12/11/30		12
O'Connor, Jack	C-1B	1899–1900	3/3/67	11/14/37	94
O'Connor, Patrick	C	1914	8/4/79	8/17/50	10
O'Dea, Ken	C	1942–46	3/16/13		336

Name	Pos.	Years	Born	Died	Games
O'Farrell, Bob	C	1925-28, 33	10/19/96		387
Ogrodowski, Brusie	C	1936-37	2/17/12	3/5/56	184
O'Hara, Bill	OF-1B	1910	8/14/83	6/15/31	9
O'Hara, Tom	OF	1906-07	7/13/85	6/8/54	62
O'Leary, Charley	SS-2B	1913	10/15/81	1/6/41	120
Olivares, Ed	2B-OF	1960-61	11/5/38		24
Oliver, Gene	OF-C-1B	1959, 61-63	3/22/36		251
O'Neil, Dennie	1B	1893	1861	(deceased)	7
O'Neil, Jack	C	1902-03	1/10/73	6/29/35	138
Orengo, Joe	IF	1939-40	11/29/14		136
O'Rourke, Charlie	PH	1959	6/22/37		2
O'Rourke, Joseph	SS	1908	4/13/81	4/18/56	53
O'Rourke, Tim	IF-OF	1894	5/18/64	4/20/38	18
Orsatti, Ernie	OF-1B	1927-35	9/8/03	9/4/68	709
Osteen, Champ	IF	1908-09	2/24/77	12/14/62	45
Otten, Joe	C-OF	1895	(unknown)	(deceased)	26
Owen, Mickey	C	1937-40	4/4/16		450
Padden, Dick	2B-SS	1901	9/17/70	10/31/22	123
Padgett, Don	OF-1B-C	1937-41	12/5/11	12/9/80	525
Papi, Stan	SS-2B	1974	2/4/51		8
Parent, Freddy	2B	1899	11/25/75	11/2/72	2
Paris, Kelly	IF	1982	10/17/57		12
Pasquriello, Mike	PH	1919	11/7/98	4/5/65	1
Paulette, Gene	IF-OF-P	1917-19	5/26/91	2/8/66	263
Paynter, George	OF	1894	7/6/71	10/1/50	1
Pearce, Dickey	SS	1876-77	1/2/36	10/12/08	8
Peel, Homer	OF	1927	10/10/02		2
Peete, Charlie	OF	1956	2/22/31	11/27/56	23
Peitz, Heinie	C OF-IF-P	1892-95 1913	11/28/70	10/23/43	289
Peitz, Joe	OF	1892	(unknown)	(deceased)	7
Pepper, Ray	OF	1932-33	8/5/05		24
Phelps, Ed	C	1909-10	3/3/79	1/31/42	193
Phillips, Ed	PH	1953	7/8/31		9
Phillips, Mike	IF	1977-80	8/19/50		231
Pike, Lipman	OF	1876	5/25/45	10/10/93	63
Pinckney, George	3B	1892	1/11/62	11/9/26	78
Pinson, Vada	OF	1969	8/28/43		132
Porter, Darrell	C	1981-82	1/17/52		181
Porter, J. W.	C	1959	1/17/33		23
Potter, Mike	OF	1976-78	5/16/51		14
Puccinelli, George	OF	1930	6/22/06	4/16/56	42
Quinlan, Finners	OF	1913	10/21/87	2/17/66	13
Quinn, Joe	OF-IF	1885-86, 93-96, 98	12/25/64	11/12/40	720
Rader, Dave	C	1977	12/26/48		66
Ramirez, Milt	SS-3B	1970-71	4/2/50		66
Ramsey, Mike	SS	1978, 80-82	3/29/54		130
Rand, Dick	C	1953	3/7/31		12
Raub, Tommy	C	1906	12/1/70	2/16/49	24

Non-Pitchers (continued)

Name	Pos.	Years	Born	Died	Games
Rebel, Art	OF	1945	3/4/15		26
Reed, Milt	PH	1911	7/4/90	7/27/38	1
Reese, Jimmy	2B	1932	10/1/04		90
Reilly, Tom	SS	1908-09	8/3/84	10/18/18	34
Reitz, Ken	3B-SS	1972-75, 77-80	6/24/51		1100
Remsen, Jack	OF	1876	1851	(deceased)	33
Repass, Bob	2B	1939	11/6/17		3
Repulski, Rip	OF	1953-56	10/4/27		564
Rice, Del	C	1945-55, 60	10/27/22		1038
Rice, Hal	OF	1948-53	2/11/24		267
Richard, Lee	IF	1976	9/18/48		66
Richardson, Bill	1B	1901	10/8/77	4/11/54	15
Richmond, Don	3B	1951	10/27/19	5/24/81	12
Ricketts, Dave	C	1963, 65 67-69	7/12/35		116
Ricks, John	3B	1894	(unknown)	(deceased)	1
Riggert, Joe	OF	1914	12/11/86	10/10/73	34
Riggs, Lew	PH	1934	4/22/10		2
Roberts, Clarence	C	1913	1/11/88	12/24/63	26
Robinson, Wilbert	C	1900	6/2/63	8/8/34	60
Roche, Jack	C	1914-15, 17	11/22/90		59
Roettger, Wally	OF	1927-29, 31	8/28/02	9/14/51	197
Rojas, Cookie	IF	1970	3/6/39		23
Rojek, Stan	SS	1951	4/21/19		51
Rolling, Ray	2B	1912	9/8/86	8/25/66	5
Romano, John	C	1967	8/23/34		24
Roof, Eugene	OF	1981-82	1/13/58		34
Roque, Jorge	OF	1970-72	4/28/50		40
Rothrock, Jack	OF-2B	1934-35	3/14/05	2/2/80	283
Rudolph, Ken	C	1975-76	12/29/46		71
Russell, Paul	OF-3B-2B	1894	1870	(deceased)	3
Ryan, J.	3B	1895	(unknown)	(deceased)	2
Ryan, John	C-P-OF-IF	1901-03	11/12/68		226
Sadowski, Bob	2B	1960	1/15/37		1
Samuels, Ike	3B-SS	1895	2/20/76	(deceased)	24
Sanchez, Orlando	C	1981-82	9/7/56		53
Sanders, Ray	1B	1942-45	12/4/16		536
Sarni, Bill	C	1951-52, 54-56	9/19/27		312
Sauer, Ed	OF	1949	1/3/20		24
Sauer, Hank	OF	1956	3/17/19		75
Savage, Ted	OF	1965-67	2/21/37		55
Sawatski, Carl	C	1960-63	11/4/27		305
Schaffer, Jimmy	C	1961-62	4/5/36		138
Schang, Bobby	C	1927	12/7/86	8/29/66	3
Scheffing, Bob	C	1951	8/11/15		12

Name	Pos.	Years	Born	Died	Games
Scheinblum, Richie	OF	1974	11/5/42		6
Schindler, Bill	C	1920	7/10/96		1
Schmidt, Walter	C	1925	3/20/87	7/4/73	37
Schoendienst, Albert "Red"	OF-IF	1945-56, 61-63	2/2/23		1619
Schofield, Dick	SS	1953-58, 68, 71	1/7/35		242
Schreckengost, Ossee	C-IF	1899	4/11/75	7/19/14	72
Schriver, William	C-1B	1901	6/11/66	12/27/32	53
Schuble, Heinie	SS-3B	1927, 36	11/1/06		67
Schulte, Johnny	C	1927	9/8/96	6/28/78	64
Schultz, Joe	OF-3B-1B	1919-24	7/24/93	4/13/41	405
Scoffic, Lou	OF	1936	5/20/13		4
Scott, Tony	OF	1977-80	9/18/51		487
Seery, Emmett	OF	1885-86	2/13/67	(deceased)	185
Selph, Carey	2B	1929	12/5/01	2/24/76	25
Sessi, Walter	OF	1941	7/23/18		20
Shaffer, George	OF	1885	1852	(deceased)	69
Shannon, Mike	OF-C-3B	1962-70	7/15/39		879
Shannon, Wally	SS-2B	1959-60	1/23/34		65
Shannon, William	OF	1904-06	2/7/78		354
Shaw, Al	OF-SS-3B	1907-09	3/1/81	12/30/74	229
Shay, Danny	SS-2B	1904-05	11/8/76	12/1/27	177
Shea, Gerry	C	1905	1881	5/4/64	2
Sheckard, Jimmy	OF	1913	11/23/78	1/15/47	52
Sheehan, Biff	OF-1B	1895-96	2/13/68	10/21/23	58
Shepherdson, Ray	C	1924	5/3/97		3
Shinners, Ralph	OF	1925	10/4/95	7/23/62	74
Shotton, Burt	OF	1919-23	10/18/84	7/29/62	220
Shugart, Frank	OF-IF	1893-94	1867	(deceased)	133
Simmons, Ted	C-OF-IF	1968-80	8/9/49		1564
Simpson, Dick	OF	1968	7/28/43		26
Sisler, Dick	1B-OF	1946-47, 52-53	11/2/20		280
Sizemore, Ted	IF-OF	1971-75	4/15/46		679
Skinner, Bob	OF	1964-66	10/3/31		184
Slade, Gordon	SS-2B	1933	10/9/04	1/2/74	39
Slattery, Jack	C	1906	1/6/77	7/17/49	3
Slaughter, Enos	OF	1938-42, 46-53	4/27/16		1820
Smith, Bobby Gene	OF	1957-59, 62	5/28/34		164
Smith, Charlie	3B-SS	1966	9/15/37		116
Smith, Earl	C	1928-30	2/14/97	6/9/63	99
Smith, Fred	IF	1917	7/29/91	5/28/61	56
Smith, George	SS	1898	4/21/63	12/1/27	51
Smith, Hal	C	1956-61	6/1/31		566
Smith, Jack	OF	1915-26	6/23/95	5/2/72	1111
Smith, Jud	IF-OF	1893	1/13/69	12/7/47	4
Smith, Keith	OF	1979-80	5/3/53		30
Smith, Lonnie	OF	1982	12/22/55		156
Smith, Ozzie	SS	1982	12/26/54		140
Smith, Reggie	OF-IF	1974-76	4/2/45		325

Name	Pos.	Years	Born	Died	Games
Smith, Wally	IF-OF	1911–12	3/13/89		156
Smoot, Homer	OF	1902–06	3/23/78	3/25/28	620
Smyth, Red	OF-2B	1917–18	1/30/93	4/14/58	68
Snyder, Frank	C-1B-SS	1912–19	5/27/93	1/5/62	598
Sommers, Kid	OF-C	1893	(unknown)	10/16/95	2
Southworth, Billy	OF	1926–27, 29	3/9/93	11/15/69	210
Spencer, Daryl	IF	1960–61	7/13/29		185
Spiezio, Ed	3B-OF	1964–68	10/31/41		132
Sprinz, Joe	C	1933	8/3/02		3
Stainback, Tucker	OF	1938	8/4/10		6
Stallcup, Virgil	SS	1952–53	1/3/22		30
Stanky, Eddie	2B	1952–53	9/3/16		70
Stanton, Harry	C	1900	(unknown)	(deceased)	1
Stein, Bill	OF-3B-1B	1972–73	1/21/47		46
Stenzel, Jake	OF	1898–99	6/24/67	1/6/19	108
Stephenson, Bobby	IF	1955	8/11/28		67
Stewart, Stuffy	2B-OF	1916–17	1/31/94	12/30/80	22
Stinson, Bob	C-OF	1971	10/11/45		17
Stock, Milt	IF	1919–23	7/11/93	7/16/77	741
Stone, Tige	OF-P	1923	9/18/01	1/1/60	5
Storke, Alan	IF	1909	9/27/84	3/18/10	48
Street, Gabby	C	1931	9/30/82	2/6/51	1
Stricker, John	2B	1892	6/8/59	(deceased)	28
Stripp, Joe	3B	1938	2/3/03		54
Sugden, Joe	C-OF-1B	1898	7/31/70	6/28/59	89
Sullivan, Joe	OF-IF	1896	1/6/70	11/2/97	51
Sullivan, Suter	IF-OF-P	1898	1872	(deceased)	42
Sutherland, Gary	2B	1978	9/27/44		10
Swindell, Charlie	C	1904	10/26/77	7/22/40	3
Swisher, Steve	C	1978–80	8/9/51		101
Tamargo, John	C	1976–78	11/7/51		20
Tate, Lee	IF	1958–59	3/18/32		51
Taussig, Don	OF	1961	2/19/32		98
Taylor, Carl	OF-1B-3B	1970	1/20/44		104
Taylor, Joe	OF	1958	12/30/29		18
Tebeau, Oliver "Patsy"	IF	1899–1900	12/5/64	5/15/18	78
Templeton, Garry	SS	1976–81	3/24/56		713
Tenace, Gene	C	1981–82	10/10/46		124
Thacker, Moe	C	1963	5/21/34		3
Thevenow, Tommy	IF	1924–28	9/6/03	7/29/57	357
Tolan, Bobby	OF-1B	1965–68	11/19/45		262
Toporcer, George	IF-OF	1921–28	2/9/99		546
Torre, Joe	3B-1B-C	1969–74	7/18/40		918
Triplett, Coaker	OF	1941–43	12/18/11		149
Tucker, Tommy	1B	1898	10/28/63	10/22/35	72
Turner, George	OF	1896–98	1870	7/16/45	189
Twineham, Arthur	C	1893–94	11/26/66	(deceased)	52

Name	Pos.	Years	Born	Died	Games
Tyson, Mike	2B-SS	1972-79	1/13/50		844
Uecker, Bob	C	1964-65	1/26/35		93
Ury, Lou	1B	1903	(unknown)		2
Valenzuela, Benny	3B	1958	6/2/33		10
Van Dyke, Bill	OF	1892	12/15/63	5/5/33	4
Vann, John	PH	1913	6/7/93	6/10/58	1
Van Noy, Jay	OF	1951	11/4/28		6
Verban, Emil	2B	1944-46	8/27/15		302
Vergez, Johnny	3B	1936	7/9/06		8
Vick, Ernie	C	1922, 24-26	7/2/00	7/18/80	57
Virdon, Bill	OF	1955-56	6/9/31		168
Voss, Bill	OF	1972	10/31/45		11
Wagner, Leon	OF	1960	5/13/34		39
Walker, Harry	OF-2B-1B	1940-43, 46-47, 50-51, 55	10/22/18		
Walker, Joe	1B	1923	1/23/01	6/20/59	2
Wallace, Bobby	IF	1899-1901, 17-18	11/4/73	11/30/60	455
Waller, Ty	IF	1980	3/14/57		5
Warner, John	C	1905	8/15/72	12/21/43	41
Warwick, Bill	C	1925-26	11/26/97		22
Warwick, Carl	OF	1961-62, 64-65	2/27/37		151
Watkins, George	OF-1B-2B	1930-33	6/4/02	6/1/70	525
Weaver, Art	C	1902-03	4/7/79	3/23/17	27
Webb, James	SS	1932	11/4/09		1
Werden, Perry	1B-OF	1892-93	7/21/65	1/9/34	274
Westlake, Wally	OF-3B	1951-52	11/8/20		94
Wheeler, Dick	OF	1918	(unknown)	(deceased)	3
Whelan, Jim	PH	1913	1890		1
Whisenant, Pete	OF	1955	12/14/29		58
Whistler, Lew	1B-OF	1893	3/10/68	12/30/59	10
White, Bill	1B-OF	1959-65, 69	1/28/34		1113
Whitehead, Burgess	IF	1933-35	6/29/10		219
Whitfield, Fred	1B	1962	1/7/38		73
Whitted, George	OF-IF	1912-14	2/4/90	10/16/62	154
Wicker, Floyd	OF	1968	9/12/43		5
Wilber, Del	C	1946-49	2/14/19		84
Wilie, Denney	OF	1911-12	9/22/90	6/20/66	58
Williams, Jim	SS-2B	1966-67	10/4/43		14
Williams, Otto	IF	1902-03	11/2/77	3/19/37	55
Williamson, Howie	PH	1928	12/23/04		10
Wilson, Charlie	SS-3B	1932-33, 35	1/13/05		41
Wilson, Jimmy	C-IF	1928-33	7/23/00	5/31/47	667
Wilson, Owen	OF	1914-16	8/21/83	2/22/54	377
Wingo, Ivey	C-1B-OF	1911-14	7/8/90	3/1/41	316
Winsett, Tom	OF	1935	11/24/09		7

Non-Pitchers (continued)

Name	Pos.	Years	Born	Died	Games
Withrow, Raymond	OF	1963	11/28/37		6
Wolf, William	OF	1892	5/12/62	5/16/03	3
Wolter, Harry	OF-P	1907	7/11/84	7/7/70	16
Worthington, Robert	OF	1934	4/24/06	12/8/63	1
Young, Bobby	3B	1948	1/22/25		3
Young, Dave	1B	1895	10/6/72	10/25/24	1
Young, Lemuel	IF	1941	8/29/07	1/14/62	29
Young, Norman	1B	1948	7/1/15		41
Youngblood, Joel	OF-1B	1977	8/28/51		25
Yvars, Sal	C	1953–54	2/20/24		68
Zacher, Elmer	OF	1910	9/17/83	12/20/44	47
Zearfoss, Dave	C	1904–05	1/1/68	9/12/45	47
Zeller, Bart	C	1970	7/22/41		1
Zimmerman, Eddie	3B	1906	1/4/83	5/6/45	5

TRADES

The 10 Best Cardinal Trades

1. Getting outfielder Lou Brock from the Chicago Cubs for pitchers Ernie Broglio and Bobby Shantz and outfielder Doug Clemens. The Cards also got pitchers Jack Spring and Paul Toth in the deal (1964).
2. Getting second baseman Frank Frisch from the New York Giants for second baseman Rogers Hornsby. The Cards also sent pitcher Jimmy Ring to the Giants (1926).
3. Receiving outfielder Curt Flood from the Cincinnati Reds for pitchers Marty Kutyna, Willard Schmidt and Ted Wieand. The Reds also sent outfielder Joe Taylor to St. Louis (1957).
4. Signing pitcher Curt Simmons as a free agent following his release by the Philadelphia Phillies at age 31 (1960).
5. Getting first baseman-outfielder Bill White from the San Francisco Giants for pitchers Don Choate and Sam Jones. The Cards also received third baseman Ray Jablonski in the deal (1959).
6. Getting first baseman Orlando Cepeda from the San Francisco Giants for pitcher Ray Sadecki (1966).
7. Obtaining outfielder Roger Maris from the New York Yankees for third baseman Charlie Smith (1966).
8. Obtaining outfielder George Hendrick from the San Diego Padres for pitcher Eric Rasmussen (1978).
9. Receiving infielder Dick Groat from the Pittsburgh Pirates for pitcher Don Cardwell and infielder Julio Gotay. The Cards also received pitcher Diomedes Olivo (1962).
10. Getting outfielder Billy Southworth from the New York Giants for outfielder Clarence Mueller (1926).

The 10 Worst Cardinal Trades

1. Trading pitcher Steve Carlton to the Philadelphia Phillies for pitcher Rick Wise.

2.　Sending first baseman Johnny Mize to the New York Giants for catcher Jim O'Dea, pitcher Bill Lohrman, first baseman Johnny McCarthy, and $50,000 (1941).

3.　Shipping outfielder Joe Medwick to the Brooklyn Dodgers for pitchers Carl Doyle and Sam Naham, outfielder Ernie Koy, and infielder-outfielder Bert Haas and $125,000. Cards also sent pitcher Curt Davis to the Dodgers (1940).

4.　Trading pitcher Harvey Haddix to the Philadelphia Phillies for pitchers Murry Dickson and Herman Wehmeier. The Cards also sent pitchers Ben Flowers and Stu Miller to the Phils (1956).

5.　Trading outfielder Wally Moon to the Los Angeles Dodgers for outfielder Gino Cimoli. The Dodgers also received pitcher Phil Pane from the Cards (1958).

6.　Trading outfielder Larry Hisle to the Minnesota Twins for pitcher Wayne Granger. The Cards also sent pitcher John Cumberland to the Twins (1972).

7.　Trading outfielder Bill Virdon to the Pittsburgh Pirates for outfielder Bobby Del Greco and pitcher Dick Littlefield (1965).

8.　Trading outfielder Mike Easler to the California Angels for a player to be named. The player was infielder Ron Farkas (1976).

9.　Trading pitcher Jerry Reuss to the Houston Astros for pitchers Scipio Spinks and Lance Clemons (1972).

10. (tie)　Trading pitcher Mike Cuellar to the Houston Astros for pitchers Hal Woodeshick and Chuck Taylor. The Cards also sent pitcher Ron Taylor to Houston (1965).

Sending outfielder Bobby Tolan to Cincinnati Reds for outfielder Vada Pinson. Cards also sent pitcher Wayne Granger to the Reds (1968).

1919

January 21　The Cards trade infielders Doug Baird and Stuffy Stewart, pitcher Gene Packard, and cash to the Phillies for catcher Bill Dillhoefer, pitcher Frank Davis, and infielder Milt Stock. Baird and Packard both had short stays with Philadelphia. Stewart never played for the Phillies. Dillhoefer became a popular catcher in St. Louis before dying of pneumonia Feb. 23, 1922. Davis never pitched in the majors. Stock had four seasons in which he hit .305 or better with the Redbirds.

1920

(Nothing)

1921

June 18　The Cards trade pitcher Ferdinand Schupp and infielder Hal Janvrin to the Dodgers for pitcher Jeff Pfeffer.

1922

May 30　The Cards trade outfielder Cliff Heathcote to the Cubs for outfielder Max Flack. Heathcote spent several seasons with Chicago, batting better than .300 a couple of times. Flack hit .292 in 66 games with the Cards in '22 and hit .291 the following year.

1923

February 15   The Cards trade first baseman Jacques Fournier to Brooklyn for outfielder Hal Myers and first baseman Randy Schmandt. Fournier became expendable with future Hall of Famer Jim Bottomley ready to step in at first base. Myers, who was by then pretty well along in his career, slumped to .210 in his first year with the Cards in '24. Schmandt's career ended without his ever having played for the Redbirds.

1924

(Nothing)

1925

May 23   The Cards trade catcher Mike Gonzalez and infielder Howard Freigau to the Cubs for catcher Bob O'Farrell. O'Farrell had a truly magnificent year for the Redbirds, catching 146 games and hitting .293 in '26. He became their manager in '27, but a sore arm diminished his effectiveness behind the plate. Gonzalez became a reserve backstop for Gabby Hartnett at Chicago. Freigau donned a Cub uniform and hit .307 in 117 games that season before tailing off in subsequent years.

1926

June 14   The Cards trade outfielder Clarence Mueller to the Giants for outfielder Billy Southworth. This is often called the worst deal made by John McGraw of the Giants. Mueller became an ordinary performer in New York. Southworth hit .320 and did a masterful job in right field as the Cardinals won the pennant.

June 22   The Cubs waive Grover Cleveland Alexander to the Cards. Despite his drinking problems, Alexander became the star of the 1926 World Series for the Redbirds and racked up 21 victories in '27 while enjoying four fine seasons.

December 20   The Cards trade infielder Rogers Hornsby to the Giants for infielder Frankie Frisch and pitcher Jimmy Ring. The trade was a highly unpopular one in St. Louis, but Hornsby was destined to go after a falling out with Cardinal management. The great Hornsby hit .361, .387, and .380 the next three seasons while bouncing between the Giants, Braves, and Cubs. The Fordham Flash, however, came close to making Cardinal fans forget Hornsby, batting .300 or better in seven of his next eight seasons and successfully managing the team for six years. Ring was a throw-in.

1927

(Nothing)

1928

March 20   The Cards trade third baseman-shortstop Les Bell to the Braves for infielder Andy High and $20,000. Bell hit .277 and .298 in two seasons as Boston's regular third baseman. High had his best of four seasons with the Redbirds by batting .295 as a regular at the hot corner in '29.

May 10   The Cards trade catcher Bob O'Farrell to the Giants for outfielder George Harper. The Cards finally gave up on O'Farrell when he failed to regain his 1926 form. Harper batted .305 during a brief 99-game stint with the Cardinals.

May 11   The Cards trade catcher Spud Davis and outfielder Homer Peel to the Cubs for catcher Jimmy Wilson. Wilson, then one of the game's outstanding catchers, plugged the vacancy left by O'Farrell's departure through '33. Davis became a fine catcher himself, compiling a long string of .300 seasons. Peel was no great loss.

1929

December 11   The Cards trade pitcher Grover Cleveland Alexander and catcher Harry McCurdy to the Phillies for outfielder Homer Peel and catcher Bob McGraw. Alexander lost a tough season opener in '30 to the Giants' Carl Hubbell 2-1 and never won again. McCurdy became a backup for four seasons with the Phillies. Peel had one poor season in St. Louis.

1930

June 16   The Cards trade pitchers Bill Sherdel and Fred Frankhouse to the Braves for pitcher Burleigh Grimes. Grimes, who was happy to leave his second-division surroundings in Boston, paid rich dividends for the Cardinals when his 17-9 record in '31 helped win the pennant. The promising young Frankhouse went on to win 17 games for the Braves in '34. Sherdel was 6-10 with the Braves over parts of two seasons.

1931

June 15   The Cards trade outfielder Taylor Douthit to the Reds for outfielder Walter Roettger. Douthit dropped off sharply after leaving the Cardinals. Roettger played in only 45 games with St. Louis.

December 10   The Cards trade pitcher Burleigh Grimes to the Chicago Cubs for outfielder Hack Wilson and pitcher Art Teachout. Grimes had three losing seasons after the trade and retired. Wilson never played with the Redbirds and Teachout appeared in only one game.

1932

January 23   The Cards trade outfielder Hack Wilson to Brooklyn for outfielder Bob Parkham and $45,000. Wilson had one spark left in him as he batted .297 in '32. Parkham failed to make it with the Redbirds.

April 11   Cards trade outfielder Chick Hafey to Cincinnati for pitchers Harvey Hendrick and Benny Frey and cash. A salary dispute precipitated Hafey's departure. In two full seasons with the Reds, he batted .303 and .293. Hendrick lasted the remainder of the season with the Redbirds, batting .250 in 28 games. Frey was sold back to Cincinnati a month later.

181

October 10	The Cards trade catcher Gus Mancuso and pitcher Ray Starr to the Giants for outfielder Ethan Allen, catcher Bob O'Farrell, and pitchers Jim Mooney and Bill Walker. The deal worked out better for New York as Mancuso became a regular catcher for four years, including '36 when he batted .301. Starr didn't come into his own until '42, when he went 15-13 with a 2.67 ERA in 277 innings. Walker won 39 games in four years with the Cardinals; O'Farrell and Mooney did little.
October 24	The Cards sign second baseman Rogers Hornsby. The old master got into 46 games, at second base and as a pinch-hitter, and showed he still had the old batting touch by hitting .325.
December 27	The Cards trade first baseman Jim Bottomley to Cincinnati for pitcher Owen Carroll and outfielder Estel Crabtree. Sunny Jim was shipped out to clear the first base job for Rip Collins. Carroll, a college wonder at Holy Cross, never lived up to expectations. Crabtree batted 34 times in '33 and later returned during the manpower shortage of World War II.

1933

| February 9 | The Cards trade infielder Jake Flowers and pitcher Owen Carroll to the Dodgers for pitcher Dazzy Vance and infielder Gordon Slade. The old fireballer Vance was fairly washed up by this time. Slade hit only .113 for St. Louis. Flowers and Carroll had unimpressive stays with Brooklyn. |
| May 7 | The Reds trade shortstop Leo Durocher and pitchers John Ogden and John Henry to the Cards for pitchers Paul Derringer and Allyn Stout and infielder Earl Adams. The addition of Durocher, a fine fielder, plugged a glaring weakness in the Cardinal infield. The Reds strengthened a poor pitching staff and also gained a useful utility infielder. Shortstop had been a vexing problem for the Cards ever since Charley Gelbert suffered accidental gunshot wounds during the winter. |

1934

| November 21 | The Cards trade pitcher Tex Carleton to the Cubs for pitchers Lyle Tinning and Dick Ward and cash. Carleton went on to win 51 games in the next four seasons with the Cubs. Tinning appeared in four games, Ward in one, for the Redbirds. |

1935

| December 9 | The Cards trade infielder Burgess Whitehead to the Giants for pitcher Leroy Parmelee, first baseman Phil Weintraub, and cash. Whitehead had varying degrees of success in five seasons with the Giants. Parmelee had an 11–11 mark in one season with St. Louis. Weintraub never played for the Cards. |

1936

| August 6 | The Cards trade pitcher Bill Walker to Cincinnati for pitcher Si Johnson. Walker was about through. In his 17-year career, Johnson distinguished himself by twice leading the league in defeats with Cincinnati. |

October 8	The Cards trade first baseman Rip Collins and pitcher Leroy Parmelee to the Cubs for pitcher Lon Warneke. It looked like a good trade for both clubs and St. Louis fans believed it would bring them the pennant. Warneke, known as the Arkansas Hummingbird, did his bit, winning 18 games while losing 11. Collins was slipping following several excellent seasons with the Redbirds. Parmelee went 7-8 in one season with the Cubs.

1937

October 4	The Cards trade shortstop Leo Durocher to Brooklyn for outfielder-first baseman Johnny Cooney, infielder Jim Bucher, third baseman Joe Stripp, and pitcher Roy Henshaw. A case of incompatibility had developed between St. Louis Manager Frankie Frisch and The Lip. The deflation of Durocher's batting average from .286 in '36 to .203 in '37 didn't help either. The players that were obtained by the Cardinals failed to last more than one season.

1938

April 16	The Cards trade pitcher Dizzy Dean to the Cubs for pitchers Clyde Shoun and Curt Davis, outfielder Tuck Stainback, and $185,000. Dizzy's sore arm never improved in Chicago, but in '38 he still helped the Cubs to the pennant by beating Pittsburgh during the final week of the season. Shoun led the league in appearances during '39 and '40 as a starter-reliever with the Redbirds. Davis never won a game for the Cards. Stainback's stay with St. Louis encompassed six games.

1939

December 27	The Cards recall pitcher Ken Raffensberger from Rochester, then trade him to the Cubs for infielders Gene Lillard and Steve Mesner and cash. Raffensberger was a consistent loser during his 15-year career. Lillard appeared in only two games with the Cards. Mesner hit .145 during a brief stay in St. Louis.

1940

June 12	The Cards trade outfielder Joe Medwick and pitcher Curt Davis to Brooklyn for pitcher Carl Doyle, outfielder Ernie Koy, pitcher Sam Nahem, infielder-outfielder Bert Haas, and cash. Medwick's batting average had been tapering off after .374 in '37 and he had been unhappy in St. Louis following a contract holdout in '39. Davis never came close to duplicating the 22 victories he had with the Redbirds in '39. Doyle split six decisions later that year with St. Louis and disappeared. Koy batted .310 during the same span before his batting average nose-dived. Haas later turned into a pretty good ball player with the Cincinnati Reds. Nahem was 5-2 and had a 2.98 ERA with Cards in 1941.
June 13	The Cards purchase pitcher in Ira Hutchinson from Brooklyn. As a reliever with the Redbirds in '41, his only full season, he saved five games with a 3.86 ERA in 47 innings.

| December 4 | The Cards trade Mickey Owen to Brooklyn for catcher Gus Mancuso, pitcher John Pintar, and $60,000. The Cardinals peddled Owen with the promising young Walker Cooper ready to step in and handle the catching chores. Mancuso batted a meager .229 as St. Louis's regular catcher in '41 and shortly thereafter was traded away. Pinter never made the team. |

1941

| May 14 | The Cards trade pitcher Bill McGee to the Giants for pitchers Harry Gumbert and Paul Dean and cash. It turned into a good deal for the Cardinals as McGee—who had once shown so much promise—won two games that season and never regained his early form. Dean never pitched for the Cards again, but Gumbert won 19 games in two years. |
| December 11 | The Cards trade outfielder Johnny Mize to the Giants for catcher Ken O'Dea, first baseman Johnny McCarthy, pitcher Bill Lohrman, and $50,000 cash. O'Dea, once a prominent Cardinal farmhand, became a useful reserve backstop. Lohrman was later sold back to New York. McCarthy never played for the Cards. Mize, whose home-run production had dropped from 43 to 16 in '41 because of injuries, later led the league in homers with 51 in '47 and 40 in '48. |

1942

| July 8 | The Cards sell pitcher Lon Warneke to the Cubs. He had just about reached the end of the line. |

1943

| June 1 | The Cards trade outfielders Buster Adams, Coaker Triplett and Dain Clay to the Phillies for outfielders Danny Litwhiler and Earl Naylor. Adams had a couple of fair seasons with Philadelphia, Triplett contributed little, and Clay never played for the Phillies. Litwhiler bounced around the majors through '51 without much success. Naylor hit .186 during a short career. |

1944

(Nothing)

1945

February 5	The Cards sell outfielder-first baseman Johnny Hopp to the Braves for a reported $40,000 and the transfer of infielder Eddie Joost to the Cards' Rochester farm team. Hopp batted .333 that season with Boston and had a couple of other fine seasons with the Pirates. Joost never played for the Cardinals.
May 8	The Cards trade infielder John Antonelli and infielder-outfielder Glen Crawford to the Phillies for outfielder Earl Naylor. None of them accomplished anything noteworthy with their new teams.
May 23	The Cards trade pitcher Mort Cooper to the Boston Braves for pitcher Red Barrett and cash. Cooper won 13 games with the

Braves in '46, but never recaptured the glory he had enjoyed with the Cardinals during the war years. Barrett won 21 games with the Redbirds in '45, but was ineffective after that.

1946

January 5 — The Cards sell catcher Walker Cooper to the Giants for $175,000. He bounced around the National League for several seasons, but remained a capable catcher.

April 16 — The Cards sell first baseman Ray Sanders to the Braves. He faded into oblivion with Boston.

May 1 — The Cards trade infielder Emil Verban to the Phillies for catcher Clyde Kluttz, who was obtained from the Giants for outfielder Vince DiMaggio the same day. Verban traveled around the majors without success after leaving the Cards. Kluttz batted .265 as he concluded his career that year with St. Louis.

July 8 — The Cards sell pitcher Blix Donnelly to the Phillies. His earned run average ballooned after he left the Cards.

The Cards sell catcher Ken O'Dea to the Braves. He batted .157 that year and retired.

1947

(Nothing)

1948

April 7 — The Cards trade first baseman-outfielder Dick Sisler to the Phillies for infielder Ralph LaPointe and a reported $20,000. Sisler had four respectable seasons with the Phillies. LaPointe hit .225 for the Cards in '48, which was his final big-league season.

1949

January 29 — The Cards sell pitcher Murry Dickson to the Pirates. He won 20 games with a terrible team in '51, then led the league in losses in '52 and '53 before going to the Phillies.

1950

April 3 — The Cards claim shortstop Eddie Miller from the New York Giants. He played in 64 games for the Cards, batting .227.

April 27 — The Cards trade pitcher Ken Johnson to the Phillies for outfielder John Blatnik. Blatnik played in only seven games for the Cards. Johnson played one season with the Phillies, compiling a record of 5-8 with a 4.57 ERA in 106 innings.

May 15 — Cards purchase Johnny Lindell, an outfielder, from the Yankees. Lindell had a troubled season in which he suffered emotionally from the trade. After a two-season absence from the big leagues, he returned with the Pirates and Phillies in 1953, and batted .303, before calling it a career after the '54 season.

May 10 — The Cards waive pitcher Jim Hearn. He pitched nine more seasons, including a fine year in '51 when he compiled a 17–9 record with a 2.49 ERA for the Giants.

1951

May 14   The Cards trade first baseman Don Bollweg and an estimated $15,000 cash to the Yankees for third baseman Bill Johnson. Bollweg reached a career high .297 with New York, and after being dealt away in 1952, never reached the .220 mark again. Johnson hit .262 with the Cards in '51, with 24 doubles, but that proved to be the last good year of his career.

May 17   The Cards trade outfielder Erv Dusak and first baseman Rocky Nelson to Pittsburgh for shortstop Stan Rojek. Dusak was seldom used. Nelson was claimed on waivers by the White Sox in September. Rojek was about finished and spent only one season with St. Louis.

June 15   The Cards trade pitchers Howie Pollet and Ted Wilks, outfielder Bill Howerton, catcher Joe Garagiola, and infielder Dick Cole to Pittsburgh for outfielder Wally Westlake and pitcher Cliff Chambers. Chambers won 11 games in '51 with St. Louis, but never equaled the brilliance of his no-hit performance. Westlake didn't have much success with the Cardinals and was gone in '52. Pollet and Wilks were well past their primes and neither was much help to the Pirates. Cole had one good year in '54, playing short and third. Garagiola shared the catching duties in Pittsburgh before he was traded in '53.

August 1   The Cards purchase catcher Bob Scheffing from Cincinnati on waivers. He batted .111 in 12 games and retired after the season.

December 10   The Cards trade pitcher Max Lanier and outfielder Chuck Diering to Giants for second baseman Eddie Stanky, who is in turn named manager. Stanky became an innovative manager with the Cards for four seasons and stayed on as a scrappy player during the first two. Age had caught up to Lanier and he played two more seasons before retiring. Diering lasted two more seasons, but failed to top the .258 mark.

1952

January 24   The Cards sell infielder Stan Rojek on waivers to the Browns.

March 26   The Cards purchase infielder Gene Mauch on waivers from the Yankees. He was a utility player, who was released to Milwaukee May 21.

May 3   The Cards trade pitcher George Munger to the Pirates for pitcher Bill Werle. Neither pitcher was a factor with his new team.

May 13   The Cards trade outfielder Wally Westlake and third baseman Eddie Kazak to the Reds for first baseman Dick Sisler and shortstop Virgil Stallcup. Sisler became St. Louis' regular first baseman that year and batted .261. Stallcup contributed little as a backup shortstop. Westlake bounced around the big leagues for the next four seasons. Kazak played a total of 13 games for the Reds.

August 30   The Cards sell infielder Tom Glaviano to the Phillies on waivers.

He played one season for the Phils as a utility man.

October 1
The Cards sell first baseman Ed Mickelson and pitcher Bob Habernicht to the Browns on waivers. The Browns should have saved their money.

October 2
The Cards sell Bill Werle to the Red Sox on waivers. This time the Red Sox should have saved their money.

1953

May 23
The Cards trade pitcher Jackie Collum to the Reds for pitcher Eddie Erautt. Collum turned into a fine middleman and the Cards reacquired him for the '56 season. Erautt amounted to nothing.

June 2
The Cards acquire pitcher Hal White on waivers from the Browns. He was at the end of a 12-year career.

June 14
The Cards trade outfielder Hal Rice to the Pirates for infielder Pete Castiglione. Rice had a good season with the Pirates in '53, but got off to a bad start in '54. Castiglione was at the end of his career and of little help to the Cardinals.

June 15
The Cards purchase Sal Yvars from the Giants. Yvars was an adequate reserve catcher.

December 2
The Cards trade pitcher Jack Crimian and approximately $75,000 to the Reds for shortstop Alex Grammas. Grammas became the starting shortstop for the next two seasons, despite his anemic bat. Crimian never played for the Reds.

1954

February 2
The Cards purchase Vic Raschi from the Yankees for a reported $85,000. He lasted two years, but was unable to pitch .500 ball.

April 11
The Cards trade outfielder Enos Slaughter to the Yankees for pitcher Mel Wright and outfielders Bill Virdon and Emil Tellinger —both transferred to Card farm clubs—and catcher Hal Smith. Slaughter saw two tours of action with New York, the first being the less successful, largely because Slaughter was upset about the trade. He was dealt to Kansas City in 1955 and returned to New York in 1956, and enjoyed nearly three solid seasons over a four-year span. Wright spent four seasons in the majors, compiling a 2-4 mark and a 7.61 ERA. Virdon established himself as a fine outfielder and came back to haunt the Yankees with the Pirates in the '60 World Series. Tellinger never made it. Smith had three good seasons with St. Louis and also came back to haunt the Yanks in the '60 World Series.

April 30
The Cards sell first baseman Steve Bilko to the Cubs. Bilko was a big minor-league home-run hitter, but couldn't field.

May 7
The Cards conditionally purchase pitcher Carl Scheib from the A's. He was returned to the A's and released June 1.

August 8
The Cards purchase pitcher Ben Wade from the Dodgers on waivers. He appeared in 13 games for the Redbirds without a decision.

August 24
The Cards sell second baseman Lou Ortiz to the Phillies.

December 8	The Cards trade third baseman Ray Jablonski and pitcher Gerry Staley (and a minor-league player to be named later) to the Reds for pitcher Frank Smith. Jablonski played with several teams, including another stint with the Cards in '59, but never matched his .296 average of '54. Staley became a dependable reliever with the White Sox starting in 1956 through 1960. Smith went 3-1 in one season with the Cards.

1955

January 11	The Cards trade pitcher Ben Wade to the Pirates for pitcher Paul LaPalme. LaPalme spent just one season in St. Louis. Wade never won a game for Pittsburgh.
April 28	The Cards release pitcher Vic Raschi. He spent the remainder of the season with Kansas City and retired.
June 3	The Cards trade catcher Del Rice to the Milwaukee Braves for outfielder Pete Whisenant and catcher Charles White. Rice, a strong defensive catcher, became the backup to Del Crandall at Milwaukee. Whisenant and White did nothing of note for the Cards.
December 5	The Cards purchase pitcher Ellis Kinder from the Red Sox. He had three fine seasons with the Red Sox earlier in the decade, but only pitched briefly with St. Louis.
December 15	The Cards sign catcher Walker Cooper. He was in the twilight of a fine major-league career, which began with the Cards in 1940, and served as a pinch-hitter for the next two seasons.

1956

January 31	The Cards trade pitcher Brooks Lawrence and third baseman Sonny Senerchia to the Reds for pitcher Jackie Collum. Lawrence became a solid pitcher with Cincinnati, winning 19 games in '56 and 16 the following season. Senerchia never saw the light of day in the big leagues. Collum made his second stint with the Cards a forgettable one.
March 30	The Cards trade outfielder Pete Whisenant and an undisclosed amount of cash to the Cubs for Hank Sauer. A big long-ball hitter in his prime with the Reds and Cubs, Sauer was just about washed up and mainly saw action as a pinch-hitter. Whisenant batted .239 as a regular outfielder for the Cubs that year.
April 10	The Cards sell pitcher Frank Smith to the Reds. He worked in only two games for the Reds.
May 1	The Cards trade pitcher Paul LaPalme to the Reds for third baseman Milt Smith. An insignificant transaction.
May 6	The Cards trade pitcher Luis Arroyo and an undisclosed amount of cash to the Pirates for pitcher Max Surkont. Surkont was about finished and retired after the '57 season. Arroyo had little success with the Pirates, but moved on to New York, where he had two great years as a relief pitcher for the Yankees, especially in 1961 when he won 15 games and saved 19.
May 11	The Cards trade pitchers Harvey Haddix, Stu Miller, and Ben

Flowers to the Phillies for pitchers Herman Wehmeier and Murry Dickson. The deal was completed May 14 as Solly Hemus was traded for another infielder, Bobby Morgan. The deal, engineered by Card General Manager Frankie Lane, defied logic in some ways. Although Flowers never blossomed, Haddix and Miller still had life left. Haddix eventually landed in Pittsburgh and pitched 12 perfect innings in one game. Miller later became a star reliever with San Francisco and Baltimore. Wehmeier, a big right-hander, had been 0–14 against the Cards and with them won 12 games in '56 and 10 in '57. Dickson had seen his better days. Hemus rode the bench in Philadelphia and Morgan never became the starting shortstop that St. Louis sought.

The Cards purchase third baseman Grady Hatton from the Red Sox. Hatton was going downhill in a fair career and was gone less than three months later.

May 16	The Cards trade shortstop Alex Grammas and outfielder Joe Frazier to the Reds for infielder-outfielder Chuck Harmon. Grammas spent two seasons with the Reds and came back to the Cardinals. Frazier was shipped to Baltimore before the end of the season. Harmon was never a success.
May 17	The Cards trade outfielder Bill Virdon to Pittsburgh for pitcher Dick Littlefield and outfielder Bobby Del Greco. Virdon was off to a bad start after being named Rookie of the Year in 1955. The Redbirds would regret the trade as Virdon righted himself and remained an outstanding defensive center fielder with the Pirates until 1965. Del Greco and Littlefield were out of St. Louis by 1957.
June 4	The Cards sign pitcher Jim Konstanty. He pitched in 27 games for the Redbirds that year with a 1–1 mark.
June 14	The Cards trade second baseman Red Schoendienst, catcher Bill Sarni, outfielder Jackie Brandt, and pitcher Dick Littlefield to the Giants for shortstop Alvin Dark, outfielder-first baseman Whitey Lockman, catcher Ray Katt, and pitcher Don Liddle. The Cards also transferred Bobby Stephenson from Omaha to Minneapolis as part of the deal. A fine rookie prospect at second base, Don Blasingame, made Schoendienst an expandable commodity. Sarni was nothing more than a backup, but Brandt became a regular with Baltimore in the '60s. Dark filled a hole at shortstop for the Cards for a season and a half. Lockman was a reserve with the Cards before going back to the Giants and becoming a starter in '57. Katt, Littlefield, and Stephenson were basically throw-ins.
July 11	The Cards sell Ellis Kinder to the White Sox. He was at the tail end of a 12-year major-league career.
July 30	The Cards purchase first baseman Rocky Nelson from the Dodgers. He batted .232 in 38 games for the Redbirds.
July 31	The Cards sell infielder Grady Hatton to the Orioles. His value had been diminished by age.
September 31	The Cards sell pitcher Gordon Jones to the Giants. He had an undistinguished 11-year career with several teams.
October 8	The Cards release Walker Cooper and sign him as a coach, and also release pitcher Jim Konstanty.

189

October 26	The Giants sign Hank Sauer, who had been released by the Cards.
November 20	The Cards trade outfielder Rip Repulski and infielder Bobby Morgan to the Phillies for outfielder Del Ennis and a minor-leaguer to be named. Ennis' 24 home runs in '57, making an explosive one-two combination with Stan Musial, made the Cards forget about the power-hitting Repulski.
December 10	The Cards trade pitchers Tom Poholsky and Jackie Collum, catcher Ray Katt, infielder Wally Lammers, and two minor-leaguers to be named to the Cubs for pitchers Sam Jones and Jim Davis, infielder Eddie Miksis, and catcher Hobie Landrith. Landrith was a backup catcher and Davis a journeyman pitcher and Miksis was washed up. But the Cards reaped benefits from the trade as Jones compiled a 12–9 record in '57 and 14–13 in '58. None of the players sent to the Cubs panned out.

1957

February 26	The Cards trade first baseman Whitey Lockman to the Giants for pitcher Hoyt Wilhelm. Lockman batted .249 in 70 games for the Cards while splitting the '56 season between St. Louis and New York. The knuckleball-throwing Wilhelm, one of the greatest bull-pen stars the game has ever seen, pitched in 40 games for the Cards in '57 with a 1–4 record.
April 20	The Cards trade outfielder Bobby Del Greco and pitcher Ed Mayer to the Cubs for outfielder Jim King. Del Greco never batted higher than .254 in nine limited seasons in the majors. Mayer had a meager 2–2 record in two seasons with the Cubs. King batted only 22 times for the Redbirds.
May 11	The Cards trade infielder-outfielder Chuck Harmon for outfielder Glen Gorbous. The trade amounted to nothing.
May 14	The Cards sell pitcher R. G. Smith to the Pirates.
June 4	The Cards sell pitcher Jim Davis to the Giants.
July 31	The Cards purchase outfielder Irv Noren from the A's. He became a respectable pinch-hitter, batting .264 in '58.
September 19	The Cards sell infielder Eddie Miksis to the Orioles.
September 21	The Cards sell pitcher Hoyt Wilhelm to the Indians.
October 11	The Cards release pitcher Murry Dickson and catcher Walker Cooper.
December 5	The Cards trade pitchers Willard Schmidt, Ted Wieand, and Marty Kutyna to the Reds for outfielders Curt Flood and Joe Taylor. This was the first trade by Card General Manager Bing Devine and turned into a gem. None of the players given up amounted to anything for the Reds. Joe Taylor was a big outfielder of little achievement. Flood became a premier outfielder through the 1960s.

1958

April 2	The Cards trade outfielder Jim King to the Giants for catcher Ray Katt. King later developed into a fair power hitter with Washing-

190

ton. Katt saw little action with the Redbirds in two seasons.

April 19	The Cards purchase pitcher Phil Paine from the Braves. He went 5-1 in '58, which was his final season in the big leagues.
May 9	The Cards sell Herm Wehmeier to the Tigers. He was finished.
May 20	The Cards trade third baseman Al Dark to the Cubs for pitcher Jim Brosnan. Dark became expendable as Ken Boyer took over the hot corner for the Birds. Brosnan hurled in 33 games for the Cards that year, producing an 8-4 mark.
May 21	The Cards sign pitcher Bill Wight. He won three games for the Redbirds.
June 2	The Cards sell pitcher Morrie Martin to the Indians. He was nearing the close of a lackluster 10-year career in the big leagues.
June 14	The Cards obtain pitcher Sal Maglie from the Yankees for cash and the assignment of pitcher Joe McClain from Rochester to the Yanks' Denver farm club for the balance of the season. Maglie went 2-6 for the Cards and retired after the season.
June 15	The Cards trade shortstop Dick Schofield and cash to the Pirates for infielders Gene Freese and Johnny O'Brien. Schofield had the misfortune to join the Pirates when Bill Mazeroski and Dick Groat had the keystone positions tied down. He probably spent the best years of his career on the bench until he replaced Groat in '63. Freese had three good years with three teams and returned to the Bucs in '64. O'Brien had no success with the Cards.
July 9	The Cards purchase Chuck Stobbs from the Senators. He won 107 games during a 15-year carrer in the majors, but only one victory occurred in a St. Louis uniform.
July 25	The Cards sell outfielder Joe Taylor to the Orioles.
September 29	The Cards trade infielder Gene Freese to the Phillies for second baseman Solly Hemus, who is named manager. Hemus, who was the last of the playing managers in the National League, lacked the experience to effectively lead the Redbirds. Freese played one season with the Phillies and traveled around the majors through 1966.
October 3	The Cards trade outfielder Del Ennis, infielder Eddie Kasko, and pitcher Bob Mabe to the Reds for first baseman George Crowe, pitcher Alex Kellner, and infielder Alex Grammas. Ennis was washed up by that time. Kasko promptly became Cincinnati's regular shortstop and toiled in the Reds' infield through 1963, after which he went to Houston. Mabe finished '59 with a 4-2 mark and 5.46 ERA for the Reds. Crowe saw action mainly as a pinch-hitter during the next three seasons with the Redbirds. Kellner threw only 37 innings for the Cards in '59. Grammas lasted into the '62 season with St. Louis as a utility infielder.
October 7	The Cards trade catcher Hobie Landrith, pitcher Billy Muffett, and third baseman Benny Valenzuela to the Giants for pitchers Marv Grissom and Ernie Broglio. Landrith would spend the next five years with four teams as a backup catcher. Muffett won just nine games in the next four seasons. Valenzuela never played in the majors after '58. Grissom threw only two innings in '59 with the Cards. Broglio, however, became a 21-game winner in '60,

191

before gaining his greatest notoriety as a principal figure in the 1964 Lou Brock trade.

October 17	The Cards release pitcher Bill Wight.
November 19	The Cards release Ray Katt as a player and sign him as a coach.
December 3	The Cards trade shortstop Ruben Amaro to the Phillies for outfielder Chuck Essegian. Essegian batted .179 in 17 games before the Cards shipped him to Los Angeles in '59. Amaro was a slick-fielding backup infielder with the Phillies for six years before closing out his career with the Yankees and Angels.
December 4	The Cards trade outfielder Wally Moon and pitcher Phil Paine to the Dodgers for outfielder Gino Cimoli. Moon was a valuable acquisition for the Dodgers, batting .302, .299, and .328 during the next three seasons. Cimoli, a journeyman outfielder, batted .279 as a regular outfielder with the Birds in '59. Paine never made it to the majors with the Dodgers.

1959

February 2	The Cards purchase Billy Harrell from the Indians. He never played for the Cards.
March 3	The Senators sign pitcher Chuck Stobbs, who was released by the Cards.
March 15	The Cards trade pitcher Nelson Chittum to the Red Sox for pitcher Dean Stone. Chittum pitched in 21 games for Boston during the '60 season, winning three. Stone had a record of 0–1 during one season in St. Louis.
March 25	The Cards trade pitchers Sam Jones and Don Choate to the Giants for first baseman-outfielder Bill White and third baseman Ray Jablonski. Jones had two fine seasons with the Giants, winning 21 games in '59 and 18 in '60. In 1963 he resurfaced and pitched 11 games for the Cards. Choate's major-league career consisted of four games with the Giants in '60. Jablonski was sold to Kansas City before the end of the year. However, White made the trade a sparkling one from St. Louis' point of view by becoming an All-Star first baseman during his six seasons in St. Louis.
April 10	The Cards release pitcher Sal Maglie.
May 19	The Cards trade outfielder Irv Noren to the Cubs for outfielder Chick King. Noren saw limited action with the Cubs and Dodgers that year and vanished. King appeared in five games for the Cards that year before likewise disappearing.
June 8	The Cards trade pitcher Jim Brosnan to the Reds for pitcher Hal Jeffcoat. Brosnan had a couple of fair seasons with Cincinnati. Jeffcoat finished a mediocre career that year with a record of 0–1 in 11 games with the Cards. Brosnan later authored two baseball books, *The Long Season* and *Pennant Race*.
June 15	The Cards purchase third baseman Dick Gray from the Dodgers. Gray hit .314 as a reserve for the Redbirds that year and batted five times in '60 before his brief career ended.
June 25	The Cards purchase catcher J. W. Porter from the Senators.

Porter, a hanger-on throughout his six-year career, batted .212 in 23 games with St. Louis.

June 26   The Cards sell pitcher Gary Blaylock to the Yankees. Blaylock hurled in 15 games for New York with a mark of 0–1.

August 20   The Cards sell third baseman Ray Jablonski to the A's. It was his last big-league season.

October 13 The Cards release pitcher Hal Jeffcoat.

December 2 The Cards trade outfielder-catcher Gene Green to the Orioles for outfielder Bob Nieman. The Cards also assigned catcher Charles Stainland from Rochester to Miami as part of the deal. Baltimore got a long-ball hitting reserve while St. Louis gained a backup man who hit .287 in 81 games during '60.

December 4 The Cards trade outfielder Bobby Gene Smith to the Phillies for catcher Carl Sawatski. St. Louis later assigned pitcher Bill Smith from Rochester to Buffalo to complete the deal. Smith had been a good-field, no-hit outfielder who played sparingly in three seasons with the Redbirds. Sawatski was a second-string catcher with the Cards for the period 1960–63. Smith pitched in 24 games with the Phils during '62, posting a 1–5 mark.

December 15 The Cards trade second baseman Don Blasingame to the Giants for infielder Daryl Spencer and outfielder Leon Wagner. Blasingame never matched his early success with the Redbirds in his remaining seven seasons. Wagner became a feared power-hitter with the Angels and Indians. Spencer played extensively at shortstop and second base for the Cards in '60, hitting .258 with 16 home runs.

December 21 The Cards trade outfielder Gino Gimoli and pitcher Tom Cheney to Pittsburgh for pitcher Ron Kline. Kline left St. Louis after one season but later became a good reliever in the American League. Cimoli saw a good deal of action with the Bucs, mostly in the infield. Cheney was used as a spot starter.

1960

May 19   The Cards sell pitcher Frank Barnes to the White Sox, who option him to San Diego.

May 20   The Cards sign pitcher Curt Simmons, who was released by the Phillies. Simmons was thought to have a bad arm, but he pitched well for the Redbirds, especially in their pennant-winning year of '64, when he won 18 games.

May 27   The Cards trade pitcher Wilmer Mizell and infielder Dick Gray, the latter assigned to Columbus, to Pittsburgh for second baseman Julian Javier and pitcher Ed Bauta, both on the Columbus roster. The trade paid dividends for both teams. Mizell won 13 games for the Pirates in '60 and his addition gave Pittsburgh the added mound strength to win the World Championship. Javier became the Cards' starting second baseman and helped them to pennants in '64, '67, and '68.

June 15   The Cards trade infielder Jim McKnight to the Cubs, who assign him from Memphis to Houston, for outfielder Walt "Moose"

Moryn. The Cubs also got some cash. McKnight was nothing for Chicago, but Moryn did a good job in a reserve role for St. Louis.

June 15 — The Cards trade pitcher Jim Donohue to the Dodgers for outfielder John Glenn, who is on the St. Paul roster. Donohue was transferred from Rochester to St. Paul and pitched unimpressively during two seasons. Glenn batted .258 in 32 games with the Cards that year.

July 29 — The Cards purchase pitcher Bob Grim from the Reds. Grim had an outstanding rookie year (20–6) with the Yankees in '54, but never came close to matching it.

August 2 — The Cards sell pitcher Marshall Bridges to the Reds. He hung around through '65 without success.

September 2 — The Cards purchase Rocky Bridges from the Indians. He played in three games for the Redbirds and was released Oct. 11.

1961

March 15 — The Cards sign second baseman Red Schoendienst as a free agent. He became a valuable addition as a pinch-hitter, batting .300 in each of the next two seasons.

April 10 — The Cards sell pitcher Ron Kline to the Angels.

The Cards sign pitcher Mickey McDermott as a free agent. He appeared in 19 games with St. Louis and finished the season with Kansas City.

May 10 — The Cards trade outfielder Bob Nieman to the Indians for infielder Joe Morgan, who is assigned to San Juan, and a player to be named. The Indians assigned pitcher Mike Lee to the Card organization Sept. 25 to complete the deal. Nieman batted .354 with the Indians during the remainder of the season, although he appeared in only 39 games. Morgan was not *the* Joe Morgan, but rather a much-traveled ball player who appeared in three games with the Cards in '64. Lee eventually pitched in 13 big-league games with the Indians and Angels.

May 30 — The Cards trade infielder Daryl Spencer to the Dodgers for infielder Bob Lillis and outfielder Carl Warwick. Spencer became the Dodgers' regular third baseman in '62. Warwick served as a backup outfielder with the Redbirds. Lillis went to Houston in the expansion draft following the season.

June 15 — The Cards sell outfielder Walt Moryn to the Pirates. He contributed little in parts of two seasons with St. Louis.

July 8 — The Cards release catcher Darrell Johnson as a coach. The next day he was signed by the Phillies as an active player.

July 21 — The Cards sell pitcher Mickey McDermott to the Athletics.

October 13 — The Colt .45s purchase pitcher Al Cicotte from the Cards.

October 24 — The Cards release pitcher Red Schoendienst as a player and sign him as a coach.

November 27 — The Cards trade first baseman Joe Cunningham to the White Sox for outfielder Minnie Minoso. Cunningham could never crack the Cardinal lineup at first base. The Cards had hoped the ageless

194

Minoso would lend experience to the outfield, but two serious injuries hampered his effectiveness.

December 1   The Cards trade infielder Ron Kabbes to Baltimore for pitcher Johnny Kucks. Kucks had won 18 games with the Yankees in '56 but never pitched with the Redbirds. Kabbes failed to reach the majors.

1962

March 30   The Cards sell first baseman Frank Leja to the Angels. He spent most of his career buried in the minor leagues.

April 7   The Cards trade outfielder Al Herring, transferred from Tulsa to San Antonio, and cash to the Cubs for pitcher Bobby Locke. Nothing more need be said.

May 6   The Cards trade outfielder Carl Warwick and pitcher John Anderson to the Colt .45s for pitcher Bobby Shantz. The deal worked out well for the Redbirds because they gave up two players of marginal value for a veteran left-handed relief pitcher, who still had mileage left on him.

June 5   The Cards trade infielder Alex Grammas and outfielder Don Landrum to the Cubs for outfielder Bobby Gene Smith and infielder Daryl Robertson, who is assigned to Tulsa. Grammas had outlived his usefulness by this time. Landrum became the Cubs' regular center fielder for a couple of seasons, but never distinguished himself. Smith would go around with St. Louis a second time and bat a weak .231 in 91 games. Robertson lasted only briefly in the majors.

September 1   The Cards trade pitcher Paul Toth to the Cubs for pitcher Harvey Branch, who is on the San Antonio roster. Toth played a couple of seasons with the Cubs but never amounted to much. Branch became a one-game Cardinal and a one game major leaguer

October 5   The Cards release second baseman Red Schoendienst as a player and sign him as a coach.

October 17   The Cards trade pitchers Larry Jackson and Lindy McDaniel and catcher Jim Schaffer to the Cubs for outfielder George Altman, pitcher Don Cardwell, and catcher Moe Thacker, the latter assigned to Atlanta. Jackson bolstered the Cubs' staff, serving as their top starter until 1966. McDaniel became the cornerstone of their bull pen during that time, his 22 saves in 1963 leading the league. Schaffer was a light-hitting, second-rate catcher. Altman followed his .318 average for the Cubs in '62 with a .274 clip with the Redbirds in '63. Cardwell, who pitched a no-hitter against the Cards with the Cubs in '60, was traded away before ever wearing a St. Louis uniform. Thacker played in only three games for the Cards.

November 19   The Cards trade pitcher Don Cardwell and infielder Julio Gotay to Pittsburgh for infielder Dick Groat and pitcher Diomedes Olivo. Olivo fell apart after becoming a great relief pitcher in 1962, but Groat filled a hole at shortstop and helped the Cards to the World Championship. Cardwell had a fair year in '63, then hurt his arm and won only once in '64. He was never the outstanding starter the Pirates had hoped for and was traded to the Mets after the '66 season. Gotay was a throw-in and never played much.

December 15   The Cards trade first baseman Fred Whitfield to the Indians for pitcher Ron Taylor and infielder Jack Kubiszyn, the latter assigned from Jacksonville to Atlanta. Taylor became a valuable relief man for the Cards in '63 and '64. Whitfield rode the bench most of the time during his career. Kubiszyn never surfaced in the big leagues with St. Louis.

1963

April 2   The Cards sell outfielder Minnie Minoso to the Senators for cash and a player to be named. Minoso, age 40 at the time, had suffered through an injury-riddled year with the Cards and his value from a talent standpoint had been greatly diminished. He had only 93 at-bats, a .196 average and 19 hits in 97 at-bats.

June 15   The Cards trade catcher-outfielder Gene Oliver and pitcher Bob Sadowski to the Braves for pitcher Lou Burdette. Oliver had one good season in the majors, walloping 21 homers for Milwaukee in '65. Sadowski had a couple of so-so years with the Braves as a starter and long reliever. Burdette sadly took too long before retiring, trying in vain to recapture the glory he achieved with the Braves in the '50s.

June 24   The Cards trade infielder Leo Burke to the Cubs for pitcher Barney Schultz. Burke was a utility infielder. Acquiring Schultz paid great dividends as his steady relief pitching for the Cards in late '64 was crucial in winning the pennant.

July 29   The Cards trade outfield-first baseman Duke Carmel to the Mets for cash and outfielder Jacke Davis, who was assigned from Buffalo to Atlanta. A trade hardly worth mentioning.

July 5   The Cards trade pitcher Ed Bauta to the Mets for pitcher Ken MacKenzie. Neither team derived any benefits from the deal.

October 1   The Cards trade pitcher Ken MacKenzie to the Giants for catcher Jim Coker. A couple of warm bodies were moved, but nothing in terms of talent.

October 9   The Cards release pitcher Sam Jones. He had reached the end of the line.

November 4   The Cards trade outfielder George Altman and pitcher Bill Wakefield to the Mets for pitcher Roger Craig. Altman and Wakefield helped make the Mets what they were in their formative years— terrible. Craig recovered from the humiliation of losing 24 games with the Mets in '62 to finish at 7-9 for the Cards in '64 with a respectable 3.25 ERA.

December 6   The Cards release catcher Carl Sawatski. His 11-year career was finished.

1964

February 17   The Cards trade outfielder Jim Beauchamp and pitcher Chuck Taylor, the latter on the Tulsa roster, to Houston for outfielder Carl Warwick. Beauchamp was a journeyman reserve during his 10-year career in the big leagues. Taylor had a big season with

196

	Montreal in '74, hurling 108 innings in relief with a 6-2 record and 2.17 ERA. Warwick batted .259 as a reserve with the Cards in '64.
April 9	The Cards trade catcher Jim Coker and outfielder Gary Kolb to the Braves for catcher Bob Uecker. The Cards surrendered two players of little value for a superb defensive catcher to play behind Tim McCarver.
June 2	The Cards trade pitcher Lou Burdette to the Cubs for pitcher Glen Hobbie. Hobbie was a bright prospect who never panned out. Burdette should have retired long before that time.
June 15	The Cards trade pitchers Ernie Broglio and Bobby Shantz and outfielder Doug Clemens to the Cubs for outfielder Lou Brock and pitcher Paul Toth, the latter assigned to Jacksonville. It probably ranked as the most lopsided deal in history, except for the Red Sox selling Babe Ruth to the Yankees in 1919. After finishing above .500 in '63, the Cubs hoped Broglio would propel them into pennant contention. But he won only seven games for them before the end of his career in '66. Cardinal fans well know Brock's accomplishments. He became the most prolific base stealer in history, as well as a member of the 3,000 hit club. He ended a fabulous 19-year career with a .293 batting average.
July 17	The Cards sell first baseman Jeoff Long to the White Sox.
December 7	The Cards trade pitcher Gordon Richardson and outfielder Johnny Lewis to the Mets for pitcher Tracy Stallard and a player to be named. Infielder Elio Chacon was transferred from Buffalo to Jacksonville in February to complete the deal. Stallard is most remembered for yielding Roger Maris' 61st home run in 1961. A 20-game loser in '64, Stallard compiled a mark of 11–8 in '65. Richardson and Lewis didn't contribute much to the Mets.
December 14	The Cards trade pitcher Roger Craig and outfielder Charlie James to the Reds for pitcher Bob Purkey and a player to be named later. The veteran Craig was in the twilight of his career. The crowded Cincinnati outfield had no room for James. Purkey, who had several fine seasons with the Reds, won 10 games with the Cards in '65 but had a whopping 5.79 ERA.
December 15	The Cards trade cash and a player to be named to the Indians for first baseman-outfielder Tito Francona. The Redbirds added Francona for left-handed bench power, but he hit only .259 and .212 in two seasons with a total of nine homers.

1965

March 19	The Astros claim catcher Ed Pacheo from the Cards on first-year waivers.
March 22	The Cards claim pitcher Mike Buist from the Mets on first-year waivers.
April 7	The Cards trade pitcher Bob Humphreys to the Cubs for pitcher Hal Gilson and infielder Bob Pfeil. Humphreys spent one season with Chicago and several with Washington, achieving fair success. Gilson pitched 13 games with the Cards in '68. Pfeil had quick stays with the Mets in '69 and the Phillies in '71.
June 15	The Cards trade pitcher Ron Taylor and Mike Cuellar, the latter

197

on the Jacksonville roster, to the Astros for pitcher Hal Woodeshick. The Astros assigned pitcher Chuck Taylor from Oklahoma City to Jacksonville to complete the deal. The Cards goofed on this deal because Cuellar had several outstanding seasons with the Orioles during the '70s and Ron Taylor developed into a reliable reliever with the Mets. Woodeshick, a bull-pen specialist, pitched well during '65 and '66 in St. Louis. Chuck Taylor had three good seasons with the Redbirds beginning in '69, but he and Woodeshick together never matched Cuellar's value.

July 24	The Cards sell outfielder Carl Warwick to the Orioles.
October 20	The Cards trade third baseman Ken Boyer to the Mets for third baseman Charlie Smith and pitcher Al Jackson. Boyer had dropped off sharply from an excellent season in '64, when he was named the league's Most Valuable Player. Smith batted .266 in one season with St. Louis. Jackson went 13–15 in '66 and 9–4 in '67 and was returned to the Mets.
October 27	The Cards trade first baseman Bill White, shortstop Dick Groat, and catcher Bob Uecker to the Phillies for pitcher Art Mahaffey, outfielder Alex Johnson, and catcher Pat Corrales. By sending White and groat to Philadelphia, Cardinal General Manager Bob Howsam all but completed the desecration of the infield that won the World Championship in '64. Howsam was looking for speed because the Cards were to move into a new, bigger ballpark the next spring. Although the trade shocked St. Louis fans at the time, none of the players involved, except Johnson, had much of a future.

1966

April 7	The Cards sell pitcher Bob Purkey to the Pirates.
May 8	The Cards trade pitcher Ray Sadecki to the Giants for first baseman Orlando Cepeda. Sadecki's career began a downhill slide after he won 20 games in '64. Cepeda, bothered by chronically sore knees, had no place in the Giant lineup with Willie McCovey at first base. After hitting .303 with the Cards in '66, he batted .325 and hit 25 home runs in '67 to win the National League's Most Valuable Player Award.
June 22	The Cards sell pitcher Curt Simmons to the Cubs. He was washed up.
October 5	The Cards release outfielder Bob Skinner and pitcher Barney Schultz. They both retired.
December 8	The Cards obtain Roger Maris from the Yankees for third baseman Charlie Smith. Maris helped the Redbirds win the pennant, while Smith helped the Yankees finish in ninth place.
December 14	The Cards trade pitcher Don Dennis and outfielder Walt Williams to the White Sox for catcher Johnny Romano and pitcher Lee White, the latter transferred from Indianapolis to Little Rock. Dennis appeared briefly with the Cards in '65–'66, but never made the big leagues in Chicago. Williams had a few fair seasons in Chicago during his 10-year career in the majors. Romano, who had his best year in '62 when he hit 25 homers for Cleveland, played in only 20 games with St. Louis and retired. White never reached the majors.

1967

April 1	The Cards trade infielder Jerry Buchek, pitcher Art Mahaffey, and shortstop Tony Martinez to the Mets for shortstop Eddie Bressoud and outfielder Dan Napoleon. Mahaffey and Martinez were transferred from Tulsa to Jacksonville and Napoleon from Jacksonville to Tulsa. Although a lot of bodies exchanged uniforms, the trade didn't improve either side.
April 10	The Cards sell Tito Francona to the Phillies.
May 14	The Cards sell outfielder Ted Savage to the Cubs. He was a journeyman ball player who had reached the end of the road.
July 16	The Cards get pitcher Jack Lamabe from the Mets for a player to be named; the Cards option pitcher Jim Cosman to Jacksonville as part of the deal. The Mets got Al Jackson from the Cards Oct. 13 to complete the deal. Lamabe appeared in 23 games for St. Louis that year and was sent elsewhere. Cosman never pitched for the Mets. Jackson was used up.
September 3	The Cards sign pitcher Barney Schultz as a free agent to enable him to qualify for a major-league player pension.
October 20	The Cards release pitchers Barney Schultz and Hal Woodeshick and catcher John Romano.

1968

January 11	The Cards trade outfielder Alex Johnson to the Reds for outfielder Dick Simpson. Johnson, beset by attitude problems, had two solid years in Cincinnati and one in California. Simpson hit a disappointing .232 in 26 games for the Cards.
February 8	The Cards trade infielder Jimy Williams and catcher Pat Corrales, the latter assigned to Indianapolis, to the Reds for catcher Johnny Edwards. Edwards, an All-Star catcher in his prime, had seen his better days, but still proved a valuable backup to Tim McCarver. Corrales was a good defensive catcher but no threat with a bat. Williams' major-league career consisted of 14 games with the Cards in '66–'67.
April 1	The Cards sign free-agent infielder Dick Schofield. He batted only .227 during his career, which amazingly lasted 19 years.
April 22	The Cards trade pitchers Jack Lamabe and Ron Piche, both on the Tulsa roster, to the Cubs for pitchers Pete Mikkelsen and Dave Dowling, the latter on the Tacoma roster. Piche was assigned to Tacoma; Mikkelsen and Dowling were assigned to Tulsa. Lamabe, a veteran reliever, lasted one season with the Cubs and hung it up. Piche never played in the majors after '66. Mikkelsen had some fair seasons ahead, but with the Dodgers rather than the Cards. Dowling, originally touted as a fine mound prospect, appeared in just two games in the big leagues.
June 15	The Cards trade outfielder Dick Simpson and pitcher Hal Gilson to the Astros for outfielder Ron Davis. Neither side gained or lost much.
September 27	The Cards again sign free-agent pitcher Barney Schultz to get him pension time. They released him Oct. 8.

October 11	The Cards trade catchers Johnny Edwards and Tommy Smith, the latter transferred from Tulsa to Oklahoma City, to the Astros for pitcher Dave Giusti and catcher Dave Adlesh. Giusti was the key man for the Cards, who sought to improve their bull pen. He pitched one season in St. Louis and made 22 appearances but failed to post a save. Adlesh was a throw-in to compensate the Cards for the loss of Edwards as a backup catcher. Edwards played six more seasons, but never came close to matching the success he achieved earlier in his career with Cincinnati. Tommy Smith never made it.
	The Cards trade outfielder Bobby Tolan and pitcher Wayne Granger to the Reds for outfielder Vada Pinson. Pinson cost the Cards one of their most promising young players, the speedy Tolan, and a proven reliever, Granger. The Cards hoped he would replace Roger Maris in right field, but a broken leg sidelined him in '69 and he batted only .255.
December 3	The Cards trade third baseman Ed Spiezio, outfielder Ron Davis, catcher Dan Breeden, and pitcher Phil Knuckles to the Padres for pitcher Dave Giusti. The Cards, unable to protect Giusti in the expansion draft, had to sacrifice several young players to reacquire him, although only Spiezio became a regular with the Padres.

1969

March 17	The Cards trade first baseman Orlando Cepeda to the Braves for catcher-first baseman Joe Torre. Cepeda in slumping to .248 during '68 fell from good graces in St. Louis. Torre was having contract problems in Atlanta. He had several fine seasons in St. Louis, including '71 when he batted .363. He went on to further fame with the New York Mets as a player and later manager.
March 25	The Cards trade catcher Dave Adlesh to the Braves for infielder Bob W. Johnson. Adlesh never played in the major leagues again. Johnson batted .207 in 19 games with the Cards.
April 3	The Cards trade infielder Jim Hutton, assigned to Eugene, and infielder Jerry Buchek, assigned from Tulsa to Eugene, to the Phillies for first baseman Bill White. Hutton's career in the big leagues consisted of 57 games with the Phillies in '70 and four with the Orioles in '75. Buchek retired without playing for the Phillies. The aging White batted 57 times with the Cards in '69 and retired.
May 22	The Cards trade shortstop John Sipin and catcher Sonny Roberts, the latter on the Tulsa roster, to the Padres for shortstop Jerry DaVanon and first baseman Bill Davis, both assigned to Tulsa. Sipin was platooned at second base for the Padres in '69. Roberts never made it to the majors. The Cards rarely used DaVanon in '69 and '70. Davis never played in a big-league game for St. Louis.
May 30	The Cards trade outfielder Jim Hicks to the Angels for outfielder Vic Davalillo. Hicks had a lifetime average of .163 in a brief career. Davalillo was a fine addition as a pinch-hitter for the Redbirds.
July 12	The Cards trade infielder Bob W. Johnson to the A's for outfielder Joe Nossek, who is assigned from Des Moines to Tulsa. Neither

had a major-league career worth noting.

August 8	The Cards sell pitcher Ron Willis to the Astros. On Oct. 15 Houston returned him to the Cards, who shipped him to Tulsa. The Astros picked up Willis to bolster their bull pen for the '69 pennant race, but he contributed little.
October 2	The Cards place first baseman Bill White on the voluntary retired list.
October 7	The Cards trade catcher Tim McCarver, outfielders Curt Flood and Byron Browne, and pitcher Joe Hoerner to the Phillies for first baseman Richie Allen, infielder Cookie Rojas, and pitcher Jerry Johnson. The trade led to Flood's historic challenge of the legality of baseball's reserve clause. He subsequently sat out the '70 season. McCarver still had several seasons ahead as a durable backup catcher with several teams. Hoerner had two good seasons in Philadelphia before a youth movement swept him away. Browne was a throw-in. Rojas failed to last the '70 season with the Cards. Johnson pitched in only seven games with St. Louis. Allen was the key for the Redbirds. They found his power intriguing and drooled over the prospect of teaming him with Joe Torre in the lineup.

1970

March 31	The Cards release pitcher Ramon Hernandez. He resurfaced in '71 with Pittsburgh and became a steady reliever for several seasons.
April 8	The Cards trade Willie Montanez to the Phillies as partial compensation for the loss of Curt Flood. Traded Oct. 7, '69, Flood remained out of baseball for the 1970 season. Montanez was assigned to Eugene. The Cardinals let a player who was destined to become a fine power-hitter and slick infielder slip away.
April 22	The Cards trade shortstop Steve Huntz to the Padres for pitcher Billy McCool, who is assigned to Tulsa. Huntz was a second-rate infielder. A good reliever with Cincinnati several years earlier, McCool pitched briefly with St. Louis and retired.
May 15	The Cards sell pitcher Rich Nye to the Expos, who assign him to Buffalo. His major-league career ended when the season came to a close.
May 18	The Cards trade Jerry Johnson to the Giants for pitcher Frank Linzy. Johnson lasted several years, but never won more than 12 games in a season. Linzy pitched well for the Cards in '71 (59 innings, 2.14 ERA, 6 saves) and then had a couple of fair seasons as a reliever in the American League.
May 29	The Cards trade infielder Phil Gagliano to the Cubs for pitcher Ted Abernathy. Gagliano stayed a utility infielder. Abernathy, whose trademark was a submarine delivery, made 11 appearances with St. Louis.
June 13	The Cards trade pitcher George Culver to the Astros for outfielder-first baseman Jim Beauchamp and shortstop Leon McFadden, the latter assigned from Oklahoma City to Tulsa. Culver struggled in the majors, never winning more than 11 games in any single season. Beauchamp, a bench-warmer throughout his career, played another year and a half without contributing

201

much. McFadden never played again in the majors.

June 13   The Cards trade second baseman Cookie Rojas to the Royals for outfielder Fred Rico, who is assigned from Omaha to Tulsa. Rojas played seven more years, having his best season in '71 when he batted .300. Rico never played with the varsity in St. Louis.

July 1   The Cards trade pitcher Ted Abernathy to the Royals for pitcher Chris Zachary, who is assigned from Omaha to Tulsa. Although pushing age 40, Abernathy saved 23 games with the Royals in '71. Zachary went 3–10 with a 5.30 ERA with the Cards the same year.

July 21   The Cards release pitcher Chuck Hartenstein, who is signed by the Red Sox and assigned to Louisville. He pitched in 17 games with the Red Sox that season, then dropped from the majors until '77 when he came back with Toronto.

August 14   The Cards purchase pitcher Frank Bertaina from Rochester in the Baltimore farm system. He finished the season in St. Louis and retired.

August 30   The Cards send pitcher Jim Browning to the Phillies as final payment for the Curt Flood deal of Oct. 7, 1969. He was assigned from St. Petersburg to Phillies' Peninsula farm club.

September 17   The Cards purchase pitcher Fred Reahm from the Mets.

September 28   The Cards purchase pitcher Fred Norman from the Dodgers. He never won a game in St. Louis, but later had several good seasons with Cincinnati.

October 5   The Cards trade first baseman-third baseman Richie Allen to the Dodgers for infielder Ted Sizemore and catcher Bob Stinson. Allen quickly fell out of favor in St. Louis, despite knocking 34 homers and batting in 101 runs in '70. The Redbirds received nothing of comparable value, however. Sizemore became their regular second baseman for five seasons with a batting average that hovered around .260. Stinson batted only 19 times with the Cards and drifted around the majors and minors before finding a home with the Seattle expansion team in '77.

October 20   The Cards trade pitcher Sal Campisi and infielder Jim Kennedy, the latter on the Tulsa roster, to the Twins for outfielders Herman Hill and Charles Wissler, the latter assigned from Evansville to Tulsa. Hill drowned in the Caribbean Sea near Valencia, Venezuela Dec. 14, 1970.

The Cards trade outfielder-first baseman Carl Taylor and pitcher Jim Ellis, the latter assigned from Arkansas to Portland, to the Brewers for catcher Jerry McNertney and pitchers George Lauzerique and Jesse Higgins, the latter two assigned from Portland to Tulsa. Taylor had a fine season in '69 with the Pirates as he batted .348, but he dropped to .249 with the Cards. McNertney, the other principal in the trade, had a combined average of .239 in nine seasons.

October 21   The Cards trade first baseman Jim Campbell, who is assigned from Tulsa to Louisville, to the Red Sox for infielder Dick Schofield. Campbell's entire big-league career encompassed 13 at-bats with the Cards in '70. Schofield, who would embark on his third stint in St. Louis, was at the end of the line.

202

| November 30 | The Cards trade infielder Jerry DaVanon to the Orioles for pitcher Moe Drabowsky. Drabowsky, who was most remembered as the hero of the '66 World Series, had reached the end of a long career. DaVanon returned to the Cards and remained relegated to a backup role. |

1971

| January 29 | The Cards trade pitcher Nelson Briles and outfielder Vic Davalillo to the Pirates for outfielder Matty Alou and pitcher George Brunet. Alou had a great season in '71 for the Cards, batting .315 while alternating between first base and the outfield. Briles became one of the Pirates' most dependable pitchers as a reliever and spot starter. Davalillo was an excellent pinch-hitter and reserve outfielder. |

| February 2 | The Cards trade pitcher Fred Reahm, who is assigned from Tulsa to Evansville, to the Brewers for first baseman-outfielder Bob Burda. Burda played in 65 games for the Cards in '71, batting .296. |

| May 10 | The Cards release pitcher George Brunet. He became a star in the Mexican leagues. |

| June 11 | The Cards trade outfielder Leron Lee and pitcher Fred Norman, the latter on the Tulsa roster, to the Padres for pitcher Al Santorini. Lee had been one of St. Louis' hottest prospects but never panned out. Norman later had several good years with the Reds. Santorini compiled an unimpressive 8–13 record during three seasons in St. Louis. |

| June 15 | The Cards trade pitcher Mike Torrez to Winnipeg, the Expos' affiliate, for pitcher Bob Reynolds. Torrez became a 20-game winner with the Orioles in '75. Reynolds appeared in just four games for the Redbirds. |

| June 25 | The Cards purchase pitcher Daryl Patterson from the A's. They returned him Oct. 21. |

| July 15 | The Cards purchase Dennis Higgins from the Indians and assign him to Tulsa. |

| July 29 | The Cards trade outfielder Jose Cardenal, infielder Dick Schofield, the latter on the Tulsa roster, and pitcher Bob Reynolds to the Brewers for infielder Ted Kubiak and pitcher Charlie Loseth, the latter on the Raleigh-Durham roster. The speedy Cardenal later became a fine outfielder with the Cubs. The rest of the players in the trade amounted to nothing. |

| September 1 | The Cards get pitcher Stan Williams from the Twins for two players to be named. The Cards assigned outfielder Dan Ford from Arkansas to Portland, and catcher-outfielder Fred Rico from Tulsa to Portland Sept. 14 to complete the deal. Williams appeared in 10 games with the Cards. Ford became a starter in the Minnesota outfielder for several seasons. |

| September 13 | The Cards purchase pitcher Mike Jackson from the Royals' Omaha affiliate. They returned him to Omaha Oct. 18. |

| October 18 | The Cards trade first baseman-outfielder Jim Beauchamp, pitcher Charles G. Taylor, pitcher Harry Parker, and infielder Chip Coul- |

203

ter, the latter two assigned to Tidewater by the Mets, to the Mets for outfielder-first baseman Art Shamsky and pitchers Jim Bibby, Rich Folkers, and Charlie Hudson, the last-named on the Memphis roster. Bibby had not yet learned to harness his blazing fastball, but once he did he became an overpowering pitcher. Beauchamp played two seasons with the Mets. Taylor had a great season in Montreal. Parker had a couple of fair seasons with the Mets in relief before returning to St. Louis. Shamsky never played in a Redbird uniform. Folkers was ineffective as a reliever.

November 3   The Cards trade catcher Bob Stinson to the Astros for infielder Orlando Marty Martinez. Hardly a memorable trade for either club.

The Cards trade shortstop Ted Kubiak to the Rangers for pitcher Joe Grzenda. Kubiak failed to last the '72 season with the Rangers. Grzenda's ERA skyrocketed to 5.66 in 30 games with the Cards during '72.

December 9   The Cards sign first baseman Donn Clendenon, released by the Mets. The curtain had just about fallen on Clendenon's fine career.

1972

January 4   The Cards sign pitcher Jim Maloney, released by the Angels. He retired.

February 25   The Cards trade pitcher Steve Carlton to the Phillies for pitcher Rick Wise. The Cards traded Carlton when he asked for the "exorbitant" contract of $75,000 per year. An insider close to the Cards said the trade cost the team at least two pennants. Carlton was one of the National League's premier pitchers through the decade. Wise, a good pitcher in his own right but hardly in Carlton's class, had consecutive 16-victory seasons with the Cards.

March 20   The Cards trade outfielder-first baseman Bob Burda to the Red Sox for first baseman Mike Fiore, the latter assigned to Tulsa. Nothing for nothing is still nothing.

March 24   The Cards trade second baseman Julian Javier to the Reds for pitcher Tony Cloninger. Both players had passed their primes.

March 26   The Cards trade pitcher Frank Linzy to Milwaukee for pitcher Rich Stonum, the latter assigned from Evansville to Arkansas. Linzy had two mildly successful seasons with the Brewers. Stonum never pitched in the big leagues.

April 9   The Cards release pitchers Jim Maloney and Stan Williams.

April 14   The Cards release first baseman-outfielder Art Shamsky; the Cubs sign him the same day.

April 15   The Cards trade pitcher Jerry Reuss to the Astros for pitchers Scipio Spinks and Lance Clemons. The Cards gave up one of their best pitchers for basically nothing. Spinks tore up his knee and never came back.

May 15   The Cards trade pitcher Don Shaw to the A's for infielder Dwain Anderson. Shaw appeared in only three games for Oakland and retired. Anderson played parts of two seasons in St. Louis.

204

May 18	The Cards trade infielder Orlando "Marty" Martinez to the A's for outfielder Brandt Alyea. Martinez hit .125 in 22 games with the A's. Alyea batted .158 in 13 games with the Cards.
May 19	The Cards trade first baseman Joe Hague to the Reds for outfielder Bernie Carbo. Hague played sparingly with Cincinnati and retired after '73. Carbo had one good season with the Cards, hitting .286 in '73.
June 7	The Cards purchase Diego Segui from the A's. He pitched surprisingly well as a reliever in St. Louis through '73.
June 16	The Cards purchase pitcher John Cumberland from the Giants. He floundered badly during his brief stay in St. Louis.
June 20	The Cards trade first baseman Mike Fiore and pitcher Bob Chlupsa, the latter transferred from Tulsa to Hawaii, to the Padres for infielder Rafael Robles, who is then assigned to Tulsa.
July 3	The Padres return first baseman Mike Fiore to the Cards, who assign him to Tulsa.
July 26	The Cards release pitcher Tony Cloninger.
July 27	The Cards return Brandt Alyea to the A's, who assign him to Tulsa.
August 7	The Cards release first baseman Donn Clendenon.
August 15	The Cards release pitcher Moe Drabowsky. He was signed by the White Sox and released Oct. 6.
August 27	The Cards trade outfielder Matty Alou to the A's for outfielder Bill Voss and pitcher Steve Easton, the latter assigned from Birmingham to Arkansas. The deal was a follow-up to the purchase of Diego Segui by the Cards June 7. Alou batted .281 in 32 games with Oakland. Voss hit .267 in 11 games with St. Louis.
August 30	The Cards trade shortstop Dal Maxvill to the A's for infielder Joe Lindsey, assigned from Birmingham to Arkansas, and a player to be named. A's sent catcher Gene Dusan to Cards October 27 to complete deal. Maxvill lasted through the '75 season, but true to form kept an anemic batting average.
September 1	The Cards sell pitcher Dennis Higgins to the Padres.
September 18	The Cards sell pitcher Lowell Palmer to the Indians.
October 26	The Cards trade pitchers Rudy Arroyo and Greg Millikan, the latter transferred from Arkansas to Albuquerque, to the Dodgers for Larry Hisle, who is on the Albuquerque roster. The trade could have been a great one for the Cards, had they only hung on to Hisle. (See Nov. 29.)
October 27	The Cards release catcher Jerry McNertney.
November 6	The Cards trade outfielder Jorge Roque to the Expos for catcher Tim McCarver. Roque batted 61 times for the Expos in '73 and disappeared. McCarver became a good backup for Ted Simmons at catcher.
November 29	The Cards trade outfielder Larry Hisle and pitcher John Cumberland, the latter assigned from Arkansas to Tacoma, to the Twins for pitcher Wayne Granger. Hisle became a superstar with the

Twins, Granger failed to last the following season with the Redbirds and Cumberland won one game with St. Louis.

1973

January 24   The Cards trade a player to be named to the Red Sox for pitcher Mike Nagy. St. Louis assigned pitcher Lance Clemons to the Red Sox Pawtucket affiliate March 29 to complete the deal.

February 1   The Cards trade pitcher Charlie Hudson to the Rangers for a player to be named. The Rangers satisfied their obligation March 31 in the deal which gave the Redbirds pitcher Mike Thompson.

March 31   The Cards trade pitcher Mike Nagy to the Rangers for pitcher Mike Thompson. Nagy was assigned to Spokane, Thompson to Tulsa.

April 3   The Cards purchase pitcher Alan Foster from the Angels. He had a decent year in '73 for St. Louis, winning 13 games, and then dropped off.

May 8   The Cards trade pitcher Al Santorini, who is assigned to Omaha by Kansas City, to the Royals for pitcher Tom Murphy. Santorini never pitched again in the majors. Murphy went 3-7 with a 3.76 ERA with St. Louis in '73.

June 6   The Cards trade pitcher Jim Bibby to the Rangers for pitcher Mike Nagy and catcher John Wockenfuss, both assigned from Spokane to Tulsa. Bibby matured into a fine pitcher later with the Pirates. Nagy, who had one good year in the majors with Boston in '69, worked in 9 games with the Redbirds. Wockenfuss never played for St. Louis, but had some good seasons with Detroit.

June 7   The Cards trade infielder Dwain Anderson to the Padres for second baseman Dave Campbell. Both players spent the remainders of their short careers trying to hit their weights.

June 8   The Cards trade shortstop Ray Busse to the Astros for infielder Stan Papi, who is assigned to Tulsa. Busse had a .148 average in three big-league seasons. Papi appeared in eight games with St. Louis in '74.

June 15   The Cards purchase pitcher Orlando Pena from the Orioles. He pitched well in parts of two seasons with the Redbirds.

July 16   The Cards trade pitcher Don Durham to the Rangers for pitcher Jim Kremmel, who is assigned to Tulsa. Durham went 0-4 with the Redbirds in '73. Kremmel pitched briefly with the Rangers and White Sox.

July 27   The Cards trade infielder Ed Crosby and catcher Gene Dusan, the latter assigned to Indianapolis by the Reds, to the Reds for pitcher Ed Sprague and a player to be named. First baseman-outfielder Roe Skidmore was assigned from Indianapolis to Tulsa Sept. 30 to complete the deal. Crosby was a very mediocre infielder. Dusan never made it. Skidmore's career consisted of one at-bat with the Cubs. Sprague failed to register a decision in eight games with the Cards.

August 7   The Cards trade pitcher Wayne Granger to the Yankees for two players to be named. The deal was completed Sept. 12 when the

Yankees assigned pitcher Ken Crosby from Syracuse to Tulsa and gave the Cards cash in lieu of another player. Granger was over the hill. Crosby never made it in St. Louis.

August 18   The Cards trade infielder Dave Campbell and cash to the Astros for outfielder Tommie Agee. Agee, a fine outfielder with the Miracle Mets during his prime, batted .177 in 26 games with the Cards that year and retired. Campbell was no loss.

August 29   The Cards purchase Eddie Fisher from the White Sox. The aging reliever appeared in six games and called it quits.

September 1   The Cards purchase Lew Krausse Jr. and catcher Larry Haney from Tucson, an Oakland affiliate. Krausse pitched in one game, and Haney caught in 10.

September 4   The Cards sell pitcher Ed Sprague, who is on the Tulsa roster, to the Brewers. Sprague got off to a fast start with the Brewers the following season, but a serious knee injury finished him.

September 6   The Cards purchase Matty Alou from the Yankees. No gain.

October 23   The Cards sell shortstop Mick Kelleher to the Astros. He was long on desire, short on talent.

October 25   The Cards sell Matty Alou to the Padres.

October 26   The Cards trade pitcher Jim Kremmel, who is on the Tulsa roster, to the White Sox for pitcher Dennis O'Toole, who is assigned from Iowa to Tulsa.

The Cards release pitchers Eddie Fisher and Lew Krausse Jr. The Cards trade pitcher Rick Wise and outfielder Bernie Carbo to the Red Sox for outfielder Reggie Smith and pitcher Ken Tatum. The power-hitting Smith had two excellent seasons in St. Louis before dropping off in '76. Tatum never pitched for the Cards. Wise helped lead the Red Sox to the pennant in '75. Carbo never became an established player.

The Cards trade outfielder Cirilio Cruz to the Rangers for pitcher Sonny Siebert. Cruz' major-league career consisted of two at-bats. Siebert, who had been a good pitcher with the Indians and Red Sox during his prime, produced an 8-8 record in one season with the Redbirds.

December 5   The Cards trade outfielder Tommie Agee to the Dodgers for pitcher Pete Richert. Both players had long since seen their better days.

December 6   The Cards trade pitcher John Andrews to the Angels for catcher Jeff Torborg. Neither player appeared in the majors again.

December 7   The Cards trade pitchers Reggie Cleveland and Diego Segui and infielder Terry Hughes to the Red Sox for pitchers Lynn McGlothen, John Curtis, and Mike Garman. Cleveland became a key man on the Boston pitching staff for the next four years. Segui struggled in the Boston bull pen. Hughes had limited playing time with the Red Sox in '74, which was his last big-league season. McGlothen pitched well in streaks for the Cards in three years. Curtis had three losing seasons in St. Louis as a starter and long relief man. Garman had two good seasons in the St. Louis bull pen.

January 9	The Cards purchase outfielder Jay Johnstone from the A's Tucson affiliate. He was released March 26.
March 23	The Cards trade Scipio Spinks to the Cubs for first baseman-outfielder Jim Hickman. Spinks was assigned to Wichita by the Cubs. Hickman was washed up.
March 25	The Cards release catcher Jeff Torborg.
March 26	The Cards sell catcher Larry Haney to the A's.
March 29	The Cards purchase infielder Ed Crosby from the Phillies, and assign him to Tulsa.
April 27	The Cards trade pitcher Ken Tatum to the White Sox for infielder Luis Alvarado. Tatum pitched in only 10 games for Chicago in '74. Alvarado batted .139 in 17 games with the Cards.
June 1	The Cards trade infielders Luis Alvarado and Ed Crosby, who is on the Tulsa roster, to the Indians for shortstop Jack Heidemann. Heidemann batted .271 in 47 games with St. Louis during a brief stay. Alvarado and Crosby were reserves in Cleveland.
June 21	The Cards sell pitcher Pete Richert to the Phillies.
July 16	The Cards release first baseman-outfielder Jim Hickman.
July 31	The Cards trade infielder Bob Heise, who is on the Tulsa roster, to the Angels for a player to be named. The Angels assigned out-fielder Doug Howard to Tulsa Oct. 7 to complete the deal. Another forgettable trade.
August 5	The Cards purchase outfielder Richie Scheinblum from the Roy-als and assign him to Tulsa. He concluded his big-league career by playing in six games with St. Louis.
August 11	The Cards sign pitcher Steve Barber, released by the Giants, and assign him to Tulsa. His arm was shot and he retired.
August 12	The Cards purchase catcher Rick Billings from the Rangers and assign him to Tulsa. He batted three times with the Redbirds.
August 15	The Cards trade pitcher Ron Selak, who is assigned from Arkan-sas to Columbus, and a player to be named later, to the Astros for pitcher Claude Osteen. The Cards assigned pitcher Dan Larsen to Denver Oct. 14 to complete the deal. Osteen was a solid starter on the Dodger staff during his heyday, but was over the hill by this time.
September 1	The Cards sell Tim McCarver to the Red Sox. He lasted several more years as a steady reserve with Boston and Philadelphia.
September 5	The Cards release pitcher Orlando Pena, who is signed by the Angels. In a related deal, pitcher Rich Hand was assigned to Tulsa by the Angels Oct. 15.
	The Cards purchase infielder Ron Hunt from the Expos. He had been an All-Star second baseman during his prime, but no longer had much to contribute.
September 10	The Cards sell pitcher Mike Thompson to the Braves. In a related deal, the Cards bought pitcher Barry Lersch from Richmond Sept.

14. Thompson had one lousy year with the Braves. Lersch never played for the Redbirds.

October 13	The Cards trade first baseman-third baseman Joe Torre to the Mets for pitchers Ray Sadecki and Tommy Moore, the latter on the Tidewater roster. Torre and Sadecki were about through. Moore never left a mark.
October 14	The Cards trade catcher Marc Hill to the Giants for pitcher Elias Sosa and catcher Ken Rudolph. Hill and Rudolph were both reserve catchers of average talent. Sosa blossomed into a fine reliever, but with the Dodgers. The Cards trade second baseman Tom Heintzelman, who is on the Tulsa roster, to the Giants for pitcher Jim Willoughby, who is assigned from Phoenix to Tulsa.
October 24	The Cards sell outfielder Jose Cruz to the Astros. He became a fine outfielder in Houston, having an outstanding year in '78 when he batted .315.
November 18	In a three-club deal, the Padres trade first baseman Nate Colbert to the Tigers for shortstop Ed Brinkman, pitcher Bob Strampe, and outfielder Dick Sharon; the Padres then trade Brinkman and a player to be named later to the Cards for pitchers Alan Foster, Rick Folkers, and Sonny Siebert. The deal was completed Dec. 12 when the Padres assigned catcher Dan Breeden from Hawaii to the Cards' Tulsa affiliate. The Redbirds basically gave up three pitchers of little value to obtain Brinkman, who was supposed to be a shortstop who could handle the AstroTurf at Busch Memorial Stadium. But he played only 28 games in St. Louis and was shipped out.
December 2	The Cards purchase pitcher Bill Parsons from the A's. He never threw again in the majors.
December 6	The Cards trade infielder Rudy Kinard and first baseman Ed Kurpiel, the latter assigned from Tulsa to Memphis, to the Expos for first baseman-outfielder Ron Fairly. Fairly proved a valuable addition, batting .301 in '75.
December 11	The Cards trade infielder Jack Heidemann and outfielder Mike Vail, the latter assigned from Tulsa to Tidewater, to the Mets for infielder Teddy Martinez. Heidemann's limited talent kept him on the bench with most teams. Vail occasionally hit for power but, like Heidemann, seldom found himself in anyone's starting lineup. Martinez hit .190 in 16 games with the Cards.
December 13	The Cards purchase shortstop Mick Kelleher from the Astros and assign him to Tulsa. He played in seven games with the Redbirds the second time around.

1975

March 27	The Cards release infielder Ron Hunt. He retired.
March 29	The Cards trade outfielder Danny Godby, who is assigned to Pawtucket, to the Red Sox for first baseman Danny Cater. Fodby's career in the big leagues consisted of 13 at-bats with the Cards in '74. Cater played in 29 games with the Redbirds, batting .229.

April 4	The Cards purchase shortstop Mario Guerrero from the Red Sox and assign him to Tulsa. The Red Sox acquired pitcher Jim Willoughby from Tulsa July 4 to complete the deal. Guerrero played one season in St. Louis, batting a paltry .239. Willoughby spent three seasons in the Boston bullpen, leading all A.L. relievers in losses (12) in '76.
	The Cards sell pitcher Ray Bare to the Tigers. He went 8–13 that season with Detroit.
April 11	The Cards release pitcher Claude Osteen, who is signed by the White Sox. He compiled a 7–16 record in '75 with Chicago and retired.
May 9	The Cards trade outfielder Larry Herndon and pitcher Luis Gonzalez to the Giants, who assign them to Phoenix, for pitcher Ron Bryant. Herndon became a fair outfielder with San Francisco. Gonzalez never reached the big leagues. Bryant, who had a super year in '73 by winning 24 games with the Giants, pitched only nine innings for the Redbirds.
May 18	The Cards trade infielder Ted Martinez to the A's for pitcher Steve Stainland, who is assigned from Modesto to St. Petersburg, and a player to be named. Pitcher Mike Barlow was assigned from Tucson to Tulsa May 23 to complete the deal. Neither side derived anything of value from this deal.
May 21	The Cards sign outfielder Don Hahn, released by the Phillies. He batted .125 in seven games with the Redbirds.
May 28	The Cards trade pitchers Elias Sosa and Ray Sadecki to the Braves for pitcher Ron Reed and a player to be named. The Braves assigned outfielder Wayne Nordhagen from Richmond to Tulsa June 2 to complete the deal. The Cards should have held on to Sosa, who had a fine 1.97 ERA in 64 innings with Los Angeles during '77. Sadecki bounced around the majors before ending his career after the '77 season. Reed pitched less than one season with the Redbirds. Nordhagen never played with the Cards, but later became a fine reserve with the White Sox.
June 4	The Cards trade shortstop Ed Brinkman and pitcher Tommy Moore, the latter assigned to Spokane, to the Rangers for outfielder Willie Davis. Davis hit .291 in 98 games with the Cards. Brinkman retired following the season. Moore was a throw-in.
June 13	The Cards purchase pitcher Mike Wallace from the Yankees and assign him to Tulsa.
June 24	The Cards sell outfielder Don Hahn to the Padres.
June 30	The Cards trade cash and a player to be named to the White Sox for outfielder Buddy Bradford. The Cards assigned pitcher Bill Parsons from Tulsa to Denver July 7 to complete the deal. Bradford batted .272 in 50 games with St. Louis.
July 25	The Cards trade outfielder Jim Dwyer, on the Tulsa roster, to the Expos for infielder Larry Lintz. Dwyer had a terrible year in '76 with the Expos and Mets, batting .181. Lintz hit .278 in 27 games with the Redbirds.
July 31	The Cards release pitcher Ron Bryant.

August 1	The Cards purchase pitcher Lloyd Allen from the White Sox and assign him to Tulsa.
August 4	The Cards purchase pitcher Harry Parker from the Mets. He posted one losing decision in his second stint with the St. Louis.
September 19	The Cards sign pitcher John Sielick, released by the Giants, and assign him to Tulsa.
September 29	The Cards release catcher Rich Billings.
September 30	The Cards trade pitcher Mike Barlow to the Astros for outfielder Mike Easler. Barlow appeared in just 16 games with the Astros during '76. Easler never made it with St. Louis, but went on to stardom at Pittsburgh.
	The Cards assign first baseman Doug Howard to Oklahoma City, an Indian affiliate, to complete a deal in which Tulsa acquired shortstop Luis Alvarado from Oklahoma City.
October 20	The Cards trade outfielder Willie Davis to the Padres for outfielder Dick Sharon, who is assigned to Tulsa. Davis played one more season. Sharon never played in the majors again.
October 28	The Cards trade pitcher Mike Garman and a player to be named to the Cubs for shortstop Don Kessinger. Garman later had a good year with the Dodgers in '77. Kessinger remained a steady player, although unintimidating at the plate.
	The Cards trade infielder Larry Lintz to the A's for outfielder Charlie Chant.
December 8	The Cards trade third baseman Ken Reitz to the Giants for pitcher Pete Falcone. Reitz hit .267 in one season with San Francisco. Falcone went through three losing seasons in St. Louis.
December 9	The Cards trade pitcher Ron Reed to the Phillies for outfielder Mike Anderson. Reed helped pitch Philadelphia to three divisional crowns. Anderson, a fine defensive outfielder, hit .291 and .221 in two seasons with the Birds.
December 12	The Cards trade outfielder Buddy Bradford and pitcher Greg Terlecky to the White Sox for infielder Lee Richard. Bradford and Richard had poor years with their new teams during '76 and vanished. Terlecky never threw in the majors again.
December 22	The Cards trade shortstop Mick Kelleher to the Cubs for second baseman Vic Harris. Harris had been a hot prospect who never lived up to his advance billing. Kelleher became a reserve in Chicago.

1976

January 9	The Cards purchase infielder Terry Hughes from Rhode Island Red Sox farm and assign him to Tulsa. He never played in the big leagues again.
January 12	The Cards trade outfielder Dick Sharon, who is on the Tulsa roster, to the Angels for pitcher Bill Rothan. Rothan was assigned to Arkansas, Sharon to Salt Lake City.

211

February 3	The Cards purchase pitcher Tom Walker, who is on the Evansville roster, from the Tigers and assign him to Tulsa. Walker pitched in 19 games for St. Louis in '76 with an ERA of 4.12.
March 2	The Cards trade second baseman Ted Sizemore to the Dodgers for outfielder Willie Crawford. Crawford had a good year in '76, batting .304 with the Redbirds. Sizemore played for several more seasons, having his best effort in '77 when he batted .281 with the Phillies.
April 2	The Cards purchase pitcher Lerrin LaGrow from the Tigers and assign him to Tulsa. He pitched in only eight games with the Redbirds.
April 5	The Cards assign shortstop Bob Hrapmann from Arkansas to the Cubs' Midland farm club to complete the Don Kessinger deal.
April 7	The Cards trade pitcher Harry Parker to the Indians for pitcher Roric Harrison. Parker was assigned to Toledo, Harrison to Tulsa.
April 8	The Cards trade pitchers Ken Reynolds and Bob Stewart, the latter on the Arkansas roster, to San Diego for pitcher Dan Frisella. Reynolds was assigned to Hawaii. Frisella didn't last the season with St. Louis.
May 19	The Cards trade outfielder Luis Melendez to the Padres for pitcher Bill Grief. Melendez was another "can't miss" prospect, who somehow managed to fail. Grief went 1–5 in 47 games with St. Louis in '76.
May 28	The Cards sell pitcher Cardell Camper to the Indians, who assign him to Toledo.
May 29	The Cards trade infielder Mario Guerrero, who is on the Tulsa roster, to the Angels for catcher Ed Jordan, who is assigned from El Paso to Arkansas, and a player to be named. The Angels assigned first baseman-outfielder Ed Kurpiel from Salt Lake City to Tulsa to complete the deal.
June 15	The Cards trade outfielder Reggie Smith to the Dodgers for catcher-outfielder Joe Ferguson and infielder Freddie Tisdale, the latter assigned from Lodi to St. Petersburg. A slow start in '76 diminished Smith's value, but he quickly adapted to his new surroundings and had several fine seasons with the Dodgers. Ferguson, meanwhile, had one disastrous season in St. Louis.
June 23	The Cards trade pitcher Dan Frisella to the Brewers for a player to be named. Outfielder Sam Mejias was assigned from Tulsa June 7 to complete the deal. Frisella was killed before the '77 season in a recreational vehicle accident. Mejias batted .143 in 18 games with the Redbirds.
September 3	The Cards trade outfielder Mike Easler, who is on the Tulsa roster, to the Angels for infielder Ron Farkas. Farkas was assigned from El Paso to Tulsa Sept. 7. Easler later became a feared hitter with the Pirates. Farkas never made it.
September 14	The Cards sell first baseman-outfielder Ron Fairly to the A's. He found the A.L. more conducive with its designated hitter rule.
October 20	The Cards trade outfielder Willie Crawford, infielder-outfielder

212

Vic Harris, and pitcher John Curtis to the Giants for pitchers John D'Acquisto and Mike Caldwell and catcher Dave Rader. Crawford's average dipped from .304 in '76 to .216 in '77. Harris was a constant disappointment throughout his career. Curtis posted a horrendous ERA of 5.49 with the Giants in '77. D'Acquisto failed to register a decision in three games with St. Louis. Caldwell never pitched for the Cards. Rader lasted one season without distinction.

October 22   The Cards trade pitcher Mike Wallace to the Rangers for pitcher Johnny Ike Sutton, who is assigned from Sacramento to New Orleans.

November 6   The Cards trade pitchers Bill Greif and Angel Torres and outfielder Sam Mejias to the Expos for pitcher Steve Dunning, infielder Pat Scanlon, and outfielder Tony Scott, the last-named from the Denver roster. The deal paid dividends for the Cards as Scott blossomed into a versatile outfielder with good defensive ability. Greif and Torres had no subsequent big-league days. Dunning, Mejias, and Scanlon played only briefly.

The Cards release pitcher Lloyd Allen and infielder Bee Bee Richard.

The Cards sell infielder Luis Alvarado to the Tigers.

November 23   The Cards trade catcher-outfielder Joe Ferguson and outfielder Bobby Detherage, the latter assigned to Memphis, to the Astros for pitcher Larry Dierker and infielder Jerry DaVanon. Ferguson had years left, but none of them was outstanding. Dierker was at the end of the line. DaVanon played in nine games with the Cards in '77, his final season.

December 9   The Cards trade first baseman-outfielder Ed Kurpiel, on the New Orleans roster, to the Mets for outfielder Leon Brown and first baseman Brock Pemberton, both on the Tidewater roster. Kurpiel was assigned to Tidewater, Brown and Pemberton to New Orleans.

December 10   The Cards trade pitcher Lynn McGlothen to the Giants for third baseman Ken Reitz. Reitz was needed back at St. Louis after rookie Heity Cruz failed miserably at third. McGlothen's effectiveness was reduced by arm trouble.

1977

February 28   The Cards trade pitcher Mark Covert to the Cubs for pitcher Buddy Schultz. Schultz was assigned to New Orleans, Covert to Wichita.

March 23   The Cards trade pitcher Lerrin LaGrow to the White Sox for pitcher Clay Carroll. LaGrow had an outstanding year in '77, when he compiled a 7-3 record with a 2.45 ERA in 99 innings. Carroll had a 4-2 mark in 51 games with the Redbirds.

March 24   The Cards release pitcher Tom Walker.

March 25   The Cards purchase infielder Tommy Sandt from the A's and assign him to New Orleans.

March 28   The Cards trade pitcher Bill Caudill to the Reds for outfielder-

213

third baseman Joel Youngblood. Caudill has shown potential, but not harnessed his fastball. Youngblood hit .185 in 25 games with St. Louis.

March 29   The Cards release pitcher Roric Harrison.

The Cards trade pitcher Mike Caldwell to the Reds for pitcher Pat Darcy, who is assigned to New Orleans. Caldwell posted a 22-9 record with a 2.36 ERA the next season with Milwaukee. Darcy never made it with the Redbirds.

March 30   The Cards trade infielder Doug Clarey to the Mets for outfielder Benny Ayala. Ayala was assigned to New Orleans, Clarey to Tidewater.

March 31   The Cards' New Orleans farm club sells catcher Ken Rudolph to the Giants.

May 11   The Cards release infielder Jerry DaVanon.

May 17   The Cards trade pitcher John D'Acquisto and infielder Pat Scanlon, the latter transferred from New Orleans to Hawaii, to the Padres for pitcher Butch Metzger. D'Acquisto has been a losing pitcher throughout his career. Scanlon was an obscure infielder. Metzger went 4-2 in 58 games with the Redbirds in '77.

June 15   The Cards trade pitcher Doug Capilla to the Reds for pitcher Rawly Eastwick. Eastwick went 3-7 during the remainder of the season with the Redbirds and opted for free agency. Capilla didn't appear in the majors until '79.

The Cards trade outfielder Arnold "Bake" McBride and pitcher Steve Waterbury to the Phillies for pitcher Tom Underwood, first baseman Dane Iorg, and outfielder Rick Bosetti. McBride's .339 average helped carry the Phillies to the divisional championship in '77 and he has remained a good outfielder. Underwood had a 6-9 record the rest of the way with the Cards. Iorg had his busiest season in '80, batting .303 in 104 games and followed with a .327 percentage in 75 games during '81. Bosetti batted .232 in a short engagement with the Redbirds in '77.

The Cards trade infielder Joel Youngblood to the Mets for infielder Mike Phillips. Phillips settled into a reserve role with the Redbirds. Youngblood has blossomed into an outstanding outfielder with the Mets, batting .350 during the abbreviated '81 season.

August 20   The Cards trade shortstop Don Kessinger to the White Sox for a player to be named. The aging Kessinger became a player-manager in Chicago. (See next entry for player named later.)

August 31   The Cards trade pitcher Clay Carroll to the White Sox for a player to be named later. This deal and the deal of August 20 in which the Cardinals sent infielder Don Kessinger to the White Sox were completed with the transfer of outfielder Nyls Nyman to the Cards' New Orleans affiliate, Sept. 2, the transfer of pitcher Steve Stainland to the White Sox's Iowa affiliate Aug. 20, and the release of pitchers Dave Hamilton and Silvio Martinez by the White Sox to the Cards Nov. 28. Carroll, who was on his last legs, had a 1-3 record with the Sox during the final part of the season. Martinez became the most valuable property in the trade, having

214

his best year in '79 when he compiled a 15–9 mark for the Redbirds.

October 25	Purchase pitcher Frank Riccelli from Giants.
October 26	The Cards purchase infielder Aurelio Lopez from the Mexico City Reds.
December 6	The Cards trade pitchers Tom Underwood and Victor Cruz, the latter on the Arkansas roster, to the Blue Jays for pitcher Pete Vuckovich and a player to be named later. Cruz was assigned to Syracuse. Outfielder John Scott was assigned to the Cards Dec. 16 to complete the deal. While Underwood suffered through two losing seasons in Toronto, Vuckovich developed into a steady hurler for the Cards.
December 8	The Cards trade catcher Dave Rader and outfielder-third baseman Hector Cruz to the Cubs for outfielder Jerry Morales, catcher Steve Swisher, and a player to be named later. Cruz, a bright prospect, never bore fruit at third base for the Cards. Morales, who underwent knee surgery before the season, hit a disappointing .239 with the Redbirds in '78. The Cubs hoped that Rader would fill a hole at catcher, but he hit a weak .203 the next season in a Chicago uniform. Swisher became a fair backup with St. Louis for a few seasons.

The Cards trade pitcher Al Hrabosky to the Royals for pitcher Mark Littell and catcher John (Buck) Martinez; the Cardinals then trade Martinez to the Brewers for pitcher George Frazier, who is assigned from Spokane to New Orleans. Hrabosky dropped off after an outstanding season as a reliever with the Redbirds in '75. He went on to have a couple of decent seasons with the Royals. Littell had an excellent '79 season with the Cards, posting the lowest ERA (2.20) on the staff, before soreness in his pitching elbow reduced his effectiveness. Martinez was a defensive specialist with a poor bat. Frazier bounced between the Springfield minor-league club and the parent club during three seasons with St. Louis.

1978

February 2	The Cards sign catcher Ken Rudolph, a free agent released by the Orioles Jan. 6, and assign him to Springfield. He never made the team.
March 15	The Cards sell outfielder Rick Bosetti to the Blue Jays. He became a regular outfielder with Toronto.
March 28	The Cards release pitcher Larry Dierker.
April 5	The Cards sell pitcher Butch Metzger to the Mets.
May 26	The Cards trade pitcher Eric Rasmussen to the Padres for outfielder George Hendrick. Rasmussen was never much of a factor after winning 12 games the rest of the way with San Diego. Hendrick made the trade a steal for the Cards by hitting better than .300 in '79 and '80.

The Cards release infielder Gary Sutherland.

215

May 28	The Cards sell pitcher Dave Hamilton to the Pirates.
June 8	The Cards trade pitcher Frank Riccelli to the Astros for outfielder Bob Coluccio. Riccelli was assigned to Charleston.
June 15	The Cards assign outfielder Jim Dwyer to the Giants to complete the deal Oct. 25, 1977 in which the Cards acquired pitcher Frank Riccelli. Dwyer eventually spent a couple of seasons as a backup with the Red Sox.
June 23	The Cards purchase pitcher Roy Thomas from the Astros.
June 26	The Cards trade a player to be named to the Mariners for infielder Jose Baez. Baez was assigned to Springfield. The Mariners purchased outfielder Mike Potter to complete the deal Oct. 27.
July 18	The Cards trade catcher John Tamargo to the Giants for a player to be named. The Giants assigned pitcher Rob Dressler from Phoenix to Springfield to complete the deal July 24.
July 21	The Cards buy infielder Wayne Garrett from the Expos.
October 2	The Cards trade outfielder Bob Coluccio to the Mets for pitcher Paul Siebert, who is assigned to Springfield.
October 23	The Cards trade outfielder John Scott to the White Sox for pitcher Jim Willoughby. Neither player made it with his new team.
December 4	The Cards trade outfielder Jerry Morales and pitcher Aurelio Lopez to the Tigers for pitchers Bob Sykes and Jack Murphy. Morales never hit well after leaving the Cards, but Lopez developed into a fine reliever. Sykes underwent shoulder surgery in '79 and didn't contribute much with the Cards through '81. Murphy never reached the big leagues.
December 5	The Cards trade pitcher Pete Falcone to the Mets for outfielder Tom Grieve and pitcher Kim Seaman. Falcone suffered through two losing seasons with New York before righting himself with a 5-3 record and a 2.56 ERA during '81. Grieve hit .200 in one season with St. Louis. Seaman pitched only briefly with the big-league club in St. Louis.

1979

January 16	The Cards acquire pitcher Darold Knowles, who was formerly with the Expos, as their first re-entry signing. He went 2-5 with a 4.04 ERA in '79 and then appeared in two games the following season.
February 15	The Cards release infielder Jose Baez.
February 19	The Cards sign pitcher Will McEnaney as a free agent and assign him to Arkansas. He threw in just seven games with the Redbirds.
March 2	The Cards sign outfielder Bernie Carbo, who was formerly with the Indians, after selecting him in the re-entry draft. Carbo hit .281 for the Redbirds that year before dropping sharply to .182 in '80.
March 30	The Cards release pitcher Jim Willoughby.
April 5	The Cards release pitcher Paul Siebert.
May 9	The Cards release outfielder Tom Grieve.

October 17	The Cards trade second baseman Mike Tyson to the Cubs for pitcher Donnie Moore. The Cards no longer had any use for Tyson with Ken Oberkfell at second base. Moore went 1-1 with the Redbirds in '80.
November 9	The Cards sell pitcher Dan O'Brien to the Mariners.
December 7	The Cards trade outfielder Jerry Mumphrey and pitcher John Denny to the Indians for outfielder Bobby Bonds. Mumphrey hit .298 in '80 and followed up with a .307 clip for the Yankees in '81. Denny came on strong in '81, compiling a 10-6 mark with a 3.14 ERA. The much-traveled Bonds batted a miserable .203 in '80 with the Redbirds.

1980

March 13	The Cards sign pitcher Don Hood, a re-entry free agent, formerly with the Yankees. Hood had a 4-6 record and a 3.40 ERA in 33 games that season.
March 31	The Cards release pitchers Will McEnaney and Tom Bruno.
April 2	The Cards release outfielder-first baseman Roger Freed. He was signed by the Phillies April 7.
April 30	The Cards sign pitcher Pedro Borbon, a free agent; purchase pitcher Jim Kaat from the Yankees; and release pitcher Darold Knowles. Borbon pitched in only 10 games for the Cards, who were desperate for relief help at the time. The ageless Kaat pitched surprisingly well through '81.
May 27	The Cards release pitcher Pedro Borbon and outfielder Bernie Carbo.
June 2	The Cards trade outfielder Jim Lentine, who is on the Springfield roster, to the Tigers for pitcher John Martin and outfielder Al Green, both assigned from Evansville to Springfield. Martin went 2-3 in '80 and 8-5 in '81 with the Redbirds. Lentine hit .261 with the Tigers in '80.
October 25	The Cards release pitcher Don Hood.
December 7	The Cards sign catcher Darrell Porter, a re-entry free agent formerly with the Royals. Porter hit a disappointing .224 with the Cards in '81.
December 8	The Padres trade pitchers Rollie Fingers and Bob Shirley, catcher-first baseman Gene Tenace, and a player to be named to the Cardinals for catchers Terry Kennedy and Steve Swisher, infielder Mike Phillips, and pitchers John Littlefield, John Urrea, Kim Seaman, and Al Olmstead. Catcher Bob Geren was assigned from Gastonia to complete the deal Dec. 10. The Cards, desperate for bull pen help, acquired the sturdy Fingers, only to trade him away days later. Shirley went 6-4 with a 4.10 ERA in '81. Tenace batted .233. Kennedy, a bright prospect, hit .301 during the strike-plagued '81 campaign while Swisher struggled through at a .143 clip. Littlefield and Urrea both won only two games. The jury was still out on Olmstead, Geren, and Seaman.
December 9	The Cubs trade pitcher Bruce Sutter to the Cardinals for outfielder-first baseman Leon Durham, third baseman Ken Reitz,

217

and a player to be named. The Cubs acquired infielder Ty Waller to complete the deal Dec. 22. Sutter, who had fallen from good graces in Chicago because of a contract squabble, posted a 2.63 ERA in 82 innings during '81 to help shore up the St. Louis bull pen. Reitz hit a low .215 for the Cubs while plugging a hole at third base. Durham and Waller both held the promise of future stardom.

December 12   The Cards trade pitchers Pete Vuckovich and Rollie Fingers and catcher Ted Simmons to the Brewers for outfielders Sixto Lezcano and David Green, the latter assigned from Holyoke to Arkansas, and pitchers Lary Sorensen and David LaPointe. The trade was a most unpopular one in St. Louis and probably for good reason. Vuckovich, Fingers, and Simmons all made big contributions to Milwaukee's drive for the second-season championship in '81. Fingers was nothing short of phenomenal as he captured both the Fireman of the Year and Most Valuable Player awards with 28 saves and a 1.04 ERA. After a quick start, Sorensen slowed down and finished with a 7–7 mark in '81. Lezcano hit .266, far below his potential. However, Green and LaPointe needed seasoning but possessed the talent to still make the trade pay off.

December 22   The Cards release outfielder Bobby Bonds. Bonds was on the road again after hitting a disastrous .203.

1981

February 16   Conditionally purchase shortstop Rafael Santana from New York Yankees. Santana hits .233 at Arkansas in the Texas League and Cards send pitcher George Frazier to New York on June 7. Frazier is 0–1 in 16 games with New York, but posts a 1.61 ERA in relief. He wins the only American League Championship Series game he plays, with a series record of five strikeouts in 5⅔ innings October 14 against Oakland. He pitches 3⅔ innings of relief in the World Series against Los Angeles and is charged with three loses.

March 3   Sign free-agent outfielder Steve Braun. He hits .196 in 44 games.

April 3   Sign free-agent second baseman Julio Gonzalez. He hits .318 in 20 games with the Cards.

April 3   Reclaim catcher George Bjorkman from the Giants, who had selected him from Springfield in the 1980 major-league draft. He hits .254 in 107 games for Springfield, including an American Association leading 28 homers.

June 7   Trade outfielder Tony Scott to Astros for pitcher Joaquin Andujar. Scott, who was batting .227 at the time, hits .293 for Houston; .264 composite for the year. Andujar, who was 2–3 with a 4.88 ERA at Houston, posts a 6–1 record and 3.76 ERA in Cardinal livery.

September 10   Trade second baseman Neil Fiala and pitcher Joe Edelen to Cincinnati for pitcher Doug Bair. Bair, who was 2–2 with a 5.77 ERA for the Reds, is 2–0 and posts a 3.38 ERA for the Cards. Edelen equals his 1–0 Card record with Cincinnati but lowers his ERA from 9.53 to 0.69. Fiala, who was hitless in three at-bats for the Cards, goes 1-for-2 with Cincinnati.

October 21	Trade pitcher Bob Sykes to the New York Yankees for outfielder Willie McGee.
November 20	In a three-club deal, Cards receive outfielder Lonnie Smith from Cleveland, who had obtained him from Philadelphia, with a player to be named, for catcher Bo Diaz. Cards send pitchers Lary Sorensen and Silvio Martinez to Cleveland as their part of the swap.
December 10	Trade outfielder Sixto Lezcano and a player to be named to San Diego for pitcher Steve Mura and a player to be named. Deal is completed February 10, 1982, when Cards send shortstop Garry Templeton to San Diego for shortstop Ozzie Smith. Smith proved to be one of the key reasons for the '82 Cardinal pennant drive.

OPENING GAMES

Cardinal Opening Day Lineups

1876

Ned Cuthbert	LF	
John Clapp	C	
Mike McGeary	2B	
Lipman Pike	CF	
Joe Battin	3B	
Joe Blong	RF	
George Bradley	P	
Harmon Dehlman	1B	
Dennis Mack	SS	

Cincinnati 2, St. Louis 1
at Cincinnati—April 25

1877

Mike Dorgan	LF
John Clapp	C
Mike McGeary	2B
Joe Battin	3B
Davy Force	SS
Jack Remsen	CF
Art Croft	1B
Joe Blong	RF
Fred Nichols	P

St. Louis 3, Boston 2
at St. Louis—May 8

1885

Fred Dunlap	2B
George Shaffer	RF
Charlie Sweeney	P
Fred Lewis	LF
Jack Glasscock	SS
Henry Boyle	CF
Joe Quinn	1B
George Baker	C
Billy Alvord	3B

St. Louis 3, Chicago 2
at St. Louis—April 30

1886

Jack Glasscock	SS
Fred Dunlap	2B
Emmett Seerey	LF
Alex McKinnon	1B
Jerry Denny	3B
Charlie Sweeney	P
Tom Dolan	C
John Cahill	RF
Joe Quinn	CF

Detroit 9, St. Louis 2
at St. Louis—April 29

1892

John Crooks	2B
Cliff Carroll	LF
Perry Werden	1B
George Pickney	3B
Steve Brodie	RF
Jack Glasscock	SS
Bill Van Dyke	CF
Dick Buckley	C
Kid Gleason	P

Chicago 14, St. Louis 10
at St. Louis—April 12

1893

John Crooks	2B
Tommy Dowd	RF
Jack Glasscock	SS
Perry Werden	1B
Steve Brodie	CF
Joe Quinn	2B
Sandy Griffen	CF
Dick Buckley	C
Pink Hawley	P

St. Louis 4, Louisville 2
at St. Louis—April 27

219

Cardinal Opening Day Lineups (continued)

1894

Tommy Dowd	RF
Charlie Frank	LF
Frank Shugart	CF
George Miller	3B
Heinie Peitz	1B
Joe Quinn	2B
Fred Ely	SS
Dick Buckley	C
Ted Breitenstein	P

St. Louis 11, Pittsburgh 3
at St. Louis—April 19

1895

Tommy Dowd	LF
George Miller	RF
Roger Connor	1B
Joe Quinn	2B
Denny Lyons	3B
Fred Ely	SS
Marty Hogan	CF
Heinie Peitz	C
Ted Breitenstein	P

Chicago 10, St. Louis 7
at St. Louis—April 18

1896

Arlie Latham	3B
Duff Cooley	LF
Tommy Dowd	CF
Joe Quinn	2B
Roger Connor	1B
Biff Sheehan	RF
Ed McFarland	C
Monte Cross	SS
Ted Breitenstein	P

St. Louis 5, Cleveland 2
at St. Louis—April 16

1897

Bill Douglas	LF
Tommy Dowd	CF
Tuck Turner	RF
Roger Connor	1B
Fred Hartman	3B
Lou Bierbauer	2B
Monte Cross	SS
Ed McFarland	C
Red Donahue	P

Pittsburgh 4, St. Louis 1
at St. Louis—April 22

1898

Tommy Dowd	CF
Tuck Turner	RF
Jim Holmes	LF
Joe Sugden	C
Lave Cross	SS
Mike Mahoney	1B
Russ Hall	3B
Lou Bierbauer	2B
Jack Taylor	P

Chicago 2, St. Louis 1
at St. Louis—April 15

1899

Jesse Burkett	LF
Clarence Childs	2B
Ed McKean	SS
Bobby Wallace	3B
John Heidrick	RF
Patsy Tebeau	1B
Jack O'Connor	C
Harry Blake	CF
Cy Young	P

St. Louis 10, Cleveland 1
at St. Louis—April 15

1900

Jesse Burkett	LF
John Heidrick	CF
Patsy Donovan	RF
Bill Keister	2B
Dan McGann	1B
Bobby Wallace	SS
Lave Cross	3B
Jack O'Connor	C
Cy Young	P

St. Louis 3, Pittsburgh 0
at St. Louis—April 19

1901

Jesse Burkett	LF
John Heidrick	CF
Patsy Donovan	RF
Dan McGann	1B
Bobby Wallace	SS
Dick Padden	2B
Otto Kruger	3B
John Ryan	C
Jack Powell	P

Chicago 8, St. Louis 7
at St. Louis—April 19

1902

John Farrell	2B
George Barclay	LF
Fred Hartman	3B
Homer Smoot	CF
Otto Kruger	3B
Patsy Donovan	RF
Doc Hazleton	1B
John Ryan	C
Stan Yerkes	P

Pittsburgh 1, St. Louis 0
at St. Louis—April 17

1903

John Farrell	2B
Homer Smoot	CF
Dave Brain	3B
George Barclay	LF
Patsy Donovan	RF
Art Nichols	1B
Otto Williams	SS
John Ryan	C
Clarence Currie	P

St. Louis 2, Chicago 1
at St. Louis—April 16

1904

John Farrell	2B
Spike Shannon	RF
Homer Smoot	CF
Jake Beckley	1B
Danny Shay	SS
Jimmy Burke	3B
George Barclay	LF
Bill Byers	C
Jack Taylor	P

Pittsburgh 5, St. Louis 4
at Pittsburgh—April 15

1905

John Farrell	2B
Spike Shannon	LF
Homer Smoot	CF
Dave Brain	SS
Mike Grady	1B
John Dunleavy	RF
Jimmy Burke	3B
John Warner	C
Charles McFarland	P

Chicago 6, St. Louis 1
at St. Louis—April 14

1906

Pug Bennett	2B
Spike Shannon	LF
Mike Grady	C
Homer Smoot	RF
Jake Beckley	1B
John Himes	CF
Harry Arndt	3B
George McBride	SS
Jack Taylor	P

Pittsburgh 2, St. Louis 1
(13 innings)
at Pittsburgh—April 12

1907

John Kelly	RF
Tom O'Hara	LF
Pug Bennett	2B
Jake Beckley	1B
Bobby Byrne	3B
Ed Holly	SS
Al Burch	CF
Doc Marshall	C
Art Fromme	P

Chicago 6, St. Louis 1
at Chicago—April 11

1908

Chappy Charles	3B
Shad Barry	RF
Joe Delahanty	LF
Ed Konetchy	1B
Red Murray	CF
Bobby Byrne	SS
Billy Gilbert	2B
Art Hostetter	C
Johnny Lush	P

Pittsburgh 3, St. Louis 1
at St. Louis—April 15

1909

Bobby Byrne	3B
Al Shaw	CF
Roger Bresnahan	C
Ed Konetchy	1B
Steve Evans	RF
Joe Delahanty	CF
Chappy Charles	2B
Champ Osteen	SS
Johnny Lush	P

Chicago 3, St. Louis 1
at Chicago—April 14

1910

Miller Huggins	2B
Rube Ellis	LF
Ennis Oakes	CF
Ed Konetchy	1B
Steve Evans	RF
Roger Bresnahan	C
Rudy Hulswitt	SS
Jap Barbeau	3B
Vic Willis	P

Pittsburgh 5, St. Louis 1
at St. Louis—April 14

1911

Miller Huggins	2B
Rube Ellis	LF
Mike Mowrey	3B
Ed Konetchy	1B
Steve Evans	RF
Roger Bresnahan	C
Ennis Oakes	CF
Arnold Hauser	SS
Slim Sallee	P

St. Louis 3, Chicago 3
(darkness)
at Chicago—April 12

1912

Miller Huggins	2B
Rube Ellis	LF
Ennis Oakes	CF
Ed Konetchy	1B
Steve Evans	RF
Mike Mowrey	3B
Arnold Hauser	SS
John Bliss	C
Bob Harmon	P

St. Louis 7, Pittsburgh 0
at St. Louis—April 11

1913

Miller Huggins	2B
Lee Magee	LF
Mike Mowrey	3B
Ed Konetchy	1B
Steve Evans	RF
Ennis Oakes	CF
Charlie O'Leary	SS
Ivey Wingo	C
Dan Griner	P

St. Louis 5, Chicago 3
at Chicago—April 12

1914

Miller Huggins	2B
Lee Magee	CF
Art Butler	SS
John Miller	1B
Owen Wilson	RF
Cozy Dolan	3B
Walt Cruise	LF
Ivey Wingo	C
Dan Griner	P

St. Louis 2, Pittsburgh 1
at St. Louis—April 14

1915

Cozy Dolan	CF
Miller Huggins	2B
Bob Bescher	LF
John Miller	1B
Owen Wilson	RF
Zinn Beck	3B
Rolla Daringer	SS
Frank Snyder	C
Slim Sallee	P

Chicago 7, St. Louis 2
at Chicago—April 14

1916

Bob Bescher	LF
Zinn Beck	3B
Jack Smith	CF
John Miller	1B
Tommy Long	RF
Bruno Betzel	2B
Rogers Hornsby	SS
Frank Snyder	C
Bill Doak	P

St. Louis 2, Pittsburgh 1
at St. Louis—April 12

1917

Bob Bescher	LF
Bruno Betzel	2B
Tommy Long	RF
John Miller	1B
Rogers Hornsby	SS
Walt Cruise	CF
Fred Smith	3B
Frank Snyder	C
Lee Meadows	P

Cincinnati 3, St. Louis 1
at Cincinnati—April 12

1918

Red Smyth	RF
Jack Smith	CF
Doug Baird	3B
Rogers Hornsby	SS
Walt Cruise	LF
Gene Paulette	1B
Mike Gonzalez	C
Bruno Betzel	2B
Lee Meadows	P

St. Louis 4, Chicago 2
at St. Louis—April 16

1919

Burt Shotton	LF
Jack Smith	RF
Austin McHenry	CF
Rogers Hornsby	SS
Milt Stock	3B
Gene Paulette	1B
Bobby Fisher	2B
Frank Snyder	C
Jakie May	P

Cincinnati 6, St. Louis 2
at Cincinnati—April 23

1920

Burt Shotton	LF
Cliff Heathcote	RF
Milt Stock	3B
Rogers Hornsby	2B
Jacques Fournier	1B
Austin McHenry	CF
Hal Janvrin	SS
Vern Clemons	C
Bill Doak	P

Pittsburgh 5, St. Louis 4
at St. Louis—April 14

1921

Heinie Mueller	LF
Cliff Heathcote	CF
Milt Stock	3B
Rogers Hornsby	LF
Jacques Fournier	1B
Doc Lavan	SS
Vern Clemons	C
George Toporcer	2B
Jesse Haines	P

Chicago 5, St. Louis 2
at Chicago—April 13

1922

Les Mann	CF
Del Gainor	1B
Milt Stock	3B
Rogers Hornsby	2B
Joe Schultz	RF
Austin McHenry	LF
George Toporcer	SS
Vern Clemons	C
Bill Sherdel	P

St. Louis 10, Pittsburgh 1
at St. Louis—April 12

1923

Ray Blades	LF
Jack Smith	RF
Rogers Hornsby	2B
Jim Bottomley	1B
Milt Stock	3B
Heinie Mueller	CF
Howard Freigau	SS
Eddie Ainsmith	C
Jeff Pfeffer	P

Cincinnati 3, St. Louis 2 (11 innings)
at Cincinnati—April 17

1924

Max Flack	RF
Jack Smith	CF
Rogers Hornsby	2B
Jim Bottomley	1B
Howard Freigau	3B
Ray Blades	LF
Doc Lavan	SS
Ernie Vick	C
Jeff Pfeffer	P

Chicago 12, St. Louis 1
at Chicago—April 23

1925

Max Flack	RF
Heinie Mueller	CF
Rogers Hornsby	2B
Jim Bottomley	1B
Les Bell	3B
Wattie Holm	LF
Walter Schmidt	C
Tommy Thevenow	SS
Jesse Haines	P

Cincinnati 4, St. Louis 0
at Cincinnati—April 14

Cardinal Opening Day Lineups (continued)

1926
Ray Blades	LF
Heinie Mueller	CF
Rogers Hornsby	2B
Jim Bottomley	1B
Chick Hafey	RF
Les Bell	3B
Bob O'Farrell	C
Tommy Thevenow	SS
Flint Rhem	P

St. Louis 7, Pittsburgh 6
at St. Louis—April 14

1930
Taylor Douthit	CF
Sparky Adams	2B
Frank Frisch	3B
Jim Bottomley	1B
Chick Hafey	LF
George Fisher	RF
Charlie Gelbert	SS
Jimmy Wilson	C
Flint Rhem	P

Chicago 9, St. Louis 8
at St. Louis—April 15

1927
Taylor Douthit	CF
Billy Southworth	RF
Frank Frisch	2B
Jim Bottomley	1B
Les Bell	3B
Chick Hafey	LF
Bob O'Farrell	C
Tommy Thevenow	SS
Grover Cleveland Alexander	P

Chicago 10, St. Louis 1
at Chicago—April 12

1931
Taylor Douthit	CF
Ernie Orsatti	LF
Frank Frisch	2B
Jim Bottomley	1B
George Watkins	RF
Charlie Gelbert	SS
Sparky Adams	3B
Jimmy Wilson	C
Flint Rhem	P

St. Louis 7, Cincinnati 3
at Cincinnati—April 14

1928
Taylor Douthit	CF
Wattie Holm	3B
Frank Frisch	2B
Jim Bottomley	1B
Chick Hafey	RF
Wally Roettger	LF
Tommy Thevenow	SS
Bob O'Farrell	C
Jesse Haines	P

St. Louis 14, Pittsburgh 7
at St. Louis—April 11

1932
Sparky Adams	3B
Ray Blades	RF
Frank Frisch	2B
Jim Bottomley	1B
Rip Collins	LF
Pepper Martin	CF
Jimmy Wilson	C
Charlie Gelbert	SS
Flint Rhem	P

St. Louis 10, Pittsburgh 2
at St. Louis—April 12

1929
Taylor Douthit	CF
Fred Haney	3B
Frank Frisch	2B
Jim Bottomley	1B
Chick Hafey	LF
Wally Roettger	RF
Charlie Gelbert	SS
Bubber Jonnard	C
Grover Cleveland Alexander	P

St. Louis 5, Cincinnati 2
at Cincinnati—April 16

1933
Sparky Adams	3B
George Watkins	RF
Frank Frisch	2B
Rip Collins	1B
Joe Medwick	LF
Ernie Orsatti	CF
Jimmy Wilson	C
Gordon Slade	SS
Dizzy Dean	P

Chicago 3, St. Louis 0
at Chicago—April 13

1934

Gene Moore	CF
Frank Frisch	2B
Pepper Martin	3B
Jack Rothrock	LF
Joe Medwick	RF
Rip Collins	1B
Spud Davis	C
Leo Durocher	SS
Dizzy Dean	P

St. Louis 7, Pittsburgh 1
at St. Louis—April 17

1935

Pepper Martin	3B
Jack Rothrock	RF
Frank Frisch	2B
Joe Medwick	LF
Rip Collins	1B
Bill DeLancey	C
Terry Moore	CF
Leo Durocher	SS
Dizzy Dean	P

Chicago 4, St. Louis 3
at Chicago—April 16

1936

Terry Moore	CF
Frank Frisch	2B
Pepper Martin	RF
Joe Medwick	LF
Rip Collins	1B
Spud Davis	C
Charlie Gelbert	3B
Leo Durocher	SS
Dizzy Dean	P

Chicago 12, St. Louis 7
at St. Louis—April 14

1937

Terry Moore	CF
Stu Martin	2B
Frenchy Bordagaray	3B
Joe Medwick	LF
Johnny Mize	1B
Pepper Martin	RF
Leo Durocher	SS
Brusio Ogrodowski	C
Dizzy Dean	P

St. Louis 2, Cincinnati 0
(10 innings)
at Cincinnati—April 20

1938

Don Gutteridge	SS
Stu Martin	2B
Enos Slaughter	CF
Don Padgett	LF
Johnny Mize	1B
Pepper Martin	3B
Terry Moore	CF
Mickey Owen	C
Bob Weiland	P

Pittsburgh 4, St. Louis 3
at St. Louis—April 19

1939

Jimmy Brown	2B
Don Gutteridge	3B
Enos Slaughter	RF
Joe Medwick	LF
Johnny Mize	1B
Terry Moore	CF
Mickey Owen	C
Joe Orengo	SS
Bob Weiland	P

St. Louis 3, Pittsburgh 2
at Pittsburgh—April 18

1940

Jimmy Brown	3B
Stu Martin	2B
Enos Slaughter	RF
Johnny Mize	1B
Don Padgett	C
Pepper Martin	LF
Terry Moore	CF
Marty Marion	SS
Curt Davis	P

Pittsburgh 6, St. Louis 4
at St. Louis—April 16

1941

Ernie Koy	LF
Jimmy Brown	3B
Terry Moore	CF
Johnny Mize	1B
Enos Slaughter	RF
Gus Mancuso	C
Marty Marion	SS
Creepy Crespi	2B
Lon Warneke	P

St. Louis 7, Cincinnati 3
at Cincinnati—April 15

Cardinal Opening Day Lineups (continued)

1942

Creepy Crespi	2B
Stan Musial	LF
Terry Moore	CF
Enos Slaughter	RF
Ray Sanders	1B
Jimmy Brown	3B
Ken O'Dea	C
Marty Marion	SS
Mort Cooper	P

Chicago 5, St. Louis 4
at St. Louis—April 14

1946

Lou Klein	2B
Terry Moore	CF
Stan Musial	LF
Enos Slaughter	RF
Whitey Kurowski	3B
Dick Sisler	1B
Marty Marion	SS
Del Rice	C
Johnny Beazley	P

Pittsburgh 6, St. Louis 4
at St. Louis—April 16

1943

Jimmy Brown	2B
Frank Demaree	RF
Stan Musial	LF
Whitey Kurowski	3B
Walker Cooper	C
Buster Adams	CF
Johnny Hopp	1B
Lou Klein	SS
Mort Cooper	P

Cincinnati 1, St. Louis 0
at Cincinnati—April 21

1947

Red Schoendienst	2B
Harry Walker	CF
Stan Musial	1B
Enos Slaughter	RF
Whitey Kurowski	3B
Dick Sisler	LF
Marty Marion	SS
Joe Garagiola	C
Howie Pollet	P

Cincinnati 3, St. Louis 1
at Cincinnati—April 15

1944

Emil Verban	2B
Johnny Hopp	CF
Stan Musial	RF
Walker Cooper	C
Ray Sanders	1B
Whitey Kurowski	3B
Danny Litwhiler	LF
Marty Marion	SS
Max Lanier	P

St. Louis 2, Pittsburgh 0
at St. Louis—April 18

1948

Erv Dusak	CF
Red Schoendienst	2B
Stan Musial	RF
Enos Slaughter	LF
Whitey Kurowski	3B
Nippy Jones	1B
Del Wilber	C
Marty Marion	SS
Murry Dickson	P

St. Louis 4, Cincinnati 0
at St. Louis—April 20

1945

Augie Bergamo	RF
Johnny Hopp	CF
Red Schoendienst	LF
Walker Cooper	C
Ray Sanders	1B
Whitey Kurowski	3B
Marty Marion	SS
Emil Verban	2B
Ted Wilks	P

Chicago 3, St. Louis 2
at Chicago—April 17

1949

Tom Glaviano	3B
Red Schoendienst	2B
Stan Musial	CF
Enos Slaughter	LF
Nippy Jones	1B
Ron Northey	RF
Marty Marion	SS
Del Rice	C
Harry Brecheen	P

Cincinnati 3, St. Louis 1
at Cincinnati—April 19

1950

Harry Walker	CF
Red Schoendienst	2B
Stan Musial	RF
Enos Slaughter	LF
Ed Kazak	3B
Rocky Nelson	1B
Joe Garagiola	C
Eddie Miller	SS
Gerry Staley	P

St. Louis 4, Pittsburgh 2
at St. Louis—April 18

1951

Peanuts Lowrey	CF
Red Schoendienst	2B
Enos Slaughter	RF
Stan Musial	LF
Don Richmond	3B
Steve Bilko	1B
Joe Garagiola	C
Solly Hemus	SS
Tom Poholsky	P

Pittsburgh 5, St. Louis 4
at Pittsburgh—April 17

1952

Solly Hemus	SS
Red Schoendienst	2B
Stan Musial	LF
Enos Slaughter	RF
Wally Westlake	CF
Steve Bilko	1B
Billy Johnson	3B
Del Rice	C
Gerry Staley	P

St. Louis 3, Pittsburgh 2
at St. Louis—April 15

1953

Solly Hemus	SS
Red Schoendienst	2B
Stan Musial	LF
Steve Bilko	1B
Enos Slaughter	RF
Ray Jablonski	3B
Rip Repulski	CF
Del Rice	C
Les Fusselman	P

Milwaukee 3, St. Louis 2
(10 innings)
at Milwaukee—April 14

1954

Rip Repulski	RF
Wally Moon	CF
Red Schoendienst	2B
Stan Musial	LF
Ray Jablonski	3B
Steve Bilko	1B
Alex Grammas	SS
Del Rice	C
Vic Raschi	P

Milwaukee 7, St. Louis 6
(11 innings)
at Milwaukee—April 15

1955

Wally Moon	LF
Bill Virdon	CF
Stan Musial	1B
Rip Repulski	RF
Red Schoendienst	2B
Ken Boyer	3B
Bill Sarni	C
Alex Grammas	SS
Brooks Lawrence	P

Chicago 14, St. Louis 4
at Chicago—April 12

1956

Wally Moon	1B
Red Schoendienst	2B
Stan Musial	RF
Hank Sauer	LF
Ken Boyer	3B
Bill Virdon	CF
Bill Sarni	C
Alex Grammas	SS
Vinegar Bend Mizell	P

St. Louis 4, Cincinnati 2
at Cincinnati—April 17

1957

Don Blasingame	2B
Al Dark	SS
Stan Musial	1B
Del Ennis	RF
Ken Boyer	3B
Wally Moon	LF
Hal Smith	C
Bobby Gene Smith	CF
Herman Wehmeier	P

St. Louis 14, Cincinnati 4
at Cincinnati—April 16

1958

Don Blasingame	2B
Al Dark	SS
Stan Musial	1B
Del Ennis	LF
Ken Boyer	3B
Wally Moon	RF
Bobby Gene Smith	CF
Hobie Landrith	C
Vinegar Bend Mizell	P

Chicago 4, St. Louis 0
at St. Louis—April 15

1959

Don Blasingame	2B
Gino Cimoli	CF
Bill White	1B
Ken Boyer	3B
Stan Musial	LF
Joe Cunningham	RF
Hal Smith	C
Alex Grammas	SS
Larry Jackson	P

St. Louis 6, San Francisco 5
at St. Louis—April 10

1960

Joe Cunningham	RF
Darryl Spencer	SS
Bill White	CF
Ken Boyer	3B
Stan Musial	1B
Leon Wagner	LF
Hal Smith	C
Mike Shannon	3B
Larry Jackson	P

San Francisco 3, St. Louis 1
at San Francisco—April 12

1961

Julian Javier	2B
Don Landrum	CF
Bill White	1B
Ken Boyer	3B
Stan Musial	LF
Darryl Spencer	SS
Joe Cunningham	RF
Hal Smith	C
Ernie Broglio	P

St. Louis 2, Milwaukee 1
(11 innings)
at Milwaukee—April 11

1962

Curt Flood	CF
Julian Javier	2B
Bill White	1B
Stan Musial	RF
Ken Boyer	3B
Minnie Minoso	LF
Gene Oliver	C
Julio Gotay	SS
Larry Jackson	P

St. Louis 11, New York Mets 4
at St. Louis—April 11

1963

Curt Flood	CF
Dick Groat	SS
Bill White	1B
George Altman	RF
Ken Boyer	3B
Stan Musial	LF
Carl Sawatski	C
Julian Javier	2B
Ernie Broglio	P

St. Louis 7, New York Mets 0
at New York—April 9

1964

Julian Javier	2B
Dick Groat	SS
Bill White	1B
Charlie James	LF
Ken Boyer	3B
Carl Warwick	RF
Curt Flood	CF
Bob Uecker	C
Ernie Broglio	P

Los Angeles 4, St. Louis 0
at Los Angeles—April 14

1965

Curt Flood	CF
Lou Brock	LF
Bill White	1B
Ken Boyer	3B
Dick Groat	SS
Mike Shannon	RF
Julian Javier	2B
Bob Uecker	C
Bob Gibson	P

St. Louis 10, Chicago 10
(darkness)
at Chicago—April 12

1966

Lou Brock	RF
Julian Javier	2B
Curt Flood	CF
Tim McCarver	C
Charlie Smith	3B
Alex Johnson	LF
George Kernek	1B
Jerry Buchek	SS
Curt Simmons	P

Philadelphia 3, St. Louis 2
at St. Louis—April 13

1967

Lou Brock	LF
Curt Flood	CF
Roger Maris	RF
Orlando Cepeda	1B
Mike Shannon	3B
Tim McCarver	C
Julian Javier	2B
Dal Maxvill	SS
Bob Gibson	P

St. Louis 5, San Francisco 0
at St. Louis—April 11

1968

Lou Brock	LF
Curt Flood	CF
Roger Maris	RF
Orlando Cepeda	1B
Tim McCarver	C
Mike Shannon	3B
Julian Javier	2B
Dal Maxvill	SS
Bob Gibson	P

St. Louis 2, Atlanta 1
at St. Louis—April 10

1969

Lou Brock	LF
Curt Flood	CF
Vada Pinson	RF
Joe Torre	1B
Tim McCarver	C
Mike Shannon	3B
Julian Javier	2B
Dal Maxvill	SS
Bob Gibson	P

Pittsburgh 6, St. Louis 2
at St. Louis—April 8

1970

Lou Brock	LF
Jose Cardenal	CF
Richie Allen	3B
Joe Torre	C
Leron Lee	RF
Joe Hague	1B
Julian Javier	2B
Dal Maxvill	SS
Bob Gibson	P

St. Louis 7, Montreal 2
at Montreal—April 8

1971

Matty Alou	CF
Ted Sizemore	SS
Lou Brock	LF
Joe Torre	3B
Jose Cardenal	RF
Joe Hague	1B
Ted Simmons	C
Julian Javier	2B
Bob Gibson	P

Chicago 2, St. Louis 1
at Chicago—April 6

1972

Lou Brock	LF
Ted Sizemore	2B
Matty Alou	RF
Joe Torre	3B
Ted Simmons	C
Joe Hague	1B
Jose Cruz	CF
Dal Maxvill	SS
Bob Gibson	P

Montreal 3, St. Louis 2
at St. Louis—April 15

1973

Lou Brock	LF
Ted Sizemore	2B
Jose Cruz	CF
Joe Torre	1B
Ted Simmons	C
Ken Reitz	3B
Bernie Carbo	RF
Ray Busse	SS
Bob Gibson	P

Pittsburgh 7, St. Louis 5
at Pittsburgh—April 6

Cardinal Opening Day Lineups (continued)

1974

Lou Brock	LF
Ted Sizemore	2B
Reggie Smith	RF
Joe Torre	1B
Ted Simmons	C
Bake McBride	CF
Ken Reitz	3B
Mike Tyson	SS
Bob Gibson	P

St. Louis 6, Pittsburgh 5
at St. Louis—April 5

1975

Lou Brock	LF
Ted Sizemore	2B
Bake McBride	CF
Reggie Smith	RF
Ted Simmons	C
Keith Hernandez	1B
Ken Reitz	3B
Ed Brinkman	SS
Bob Gibson	P

Montreal 8, St. Louis 4
at St. Louis—April 7

1976

Lou Brock	LF
Lee Richard	SS
Bake McBride	CF
Ted Simmons	C
Reggie Smith	RF
Keith Hernandez	1B
Hector Cruz	3B
Mike Tyson	2B
Lynn McGlothen	P

St. Louis 5, Chicago 1
at St. Louis—April 9

1977

Lou Brock	LF
Garry Templeton	SS
Bake McBride	CF
Hector Cruz	RF
Ted Simmons	C
Keith Hernandez	1B
Ken Reitz	3B
Mike Tyson	2B
John Denny	P

St. Louis 12, Pittsburgh 6
at St. Louis—April 7

1978

Lou Brock	LF
Garry Templeton	SS
Jerry Morales	RF
Ted Simmons	C
Keith Hernandez	1B
Ken Reitz	3B
Tony Scott	CF
Mike Tyson	2B
Bob Forsch	P

St. Louis 5, Philadelphia 1
at Philadelphia—April 7

1979

Lou Brock	LF
Garry Templeton	SS
Keith Hernandez	1B
Ted Simmons	C
George Hendrick	CF
Tony Scott	RF
Ken Reitz	3B
Mike Tyson	2B
John Denny	P

St. Louis 8, Philadelphia 1
at St. Louis—April 6

1980

Garry Templeton	SS
Ken Oberkfell	2B
Keith Hernandez	1B
Ted Simmons	C
Bobby Bonds	LF
George Hendrick	RF
Tony Scott	CF
Ken Reitz	3B
Pete Vuckovich	P

St. Louis 1, Pittsburgh 0
at St. Louis—April 10

1981

Garry Templeton	SS
Ken Oberkfell	3B
Keith Hernandez	1B
George Hendrick	RF
Darrell Porter	C
Sixto Lezcano	LF
Tony Scott	CF
Tom Herr	2B
Bob Forsch	P

Philadelphia 5, St. Louis 2
at St. Louis—April 11

1982

Lonnie Smith	CF
Tom Herr	2B
Keith Hernandez	1B
Darrell Porter	C
George Hendrick	RF
Dane Iorg	LF
Steve Braun	3B
Ozzie Smith	SS
Bob Forsch	P

St. Louis 14, Houston 3
at Houston—April 6

A Potpourri of Cardinal Opening Day Statistics

	Games	Won	Lost	Tied	Percentage
At St. Louis	53	30	23	0	.566
Road	42	13	27	2	.325
TOTAL	95	43	50	2	.462

Against Each Opponent

	HOME			ROAD				TOTAL			
	Won	Lost	Pct.	Won	Lost	Tie	Pct.	Won	Lost	Tie	Pct.
Atlanta	1	0	1.000	—	—	—	—	1	0	0	1.000
Boston	1	0	1.000	—	—	—	—	1	0	0	1.000
Chicago	4	9	.308	1	11	2	.083	5	20	2	.200
Cincinnati	1	0	1.000	6	8	0	.429	7	8	0	.467
Cleveland	2	0	1.000	—	—	—	—	2	0	0	1.000
Detroit	0	1	.000	—	—	—	—	0	1	0	.000
Houston	—	—	—	1	0	0	1.000	1	0	0	1.000
Los Angeles	—	—	—	0	1	0	.000	0	1	0	.000
Louisville	1	0	1.000	—	—	—	—	1	0	0	1.000
Milwaukee	—	—	—	1	2	0	.333	1	2	0	.333
Montreal	0	2	.000	1	0	0	1.000	1	2	0	.333
New York Mets	1	0	1.000	1	0	0	1.000	2	0	0	1.000
Philadelphia	1	2	.333	1	0	0	1.000	2	2	0	.500
Pittsburgh	16	9	.640	1	4	0	.200	17	13	0	.567
San Francisco	2	0	1.000	0	1	0	.000	2	1	0	.667

Earliest opener: April 5, 1974
Latest opener: May 8, 1877
One run games: Of 33 played, Cards won 14, lost 19, for a .424 percentage.
Extra inning games: Of six played, Cards won 2, lost 4, .333 percentage.
By innings: 10 innings, 1-1, 11 innings, 1-2; 13 innings, 0-1.
Number of players used from 1876 through 1982, 364 of a possible 855. Of those, lineups had the same nine players in two consecutive openers only once, 1967–68. Twice lineups contained no players making Card debuts, 1936 and 1968.

Cardinal Opening Day Games By Date

Date	Won	Lost	Tied
April 5	1	0	0
6	2	2	0
7	2	1	0
8	1	1	0
9	2	0	0
10	3	0	0
11	5	2	0
12	4	6	2
13	0	3	0
14	3	10	0
15	3	8	0
16	5	3	0
17	2	4	0
18	3	1	0
19	2	3	0
20	2	0	0
21	0	1	0
22	0	1	0
23	0	2	0
25	0	1	0
27	1	0	0
29	0	1	0
30	1	0	0
May 8	1	0	0

PRESIDENTS, MANAGERS, COACHES

Cardinal Club Presidents

J.B.C. Lucas	1876–77
Henry V. Lucas	1885–86
Chris Von der Ahe	1892–97
Benjamin S. Muckenfuss	1898
Frank De Hass Robison	1899–1906
M. Stanley Robison	1906–10
E.A. Steininger	1911–12
James C. Jones	1912
Schuyler P. Britton	1913–16
Mrs. Schuyler P. Britton	1916
W. Branch Rickey	1917–19
Samuel Breadon	1920–47
Robert E. Hannegan	1947–49
Fred M. Saigh Jr.	1949–53
August A. Busch Jr.	1953–73
Richard A. Meyer	1974
August A. Busch Jr.	1974–82

The Managers and Their Records

	Years	W	L	Pct.	Pnts.	Chmps.
S. Mason Graffen	1876	45	19	.703	0	0
John Lucas	1877	14	12	.538	0	0
George McManus	1877	14	20	.412	0	0
Henry Lucas	1885	36	72	.333	0	0
Gus Schmelz	1886	43	79	.352	0	0
Chris Von der Ahe	1892, 95–97	59	110	.349	0	0
Bill Watkins	1893	57	75	.432	0	0
George Miller	1894	56	76	.424	0	0
Al Buckenberger	1895	16	32	.333	0	0
Joe Quinn	1895	13	27	.325	0	0
Lew Phelan	1895	8	21	.276	0	0
Harry Diddledock	1896	7	11	.389	0	0
Arlie Latham	1896	0	2	.000	0	0
Roger Connor	1896	9	37	.196	0	0
Tommy Dowd	1896–97	30	63	.323	0	0
Hugh Nicol	1897	9	29	.237	0	0
Bill Hallman	1897	13	36	.220	0	0
Tim Hurst	1898	39	111	.260	0	0
Oliver "Patsy" Tebeau	1899–1900	132	122	.520	0	0
Louis Heilbroner	1900	17	20	.459	0	0
Patsy Donovan	1901–03	175	236	.426	0	0
Kid Nichols	1904–05	94	108	.465	0	0
Jimmy Burke	1905	17	32	.347	0	0
M. Stanley Robison	1905	22	35	.386	0	0
John McCloskey	1906–08	153	304	.335	0	0
Roger Bresnahan	1909–12	255	352	.420	0	0
Miller Huggins	1913–17	346	415	.455	0	0
Jack Hendricks	1918	51	78	.395	0	0
Branch Rickey	1919–25	458	485	.486	0	0
Rogers Hornsby	1926	153	116	.569	1	1
Bob O'Farrell	1927	92	61	.601	0	0
Bill McKechnie	1928–29	128	88	.592	1	0
Billy Southworth	1929, 40–45	620	346	.642	2	1
Gabby Street	1930–33	313	242	.564	2	1
Frankie Frisch	1933–38	457	354	.563	1	1
Mike Gonzalez	1938, 40	9	13	.409	0	0
Ray Blades	1939–40	107	85	.557	0	0
Eddie Dyer	1946–50	446	325	.578	1	1
Marty Marion	1951	81	73	.526	0	0
Eddie Stanky	1952–55	260	238	.522	0	0
Harry Walker	1955	51	67	.432	0	0
Fred Hutchinson	1956–58	232	220	.513	0	0
Stan Hack	1958	3	7	.300	0	0
Solly Hemus	1959–61	190	192	.497	0	0
Johnny Keane	1961–64	317	249	.560	1	1
Red Schoendienst	1965–76, 80	1020	936	.521	2	1
Vern Rapp	1977–78	88	89	.497	0	0
Jack Krol	1978, 80	2	2	.500	0	0
Ken Boyer	1978–80	166	191	.465	0	0
Whitey Herzog	1980–82	188	148	.560	1	1

All Time Cardinal Coaches List

Tony Auferio	1973
Joe Becker	1965–66
Vern Benson	1961 thru 64, 1970 thru 75
Ray Blades	1930 thru 32, 1951
Ken Boyer	1971–72
Walker Cooper	1957
Preston Gomez	1976
Mike Gonzalez	1934 thru 46
Stan Hack	1957–58
Chuck Hiller	1981 and 82
Al Hollingsworth	1957–58
Johnny Hopp	1956
Darrell Johnson	1960–61
Lou Kahn	1954–55
Ray Katt	1959 thru 61
Tony Kaufmann	1947 thru 50
Johnny Keane	1959 thru 61
Bill Killefer	1926
George Kissell	1969 thru 75
Hub Kittle	1981 and 82
Fred Koenig	1976
Jack Krol	1977 thru 80
Hal Lanier	1981 and 82
Johnny Lewis	1973 thru 76
Marty Marion	1950
Dal Maxvill	1979–80
Bill McKechnie	1927
Bob Milliken	1965 thru 70, 1976
Terry Moore	1949 thru 52, 1956 thru 58
Mo Mozzali	1977–78
Billy Muffett	1967 thru 70
Greasy Neale	1929
Charley O'Leary	1913 thru 17
Jack Onslow	1928
Claude Osteen	1977 thru 80
Heinie Peitz	1913
Howie Pollet	1959 thru 64
Bill Posedel	1954 thru 57
Dave Ricketts	1974–75, 1978 thru 82
John Riddle	1952 thru 55
Sonny Ruberto	1977–78
Mike Ryba	1951 thru 54
Red Schoendienst	1962 thru 64, 1979 thru 82
Barney Schultz	1971 thru 75
Joe Schultz	1963 thru 68
Burt Shotton	1923 and 25
Dick Sisler	1966 thru 70
Hal Smith	1962
Al Sothoron	1927–28
Joe Sugden	1921 thru 25
Lee Thomas	1972
Ray Thomas	1922
Tink Turner	1924

Mickey Vernon	1965
Dixie Walker	1953 and 55
Harry Walker	1959 thru 62
Buzzy Wares	1930 thru 35
Otto Williams	1926
Bart Zeller	1970
Tom Zimmer	1976

NICKNAMES

St. Louis Cardinal Nicknames

Given Name	**Nickname(s)**
Abernathy, Ted	Abby
Abbott, Ody	Toby
Adams, Charles	Babe
Adams, Earl	Sparky
Adams, Elvin	Buster
Adams, Joseph	Wagon Tongue
Alberts, Frederick	Cy
Alexander, Grover Cleveland	Pete
Alexander, William	Nin
Allen, Ethan	Curly
Allen, Richie	Dick
Alston, Tom	Tall Tom
Alston, Walter	Smokey
Altman, George	Big George
Alvarado, Luis	Pimba
Ames, Leon	Red
Anderson, Dwain	D
Anderson, Ferrell	Andy
Arroyo, Luis	Yo-Yo
Bannon, Jim	Foxy Grandpa
Barbeau, William	Jap
Barrett, Charles	Red
Barrett, Frank	Red
Barry, John	Shad
Beckley, Jake	Eagle Eye
Beecher, Ed	Scrap Iron
Bell, Herman	Hi
Benes, Joe	Bananas
Bennett, Justin	Pug
Betzel, Christian	Bruno
Bilko, Steve	Humphrey
Blades, Francis	Ray
Blake, Harry	Dude
Blake, John	Sheriff
Blasingame, Don	Blazer
Blatnik, John	Chief
Blattner, Robert	Buddy
Bloomfield, Clyde	Buddy
Bolden, Bill	Big Bill

235

Bonds, Bobby	Bo Bo Junior
Bonner, Frank	The Human Flea
Bordagaray, Stanley	Frenchy
Bottomley, Jim	Sunny Jim
Boyer, Cloyd	Junior
Boyle, Jack	Honest John
Bradford, Charles	Buddy
Bradley, George	Grin
Brandt, Jackie	Ozark, Flakey
Brashear, Robert	Kitty
Bratcher, Joe	Goobers
Brazle, Alpha	Cotton, Ol' Boots and Saddles
Brecheen, Harry	The Cat, The Weasel
Bresnahan, Roger	The Duke of Tralee
Bressler, Raymond	Rube
Bridges, Marshall	Sheriff
Bridges, Everett	Rocky
Briody, Charles	Fatty, The Alderman
Bronkie, Herman	Dutch
Brosnan, Jim	Professor
Broughton, Cecil	Cal
Brown, Charles	Buster
Brown, Jim	Moose
Brown, Mordecai	Three Finger, Miner
Brown, Willard	Big Bill, California
Browning, Louis	Pete, The Gladiator
Brunet, George	Lefty
Bryant, Ron	Bear
Buchek, Jerry	Butch
Buelow, Fred	Fritz
Burdette, Selva	Lou
Burgess, Tom	Tim
Burk, Charles	Sandy
Burke, Jim	Sunset Jimmy
Burkett, Jesse	Crab
Burns, James	Farmer
Bush, Guy	Joe, The Mississippi Mudcat
Bushong, Albert	Doc
Butler, John	Trolley Line
Byerly, Eldred	Bud
Byers, William	Big Bill
Calhoun, John	Red
Camberlain, Elton	Iceberg
Campau, Charles	Count
Cardenal, Jose	Junior
Carleton, James	Tex
Carlton, Steve	Lefty
Carmel, Leon	Duke
Carpenter, Warren	Hick
Carroll, Clay	Hawk
Carsey, Wilfred	Kid
Cartwright, Ed	Jumbo
Caruthers, Bob	Parisian Bob

Cepeda, Orlando	Baby Bull, Cha-Cha, Plo-Plo
Chambers, Cliff	Lefty
Charles, Raymond	Chappy
Childs, Clarence	Cupid
Cicotte, Al	Bozo
Clark, Mike	Old
Clarke, Josh	Pepper
Clarkson, Art	Dad
Clemons, Verne	Fats
Clough, Ed	Spec
Collins, Phil	Fidgety
Collins, James	Rip
Collum, Jackie	Half Column
Comiskey, Charles	Commy, The Old Roman
Conwell, Ed	Irish
Cooley, Duff	Sir Richard
Cooney, James	Scoops
Cooper, William	Walker
Corhan, Roy	Irish
Corridon, Frank	Fiddler
Coulter, Thomas	Chip
Crabtree, Estel	Crabby
Crandall, James	Doc
Crawford, Glenn	Shorty
Creel, Jack	Tex
Creely, August	Gus
Crespi, Frank	Creepy
Crosby, Ed	Bing, Spider
Cross, Joffre	Jeff
Cross, Lafayette	Lave
Crowe, George	Big George
Cruz, Cirilio	Tommy
Cruz, Hector	Heity
Cuellar, Miguel	Mike
Cuppy, George	Nig
Cuthbert, Edgar	Ned
Daily, Hugh	One Arm
Dark, Alvin	Blackie
Darling, Dell	Winerwurst
Davis, Curt	Coonskin
Davis, George	Kiddo
Davis, James	Jumbo
Davis, John	Daisy
Davis, Virgil	Spud
Davis, Willie	Comet
Day, Charles	Boots
Day, Clyde	Pea Ridge
Deal, Ellis	Cot
Dean, Jay	Dizzy
Dean, Paul	Daffy
Deasley, Thomas	Pat
De Groff, Edward	Rube
De Lancey, Bill	Dee
Dell, William	Wheezer

Nicknames (continued)

Demaree, Joseph	Frank
Derringer, Paul	Duke, 'Oom Paul
Dickson, Murry	Dick, The Merry Magician
Dillhoefer, William	Pickles
Distel, George	Dutch
Doak, Bill	Spittin' Bill
Dockins, George	Lefty
Dolan, Patrick	Cozy
Donahue, Charles	She
Donahue, Francis	Red
Donlin, Mike	Turkey
Donnelly , Sylvester	Blix
Donovan, Patrick	Patsy
Dorr, Charles	Bert
Douglas, William	Klondike
Dowd, Tommy	Buttermilk
Drabowsky, Myron	Moe
Duliba, Bob	Ach
Durham, Joseph	Pop
Durham, Leon	Bull
Durocher, Leo	The Lip, The Lion
Duryea, James	Cyclone
Dusak, Erv	Four Sack
Eagan, William	Bad Bill
Earle, William	Globetrotter
Earnshaw, George	Moose
Eckert, Al	Obbie
Edelen, Benny	Joe
Egan, Aloysius	Wish
Ehret, Phillip	Red
Ellis, George	Rube
Ely, Frederick	Bones
Esper, Charles	Duke
Ewing, John	Long John
Fallon, George	Flash
Fanok, Harry	Flame Thrower
Farrell, Edward	Doc
Faszholz, Jack	Preacher
Fenwick, Bobby	Bloop
Ferrarese, Don	Midget
Fiore, Mike	Lefty
Fisher, Chauncey	Peach
Fisher, Ed	Donald Duck
Fisher, George	Showboat
Flowers, D'Arcy	Jake
Force, David	Wee Davey
Ford, Horace	Hod
Fournier, Jacques	Jack
Foutz, Dave	Scissors
Fowler, Jesse	Pete
Francona, John Patsy	Tito

238

Frankhouse, Fred	Ants, Peter Pan
Frazier, Joe	Cobra Joe
Freeman, Julius	Julie
Freese, Gene	Augie
Freigau, Howard	Ty
Frisch, Frank	The Fordham Flash
Frisella, Danny	Bear
Fuller, Henry	Harry
Fuller, William	Shorty
Fullis, Charles	Chick
Galloway, James	Bad News
Galvin, James	Pud, Little Steam Engine, Gentle Jeems
Genins, Frank	Frenchy
Gerhardt, Joe	Moveup
Getzein, Charles	Pretzels
Gibson, Bob	Bullet Bob, Hoot
Gilhooley, Frank	Flash
Gilson, Hal	Lefty
Giusti, John	Dave
Glasscock, John	Pebbly Jack, Jack
Glaviano, Tom	Rabbit
Gleason, William	Kid
Gomez, Pedro	Preston
Gonzalez, Miguel	Mike
Gore, George	Piano Legs
Gorman, Jack	Stopping Jack
Grabowski, Al	Hook
Grammas, Alex	Golden Greek, Candy Kid
Grant, Jim	Mudcat
Greason, Bill	Booster
Griffith, Clark	Griff
Grimes, Burleigh	Old Stubblebeard
Grimm, Charlie	Jolly Cholly
Griner, Dan	Rusty
Gumbert, Harry	Gunboat
Habenicht, Bob	Hobby
Hack, Stan	Stanislaus
Hackett, Jim	Sunny Jim
Haddix, Harvey	The Kitten
Hafey, Charles	Chick
Hageman, Kurt	Casey
Haines, Jesse	Pop
Hall, Charles	Sea Lion
Hallahan, William	Wild Bill
Haney, Fred	Pudge
Harmon, Bob	Hickory Bob
Harrell, Ray	Cowboy
Hartenstein, Chuck	Twiggy
Hartman, Fred	Dutch
Hartnett, Pat	Happy
Hauser, Arnold	Pee Wee
Hawke, Bill	Dick
Hawley, Emerson	Pink

239

Hazleton, Willard	Doc
Healy, John	Egyptian
Hearn, Elmer	Bunny
Heathcote, Cliff	C.C.
Heidrick, John	Snags
Heise, Clarence	Lefty
Hemphill, Charlie	Eagle Eye
Hendrick, George	
Hendrick, Harvey	Gink
Herzog, Dorrell	Whitey, Relly
Heusser, Ed	Wild Elk of the Wasatch, Big Ed
High, Andy	Handy Andy
Hildebrand, Palmer	Pete
Hill, Carmen	Specs, Bunker
Holland, Howard	Mul
Holm, Roscoe	Wattie
Holmes, Howard	Ducky
Holmes, James	Ducky
Hopkins, John	Sis
Hopp, Johnny	Cotney, Hippity
Hopper, Bill	Bird Dog
Hornsby, Rogers	Rajah
Howell, Roland	Billiken
Howerton, Bill	Hopalong
Hoy, William	Dummy
Hrabosky, Al	The Mad Hungarian, Big Al
Huggins, Miller	Hug, Mighty Mite, Rabbit
Hughey, Jim	Cold Water
Hunt, Ben	Highpockets
Hunt, Joel	Jodie
Huntzinger, Walter	Shakes
Hutchison, Bill	Wild Bill
Hyatt, Robert	Ham
Irwin, Walter	Lightning
Jablonski, Ray	Jabbo
Janvrin, Hal	Childe Harold
Jasper, Harry	Hi
Javier, Julian	Hoolie, Phantom
Johnson, Ken	Hooks
Johnson, Sylvester	Si
Jones, Albert	Bronco, Cowboy
Jones, Maurice	Red
Jones, Sam	Toothpick, Sad Sam
Jones, Vernal	Nippy
Jonnard, Clarence	Bubber
Judy, Lyle	Punch
Jutze, Alfred	Skip
Kaat, Jim	Kitty, Dutchman
Keister, Bill	Wagon Tongue
Kelleher, Michael	Mick
Kimball, Newell	Newt

Kinder, Ellis	Old Folks
King, Charles Gilbert	Chick
King, Charles Frederick	Silver
King, Jim	Arkansas Hummingbird
King, Lynn	Dig
Kissinger, Bill	Shang
Klein, Lou	Chuck
Kleinke, Norbert	Nub
Knight, Elmer	Jack
Konetchy, Ed	Big Ed, Koney
Konstanty, Casimir	Jim
Koy, Ernie	Chief
Krist, Howie	Spud
Krueger, Otto	'Oom Paul
Kurowski, George	Whitey
Kuzava, Bob	Sarge
Lake, Eddie	Sparky
Lally, Daniel	Bud
Lamline, Fred	Dutch
Landrum, Terry	Tito
Lanier, Hubert	Max
Larmore, Robert	Red
Latham, Walter	Arlie, The Freshest Man on Earth
Lavan, John	Doc
Lawrence, Brooks	Bull
Lewis, Bill	Buddy
Lillard, Robert	Gene
Littell, Mark	Country
Little, Don	Jeff
Livingston, Patrick	Paddy
Locke, Lawrence	Bobby
Lockman, Carroll	Whitey
Lotz, Joe	Smokey
Lowrey, Harry	Peanuts
Lucid, Cornelius	Con
Luna, Guillermo	Mimo
Lyons, George	Smooth
McAuley, James	Ike
McBride, Arnold	Bake
McCarver, James	Tim
McDermott, Maurice	Mickey, Lefty
McDougal, James	Sandy
McFarlane, Charles	Chappie
McGann, Dan	Dennis
McGarr, James	Chippy
McGee, Willie	E.T.
McGee, Bill	Fiddler, Fibber
McGill, Willie	Kid
McGinnis, George	Jumbo
McGlynn, Ulysses	Stoney
McGraw, John	Little Napoleon
McKechnie, Bill	Deacon
McSorley, John	Trick
Maglie, Sal	The Barber

Mails, John	Duster, The Great
Mallory, James	Sunny Jim
Mancuso, August	Gus, Blackie
Maranville, Walter	Rabbit
Marion, Marty	Slats, Octopus
Marolewski, Fred	Fritz
Marshall, William	Doc
Martin, John	Pepper, Wild Horse of the Osage
Martinez, Orlando	Marty
Mattick, Walter	Chick
Mauch, Gene	Skip
May, Frank	Jakie
Meadows, Henry	Lee, Specs
Medwick, Joe	Ducky, Muscles
Meek, Frank	Dad
Metzger, Clarence	Butch
Mierkowicz, Ed	Butch
Miggins, Larry	Irish
Miller, Charles	Dusty
Miller, Eddie	Eppie
Miller, George	Doggie, Foghorn, Calliope
Miller, John	Dots
Milligan, John	Jocko
Mills, Colonel	Buster
Minoso, Saturnino	Minnie
Mitchell, Clarence	Mitch
Mize, Johnny	The Big Cat
Mizell, Wilmer	Vinegar Bend
Mollwitz, Fred	Fritz, Zip
Moore, Gene	Rowdy, Gus
Moore, Lloyd	Whitey
Morales, Julio	Jerry
Moran, Charles	Uncle Charlie
Morgan, Eddie	Pepper
Morse, Peter	Hap
Moryn, Walt	Moose
Mourey, Harry	Mike
Mozzali, Maurice	Mo
Mueller, Clarence	Heinie
Muffett, Billy	Muff
Mullane, Tony	Count
Munger, George	Red
Munns, Les	Nem, Big Ed
Murphy, John	Soldier Boy
Murray, John	Red
Musial, Stan	The Man
Myers, Henry	Hy
Neale, Earle	Greasy
Nelson, Glenn	Rocky
Nichols, Charles	Kid
Nichols, Frederick	Tricky
Niebergall, Charles	Nig

Niehoff, John	Bert, Buck, Paddles
Niland, Tom	Honest Tom
Northey, Ron	The Round Man
Oakes, Ennis	Rebel
O'Brien, Johnny	Chewing Gum
O'Connor, John	Jack, Rowdy, Peach Pie
O'Connor, Patrick	Paddy
O'Neill, James	Tip
O'Rourke, Joseph	Patsy
O'Rourke, Tim	Voiceless
Osteen, James	Champ
Padgett, Don	Red
Paine, Phil	Flip
Parmelee, Leroy	Tarzan, Bud
Parrott, Tom	Tacky
Partenheimer, Stan	Party
Pearce, Richard	Dickey
Peete, Charles	Mule
Perduc, Hubbard	The Gallatin Squash
Perritt, William	Pol
Pfeffer, Ed	Jeff
Pippen, Harold	Cotton
Posedel, Bill	Barnacle Bill
Porter, J.W.	Jay
Presko, Joseph	Little Joe
Puccinelli, George	Count
Quinlan, Thomas	Finners
Raschi, Vic	Springfield Rifle
Ramsey, Thomas	Toad
Rasmussen, Harry	Eric
Raub, Thomas	Shorty
Raymond, Arthur	Bugs
Repulski, Eldon	Rip, Al
Rhem, Charles	Flint, Shad
Rhoads, Robert	Dusty
Rice, Hal	Hoot
Richard, Lee	Bee Bee
Riddle, John	Mutt
Riviere, Arthur	Tink
Roberts, Clarence	Skipper
Robinson, Hank	Rube
Robinson, Wilbert	Uncle Robbie
Robinson, William	Yank
Roche, Jack	Red
Roe, Elwin	Preacher
Rojas, Octavio	Cookie
Romano, John	Honey
Roseman, James	Chief
Rothrock, Jack	Rocky
Ruba, Dominic	Mike
Ruberto, John	Sonny

Sadowski, Bob	Sid
Sallee, Harry	Slim
Samuels, Samuel	Ike
Sanders, Warren	War
Sauer, Ed	Horn
Sawatski, Carl	Swats
Schoendienst, Al	Red
Schofield, Dick	Ducky, Schoy
Schriver, William	Pop
Schuble, Henry	Heinie
Schultz, Charles	Buddy
Schultz, George	Barney
Schultz, Joe	Dode
Schultz, Joe	Germany
Scoffie, Lou	Weaser
Sell, Elwood	Epp
Sessi, Walter	Watsie
Shaffer, George	Orator
Shannon, Mike	Cannon, Moonman
Shannon, William	Spike
Sheckard, Samuel	Jimmy, Sheck
Sheehan, Tomothy	Biff
Sherdel, Bill	Wee Willie
Shotton, Burt	Barney
Shoun, Clyde	Hardrock
Siebert, Wilfred	Sonny
Sizemore, Ted	Size
Skinner, Bob	Dog
Slade, Gordon	Oskie
Slaughter, Enos	Country
Smith, Carl	Reggie
Smith, Earl	Oil
Smith, George	Germany
Smith, Hal	Cura
Smith, John	Jack
Smith, Lonnie	Skates
Smith, Ozzie	The Wizard of Oz
Snyder, Frank	Pancho
Solomon, Eddie	Buddy, The King
Sommers, Joseph	Kid
Southworth, Billy	Billy the Kid
Spencer, Daryl	Big D
Sprinz, Joseph	Mule
Stainback, George	Tuck, Tucker
Stallcup, Virgil	Red
Stanky, Eddie	The Brat, Muggsy
Starr, Ray	Iron Man
Steele, Bill	Big Bill
Stewart, John	Stuffy
Stinson, Gorrell	Bob, Scrap Iron
Stivetts, Jack	Happy
Stone, William	Tige
Stout, Allyn	Fish Hook
Street, Charles	Gabby, Old Sarge
Stricker, John	Cub

Stripp, Joe	Jersey Joe
Stuart, Johnny	Stud
Stuper, John	John Cosell
Sudhopp, Willie	Wee Willie
Sullivan, Don	Link
Sullivan, Thomas	Sleeper
Sunkel, Tom	Lefty
Surkont, Matthew	Max
Sutter, Howard	Bruce
Sutthoff, Jack	Sunny Jack
Sykes, Bob	Psycho
Tate, Lee	Skeeter
Taylor, Jack	Brewery Jack
Teachout, Arthur	Bud
Tebeau, Oliver	Patsy
Tenace, Fury	Gene
Thacker, Morris	Moe
Thomas, John	Lee
Thomas, Tom	Savage
Thompson, John	Gus
Tinning, Lyle	Bud
Toporcer, George	Specs
Triplett, Herman	Coaker, Trip
Tucker, Tom	Foghorn
Turner, George	Tuck
Turner, Thomas	Tink
Twineham, Arthur	Old Hoss
Valenzuela, Benny	Papeleco
Vance, Arthur Clarence	Dazzy
Verban, Emil	Dutch, Antelope
Wagner, Leon	Daddy Wags, Cheekie
Walker, Harry	The Hat, Little Dixie
Walker, Roy	Dixie
Wallace, Rhoderick	Bobby
Waller, Elliott	Ty
Ward, Dick	Ale
Wares, Clyde	Buzzy
Warmoth, Wallace	Cy
Warneke, Lon	Arkansas Hummingbird
Webb, James	Skeeter
Weiland, Bob	Lefty
Werle, Bill	Bugs
Westlake, Waldon	Wally
Weyhing, August	Gus
Whitehead, Burgess	Whitey
Whitted, George	Possum
Wight, Bill	Lefty
Wilber, Del	Babe
Wilhelm, Hoyt	The Doctor, Knuck
Wilks, Ted	Cork
Williams, James	Jimy
Williams, Rees	Steamboat
Wilson, Charles	Swamp Baby

Nicknames (continued)

Wilson, Frank	Zeke
Wilson, Jimmy	Ace
Wilson, John	Chief
Wilson, Owen	Chief
Winford, Jim	Cowboy
Wingo, Ivey	Cinder
Winsett, Tom	Long Tom
Withrow, Raymond	Corky
Wolf, William	Chicken
Worthington, Robert	Red
Young, Norman	Babe
Young, Denton True	Cy
Young, Lemuel	Pep
Zacher, Elmer	Silver
Zmich, Ed	Ike

WORLD
SERIES

Cardinal World Series Highlights

1926   Cardinals 4, New York Yankees 3

In their first World Series appearance, luck seemed to side with the Redbirds.

In the seventh inning of the seventh game, New York mounted a genuine threat, filling the bases with two out and power-hitter Tony Lazzeri at bat.

Cardinal pilot Rogers Hornsby decided he had seen enough of pitcher Jesse Haines and called upon veteran right-hander Grover Cleveland Alexander. All the 39-year-old future Hall of Famer did was strike out the Yankee shortstop on four pitches, retiring the side, and he got the New Yorkers out with no problems in the next two frames.

1928   New York Yankees 4, Cardinals 0

The Bronx Bombers never forget, as evidenced by their pasting of Cardinal pitching, avenging a Cardinal Series victory two years earlier.

Leading the Yankee attack were Babe Ruth, who hit .625, including three home runs in game four and Lou Gehrig, who belted four total round-trippers and batted .545.

After the Series, Cards prexy Sam Breadon fired Manager Bill McKechnie, blaming the team's ineptness on him.

1930   Philadelphia Athletics 4, Cardinals 2

Back in the fall classic after a one-year absence, the Cards didn't have enough to sustain the onslaught of Connie Mack and his powerful A's.

Leading the Mackmen to victory were such stalwarts as Al Simmons, Jimmy Foxx, Lefty Grove, Mickey Cochrane, and George Earnshaw.

Pitching dominated the Series, as St. Louis hit an anemic .200, the champion A's .197.

1931 Cardinals 4, Philadelphia Athletics 3

Oh, sweet revenge!

Prior to the Series, one John Leonard Martin was so obscure that the A's didn't even notice him when they were doing their Series preparatory scouting.

Pepper, or the Wild Horse of the Osage, dominated the Series like few men before or since. He stole five bases, was 12-for-24 in the batting department with five runs scored and an equal number batted in, hitting just about every Philadelphia pitcher's offering.

1934 Cardinals 4, Detroit Tigers 3

What a crazy World Series! But in the end, it was the Dean brothers, Dizzy and Daffy, who led the Redbirds to a third World Championship.

Each Dean recorded two Series victories, Dizzy in games one and seven, brother Paul in games three and six.

This was the truest of Gashouse Gang contingents, with such certified flakes as the Deans, Frank Frisch, Pepper Martin, Rip Collins, Leo Durocher, and Joe Medwick on hand for the Redbirds.

The last game, at Detroit, marked the removal of Medwick by Commissioner Landis, because of an onslaught of garbage thrown by Detroit fans.

1942 Cardinals 4, New York Yankees 1

After a seven-year absence, the Redbirds were back in the Series. And they made the most of their opportunity, clipping the defending champion Yankees in five games.

This was a young Cardinal team, the youngest ever to play in World Series competition. The players averaged 26 years old, and their oldest player, Terry Moore, was just 29.

New York took the opening contest 7-4, but it was all St. Louis after that. Speed and power took the Series for the Redbirds, Stan Musial, Enos Slaughter, and Whitey Kurowski leading the way, while Johnny Beazley notched complete game victories in games two and five.

1943 New York Yankees 4, Cardinals 1

If nothing else, the Bronx Bombers dethroned the team that handed them a similar fate one year before, and in just as many contests.

The Redbirds managed a victory in game two at New York, but not much after that. Spud Chandler limited the Cards to two runs and seven hits in the opener and came back with a seven-hit shutout in the decisive game five.

Both teams lost many players to the war effort, but St. Louis still had big guns Stan Musial, Walker Cooper, and pitcher Mort Cooper in its lineup.

1944 Cardinals 4, St. Louis Browns 2

In what has been called the greatest moment in St. Louis baseball history, the "haves," the Cardinals, took on the "have nots," the Browns, in the first and only all-St. Louis World Series.

The two teams traded victories, until the Cards won games five and six, giving them the title.

Again Stan Musial, Whitey Kurowski, and Enos Slaughter led the Redbird attack, in much the same fashion they did two Octobers earlier. The problem with the Browns was a porous defense, 10 errors, seven of which led to Cardinal runs.

1946 Cardinals 4, Boston Red Sox 3

Four simple words are remembered when the 1946 Classic comes to mind: Enos Slaughter's mad dash.

Seemingly simple, the manner in which the Redbird outfielder took things into his own hands in the deciding game seven was a piece of complex base running.

With two out and the game tied in the bottom of the eighth inning, the host Cards had Country Slaughter at first base, with a three-two count on Harry Walker. Slaughter was running with the pitch and was at second base when center fielder Leon Culberson fielded pinch-hitter Walker's low liner. Culberson fumbled the ball, then recovered and threw to shortstop Johnny Pesky, who was standing in short center field. By this time, Slaughter was flying around third, headed for the plate. For some reason, Pesky stood transfixed. Second baseman Bobby Doerr yelled for a throw to the plate, but by the time Pesky knew what was happening, Slaughter had scored what proved to be the Series' winning run.

1964   Cardinals 4, New York Yankees 3

After a 17-year drought, the Cards found themselves in the World Series again, thanks to their late-season surge, but also because of a backward surge by the Philadelphia Phillies.

The Redbirds made the most of their good fortune, but took the full slate to do it.

The hitting star for the Redbirds was Tim McCarver, who posted a .478 average. On the mound, Bob Gibson won two games, including the decisive No. 7 and struck out 31 Yankees in 27 innings of work.

1967   Cardinals 4, Boston Red Sox 3

It was the Bob and Lou show, pitcher Gibson again gaining two World Series victories, while teammate Brock stole seven bases and knocked out 12 hits.

For the sixth time, the Redbirds entered a seventh game of a Series; and for the sixth time, they were successful.

By game seven, St. Louis had a tired Red Sox pitcher Jim Lonborg as its opponent, and shelled the Boston ace for seven runs in as many innings, en route to a 7–2 victory.

1968   Detroit Tigers 4, Cardinals 3

It was the first time in Cardinal history that the club had lost a game seven, having won the previous six final game clashes.

Lefty Mickey Lolich led the Tigers with three victories, performing far better than teammate Dennis McLain, winner of 31 regular season contests.

Bob Gibson and Lou Brock again were the Redbird standouts, the righty striking out 17 Tigers in game one to break Dodger pitcher Sandy Koufax' mark and becoming the first pitcher to hit a second World Series home run, his first coming a year earlier against the Red Sox. Brock managed 13 hits and stole seven bases in a losing cause.

1982   Cardinals 4, Milwaukee Brewers 3
(See appendix for description)

The Games

1926

St. Louis N.L. 4, New York A.L. 3

Batting	Pos	G	AB	R	H	2B	3B	HR	RBI	BB	SO	SB	BA
St. Louis													
Jim Bottomley	1B	7	29	4	10	3	0	0	5	1	2	0	.345
Rogers Hornsby	2B	7	28	2	7	1	0	0	4	2	2	1	.250
Tommy Thevenow	SS	7	24	5	10	1	0	1	4	0	1	0	.417
Les Bell	3B	7	27	4	7	1	0	1	6	2	5	0	.259
Billy Southworth	RF	7	29	6	10	1	1	1	4	0	0	1	.345
Taylor Douthit	CF	4	15	3	4	2	0	0	1	3	2	0	.267
Chick Hafey	LF	7	27	2	5	2	0	0	0	0	7	0	.185
Bob O'Farrell	C	7	23	2	7	1	0	0	2	2	2	0	.304
Wattie Holm	PH-RF-CF	5	16	1	2	0	0	0	1	1	2	0	.125
Jake Flowers	PH	3	3	0	0	0	0	0	0	0	1	0	.000
Specs Toporcer	PH	1	0	0	0	0	0	0	0	1	0	0	.000
Ray Blades	Did not play—injured												
Ernie Vick	Did not play												
Grover C. Alexander	P	3	7	1	0	0	0	0	0	0	2	0	.000
Bill Sherdel	P	2	5	0	0	0	0	0	0	0	2	0	.000
Jesse Haines	P	3	5	1	3	0	0	1	2	0	1	0	.600
Flint Rhem	P	1	1	0	0	0	0	0	0	0	1	0	.000
Hi Bell	P	1	0	0	0	0	0	0	0	0	0	0	.000
Bill Hallahan	P	1	0	0	0	0	0	0	0	0	0	0	.000
Vic Keen	P	1	0	0	0	0	0	0	0	0	0	0	.000
Art Reinhart	P	1	0	0	0	0	0	0	0	0	0	0	.000
Allan Sothoron	Did not play												
Syl Johnson	Did not play												
Ed Clough	Did not play												
Team Total		7	239	31	65	12	1	4	30	11	30	2	.272

Double Plays—6   Left on Bases—43

Batting	Pos	G	AB	R	H	2B	3B	HR	RBI	BB	SO	SB	BA
New York													
Lou Gehrig	1B	7	23	1	8	2	0	0	4	5	4	0	.348
Tony Lazzeri	2B	7	26	2	5	1	0	0	3	1	6	0	.192
Mark Koenig	SS	7	32	2	4	1	0	0	2	0	6	0	.125
Joe Dugan	3B	7	24	2	8	1	0	0	2	1	1	0	.333
Babe Ruth	RF-LF	7	20	6	6	0	0	4	5	11	2	1	.300
Earle Combs	CF	7	28	3	10	2	0	0	2	5	2	0	.357
Bob Meusel	LF-RF	7	21	3	5	1	1	0	0	6	1	0	.238
Hank Severeid	C	7	22	1	6	1	0	0	1	1	2	0	.273
Ben Paschal	PH	5	4	0	1	0	0	0	0	1	2	0	.250
Pat Collins	C	3	2	0	0	0	0	0	0	0	1	0	.000
Mike Gazella	3B	1	0	0	0	0	0	0	0	0	0	0	.000
Spence Adams	PR	2	0	0	0	0	0	0	0	0	0	0	.000
Benny Bengough	Did not play—shoulder injury												
Roy Carlyle	Did not play												
Aaron Ward	Did not play												
Herb Pennock	P	3	7	1	1	1	0	0	0	0	0	0	.143
Waite Hoyt	P	2	6	0	0	0	0	0	0	0	1	0	.000
Dutch Ruether	P-PH	3	4	0	0	0	0	0	0	0	0	0	.000
Bob Shawkey	P	3	2	0	0	0	0	0	0	0	1	0	.000
Urban Shocker	P	2	2	0	0	0	0	0	0	0	2	0	.000
Myles Thomas	P	2	0	0	0	0	0	0	0	0	0	0	.000
Sam Jones	P	1	0	0	0	0	0	0	0	0	0	0	.000
Walter Beall	Did not play												
Garland Braxton	Did not play												
Herb McQuaid	Did not play												
Team Total		7	223	21	54	10	1	4	20	31	31	1	.242

Double Plays—3   Left on Bases—55

1926 World Series (continued)

Pitching	G	GS	CG	IP	H	R	ER	BB	SO	W	L	SV	ERA
St. Louis													
Grover C. Alexander	3	2	2	20⅓	12	4	3	4	17	2	0	1	1.33
Bill Sherdel	2	2	1	17	15	5	4	8	3	0	2	0	2.12
Jesse Haines	3	2	1	16⅔	13	2	2	9	5	2	0	0	1.08
Flint Rhem	1	1	0	4	7	3	3	2	4	0	0	0	6.75
Hi Bell	1	0	0	2	4	2	2	1	1	0	0	0	9.00
Bill Hallahan	1	0	0	2	2	1	1	3	1	0	0	0	4.50
Vic Keen	1	0	0	1	0	0	0	0	0	0	0	0	0.00
Art Reinhart	1	0	0	0	1	4	4	4	0	0	1	0	0.00
Syl Johnson	Did not play												
Allan Sothoron	Did not play												
Ed Clough	Did not play												
Team Total	7	7	4	63	54	21	19	31	31	4	3	1	2.71

Pitching	G	GS	CG	IP	H	R	ER	BB	SO	W	L	SV	ERA
New York													
Herb Pennock	3	2	2	22	13	3	3	4	8	2	0	0	1.23
Waite Hoyt	2	2	1	15	19	8	2	1	10	1	1	0	1.20
Bob Shawkey	3	1	0	10	8	7	6	2	7	0	1	0	5.40
Urban Shocker	2	1	0	7⅓	13	7	5	0	3	0	1	0	5.87
Dutch Ruether	1	1	0	4⅓	7	4	2	2	1	0	1	0	4.16
Myles Thomas	2	0	0	3	3	1	1	0	0	0	0	0	3.00
Sam Jones	1	0	0	1	2	1	1	2	1	0	0	0	9.00
Walter Beall	Did not play												
Garland Braxton	Did not play												
Herb McQuaid	Did not play												
Team Total	7	7	3	63	65	31	20	11	30	3	4	0	2.86

Total Attendance—328,051. Average Attendance—46,864. Winning Player's Share—$5,585. Losing Player's Share—$3,418.

LINESCORE:

FIRST GAME (Oct. 2, at New York)

ST. LOUIS	1 0 0	0 0 0	0 0 0—1 3 1
NEW YORK	1 0 0	0 0 1	0 0 x—2 6 0

Sherdel, Haines (8th)   W—Pennock
Pennock   L—Sherdel

SECOND GAME (Oct. 3, at New York)

ST. LOUIS	0 0 2	0 0 0	3 0 1—6 12 1
NEW YORK	0 2 0	0 0 0	0 0 0—2 4 0

Alexander   W—Alexander
Shocker, Shawkey (8th), Jones (9th)   L—Shocker

THIRD GAME (Oct. 5, at St. Louis)

NEW YORK	0 0 0	0 0 0	0 0 0—0 5 1
ST. LOUIS	0 0 0	3 1 0	0 0 x—4 8 0

Ruether, Shawkey (5th), Thomas (8th)   W—Haines
Haines   L—Ruether

FOURTH GAME (Oct. 6, at St. Louis)
NEW YORK .... 1 0 1 1 4 2 1 0 0—10 14 1
ST. LOUIS .... 1 0 0 3 0 0 0 0 1— 5 14 0
Hoyt   W—Hoyt
Rhem, Reinhart (5th), H. Bell (5th), Hallahan (7th), Keen (9th)   L—Reinhart

FIFTH GAME (Oct. 7, at St. Louis)
NEW YORK .... 0 0 0 0 0 1 0 0 1 1—3 9 1
ST. LOUIS .... 0 0 0 1 0 0 1 0 0 0—2 7 1
Pennock   W—Pennock
Sherdel   L—Sherdel

SIXTH GAME (Oct. 9, at New York)
ST. LOUIS .... 3 0 0 0 1 0 5 0 1—10 13 2
NEW YORK .... 0 0 0 1 0 0 1 0 0— 2 8 1
Alexander   W—Alexander
Shawkey, Shocker (7th), Thomas (8th)   L—Shocker

SEVENTH GAME (Oct. 10, at New York)
ST. LOUIS .... 0 0 0 3 0 0 0 0 0—3 8 0
NEW YORK .... 0 0 1 0 0 1 0 0 0—2 8 3
Haines, Alexander (7th)   W—Haines
Hoyt, Pennock (7th)   L—Hoyt

1928

New York A.L. 4, St. Louis N.L. 0

Batting	Pos	G	AB	R	H	2B	3B	HR	RBI	BB	SO	SB	BA
New York													
Lou Gehrig	1B	4	11	5	6	1	0	4	9	6	0	0	.545
Tony Lazzeri	2B	4	12	2	3	1	0	0	0	1	0	2	.250
Mark Koenig	SS	4	19	1	3	0	0	0	0	0	1	0	.158
Gene Robertson	3B-PH	3	8	1	1	0	0	0	2	1	0	0	.125
Babe Ruth	RF-LF	4	16	9	10	3	0	3	4	1	2	0	.625
Ben Paschal	CF-PH	3	10	0	2	0	0	0	1	1	0	0	.200
Bob Meusel	LF-RF	4	15	5	3	1	0	1	3	2	5	2	.200
Benny Bengough	C	4	13	1	3	0	0	0	1	1	1	0	.231
Cedric Durst	CF	4	8	3	3	0	0	1	2	0	1	0	.375
Joe Dugan	3B	3	6	0	1	0	0	0	1	0	0	0	.167
Leo Durocher	2B	4	2	0	0	0	0	0	0	0	1	0	.000
Pat Collins	C	1	1	0	1	1	0	0	0	0	0	0	1.000
Earle Combs	PH	1	0	0	0	0	0	0	1	0	0	0	.000
Johnny Grabowski	Did not play												
Mike Gazella	Did not play												
Bill Dickey	Did not play												
Waite Hoyt	P	2	7	0	1	0	0	0	0	0	0	0	.143
Tom Zachary	P	1	4	0	0	0	0	0	0	0	1	0	.000
George Pipgras	P	1	2	0	0	0	0	0	1	0	0	0	.000
Herb Pennock	Did not play—illness												
Fred Heimach	Did not play												
Myles Homas	Did not play												
Rosy Ryan	Did not play												
Team Total		4	134	27	37	7	0	9	25	13	12	4	.276

Double Plays—3   Left on Bases—24

Batting	Pos	G	AB	R	H	2B	3B	HR	RBI	BB	SO	SB	BA
St. Louis													
Jim Bottomley	1B	4	14	1	3	0	1	1	3	2	6	0	.214
Frankie Frisch	2B	4	13	1	3	0	0	0	1	2	2	2	.231
Rabbit Maranville	SS	4	13	2	4	1	0	0	0	1	1	1	.308
Andy High	3B	4	17	1	5	2	0	0	1	1	3	0	.294
George Harper	RF	3	9	1	1	0	0	0	0	2	2	0	.111
Taylor Douthit	CF	3	11	1	1	0	0	0	1	1	1	0	.091
Chick Hafey	LF	4	15	0	3	0	0	0	0	1	4	0	.200
Jimmie Wilson	C	3	11	1	1	1	0	0	1	0	3	0	.091
Ernie Orsatti	PH-CF	4	7	1	2	1	0	0	0	1	3	0	.286
Wattie Holm	PH-RF	3	6	0	1	0	0	0	1	0	1	0	.167
Earl Smith	C	1	4	0	3	0	0	0	0	0	0	0	.750
Ray Blades	PH	1	1	0	0	0	0	0	0	0	1	0	.000
Pepper Martin	PR	1	0	1	0	0	0	0	0	0	0	0	.000
Tommy Thevenow	SS	1	0	0	0	0	0	0	0	0	0	0	.000
Wally Roettger	Did not play—broken leg												
Howie Williamson	Did not play												
Bill Sherdel	P	2	5	0	0	0	0	0	0	0	2	0	.000
Jesse Haines	P	1	2	0	0	0	0	0	0	0	0	0	.000
Clarence Mitchell	P	1	2	0	0	0	0	0	0	0	0	0	.000
Grover C. Alexander	P	2	1	0	0	0	0	0	1	0	0	0	.000
Syl Johnson	P	2	0	0	0	0	0	0	0	0	0	0	.000
Flint Rhem	P	1	0	0	0	0	0	0	0	0	0	0	.000
Fred Frankhouse	Did not play												
Art Reinhart	Did not play												
Hal Haid	Did not play												
Team Total		4	131	10	27	5	1	1	9	11	29	3	.207

Double Plays—3   Left on Bases—27

Pitching	G	GS	CG	IP	H	R	ER	BB	SO	W	L	SV	ERA
New York													
Waite Hoyt	2	2	2	18	14	4	3	6	14	2	0	0	1.50
George Pipgras	1	1	1	9	4	3	2	4	8	1	0	0	2.00
Tom Zachary	1	1	1	9	9	3	3	1	7	1	0	0	3.00
Herb Pennock	Did not play—illness												
Fred Heimach	Did not play												
Myles Thomas	Did not play												
Rosy Ryan	Did not play												
Team Total	4	4	4	36	27	10	8	11	29	4	0	0	2.00

Pitching	G	GS	CG	IP	H	R	ER	BB	SO	W	L	SV	ERA
St. Louis													
Bill Sherdel	2	2	0	13⅓	15	7	7	3	3	0	2	0	4.73
Jesse Haines	1	1	0	6	6	6	3	3	3	0	1	0	4.50
Clarence Mitchell	1	0	0	5⅔	2	1	1	2	2	0	0	0	1.59
Grover C. Alexander	2	1	0	5	10	11	11	4	2	0	1	0	19.80
Syl Johnson	2	0	0	2	4	2	1	1	1	0	0	0	4.50
Flint Rhem	1	0	0	2	0	0	0	0	1	0	0	0	0.00
Fred Frankhouse	Did not play												
Art Reinhart	Did not play												
Hal Haid	Did not play												
Team Total	4	4	0	34	37	27	23	13	12	0	4	0	6.09

Total Attendance—199,072. Average Attendance—49,768. Winning Player's Share—$5,532. Losing Player's Share—$4,197.

LINESCORES:

FIRST GAME (Oct. 4, at New York)
```
ST. LOUIS  .........................  0 0 0  0 0 0  1 0 0—1 3 1
NEW YORK  .........................  1 0 0  2 0 0  0 1 x—4 7 0
```
Sherdel, Johnson (8th)   W—Hoyt
Hoyt   L—Sherdel

SECOND GAME (Oct. 5, at New York)
```
ST. LOUIS  .........................  0 3 0  0 0 0  0 0 0—3 4 1
NEW YORK  .........................  3 1 4  0 0 0  1 0 x—9 8 2
```
Alexander, Mitchell (3d)   W—Pipgras
Pipgras   L—Alexander

THIRD GAME (Oct. 7, at St. Louis)
```
NEW YORK  .........................  0 1 0  2 0 3  1 0 0—7 7 2
ST. LOUIS  .........................  2 0 0  0 1 0  0 0 0—3 9 3
```
Zachary   W—Zachary
Haines, Johnson (7th), Rhem (8th)   L—Haines

FOURTH GAME (Oct. 9, at St. Louis)
```
NEW YORK  .........................  0 0·0· 1 0 0  4 2 0—7 15 2
ST. LOUIS  ,,. .................  0 0 1  1 0 0  0 0 1—3 11 0
```
Hoyt   W—Hoyt
Sherdel, Alexander (7th)   L—Sherdel

1930

Philadelphia A.L. 4, St. Louis N.L. 2

Batting	Pos	G	AB	R	H	2B	3B	HR	RBI	BB	SO	SB	BA
Philadelphia													
Jimmy Foxx	1B	6	21	3	7	2	1	1	3	2	4	0	.333
Max Bishop	2B	6	18	5	4	0	0	0	0	7	3	0	.222
Joe Boley	SS	6	21	1	2	0	0	0	1	0	1	0	.095
Jimmy Dykes	3B	6	18	2	4	3	0	1	5	5	3	0	.222
Bing Miller	RF	6	21	0	3	2	0	0	3	0	4	0	.143
Mule Haas	CF	6	18	1	2	0	1	0	1	1	3	0	.111
Al Simmons	LF-CF	6	22	4	8	2	0	2	4	2	2	0	.364
Mickey Cochrane	C	6	18	5	4	1	0	2	4	5	2	0	.222
Jim Moore	PH-LF	3	3	0	1	0	0	0	0	1	1	0	.333
Eric McNair	PH	1	1	0	0	0	0	0	0	0	0	0	.000
Dib Williams	Did not play												
Wally Schang	Did not play												
Homer Summa	Did not play												
Cy Perkins	Did not play												
Pinky Higgins	Did not play												
Eddie Collins	Did not play												
George Earnshaw	P	3	9	0	0	0	0	0	0	0	5	0	.000
Lefty Grove	P	3	6	0	0	0	0	0	0	0	3	0	.000
Rube Walberg	P	1	2	0	0	0	0	0	0	0	1	0	.000
Jack Quinn	P	1	0	0	0	0	0	0	0	0	0	0	.000
Bill Shores	P	1	0	0	0	0	0	0	0	1	0	0	.000
Roy Mahaffey	Did not play												
Eddie Rommel	Did not play												
Charlie Perkins	Did not play												
Team Total		6	178	21	35	10	2	6	21	24	32	0	.197

Double Plays—2   Left on Bases—36

1930 World Series (continued)

Batting	Pos	G	AB	R	H	2B	3B	HR	RBI	BB	SO	SB	BA
St. Louis													
Jim Bottomley	1B	6	22	1	1	1	0	0	0	2	9	0	.045
Frankie Frisch	2B	6	24	0	5	2	0	0	0	0	0	1	.208
Charlie Gelbert	SS	6	17	2	6	0	1	0	2	3	3	0	.353
Sparky Adams	3B	6	21	0	3	0	0	0	1	0	4	0	.143
George Watkins	RF	4	12	2	2	0	0	1	1	1	3	0	.167
Taylor Douthit	CF	6	24	1	2	0	0	1	2	0	2	0	.083
Chick Hafey	LF	6	22	2	6	5	0	0	2	1	3	0	.273
Jimmy Wilson	C	4	15	0	4	1	0	0	2	0	1	0	.267
Ray Blades	RF-PH	5	9	2	1	0	0	0	0	2	2	0	.111
Gus Mancuso	C	2	7	1	2	0	0	0	0	1	2	0	.286
Andy High	PH-3B	1	2	1	1	0	0	0	0	0	0	0	.500
Showboat Fisher	PH	2	2	0	1	1	0	0	0	0	1	0	.500
Ernie Orsatti	PH	1	1	0	0	0	0	0	0	0	0	0	.000
George Puccinelli	PH	1	1	0	0	0	0	0	0	0	0	0	.000
Burleigh Grimes	P	2	5	0	2	0	0	0	0	0	1	0	.400
Bill Hallahan	P	2	2	0	0	0	0	0	0	1	1	0	.000
Jesse Haines	P	1	2	0	1	0	0	0	1	0	0	0	.500
Jim Lindsey	P	2	1	0	1	0	0	0	0	0	0	0	1.000
Flint Rhem	P	1	1	0	0	0	0	0	0	0	1	0	.000
Syl Johnson	P	2	0	0	0	0	0	0	0	0	0	0	.000
Hi Bell	P	1	0	0	0	0	0	0	0	0	0	0	.000
Al Grabowski	Did not play												
Team Total		6	190	12	38	10	1	2	11	11	33	1	.200

Double Plays—4 Left on Bases—37

Pitching	G	GS	CG	IP	H	R	ER	BB	SO	W	L	SV	ERA
Philadelphia													
George Earnshaw	3	3	2	25	13	2	2	7	19	2	0	0	0.72
Lefty Grove	3	2	2	19	15	5	3	3	10	2	1	0	1.42
Rube Walberg	1	1	0	4⅔	4	2	2	1	3	0	1	0	3.86
Jack Quinn	1	0	0	2	3	1	1	0	1	0	0	0	4.50
Bill Shores	1	0	0	1⅓	3	2	2	0	0	0	0	0	13.50
Roy Mahaffey	Did not play												
Eddie Rommel	Did not play												
Charlie Perkins	Did not play												
Team Total	6	6	4	52	38	12	10	11	33	4	2	0	1.73

Pitching	G	GS	CG	IP	H	R	ER	BB	SO	W	L	SV	ERA
St. Louis													
Burleigh Grimes	2	2	2	17	10	7	7	6	13	0	2	0	3.71
Bill Hallahan	2	2	1	11	9	2	2	8	8	1	1	0	1.64
Jesse Haines	1	1	1	9	4	1	1	4	2	1	0	0	1.00
Syl Johnson	2	0	0	5	4	4	4	3	4	0	0	0	7.20
Jim Lindsey	2	0	0	4⅔	1	1	1	1	2	0	0	0	1.93
Flint Rhem	1	1	0	3⅓	7	6	4	2	3	0	1	0	10.80
Hi Bell	1	0	0	1	0	0	0	0	0	0	0	0	0.00
Al Grabowski	Did not play												
Team Total	6	6	4	51	35	21	19	24	32	2	4	0	3.35

Total Attendance—212,619. Average Attendance—35,437. Winning Player's Share—$5,038. Losing Player's Share—$3,537.

LINESCORES:

FIRST GAME (Oct. 1, at Philadelphia)
```
      ST. LOUIS .......................... 0 0 2  0 0 0  0 0 0—2 9 0
      PHILADELPHIA ..................... 0 1 0  1 0 1  1 1 x—5 5 0
Grimes                                         W—Grove
Grove                                          L—Grimes
```

SECOND GAME (Oct. 2, at Philadelphia)
```
      ST. LOUIS .......................... 0 1 0  0 0 0  0 0 0—1 6 2
      PHILADELPHIA ..................... 2 0 2  2 0 0  0 0 x—6 7 2
Rhem, Lindsey (4th), Johnson (7th)             W—Earnshaw
Earnshaw                                        L—Rhem
```

THIRD GAME (Oct. 4, at St. Louis)
```
      PHILADELPHIA ..................... 0 0 0  0 0 0  0 0 0—0 7 0
      ST. LOUIS .......................... 0 0 0  1 1 0  2 1 x—5 10 0
Walberg, Shores (5th), Quinn (7th)             W—Hallahan
Hallahan                                        L—Walberg
```

FOURTH GAME (Oct. 5, at St. Louis)
```
      PHILADELPHIA ..................... 1 0 0  0 0 0  0 0 0—1 4 1
      ST. LOUIS .......................... 0 0 1  2 0 0  0 0 x—3 5 1
Grove                                          W—Haines
Haines                                         L—Grove
```

FIFTH GAME (Oct. 6, at St. Louis)
```
      PHILADELPHIA ..................... 0 0 0  0 0 0  0 0 2—2 5 0
      ST. LOUIS .......................... 0 0 0  0 0 0  0 0 0—0 3 1
Earnshaw, Grove (8th)                          W—Grove
Grimes                                          L—Grimes
```

SIXTH GAME (Oct. 8, at Philadelphia)
```
      ST. LOUIS .......................... 0 0 0  0 0 0  0 0 1—1 5 1
      PHILADELPHIA ..................... 2 0 1  2 1 1  0 0 x—7 7 0
Hallahan, Johnson (3d), Lindsey (6th), Bell (8th)  W—Earnshaw
Earnshaw                                        L—Hallahan
```

1931
St. Louis N.L. 4, Philadelphia A.L. 3

Batting	Pos	G	AB	R	H	2B	3B	HR	RBI	BB	SO	SB	BA
St. Louis													
Jim Bottomley	1B	7	25	2	4	1	0	0	2	2	5	0	.160
Frankie Frisch	2B	7	27	2	7	2	0	0	1	1	2	1	.259
Charlie Gelbert	SS	7	23	0	6	1	0	0	3	0	4	0	.261
Andy High	3B-PR	4	15	3	4	0	0	0	0	0	2	0	.267
George Watkins	RF-PR	5	14	4	4	1	0	1	2	2	1	1	.286
Pepper Martin	CF	7	24	5	12	4	0	1	5	2	3	5	.500
Chick Hafey	LF	6	24	1	4	0	0	0	0	0	5	1	.167
Jimmie Wilson	C	7	23	0	5	0	0	0	2	1	1	0	.217
Wally Roettger	RF	3	14	1	4	1	0	0	0	0	3	0	.286
Jake Flowers	PH-3B	5	11	1	1	1	0	0	0	1	0	0	.091
Sparky Adams	3B	2	4	0	1	0	0	0	0	0	1	0	.250
Ernie Orsatti	LF	1	3	0	0	0	0	0	0	0	3	0	.000
Ray Blades	PH	2	2	0	0	0	0	0	0	0	2	0	.000
Rip Collins	PH	2	2	0	0	0	0	0	0	0	1	0	.000
Gus Mancuso	PH-C	2	1	0	0	0	0	0	0	0	0	0	.000
Mike Gonzalez	Did not play												
Burleigh Grimes	P	2	7	0	2	0	0	0	2	0	2	0	.286
Bill Hallahan	P	3	6	0	0	0	0	0	0	0	3	0	.000
Paul Derringer	P	3	2	0	0	0	0	0	0	0	1	0	.000
Syl Johnson	P	3	2	0	0	0	0	0	0	0	2	0	.000
Jim Lindsey	P	2	0	0	0	0	0	0	0	0	0	0	.000
Flint Rhem	P	1	0	0	0	0	0	0	0	0	0	0	.000
Jesse Haines	Did not play												
Allyn Stout	Did not play												
Tony Kaufman	Did not play												
Team Total		7	229	19	54	11	0	2	17	9	41	8	.236

Double Plays—7 Left on Bases—40

Batting	Pos	G	AB	R	H	2B	3B	HR	RBI	BB	SO	SB	BA
Philadelphia													
Jimmie Foxx	1B	7	23	3	8	0	0	1	3	6	5	0	.348
Max Bishop	2B	7	27	4	4	0	0	0	0	3	5	0	.148
Dib Williams	SS	7	25	2	8	1	0	0	1	2	9	0	.320
Jimmy Dykes	3B	7	22	2	5	0	0	0	2	5	1	0	.227
Bing Miller	RF	7	26	3	7	1	0	0	1	0	4	0	.269
Mule Haas	CF	7	23	1	3	1	0	0	2	3	5	0	.130
Al Simmons	LF-CF	7	27	4	9	2	0	2	8	3	3	0	.333
Mickey Cochrane	C	7	25	2	4	0	0	0	1	5	2	0	.160
Jim Moore	PH-LF	2	3	0	1	0	0	0	0	0	1	0	.333
Eric McNair	PR-PH-2B	2	2	1	0	0	0	0	0	0	1	0	.000
Doc Cramer	PH	2	2	0	1	0	0	0	2	0	0	0	.500
Joe Boley	PH	1	1	0	0	0	0	0	0	0	1	0	.000
John Heving	PH	1	1	0	0	0	0	0	0	0	0	0	.000
Phil Todt	PH	1	0	0	0	0	0	0	0	1	0	0	.000
Joe Palmisano	Did not play												
Lefty Grove	P	3	10	0	0	0	0	0	0	0	7	0	.000
George Earnshaw	P	3	8	0	0	0	0	0	0	0	2	0	.000
Waite Hoyt	P	1	2	0	0	0	0	0	0	0	0	0	.000
Rube Walberg	P	2	0	0	0	0	0	0	0	0	0	0	.000
Roy Mahaffey	P	1	0	0	0	0	0	0	0	0	0	0	.000
Eddie Rommel	P	1	0	0	0	0	0	0	0	0	0	0	.000
Hank McDonald	Did not play												
Jim Peterson	Did not play												
Lew Krausse	Did not play												
Team Total		7	227	22	50	5	0	3	20	28	46	0	.220

Double Plays—4 Left on Bases—52

Pitching	G	GS	CG	IP	H	R	ER	BB	SO	W	L	SV	ERA
St. Louis													
Bill Hallahan	3	2	2	18⅓	12	1	1	8	12	2	0	1	0.49
Burleigh Grimes	2	2	1	17⅔	9	4	4	9	11	2	0	0	2.04
Paul Derringer	3	2	0	12⅔	14	10	6	7	14	0	2	0	4.26
Syl Johnson	3	1	0	9	10	3	3	1	6	0	1	0	3.00
Jim Lindsey	2	0	0	3⅓	4	4	2	3	2	0	0	0	5.40
Flint Rhem	1	0	0	1	1	0	0	0	1	0	0	0	0.00
Jesse Haines	Did not play												
Allyn Stout	Did not play												
Tony Kaufmann	Did not play												
Team Total	7	7	3	62	50	22	16	28	46	4	3	1	2.32

Pitching	G	GS	CG	IP	H	R	ER	BB	SO	W	L	SV	ERA
Philadelphia													
Lefty Grove	3	3	2	26	28	7	7	2	16	2	1	0	2.42
George Earnshaw	3	3	2	24	12	6	5	4	20	1	2	0	1.88
Waite Hoyt	1	1	0	6	7	3	3	0	1	0	1	0	4.50
Rube Walberg	2	0	0	3	3	1	1	2	4	0	0	0	3.00
Roy Mahaffey	1	0	0	1	1	1	1	1	0	0	0	0	9.00
Eddie Rommel	1	0	0	1	3	1	1	0	0	0	0	0	9.00
Hank McDonald	Did not play												
Jim Peterson	Did not play												
Lew Krausse	Did not play												
Team Total	7	7	4	61	54	19	18	9	41	3	4	0	2.66

Total Attendance—231,567. Average Attendance—33,081. Winning Player's Share—$4,468. Losing Player's Share—$3,023.

LINESCORES:

FIRST GAME (Oct. 1, at St. Louis)
```
PHILADELPHIA ................... 0 0 4  0 0 0  2 0 0—6 11 0
ST. LOUIS .................... 2 0 0  0 0 0  0 0 0—2 12 0
```
Grove   W—Grove
Derringer, Johnson (8th)   L—Derringer

SECOND GAME (Oct. 2, at St. Louis)
```
PHILADELPHIA ................... 0 0 0  0 0 0  0 0 0—0 3 0
ST. LOUIS .................... 0 1 0  0 0 0  1 0 x—2 6 1
```
Earnshaw   W—Hallahan
Hallahan   L—Earnshaw

THIRD GAME (Oct. 5, at Philadelphia)
```
ST. LOUIS .................... 0 2 0  2 0 0  0 0 1—5 12 0
PHILADELPHIA ................... 0 0 0  0 0 0  0 0 2—2 2 0
```
Grimes   W—Grimes
Grove, Mahaffey (9th)   L—Grove

FOURTH GAME (Oct. 6, at Philadelphia)
```
ST. LOUIS .................... 0 0 0  0 0 0  0 0 0—0 2 1
PHILADELPHIA ................... 1 0 0  0 0 2  0 0 x—3 10 0
```
Johnson, Lindsey (6th), Derringer (8th)   W—Earnshaw
Earnshaw   L—Johnson

1931 World Series (continued)

FIFTH GAME (Oct. 7, at Philadelphia)
```
     ST. LOUIS ....................... 1 0 0  0 0 2  0 1 1—5 12 0
     PHILADELPHIA ................... 0 0 0  0 0 0  1 0 0—1  9 0
```
Hallahan   W—Hallahan
Hoyt, Walbert (7th), Rommel (9th)   L—Hoyt

SIXTH GAME (Oct. 9, at St. Louis)
```
     PHILADELPHIA ................... 0 0 0  0 4 0  4 0 0—8 8 1
     ST. LOUIS ....................... 0 0 0  0 0 1  0 0 0—1 5 2
```
Grove   W—Grove
Derringer, Johnson (5th), Lindsey (7th), Rhem (9th)   L—Derringer

SEVENTH GAME (Oct. 10, at St. Louis)
```
     PHILADELPHIA ................... 0 0 0  0 0 0  0 0 2—2 7 1
     ST. LOUIS ....................... 2 0 2  0 0 0  0 0 x—4 5 0
```
Earnshaw, Walbert (8th)   W—Grimes
Grimes, Hallahan (9th)   L—Earnshaw

1934

St. Louis N.L. 4, Detroit A.L. 3

Batting	Pos	G	AB	R	H	2B	3B	HR	RBI	BB	SO	SB	BA
St. Louis													
Rip Collins	1B	7	30	4	11	1	0	0	3	1	2	0	.367
Frankie Frisch	2B	7	31	2	6	1	0	0	4	0	1	0	.194
Leo Durocher	SS	7	27	4	7	1	1	0	0	0	0	0	.259
Pepper Martin	3B	7	31	8	11	3	1	0	4	3	3	2	.355
Jack Rothrock	RF	7	30	3	7	3	1	0	6	1	2	0	.233
Ernie Orsatti	CF-PH	7	22	3	7	0	1	0	2	3	1	0	.318
Joe Medwick	LF	7	29	4	11	0	1	1	5	1	7	0	.379
Bill DeLancey	C	7	29	3	5	3	0	1	4	2	8	0	.172
Chick Fullis	CF-LF	3	5	0	2	0	0	0	0	0	0	0	.400
Spud Davis	PH	2	2	0	2	0	0	0	1	0	0	0	1.000
Pat Crawford	PH	2	2	0	0	0	0	0	0	0	0	0	.000
Burgess Whitehead	PR-SS	1	0	0	0	0	0	0	0	0	0	0	.000
Francis Healy	Did not play												
Dizzy Dean	P-PR	4	12	3	3	2	0	0	1	0	3	0	.250
Paul Dean	P	2	6	0	1	0	0	0	2	0	1	0	.167
Bill Hallahan	P	1	3	0	0	0	0	0	0	0	1	0	.000
Bill Walker	P	2	2	0	0	0	0	0	0	0	2	0	.000
Tex Carleton	P	2	1	0	0	0	0	0	0	0	0	0	.000
Dazzy Vance	P	1	0	0	0	0	0	0	0	0	0	0	.000
Jim Mooney	P	1	0	0	0	0	0	0	0	0	0	0	.000
Jesse Haines	P	1	0	0	0	0	0	0	0	0	0	0	.000
Team Total		7	262	34	73	14	5	2	32	11	31	2	.279

Double Plays—2   Left on Bases—49

Batting	Pos	G	AB	R	H	2B	3B	HR	RBI	BB	SO	SB	BA
Detroit													
Hank Greenberg	1B	7	28	4	9	2	1	1	7	4	9	1	.321
Charlie Gehringer	2B	7	29	5	11	1	0	1	2	3	0	1	.379
Billy Rogell	SS	7	29	3	8	1	0	0	4	1	4	1	.276
Marv Owen	3B	7	29	0	2	0	0	0	1	0	5	1	.069
Pete Fox	RF	7	28	1	8	6	0	0	2	1	4	0	.286
Jo-Jo White	CF	7	23	6	3	0	0	0	0	8	4	1	.130
Goose Goslin	LF	7	29	2	7	1	0	0	2	3	1	0	.241
Mickey Cochrane	C	7	28	2	6	1	0	0	1	4	3	0	.214
Gee Walker	PH	3	3	0	1	0	0	0	1	0	1	0	.333
Frank Doljack	PH-CF	2	2	0	0	0	0	0	0	0	0	0	.000
Ray Hayworth	C	0	0	0	0	0	0	0	0	0	0	0	.000
Flea Clifton	Did not play												
Heinie Schuble	Did not play												
Schoolboy Rowe	P	3	7	0	0	0	0	0	0	0	5	0	.000
Tommy Bridges	P	3	7	0	1	0	0	0	0	1	4	0	.143
Eldon Auker	P	2	4	0	0	0	0	0	0	0	2	0	.000
Chief Hogsett	P	3	3	0	0	0	0	0	0	0	1	0	.000
General Crowder	P	2	1	0	0	0	0	0	0	0	0	0	.000
Firpo Marberry	P	2	0	0	0	0	0	0	0	0	0	0	.000
Vic Sorrell	Did not play												
Carl Fischer	Did not play												
Luke Hamlin	Did not play												
Team Total		7	250	23	56	12	1	2	20	25	43	5	.224

Double Plays—6   Left on Bases—64

Pitching	G	GS	CG	IP	H	R	ER	BB	SO	W	L	SV	ERA
St. Louis													
Dizzy Dean	3	3	2	26	20	6	5	5	17	2	1	0	1.73
Paul Dean	2	2	2	18	15	4	2	7	11	2	0	0	1.00
Bill Hallahan	1	1	0	8⅓	6	2	2	4	6	0	0	0	2.16
Bill Walker	2	0	0	6⅓	6	7	5	6	2	0	2	0	7.11
Tex Carleton	2	1	0	3⅔	5	3	3	2	2	0	0	0	7.36
Dazzy Vance	1	0	0	1⅓	2	1	0	1	3	0	0	0	0.00
Jim Mooney	1	0	0	1	1	0	0	0	0	0	0	0	0.00
Jesse Haines	1	0	0	⅔	1	0	0	0	2	0	0	0	0.00
Team Total	7	7	4	65⅓	56	23	17	25	43	4	3	0	2.34

Pitching	G	GS	CG	IP	H	R	ER	BB	SO	W	L	SV	ERA
Detroit													
Schoolboy Rowe	3	2	2	21⅓	19	8	7	0	12	1	1	0	2.95
Tommy Bridges	3	2	1	17⅓	21	9	7	1	12	1	1	0	3.63
Eldon Auker	2	2	1	11⅓	16	8	7	5	2	1	1	0	5.56
Chief Hogsett	3	0	0	7⅓	6	1	1	3	3	0	0	0	1.23
General Crowder	2	1	0	6	6	4	1	1	2	0	1	0	1.50
Firpo Marberry	2	0	0	1⅔	5	4	4	1	0	0	0	0	21.60
Vic Sorrell	Did not play												
Carl Fischer	Did not play												
Luke Hamlin	Did not play												
Team Total	7	7	4	65	73	34	27	11	31	3	4	0	3.74

Total Attendance—28,510. Average Attendance—40,216. Winning Player's Share—$5,390. Losing Player's Share—$3,355.

LINESCORES:

FIRST GAME (Oct. 3, at Detroit)
ST. LOUIS .... 0 2 1 0 1 4 0 0 0—8 13 2
DETROIT .... 0 0 1 0 0 1 0 1 0—3 8 5
J. Dean   W—J. Dean
Crowder, Marberry (6th), Hogsett (6th)   L—Crowder

SECOND GAME (Oct. 4, at Detroit)
ST. LOUIS .... 0 1 1 0 0 0 0 0 0 0 0 0—2 7 3
DETROIT .... 0 0 0 1 0 0 0 0 1 0 0 1—3 7 0
Hallahan, W. Walker (9th)   W—Rowe
Rowe   L—W. Walker

THIRD GAME (Oct. 5, at St. Louis)
DETROIT .... 0 0 0 0 0 0 0 0 1—1 8 2
ST. LOUIS .... 1 1 0 0 2 0 0 0 x—4 9 1
Bridges, Hogsett (5th)   W—P. Dean
P. Dean   L—Bridges

FOURTH GAME (Oct. 6, at St. Louis)
DETROIT .... 0 0 3 1 0 0 1 5 0—10 13 1
ST. LOUIS .... 0 1 1 2 0 0 0 0 0— 4 10 5
Auker   W—Auker
Carleton, Vance (3d), W. Walker (5th), Haines (8th), L—W. Walker
Mooney (9th)

FIFTH GAME (Oct. 7, at St. Louis)
DETROIT .... 0 1 0 0 0 2 0 0 0—3 7 0
ST. LOUIS .... 0 0 0 0 0 0 1 0 0—1 7 1
Bridges   W—Bridges
J. Dean, Carleton (9th)   L—J. Dean

SIXTH GAME (Oct. 8, at Detroit)
ST. LOUIS .... 1 0 0 0 2 0 1 0 0—4 10 2
DETROIT .... 0 0 1 0 0 2 0 0 0—3 7 1
P. Dean   W—P. Dean
Rowe   L—Rowe

SEVENTH GAME (Oct. 9, at Detroit)
ST. LOUIS .... 0 0 7 0 0 2 2 0 0—11 17 1
DETROIT .... 0 0 0 0 0 0 0 0 0— 0 6 3
J. Dean   W—J. Dean
Auker, Rowe (3d), Hogsett (3d), Bridges (3d), Marberry (8th), L—Auker
Crowder (9th)

St. Louis N.L. 4, New York A.L. 1

Batting	Pos	G	AB	R	H	2B	3B	HR	RBI	BB	SO	SB	BA
St. Louis													
Johnny Hopp	1B	5	17	3	3	0	0	0	0	1	1	0	.176
Jimmy Brown	2B	5	20	2	6	0	0	0	1	3	0	0	.300
Marty Marion	SS	5	18	2	2	0	1	0	3	1	2	0	.111
Whitey Kurowski	3B	5	15	3	4	0	1	1	5	2	3	0	.267
Enos Slaughter	RF	5	19	3	5	1	0	1	2	3	2	0	.263
Terry Moore	CF	5	17	2	5	1	0	0	2	2	3	0	.294
Stan Musial	LF	5	18	2	4	1	0	0	2	4	0	0	.222
Walker Cooper	C	5	21	3	6	1	0	0	4	0	1	0	.286
Ray Sanders	PH	2	1	1	0	0	0	0	0	1	0	0	.000
Ken O'Dea	PH	1	1	0	1	0	0	0	1	0	0	0	1.000
Harry Walker	PH	1	1	0	0	0	0	0	0	0	1	0	.000
Creepy Crespi	PR	1	0	1	0	0	0	0	0	0	0	0	.000
Coaker Triplett	Did not play												
Sam Narron	Did not play												
Johnny Beazley	P	2	7	0	1	0	0	0	0	0	5	0	.143
Mort Cooper	P	2	5	1	1	0	0	0	2	0	1	0	.200
Ernie White	P	1	2	0	0	0	0	0	0	0	0	0	.000
Max Lanier	P	2	1	0	1	0	0	0	1	0	0	0	1.000
Harry Gumbert	P	2	0	0	0	0	0	0	0	0	0	0	.000
Howie Pollet	P	1	0	0	0	0	0	0	0	0	0	0	.000
Howie Krist	Did not play												
Murry Dickson	Did not play												
Whitey Moore	Did not play												
Team Total		5	163	23	39	4	2	2	23	17	19	0	.239

Double Plays—3   Left on Bases—32

Batting	Pos	G	AB	R	H	2B	3B	HR	RBI	BB	SO	SB	BA
New York													
Jerry Priddy	3B-1B	3	10	0	1	1	0	0	1	1	0	6	.100
Joe Gordon	2B	5	21	1	2	1	0	0	0	0	7	0	.095
Phil Rizzuto	SS	5	21	2	8	0	0	1	1	2	1	2	.381
Red Rolfe	3B	4	17	5	6	2	0	0	0	1	2	0	.353
Roy Cullenbine	RF	5	19	3	5	1	0	0	2	1	2	1	.263
Joe DiMaggio	CF	5	21	3	7	0	0	0	3	0	1	0	.333
Charlie Keller	LF	5	20	2	4	0	0	2	5	1	3	0	.200
Bill Dickey	C	5	19	1	5	0	0	0	0	1	0	0	.263
Buddy Hassett	1B	3	9	1	3	1	0	0	2	0	1	0	.333
Frankie Crosetti	3B	1	3	0	0	0	0	0	0	0	1	0	.000
Buddy Rosar	PH	1	1	0	1	0	0	0	0	0	0	0	1.000
George Selkirk	PH	1	1	0	0	0	0	0	0	0	0	0	.000
Tuck Stainback	PR	2	0	0	0	0	0	0	0	0	0	0	.000
Rollie Hemsley	Did not play												
Tommy Henrich	Not in series—military												
Red Ruffing	P-PH	4	9	0	2	0	0	0	0	0	2	0	.222
Ernie Bonham	P	2	2	0	0	0	0	0	0	1	0	0	.000
Spud Chandler	P	2	2	0	0	0	0	0	0	0	1	0	.000
Atley Donald	P	1	2	0	0	0	0	0	0	0	0	0	.000
Hank Borowy	P	1	1	0	0	0	0	0	0	0	1	0	.000
Marv Breuer	P	1	0	0	0	0	0	0	0	0	0	0	.000
Jim Turner	P	1	0	0	0	0	0	0	0	0	0	0	.000
Lefty Gomez	Did not play												
Marius Russo	Did not play												
Johnny Murphy	Did not play												
Johnny Lindell	Did not play												
Team Total		5	178	18	44	6	0	3	14	8	22	3	.247

Double Plays—2   Left on Bases—34

1942 World Series (continued)

Pitching	G	GS	CG	IP	H	R	ER	BB	SO	W	L	SV	ERA
St. Louis													
John Beazley	2	2	2	18	17	5	5	3	6	2	0	0	2.50
Mort Cooper	2	2	0	13	17	10	8	4	9	0	1	0	5.54
Ernie White	1	1	1	9	6	0	0	0	6	1	0	0	0.00
Max Lanier	2	0	0	4	3	2	0	1	1	1	0	0	0.00
Harry Gumbert	2	0	0	⅔	1	1	0	0	0	0	0	0	0.00
Howie Pollet	1	0	0	⅓	0	0	0	0	0	0	0	0	0.00
Howie Krist	Did not play												
Murry Dickson	Did not play												
Whitey Moore	Did not play												
Team Total	5	5	3	45	44	18	13	8	22	4	1	0	2.60

Pitching	G	GS	CG	IP	H	R	ER	BB	SO	W	L	SV	ERA
New York													
Red Ruffing	2	2	1	17⅔	14	8	8	7	11	1	1	0	4.08
Ernie Bonham	2	1	1	11	9	5	5	3	3	0	1	0	4.09
Spud Chandler	2	1	0	8⅓	5	1	1	1	3	0	1	1	1.08
Hank Borowy	1	1	0	3	6	6	6	3	1	0	0	0	18.00
Atley Donald	1	0	0	3	3	2	2	2	1	0	1	0	6.00
Jim Turner	1	0	0	1	0	0	0	1	0	0	0	0	0.00
Marv Breuer	1	0	0	0	2	1	0	0	0	0	0	0	0.00
Lefty Gomez	Did not play												
Marius Russo	Did not play												
Johnny Murphy	Did not play												
Johnny Lindell	Did not play												
Team Total	5	5	2	44	39	23	22	17	19	1	4	1	4.50

Total Attendance—277,101. Average Attendance—55,420. Winning Player's Share—$6,193. Losing Player's Share—$3,352.

LINESCORES:

FIRST GAME (Sept. 30, at St. Louis)
```
NEW YORK  ....................  000  110  032—7 11 0
ST. LOUIS ....................  000  000  004—4  7 4
```
Ruffing, Chandler (9th)   W—Ruffing
M. Cooper, Gumbert (8th), Lanier (9th)   L—M. Cooper

SECOND GAME (Oct. 1, at St. Louis)
```
NEW YORK  ....................  000  000  030—3 10 2
ST. LOUIS ....................  200  000  11x—4  6 0
```
Bonham   W—Beazley
Beazley   L—Bonham

THIRD GAME (Oct. 3, at New York)
```
ST. LOUIS ....................  001  000  001—2 5 1
NEW YORK  ....................  000  000  000—0 6 1
```
White   W—White
Chandler, Breuer (9th), Turner (9th)   L—Chandler

262

FOURTH GAME (Oct. 4, at New York)
```
ST. LOUIS .......................... 0 0 0   6 0 0   2 0 1—9 12 1
NEW YORK ......................... 1 0 0   0 0 5   0 0 0—6 10 1
```
M. Cooper, Gumbert (6th), Pollet (6th), Lanier (7th)   W—Lanier
Borowy, Donald (4th), Bonham (7th)   L—Donald

FIFTH GAME (Oct. 5, at New York)
```
ST. LOUIS .......................... 0 0 0   1 0 1   0 0 2—4 9 4
NEW YORK ......................... 1 0 0   1 0 0   0 0 0—2 7 1
```
Beazley   W—Beazley
Ruffing   L—Ruffing

1943

New York A.L. 4, St. Louis N.L. 1

Batting	Pos	G	AB	R	H	2B	3B	HR	RBI	BB	SO	SB	BA
New York													
Nick Etten	1B	5	19	0	2	0	0	0	2	1	2	0	.105
Joe Gordon	2B	5	17	2	4	1	0	1	2	3	3	0	.235
Frankie Crosetti	SS	5	18	4	5	0	0	0	1	2	3	1	.278
Billy Johnson	3B	5	20	3	6	1	1	0	3	0	3	0	.300
Johnny Lindell	CF-RF	4	9	1	1	0	0	0	0	1	4	0	.111
Tuck Stainback	RF-CF	5	17	0	3	0	0	0	0	0	2	0	.176
Charlie Keller	LF	5	18	3	4	0	1	0	2	2	5	1	.222
Bill Dickey	C	5	18	1	5	0	0	1	4	2	2	0	.278
Bud Methany	RF	2	8	0	1	0	0	0	0	0	2	0	.125
Snuffy Stirnweiss	PH	1	1	0	0	0	0	0	0	0	0	0	.000
Roy Weatherly	PH	1	1	0	0	0	0	0	0	0	0	0	.000
Ken Sears	Did not play												
Rollie Hemsley	Did not play												
Oscar Grimes	Did not play												
Spud Chandler	P	2	6	0	1	0	0	0	0	0	2	0	.167
Marius Russo	P	1	3	1	2	2	0	0	0	1	1	0	.667
Hank Borowy	P	1	2	1	1	1	0	0	0	0	1	0	.500
Ernie Bonham	P	1	2	0	0	0	0	0	0	0	0	0	.000
Johnny Murphy	P	2	0	0	0	0	0	0	0	0	0	0	.000
Butch Wensloff	Did not play												
Bill Zuber	Did not play												
Atley Donald	Did not play												
Jim Turner	Did not play												
Tommy Byrne	Did not play												
Marv Breuer	Did not play												
Team Total		5	159	17	35	5	2	2	14	12	30	2	.220

Double Plays—3   Left on Bases—30

1943 World Series (continued)

Batting	Pos	G	AB	R	H	2B	3B	HR	RBI	BB	SO	SB	BA
St. Louis													
Ray Sanders	1B	5	17	3	5	0	0	1	2	3	4	0	.294
Lou Klein	2B	5	22	0	3	0	0	0	0	1	2	0	.136
Marty Marion	SS	5	14	1	5	2	0	1	2	3	1	1	.357
Whitey Kurowski	3B	5	18	2	4	1	0	0	1	0	3	0	.222
Stan Musial	RF	5	18	2	5	0	0	0	0	2	2	0	.278
Harry Walker	CF-PH	5	18	0	3	1	0	0	0	0	2	0	.167
Danny Litwhiler	LF-PH	5	15	0	4	1	0	0	2	2	4	0	.267
Walker Cooper	C	5	17	1	5	0	0	0	0	0	1	0	.294
Debs Garms	PH-LF	2	5	0	0	0	0	0	0	0	2	0	.000
Johnny Hopp	CF	1	4	0	0	0	0	0	0	0	1	0	.000
Ken O'Dea	PH-C	2	3	0	2	0	0	0	0	0	0	0	.667
Frank Demaree	PH	1	1	0	0	0	0	0	0	0	0	0	.000
Sam Narron	PH	1	1	0	0	0	0	0	0	0	0	0	.000
George Fallon	Did not play												
Mort Cooper	P	2	5	0	0	0	0	0	0	0	3	0	.000
Max Lanier	P	3	4	0	1	0	0	0	1	0	0	0	.250
Al Brazle	P	1	3	0	0	0	0	0	0	0	1	0	.000
Harry Brecheen	P	3	0	0	0	0	0	0	0	0	0	0	.000
Murry Dickson	P	1	0	0	0	0	0	0	0	0	0	0	.000
Howie Krist	P	1	0	0	0	0	0	0	0	0	0	0	.000
Ernie White	PR	1	0	0	0	0	0	0	0	0	0	0	.000
Harry Gumbert	Did not play												
George Munger	Did not play												
Team Total		5	165	9	37	5	0	2	8	11	26	1	.224

Double Plays—4   Left on Bases—37

Pitching	G	GS	CG	IP	H	R	ER	BB	SO	W	L	SV	ERA
New York													
Spud Chandler	2	2	2	18	17	2	1	3	10	2	0	0	0.50
Marius Russo	1	1	1	9	7	1	0	1	2	1	0	0	0.00
Hank Borowy	1	1	0	8	6	2	2	3	4	1	0	0	2.25
Ernie Bonham	1	1	0	8	6	4	4	3	9	0	1	0	4.50
Johnny Murphy	2	0	0	2	1	0	0	1	1	0	0	1	0.00
Butch Wensloff	Did not play												
Bill Zuber	Did not play												
Artley Donald	Did not play												
Jim Turner	Did not play												
Tommy Byrne	Did not play												
Marv Breuer	Did not play												
Team Total	5	5	3	45	37	9	7	11	26	4	1	1	1.46

Pitching	G	GS	CG	IP	H	R	ER	BB	SO	W	L	SV	ERA
St. Louis													
Mort Cooper	2	2	1	16	11	5	5	3	10	1	1	0	2.81
Max Lanier	3	2	0	15⅓	13	5	3	3	13	0	1	0	1.76
Al Brazle	1	1	0	7⅓	5	6	3	2	4	0	1	0	3.68
Harry Brecheen	3	0	0	3⅔	5	1	1	3	3	0	1	0	2.45
Murry Dickson	1	0	0	⅔	0	0	0	1	0	0	0	0	0.00
Howie Krist	1	0	0	0	1	0	0	0	0	0	0	0	0.00
Harry Gumbert	Did not play												
George Munger	Did not play												
Ernie White	Did not pitch												
Team Total	5	5	1	43	35	17	12	12	30	1	4	0	2.51

Total Attendance—277,312. Average Attendance—55,462. Winning Player's Share— $6,139. Losing Player's Share—$4,322.

LINESCORES:

FIRST GAME (Oct. 5, at New York)
```
ST. LOUIS  ......................... 0 1 0  0 1 0  0 0 0—2 7 2
NEW YORK  ......................... 0 0 0  2 0 2  0 0 x—4 8 2
```
Lanier, Brecheen (8th)   W—Chandler
Chandler   L—Lanier

SECOND GAME (Oct. 6, at New York)
```
ST. LOUIS  ......................... 0 0 1  3 0 0  0 0 0—4 7 2
NEW YORK  ......................... 0 0 0  1 0 0  0 0 2—3 6 0
```
M. Cooper   W—M. Cooper
Bonham, Murphy (9th)   L—Bonham

THIRD GAME (Oct. 7, at New York)
```
ST. LOUIS  ......................... 0 0 0  2 0 0  0 0 0—2 6 4
NEW YORK  ......................... 0 0 0  0 0 1  0 5 x—6 8 0
```
Brazle, Krist (8th), Breechen (8th)   W—Borowy
Borowy, Murphy (9th)   L—Brazle

FOURTH GAME (Oct. 10, at St. Louis)
```
NEW YORK  ......................... 0 0 0  1 0 0  0 1 0—2 6 2
ST. LOUIS  ......................... 0 0 0  0 0 0  1 0 0—1 7 1
```
Russo   W—Russo
Lanier, Brecheen (8th)   L—Brecheen

FIFTH GAME (Oct. 11, at St. Louis)
```
NEW YORK  ......................... 0 0 0  0 0 2  0 0 0—2  7 1
ST. LOUIS  ......................... 0 0 0  0 0 0  0 0 0—0 10 1
```
Chandler   W—Chandler
M. Cooper, Lanier (8th), Dickson (0th)   L—M. Cooper

1944

St. Louis N.L. 4, St. Louis A.L. 2

Batting	Pos	G	AB	R	H	2B	3B	HR	RBI	BB	SO	SB	BA
St. Louis Cardinals													
Ray Sanders	1B	6	21	5	6	0	0	1	1	5	8	0	.286
Emil Verban	2B	6	17	1	7	0	0	0	2	2	0	0	.412
Marty Marion	SS	6	22	1	5	3	0	0	2	2	3	0	.227
Whitey Kurowski	3B	6	23	2	5	1	0	0	1	1	4	0	.217
Stan Musial	RF	6	23	2	7	2	0	1	2	2	0	0	.304
Johnny Hopp	CF	6	27	2	5	0	0	0	0	0	8	0	.185
Danny Litwhiler	LF	5	20	2	4	1	0	1	1	2	7	0	.200
Walker Cooper	C	6	22	1	7	2	1	0	2	3	2	0	.318
Augie Bergamo	PH-LF	3	6	0	0	0	0	0	1	2	3	0	.000
George Fallon	2B	2	2	0	0	0	0	0	0	0	1	0	.000
Ken O'Dea	PH	3	3	0	1	0	0	0	2	0	0	0	.333
Debs Garms	PH	2	2	0	0	0	0	0	0	0	0	0	.000
Pepper Martin	Did not play												
Bob Keely	Did not play												
Mort Cooper	P	2	4	0	0	0	0	0	0	0	2	0	.000
Max Lanier	P	2	4	0	2	0	0	0	1	0	0	0	.500
Harry Brecheen	P	1	4	0	0	0	0	0	0	0	1	0	.000
Ted Wilks	P	2	2	0	0	0	0	0	0	0	2	0	.000
Blix Donnelly	P	2	1	0	0	0	0	0	0	0	1	0	.000
Fred Schmidt	P	1	1	0	0	0	0	0	0	0	1	0	.000
Bud Byerly	P	1	0	0	0	0	0	0	0	0	0	0	.000
Al Jurisich	P	1	0	0	0	0	0	0	0	0	0	0	.000
George Munger	Not in series—military service												
Team Total		6	204	16	49	9	1	3	15	19	43	0	.240

Double Plays—3   Left on Bases—51

Batting	Pos	G	AB	R	H	2B	3B	HR	RBI	BB	SO	SB	BA
St. Louis Browns													
George McQuinn	1B	6	16	2	7	2	0	1	5	7	2	0	.438
Don Guttenridge	2B	6	21	1	3	1	0	0	0	3	5	0	.143
Vern Stephens	SS	6	22	2	5	1	0	0	0	3	3	0	.227
Mark Christman	3B	6	22	0	2	0	0	0	1	0	6	0	.091
Gene Moore	RF	6	22	4	4	0	0	0	0	3	6	0	.182
Mike Kreevich	CF	6	26	0	6	3	0	0	0	0	5	0	.231
Chet Laabs	LF-PH	5	15	1	3	1	1	0	0	2	6	0	.200
Red Hayworth	C	6	17	1	2	1	0	0	1	3	1	0	.118
Al Zarilla	PH-LF	4	10	1	1	0	0	0	1	0	4	0	.100
Frank Mancuso	PH-C	2	3	0	2	0	0	0	1	0	0	0	.667
Floyd Baker	PH-2B	2	2	0	0	0	0	0	0	0	2	0	.000
Milt Byrnes	PH	3	2	0	0	0	0	0	0	1	2	0	.000
Mike Chartak	PH	2	2	0	0	0	0	0	0	0	2	0	.000
Ellis Clary	PH	1	1	0	0	0	0	0	0	0	0	0	.000
Tom Turner	PH	1	1	0	0	0	0	0	0	0	0	0	.000
Denny Galehouse	P	2	5	0	1	0	0	0	0	1	1	0	.200
Jack Kramer	P	2	4	0	0	0	0	0	0	0	2	0	.000
Neis Potter	P	2	4	0	0	0	0	0	0	0	1	0	.000
Bob Muncrief	P	2	1	0	0	0	0	0	0	0	1	0	.000
Al Hollingsworth	P	1	1	0	0	0	0	0	0	0	0	0	.000
Sig Jakucki	P	1	0	0	0	0	0	0	0	0	0	0	.000
Tex Shirley	PR-P	2	0	0	0	0	0	0	0	0	0	0	.000
George Caster	Did not play												
Willis Hudlin	Did not play												
Sam Zoldak	Did not play												
Team Total		6	197	12	36	9	1	1	9	23	49	0	.183

Double Plays—4   Left on Bases—44

266

Pitching	G	GS	CG	IP	H	R	ER	BB	SO	W	L	SV	ERA
St. Louis Cardinals													
Mort Cooper	2	2	1	16	9	2	2	5	16	1	1	0	1.13
Max Lanier	2	2	0	12⅓	8	3	3	8	11	1	0	0	2.79
Harry Brecheen	1	1	1	9	9	1	1	4	4	1	0	0	1.00
Ted Wilks	2	1	0	6⅓	5	4	4	3	7	0	1	1	5.68
Blix Donnelly	2	0	0	6	2	0	0	1	9	1	0	0	0.00
Fred Schmidt	1	0	0	3⅓	1	0	0	1	1	0	0	0	0.00
Bud Byerly	1	0	0	1⅓	0	0	0	0	1	0	0	0	0.00
Al Jurisich	1	0	0	⅔	2	2	2	1	0	0	0	0	27.00
George Munger	Not in series—military service												
Team Total	6	6	2	55	36	12	12	23	49	4	2	1	1.96

Pitching	G	GS	CG	IP	H	R	ER	BB	SO	W	L	SV	ERA
St. Louis Browns													
Denny Galehouse	2	2	2	18	13	3	3	5	15	1	1	0	1.50
Jack Kramer	2	1	1	11	9	2	0	4	12	1	0	0	0.00
Neis Potter	2	2	0	9⅔	10	5	1	3	6	0	1	0	0.93
Bob Muncrief	2	0	0	6⅔	5	1	1	4	4	0	1	0	1.35
Al Hollingsworth	1	0	0	4	5	1	1	2	1	0	0	0	2.25
Sig Jakucki	1	1	0	3	5	4	3	0	4	0	1	0	9.00
Tex Shirley	1	0	0	2	2	0	0	1	1	0	0	0	0.00
George Caster	Did not play												
Willis Hudlin	Did not play												
Sam Zoldak	Did not play												
Team Total	6	6	3	54⅓	49	16	9	19	43	2	4	0	1.49

Total Attendance—206,708. Average Attendance—34,451. Winning Player's Share—$4,626. Losing Player's Share—$2,744.

LINESCORES:

FIRST GAME (Oct. 4, at Sportsman's Park)

```
BROWNS .......................... 0 0 0   2 0 0   0 0 0—2 2 0
CARDINALS ...................... 0 0 0   0 0 0   0 0 1—1 7 0
```
Galehouse   W—Galehouse
M. Cooper, Donnelly (8th)   L—M. Cooper

SECOND GAME (Oct. 5, at Sportsman's Park)

```
BROWNS ....................... 0 0 0   0 0 0   2 0 0   0 0—2 7 4
CARDINALS ................... 0 0 1   1 0 0   0 0 0   0 1—3 7 0
```
Potter, Muncrief (7th)   W—Donnelly
Lanier, Donnelly (8th)   L—Muncrief

THIRD GAME (Oct. 6, at Sportsman's Park)

```
CARDINALS ........................ 1 0 0   0 0 0   1 0 0—2 7 0
BROWNS ........................... 0 0 4   0 0 0   2 0 x—6 8 2
```
Wilks, Schmidt (3d), Jurisich (7th), Byerly (7th)   W—Kramer
Kramer   L—Wilks

FOURTH GAME (Oct. 7, at Sportsman's Park)

```
CARDINALS ...................... 2 0 2   0 0 1   0 0 0—5 12 0
BROWNS ......................... 0 0 0   0 0 0   0 1 0—1  9 1
```
Brecheen   W—Brecheen
Jakucki, Hollingsworth (4th), Shirley (8th)   L—Jakucki

1944 World Series (continued)

FIFTH GAME (Oct. 8, at Sportsman's Park)
```
    CARDINALS ........................ 0 0 0   0 0 1   0 1 0—2 6 1
    BROWNS ........................... 0 0 0   0 0 0   0 0 0—0 7 1
```
M. Cooper   W—M. Cooper
Galehouse   L—Galehouse

SIXTH GAME (Oct. 9, at Sportsman's Park)
```
    BROWNS ........................... 0 1 0   0 0 0   0 0 0—1 3 2
    CARDINALS ........................ 0 0 0   3 0 0   0 0 x—3 10 0
```
Potter, Muncrief (4th), Kramer (7th)   W—Lanier
Lanier, Wilks (6th)   L—Potter

1946

St. Louis N.L. 4, Boston A.L. 3

Batting	Pos	G	AB	R	H	2B	3B	HR	RBI	BB	SO	SB	BA
St. Louis													
Stan Musial	1B	7	27	3	6	4	1	0	4	4	2	1	.222
Red Schoendienst	2B	7	30	3	7	1	0	0	1	0	2	1	.233
Marty Marion	SS	7	24	1	6	2	0	0	4	1	1	0	.250
Whitey Kurowski	3B	7	27	5	8	3	0	0	2	0	3	0	.296
Enos Slaughter	RF	7	25	5	8	1	1	1	2	4	3	1	.320
Terry Moore	CF	7	27	1	4	0	0	0	2	2	6	0	.148
Harry Walker	LF-RF-PH	7	17	3	7	2	0	0	6	4	2	0	.412
Joe Garagiola	C	5	19	2	6	2	0	0	4	0	3	0	.316
Del Rice	C	3	6	2	3	1	0	0	0	2	0	0	.500
Erv Dusak	PH-LF	4	4	0	1	1	0	0	0	2	2	0	.250
Dick Sisler	PH	2	2	0	0	0	0	0	0	0	0	0	.000
Nippy Jones	PH	1	1	0	0	0	0	0	0	0	1	0	.000
Harry Brecheen	P	3	8	2	1	0	0	0	1	0	1	0	.125
Murry Dickson	P	2	5	1	2	2	0	0	1	0	1	0	.400
George Munger	P	1	4	0	1	0	0	0	0	0	2	0	.250
Howie Pollet	P	2	4	0	0	0	0	0	0	0	1	0	.000
Al Brazle	P	1	2	0	0	0	0	0	0	0	0	0	.000
Johnny Beazley	P	1	0	0	0	0	0	0	0	0	0	0	.000
Ted Wilks	P	1	0	0	0	0	0	0	0	0	0	0	.000
Team Total		7	232	28	60	19	2	1	27	19	30	3	.259

Double Plays—7   Left on Bases—50

Batting	Pos	G	AB	R	H	2B	3B	HR	RBI	BB	SO	SB	BA
Boston													
Rudy York	1B	7	23	6	6	1	1	2	5	6	4	0	.261
Bobby Doerr	2B	6	22	1	9	1	0	1	3	2	2	0	.409
Johnny Pesky	SS	7	30	2	7	0	0	0	0	1	3	1	.233
Pinky Higgins	3B	7	24	1	5	1	0	0	2	2	0	0	.208
Wally Moses	RF	4	12	1	5	0	0	0	0	1	2	0	.417
Dom DiMaggio	CF	7	27	2	7	3	0	0	3	2	2	0	.259
Ted Williams	LF	7	25	2	5	0	0	0	1	5	5	0	.200
Hal Wagner	C	5	13	0	0	0	0	0	0	0	1	0	.000
Tom McBride	RF-PH	5	12	0	2	0	0	0	1	0	1	0	.167
Roy Partee	PH-C	5	10	1	1	0	0	0	1	1	2	0	.100
Leon Culberson	RF-CF	5	9	1	2	0	0	1	1	1	2	1	.222
Don Gutteridge	PR-2B	3	5	1	2	0	0	0	1	0	0	0	.400
Rip Russell	PH-3B	2	2	1	2	0	0	0	0	0	0	0	1.000
George Metkovich	PH	2	2	1	1	1	0	0	0	0	0	0	.500
Paul Campbell	PR	1	0	0	0	0	0	0	0	0	0	0	.000
Dave Ferriss	P	2	6	0	0	0	0	0	0	0	1	0	.000
Mickey Harris	P	2	3	0	1	0	0	0	0	0	1	0	.333
Tex Hughson	P	3	3	0	1	0	0	0	0	0	1	0	.333
Joe Dobson	P	3	3	0	0	0	0	0	0	0	2	0	.000
Earl Johnson	P	3	1	0	0	0	0	0	0	0	0	0	.000
Jim Bagby	P	1	1	0	0	0	0	0	0	0	0	0	.000
Mace Brown	P	1	0	0	0	0	0	0	0	0	0	0	.000
Clem Dreisewerd	P	1	0	0	0	0	0	0	0	0	0	0	.000
Bob Klinger	P	1	0	0	0	0	0	0	0	0	0	0	.000
Mike Ryba	P	1	0	0	0	0	0	0	0	0	0	0	.000
Bill Zuber	P	1	0	0	0	0	0	0	0	0	0	0	.000
Team Total		7	233	20	56	7	1	4	18	22	28	2	.240

Double Plays—5   Left on Bases—53

Pitching	G	GS	CG	IP	H	R	ER	BB	SO	W	L	SV	ERA
St. Louis													
Harry Brecheen	3	2	2	20	14	1	1	5	11	3	0	0	0.45
Murry Dickson	2	2	0	14	11	6	6	4	7	0	1	0	3.86
Howie Pollet	2	2	1	10⅓	12	4	4	4	3	1	1	0	3.48
George Munger	1	1	1	9	9	3	1	3	2	1	0	0	1.00
Al Brazle	1	0	0	6⅔	7	5	4	6	4	0	1	0	5.40
Johnny Beazley	1	0	0	1	1	0	0	0	1	0	0	0	0.00
Ted Wilks	1	0	0	1	2	1	0	0	0	0	0	0	0.00
Team Total	7	7	4	62	56	20	16	22	28	4	3	0	2.32

Pitching	G	GS	CG	IP	H	R	ER	BB	SO	W	L	SV	ERA
Boston													
Tex Hughson	3	2	0	14⅓	14	8	5	3	8	0	1	0	3.14
Dave Ferriss	2	2	1	13⅓	13	3	3	2	4	1	0	0	2.03
Joe Dobson	3	1	1	12⅔	4	3	0	3	10	1	0	0	0.00
Mickey Harris	2	2	0	9⅔	11	6	4	4	5	0	2	0	3.72
Earl Johnson	3	0	0	3⅓	1	1	1	2	1	1	0	0	2.70
Jim Bagby	1	0	0	3	6	1	1	1	1	0	0	0	3.00
Bill Zuber	1	0	0	2	3	1	1	1	1	0	0	0	4.50
Mace Brown	1	0	0	1	4	3	3	1	0	0	0	0	27.00
Mike Ryba	1	0	0	⅔	2	1	1	1	0	0	0	0	13.50
Bob Klinger	1	0	0	⅔	2	1	1	1	0	0	1	0	13.50
Clem Dreisewerd	1	0	0	⅓	0	0	0	0	0	0	0	0	0.00
Team Total	7	7	2	61	60	28	20	19	30	3	4	0	2.95

Total Attendance—250,071. Average Attendance—35,724. Winning Player's Share—$3,742. Losing Player's Share—$2,141.

1946 World Series (continued)

LINESCORES:

FIRST GAME (Oct. 6, at St. Louis)

BOSTON	0 1 0	0 0 0	0 0 1	1—3	9	2
ST. LOUIS	0 0 0	0 0 1	0 1 0	0—2	7	0

Hughson, Johnson (9th)   W—Johnson
Pollet   L—Pollet

SECOND GAME (Oct. 7, at St. Louis)

BOSTON	0 0 0	0 0 0	0 0 0—	0	4	1
ST. LOUIS	0 0 1	0 2 0	0 0 x—	3	6	0

Harris, Dobson (8th)   W—Brecheen
Brecheen   L—Harris

THIRD GAME (Oct. 9, at Boston)

ST. LOUIS	0 0 0	0 0 0	0 0 0—	0	6	1
BOSTON	3 0 0	0 0 0	0 1 x—	4	8	0

Dickson, Wilks (8th)   W—Ferriss
Ferriss   L—Dickson

FOURTH GAME (Oct. 10, at Boston)

ST. LOUIS	0 3 3	0 1 0	1 0 4—	12	20	1
BOSTON	0 0 0	1 0 0	0 2 0—	3	9	4

Munger   W—Munger
Hughson, Bagby (3d), Zuber (6th), Brown (8th), Ryba (9th),   L—Hughson
Dreisewerd (9th)

FIFTH GAME (Oct. 11, at Boston)

ST. LOUIS	0 1 0	0 0 0	0 0 2—	3	4	1
BOSTON	1 1 0	0 0 1	3 0 x—	6	11	3

Pollet, Brazle (1st), Beazley (8th)   W—Dobson
Dobson   L—Brazle

SIXTH GAME (Oct. 13, at St. Louis)

BOSTON	0 0 0	0 0 0	1 0 0—	1	7	0
ST. LOUIS	0 0 3	0 0 0	0 1 x—	4	8	0

Harris, Hughson (3d), Johnson (8th)   W—Brecheen
Brecheen   L—Harris

SEVENTH GAME (Oct. 15, at St. Louis)

BOSTON	1 0 0	0 0 0	0 2 0—	3	8	0
ST. LOUIS	0 1 0	0 2 0	0 1 x—	4	9	1

Ferriss, Dobson (5th), Klinger (8th), Johnson (8th)   W—Brecheen
Dickson, Brecheen (8th)   L—Klinger

1964

St. Louis N.L. 4, New York A.L. 3

Batting	Pos	G	AB	R	H	2B	3B	HR	RBI	BB	SO	SB	BA
St. Louis													
Bill White	1B	7	27	2	3	1	0	0	2	2	6	1	.111
Dal Maxvill	2B	7	20	0	4	1	0	0	1	1	4	0	.200

Batting	Pos	G	AB	R	H	2B	3B	HR	RBI	BB	SO	SB	BA
Dick Groat	SS	7	26	3	5	1	1	0	1	4	3	0	.192
Ken Boyer	3B	7	27	5	6	1	0	2	6	1	5	0	.222
Mike Shannon	RF	7	28	6	6	0	0	1	2	0	9	1	.214
Curt Flood	CF	7	30	5	6	0	1	0	3	3	1	0	.200
Lou Brock	LF	7	30	2	9	2	0	1	5	0	3	0	.300
Tim McCarver	C	7	23	4	11	1	1	1	5	5	1	1	.478
Jerry Buchek	PR-2B	4	1	1	1	0	0	0	0	0	0	0	1.000
Julian Javier	PR-2B	1	0	1	0	0	0	0	0	0	0	0	.000
Carl Warwick	PH	5	4	2	3	0	0	0	1	1	0	0	.750
Bob Skinner	PH	4	3	0	2	1	0	0	1	1	0	0	.667
Charlie James	PH	3	3	0	0	0	0	0	0	0	1	0	.000
Bob Uecker	Did not play												
Ed Spiezio	Did not play												
Bob Gibson	P	3	9	1	2	0	0	0	0	0	3	0	.222
Curt Simmons	P	2	4	0	2	0	0	0	1	0	1	0	.500
Ray Sadecki	P	2	2	0	1	0	0	0	1	0	1	0	.500
Barney Schultz	P	4	1	0	0	0	0	0	0	0	0	0	.000
Roger Craig	P	2	1	0	0	0	0	0	0	0	0	0	.000
Ron Taylor	P	2	1	0	0	0	0	0	0	0	1	0	.000
Gordon Richardson	P	2	0	0	0	0	0	0	0	0	0	0	.000
Bob Humphreys	P	1	0	0	0	0	0	0	0	0	0	0	.000
Mike Cuellar	Did not play												
Ray Washburn	Did not play												
Team Total		7	240	32	61	8	3	5	29	18	39	3	.254

Double Plays—6 Left on Bases—47

Batting	Pos	G	AB	R	H	2B	3B	HR	RBI	BB	SO	SB	BA
New York													
Joe Pepitone	1B	7	26	1	4	1	0	1	5	2	3	0	.154
Bobby Richardson	2B	7	32	3	13	2	0	0	3	0	2	1	.406
Phil Linz	SS	7	31	5	7	1	0	2	2	2	5	0	.226
Clete Boyer	3B	7	24	2	5	1	0	1	3	1	5	1	.208
Mickey Mantle	RF	7	24	8	8	2	0	3	8	6	8	0	.333
Roger Maris	CF	7	30	4	6	0	0	1	1	1	4	0	.200
Tom Tresh	LF	7	22	4	6	2	0	2	7	6	7	0	.273
Elston Howard	C	7	24	5	7	1	0	0	2	4	6	0	.292
Hector Lopez	RF-PH	3	2	0	0	0	0	0	0	0	2	0	.000
Pedro Gonzalez	3B	1	1	0	0	0	0	0	0	0	0	0	.000
John Blanchard	PH	4	4	0	1	1	0	0	0	0	1	0	.250
Mike Hegan	PR-PH	3	1	1	0	0	0	0	0	1	1	0	.000
Archie Moore	Did not play												
Chet Trail	Did not play												
Tony Kubek	Not in series—sprained wrist												
Mel Stottlemyre	P	3	8	0	1	0	0	0	0	0	6	0	.125
Jim Bouton	P	2	7	0	1	0	0	0	1	0	2	0	.143
Al Downing	P	2	2	0	0	0	0	0	0	0	2	0	.000
Whitey Ford	P	1	1	0	1	0	0	0	1	2	0	0	1.000
Pete Mikkelsen	P	4	0	0	0	0	0	0	0	0	0	0	.000
Steve Hamilton	P	2	0	0	0	0	0	0	0	0	0	0	.000
Rollie Sheldon	P	2	0	0	0	0	0	0	0	0	0	0	.000
Hal Reniff	P	1	0	0	0	0	0	0	0	0	0	0	.000
Ralph Terry	P	1	0	0	0	0	0	0	0	0	0	0	.000
Bill Stafford	Did not play												
Stan Williams	Did not play												
Team Total		7	239	33	60	11	0	10	33	25	54	2	.251

Double Plays—6 Left on Bases—47

1964 World Series (continued)

Pitching	G	GS	CG	IP	H	R	ER	BB	SO	W	L	SV	ERA
St. Louis													
Bob Gibson	3	3	2	27	23	11	9	8	31	2	1	0	3.00
Curt Simmons	2	2	0	14⅓	11	4	4	3	8	0	1	0	2.51
Ray Sadecki	2	2	0	6⅓	12	7	6	5	2	1	0	0	8.53
Roger Craig	2	0	0	5	2	0	0	3	9	1	0	0	0.00
Ron Taylor	2	0	0	4⅔	0	0	0	1	2	0	0	1	0.00
Barney Schultz	4	0	0	4	9	8	8	3	1	0	1	1	18.00
Bob Humphreys	1	0	0	1	0	0	0	0	1	0	0	0	0.00
Gordon Richardson	2	0	0	⅔	3	3	3	2	0	0	0	0	40.50
Team Total	7	7	2	63	60	33	30	25	54	4	3	2	4.29

Pitching	G	GS	CG	IP	H	R	ER	BB	SO	W	L	SV	ERA
New York													
Mel Stottlemyre	3	3	1	20	18	8	7	6	12	1	1	0	3.15
Jim Bouton	2	2	1	17⅓	15	4	3	5	7	2	0	0	1.56
Al Downing	3	1	0	7⅔	9	8	7	2	5	0	1	0	8.22
Whitey Ford	1	1	0	5⅓	8	5	5	1	4	0	1	0	8.44
Pete Mikkelsen	4	0	0	4⅔	4	4	3	2	4	0	1	0	5.79
Rollie Sheldon	2	0	0	2⅔	0	2	0	2	2	0	0	0	0.00
Steve Hamilton	2	0	0	2	3	1	1	0	2	0	0	1	4.50
Ralph Terry	1	0	0	2	2	0	0	0	3	0	0	0	0.00
Hal Reniff	1	0	0	⅓	2	0	0	0	0	0	0	0	0.00
Team Total	7	7	2	62	61	32	26	18	39	3	4	1	3.77

Total Attendance—321,807. Average Attendance—45,972. Winning Player's Share—$8,622. Losing Player's Share—$5,309.

LINESCORES:

FIRST GAME (Oct. 7, at St. Louis)

NEW YORK .... 0 3 0   0 1 0   0 1 0—5 12 2
ST. LOUIS .... 1 1 0   0 0 4   0 3 x—9 12 0

Ford, Downing (6th), Sheldon (8th), Mikkelsen (8th)   W—Sadecki
Sadecki, Schultz (7th)   L—Ford

SECOND GAME (Oct. 8, at St. Louis)

NEW YORK .... 0 0 0   1 0 1   2 0 4—8 12 0
ST. LOUIS .... 0 0 1   0 0 0   0 1 1—3 7 0

Stottlemyre   W—Stottlemyre
Gibson, Schultz (9th), G. Richardson (9th), Craig (9th)   L—Gibson

THIRD GAME (Oct. 10, at New York)

ST. LOUIS .... 0 0 0   0 1 0   0 0 0—1 6 0
NEW YORK .... 0 1 0   0 0 0   0 0 1—2 5 2

Simmons, Schultz (9th)   W—Bouton
Bouton   L—Schultz

FOURTH GAME (Oct. 11, at New York)

ST. LOUIS .... 0 0 0   0 0 4   0 0 0—4 6 1
NEW YORK .... 3 0 0   0 0 0   0 0 0—3 6 1

Sadecki, Craig (1st), Taylor (6th)   W—Craig
Downing, Mikkelsen (7th), Terry (8th)   L—Downing

FIFTH GAME (Oct. 12, at New York)
```
ST. LOUIS  .....................  0 0 0   0 2 0   0 0 0   3—5 10 1
NEW YORK  ...................  0 0 0   0 0 0   0 0 2   0—2  6 2
```
Gibson   W—Gibson
Stottlemyre, Reniff (8th), Mikkelsen (8th)   L—Mikkelsen

SIXTH GAME (Oct. 14, at St. Louis)
```
NEW YORK  .....................  0 0 0   0 1 2   0 5 0—8 10 0
ST. LOUIS  .....................  1 0 0   0 0 0   0 1 1—3 10 1
```
Bouton, Hamilton (9th)   W—Bouton
Simmons, Taylor (7th), Schultz (8th), G. Richardson (8th),   L—Simmons
Humphreys (9th)

SEVENTH GAME (Oct. 15, at St. Louis)
```
NEW YORK  .....................  0 0 0   0 0 3   0 0 2—5  9 2
ST. LOUIS  .....................  0 0 0   3 3 0   1 0 x—7 10 1
```
Stottlemyre, Downing (5th), Sheldon (5th), Hamilton (7th),   W—Gibson
Mikkelsen (8th)   L—Stottlemyre
Gibson

1967

St. Louis N.L. 4, Boston A.L. 3

Batting	Pos	G	AB	R	H	2B	3B	HR	RBI	BB	SO	SB	BA
St. Louis													
Orlando Cepeda	1B	7	29	1	3	2	0	0	1	0	4	0	.103
Julian Javier	2B	7	25	2	9	3	0	1	4	0	6	0	.360
Dal Maxvill	SS	7	19	1	3	0	1	0	1	4	1	0	.158
Mike Shannon	3B	7	24	3	5	1	0	1	2	1	4	0	.208
Roger Maris	RF	7	26	3	10	1	0	1	7	3	1	0	.385
Curt Flood	CF	7	28	2	5	1	0	0	3	3	3	0	.179
Lou Brock	LF	7	29	8	21	2	1	1	3	2	3	7	.414
Tim McCarver	C	7	24	3	3	1	0	0	2	2	2	0	.125
Dave Ricketts	PH	3	3	0	0	0	0	0	0	0	0	0	.000
Bobby Tolan	PH	3	2	1	0	0	0	0	0	1	1	0	.000
Phil Gagliano	PH	1	1	0	0	0	0	0	0	0	0	0	.000
Ed Spiezio	PH	1	1	0	0	0	0	0	0	0	0	0	.000
Ed Bressoud	SS	2	0	0	0	0	0	0	0	0	0	0	.000
Alex Johnson	Did not play												
Bob Gibson	P	3	11	1	1	0	0	1	1	1	2	0	.091
Nelson Briles	P	2	3	0	0	0	0	0	0	0	0	0	.000
Dick Hughes	P	2	3	0	0	0	0	0	0	0	3	0	.000
Steve Carlton	P	1	1	0	0	0	0	0	0	0	0	0	.000
Jack Lamabe	P	3	0	0	0	0	0	0	0	0	0	0	.000
Ron Willis	P	3	0	0	0	0	0	0	0	0	0	0	.000
Joe Hoerner	P	2	0	0	0	0	0	0	0	0	0	0	.000
Ray Washburn	P	2	0	0	0	0	0	0	0	0	0	0	.000
Larry Jaster	P	1	0	0	0	0	0	0	0	0	0	0	.000
Hal Woodeshick	P	1	0	0	0	0	0	0	0	0	0	0	.000
Al Jackson	Did not play												
Team Total		7	229	25	51	11	2	5	24	17	30	7	.223

Double Plays—4   Left on Bases—40

1967 World Series (continued)

Batting	Pos	G	AB	R	H	2B	3B	HR	RBI	BB	SO	SB	BA
Boston													
George Scott	1B	7	26	3	6	1	1	0	0	3	6	0	.231
Jerry Adair	2B-PH	5	16	0	2	0	0	0	1	0	3	1	.125
Rico Petrocelli	SS	7	20	3	4	1	0	2	3	3	8	0	.200
Dalton Jones	3B-PH	6	18	2	7	0	0	0	1	1	3	0	.389
Jose Tartabull	PR-RF-PH	7	13	1	2	0	0	0	0	1	2	0	.154
Reggie Smith	CF	7	24	3	6	1	0	2	3	2	2	0	.250
Carl Yastrzemski	LF	7	25	4	10	2	0	3	5	4	1	0	.400
Elston Howard	C	7	18	0	2	0	0	0	1	1	2	0	.111
Joe Foy	PH-3B	6	15	2	2	1	0	0	1	1	5	0	.133
Mike Andrews	PH-2B	5	13	2	4	0	0	0	1	0	1	0	.308
Ken Harrelson	RF	4	13	0	1	0	0	0	1	1	3	0	.077
Norm Siebern	PH-RF	3	3	0	1	0	0	0	1	0	0	0	.000
George Thomas	PH-RF	2	2	0	0	0	0	0	0	0	1	0	.000
Russ Gibson	C	2	2	0	0	0	0	0	0	0	2	0	.000
Mike Ryan	C	1	2	0	0	0	0	0	0	0	1	0	.000
Jim Lonborg	P	3	9	0	0	0	0	0	0	0	7	0	.000
Jose Santiago	P	3	2	1	1	0	0	1	1	0	1	0	.500
Gary Waslewski	P	2	1	0	0	0	0	0	0	0	1	0	.000
Gary Bell	P	3	0	0	0	0	0	0	0	0	0	0	.000
Ken Brett	P	2	0	0	0	0	0	0	0	0	0	0	.000
Dave Moorehead	P	2	0	0	0	0	0	0	0	0	0	0	.000
Dan Osinski	P	2	0	0	0	0	0	0	0	0	0	0	.000
John Wyatt	P	2	0	0	0	0	0	0	0	0	0	0	.000
Lee Stange	P	1	0	0	0	0	0	0	0	0	0	0	.000
Jerry Stephenson	P	1	0	0	0	0	0	0	0	0	0	0	.000
Team Total		7	822	21	48	6	1	8	19	17	49	1	.216

Double Plays—3   Left on Bases—43

Pitching	G	GS	CG	IP	H	R	ER	BB	SO	W	L	SV	ERA
St. Louis													
Bob Gibson	3	3	3	27	14	3	3	5	26	3	0	0	1.00
Nelson Briles	2	1	1	11	7	2	2	1	4	1	0	0	1.64
Dick Hughes	2	2	0	9	9	6	5	3	7	0	1	0	5.00
Steve Carlton	1	1	0	6	3	1	0	2	5	0	1	0	0.00
Jack Lamabe	3	0	0	2⅔	5	2	2	0	4	0	1	0	6.75
Ray Washburn	2	0	0	2⅓	1	0	0	1	2	0	0	0	0.00
Hal Woodeshick	1	0	0	1	1	0	0	0	0	0	0	0	0.00
Ron Willis	3	0	0	1	2	4	3	4	1	0	0	0	27.00
Joe Hoerner	2	0	0	⅔	4	3	3	1	0	0	0	0	40.50
Larry Jaster	1	0	0	⅓	2	0	0	0	0	0	0	0	0.00
Team Total	7	7	4	61	48	21	18	17	49	4	3	0	2.66

Pitching	G	GS	CG	IP	H	R	ER	BB	SO	W	L	SV	ERA
Boston													
Jim Lonborg	3	3	2	24	14	8	7	2	11	2	1	0	2.63
Jose Santiago	3	2	0	$9\frac{2}{3}$	16	6	6	3	6	0	2	0	5.59
Gary Waslewski	2	1	0	$8\frac{1}{3}$	4	2	2	2	7	0	0	0	2.16
Gary Bell	3	1	0	$5\frac{1}{3}$	8	3	3	1	1	0	1	1	5.06
John Wyatt	2	0	0	$3\frac{2}{3}$	1	2	2	3	1	1	0	0	4.91
Dave Morehead	2	0	0	$3\frac{1}{3}$	0	0	0	4	3	0	0	0	0.00
Lee Stange	1	0	0	2	3	1	0	0	0	0	0	0	0.00
Jerry Stephenson	1	0	0	2	3	2	2	1	0	0	0	0	9.00
Ken Brett	2	0	0	$1\frac{1}{3}$	0	0	0	1	1	0	0	0	0.00
Dan Osinski	2	0	0	$1\frac{1}{3}$	2	1	1	0	0	0	0	0	6.75
Team Total	7	7	2	61	51	25	23	17	30	3	4	1	3.39

Total Attendance—304,085. Average Attendance—43,441. Winning Player's Share—$8,315. Losing Player's Share—$5,115.

LINESCORES:

FIRST GAME (Oct. 4, at Boston)

```
ST. LOUIS .........................  0 0 1  0 0 0  1 0 0—2 10 0
BOSTON ...........................  0 0 1  0 0 0  0 0 0—1  6 0
```
B. Gibson   W—Gibson
Santiago, Wyatt (8th)   L—Santiago

SECOND GAME (Oct. 5, at Boston)

```
ST. LOUIS .........................  0 0 0  0 0 0  0 0 0—0 1 1
BOSTON ...........................  0 0 0  1 0 1  3 0 x—5 9 0
```
Hughes, Willis (6th), Hoerner (7th), Lamabe (7th)   W—Lonborg
Lonborg   L—Hughes

THIRD GAME (Oct. 7, at St. Louis)

```
BOSTON ...........................  0 0 0  0 0 1  1 0 0—2  7 1
ST. LOUIS .........................  1 2 0  0 0 1  0 1 x—5 10 0
```
Bell, Waslewski (3d), Stange (6th), Osinski (8th)   W—Briles
Briles   L—Bell

FOURTH GAME (Oct. 8, at St. Louis)

```
BOSTON ...........................  0 0 0  0 0 0  0 0 0—0 5 0
ST. LOUIS .........................  4 0 2  0 0 0  0 0 x—6 9 0
```
Santiago, Bell (1st), Stephenson (3d), Morehead (5th), Brett (8th) W—Gibson
B. Gibson   L—Santiago

FIFTH GAME (Oct. 9, at St. Louis)

```
BOSTON ...........................  0 0 1  0 0 0  0 0 2—3 6 1
ST. LOUIS .........................  0 0 0  0 0 0  0 0 1—1 3 2
```
Lonborg   W—Lonborg
Carlton, Washburn (7th), Willis (9th), Lamabe (9th)   L—Carlton

SIXTH GAME (Oct. 11, at Boston)

```
ST. LOUIS .........................  0 0 2  0 0 0  2 0 0—4  8 0
BOSTON ...........................  0 1 0  3 0 0  4 0 x—8 12 1
```
Hughes, Willis (4th), Briles (5th), Lamabe (7th), Hoerner (7th)   W—Wyatt
Jaster (7th), Washburn (7th), Woodeshick (8th)   L—Lamabe
Waslewski, Wyatt (6th), Bell (8th)

1967 World Series (continued)

SEVENTH GAME (Oct. 12, at Boston
 ST. LOUIS .... 0 0 2 0 2 3 0 0 0—7 10 1
 BOSTON .... 0 0 0 0 1 0 0 1 0—2 3 1
B. Gibson   W—Gibson
Lonborg, Santiago (7th), Morehead (9th), Osinski (9th), L—Lonborg
Brett (9th)

1968

Detroit A.L. 4, St. Louis N.L. 3

Batting	Pos	G	AB	R	H	2B	3B	HR	RBI	BB	SO	SB	BA
Detroit													
Norm Cash	1B	7	26	5	10	0	0	1	5	3	5	0	.385
Dick McAuliffe	2B	7	27	5	6	0	0	1	3	4	6	0	.222
Mickey Stanley	SS-CF	7	28	4	6	0	1	0	0	2	4	0	.214
Don Wert	3B	6	17	1	2	0	0	0	2	6	5	0	.118
Al Kaline	RF	7	29	6	11	2	0	2	8	0	7	0	.379
Jim Northrup	CF-LF	7	28	4	7	0	1	2	8	1	5	0	.250
Willie Horton	LF	7	23	6	7	1	1	1	3	5	6	0	.304
Bill Freehan	C	7	24	0	2	1	0	0	2	4	8	0	.083
Eddie Mathews	PH-3B	2	3	0	1	0	0	0	0	1	1	0	.333
Ray Oyler	SS	4	0	0	0	0	0	0	0	0	0	0	.000
Dick Tracewski	3B-PR	2	0	1	0	0	0	0	0	0	0	0	.000
Tom Matchick	PH	3	3	0	0	0	0	0	0	0	1	0	.000
Jim Price	PH	2	2	0	0	0	0	0	0	0	1	0	.000
Gates Brown	PH	1	1	0	0	0	0	0	0	0	0	0	.000
Wayne Comer	PH	1	1	0	1	0	0	0	0	0	0	0	1.000
Mickey Lolich	P	3	12	2	3	0	0	1	2	1	5	0	.250
Denny McLain	P	3	6	0	0	0	0	0	0	0	4	0	.000
Earl Wilson	P	1	1	0	0	0	0	0	0	0	1	0	.000
Pat Dobson	P	3	0	0	0	0	0	0	0	0	0	0	.000
John Hiller	P	2	0	0	0	0	0	0	0	0	0	0	.000
Don McMahon	P	2	0	0	0	0	0	0	0	0	0	0	.000
Daryl Patterson	P	2	0	0	0	0	0	0	0	0	0	0	.000
Fred Lasher	P	1	0	0	0	0	0	0	0	0	0	0	.000
Joe Sparma	P	1	0	0	0	0	0	0	0	0	0	0	.000
John Warden	Did not play												
Team Total		7	231	34	56	4	3	8	33	27	59	0	.242

Double Plays—5 Left on Bases—44

Batting	Pos	G	AB	R	H	2B	3B	HR	RBI	BB	SO	SB	BA
St. Louis													
Orlando Cepeda	1B	7	28	2	7	0	0	2	6	2	3	0	.250
Julian Javier	2B	7	27	1	9	1	0	0	3	3	4	1	.333
Dal Maxvill	SS	7	22	1	0	0	0	0	0	3	5	0	.000
Mike Shannon	3B	7	29	3	8	1	0	1	4	1	5	0	.276
Roger Maris	RF-PH	6	19	5	3	1	0	0	1	3	3	0	.158
Curt Flood	CF	7	28	4	8	1	0	0	2	2	2	3	.286
Lou Brock	LF	7	28	6	13	3	1	2	5	3	4	7	.464
Tim McCarver	C	7	27	3	9	0	2	1	4	3	2	0	.333
Ron Davis	RF	2	7	0	0	0	0	0	0	0	2	0	.000
Dick Schofield	PR-SS	2	0	0	0	0	0	0	0	0	0	0	.000
Phil Gagliano	PH	3	3	0	0	0	0	0	0	0	0	0	.000
Johnny Edwards	PH	1	1	0	0	0	0	0	0	0	1	0	.000
Dave Ricketts	PH	1	1	0	1	0	0	0	0	0	0	0	1.000
Ed Spiezio	PH	1	1	0	1	0	0	0	0	0	0	0	1.000
Bobby Tolan	PH	1	1	0	0	0	0	0	0	0	1	0	.000
Bob Gibson	P	3	8	2	1	0	0	1	2	1	2	0	.125
Nelson Briles	P	2	4	0	0	0	0	0	0	0	4	0	.000
Ray Washburn	P	2	3	0	0	0	0	0	0	0	1	0	.000
Joe Hoerner	P	3	2	0	1	0	0	0	0	0	1	0	.500
Ron Willis	P	3	0	0	0	0	0	0	0	0	0	0	.000
Steve Carlton	P	2	0	0	0	0	0	0	0	0	0	0	.000
Wayne Granger	P	1	0	0	0	0	0	0	0	0	0	0	.000
Dick Hughes	P	1	0	0	0	0	0	0	0	0	0	0	.000
Larry Jaster	P	1	0	0	0	0	0	0	0	0	0	0	.000
Mel Nelson	P	1	0	0	0	0	0	0	0	0	0	0	.000
Team Total		7	239	27	61	7	3	7	27	21	40	11	.255

Double Plays—7   Left on Bases—49

Pitching	G	GS	CG	IP	H	R	ER	BB	SO	W	L	SV	ERA
Detroit													
Mickey Lolich	3	3	3	27	20	5	5	6	21	3	0	0	1.67
Denny McLain	3	3	1	16⅔	18	8	6	4	13	1	2	0	3.24
Pat Dobson	3	0	0	4⅔	5	2	2	1	0	0	0	0	3.86
Earl Wilson	1	1	0	4⅓	4	3	3	6	3	0	1	0	6.23
Daryl Patterson	2	0	0	3	1	0	0	1	0	0	0	0	0.00
Fred Lasher	1	0	0	2	1	0	0	0	1	0	0	0	0.00
John Hiller	2	0	0	2	6	4	3	3	1	0	0	0	13.50
Don McMahon	2	0	0	2	4	3	3	0	1	0	0	0	13.50
Joe Sparma	1	0	0	⅓	2	2	2	0	0	0	0	0	54.00
John Warden	Did not play												
Team Total	7	7	4	62	61	27	24	21	40	4	3	0	3.48

Pitching	G	GS	CG	IP	H	R	ER	BB	SO	W	L	SV	ERA
St. Louis													
Bob Gibson	3	3	3	27	18	5	5	4	35	2	1	0	1.67
Nelson Briles	2	2	0	11⅓	13	7	7	4	7	0	1	0	5.56
Ray Washburn	2	2	0	7⅓	7	8	8	7	6	1	1	0	9.82
Joe Hoerner	3	0	0	4⅔	5	4	2	5	3	0	1	1	3.86
Ron Willis	3	0	0	4⅓	2	4	4	4	3	0	0	0	8.31
Steve Carlton	2	0	0	4	7	3	3	1	3	0	0	0	6.75
Wayne Granger	1	0	2	2	0	0	0	1	1	0	0	0	0.00
Mel Nelson	1	0	0	1	0	0	0	0	1	0	0	0	0.00
Dick Hughes	1	0	0	⅓	2	0	0	0	0	0	0	0	0.00
Larry Jaster	1	0	0	0	2	3	3	1	0	0	0	0	0.00
Team Total	7	7	3	62	56	34	32	27	59	3	4	1	4.65

Total Attendance—379,670. Average Attendance—54,239. Winning Player's Share—$10,937. Losing Player's Share—$7,079.

LINESCORES:

FIRST GAME (Oct. 2, at St. Louis)
```
     DETROIT   ........................  0 0 0  0 0 0  0 0 0—0 5 3
     ST. LOUIS ........................  0 0 0  3 0 0  1 0 x—4 6 0
```
McLain, Dobson (6th), McMahon (8th)   W—Gibson
Gibson   L—McLain

SECOND GAME (Oct. 3, at St. Louis)
```
     DETROIT   ........................  0 1 1  0 0 3  1 0 2  8 13 1
     ST. LOUIS ........................  0 0 0  0 0 1  0 0 0—1  6 1
```
Lolich   W—Lolich
Briles, Carlton (6th), Willis (7th), Hoerner (9th)   L—Briles

THIRD GAME (Oct. 5, at Detroit)
```
     ST. LOUIS ........................  0 0 0  0 4 0  3 0 0—7 13 0
     DETROIT   ........................  0 0 2  0 1 0  0 0 0—3  4 0
```
Washburn, Hoerner (6th)   W—Washburn
Wilson, Dobson (5th), McMahon (6th), Patterson (7th), L—Wilson
Hiller (8th)

FOURTH GAME (Oct. 6, at Detroit)
```
     ST. LOUIS ........................  2 0 2  2 0 0  0 4 0—10 13 0
     DETROIT   ........................  0 0 0  1 0 0  0 0 0— 1  5 4
```
Gibson   W—Gibson
McLain, Sparma (3d), Patterson (4th), Lasher (6th),   L—McLain
Hiller (8th), Dobson (8th)

FIFTH GAME (Oct. 7, at Detroit)
```
     ST. LOUIS ........................  3 0 0  0 0 0  0 0 0—3 9 0
     DETROIT   ........................  0 0 0  2 0 0  3 0 x—5 9 1
```
Briles, Hoerner (7th), Willis (7th)   W—Lolich
Lolich   L—Hoerner

SIXTH GAME (Oct. 9, at St. Louis)
```
     DETROIT   ........................  0 2 10  0 1 0  0 0 0—13 12 1
     ST. LOUIS ........................  0 0  0  0 0 0  0 0 1— 1  9 1
```
McLain   W—McLain
Washburn, Jaster (3d), Willis (3d), Hughes (3d), Carlton (4th), L—Washburn
Granger (7th), Nelson (9th)

SEVENTH GAME (Oct. 10, at St. Louis)
```
     DETROIT   ........................  0 0 0  0 0 0  3 0 1—4 8 1
     ST. LOUIS ........................  0 0 0  0 0 0  0 0 1—1 5 0
```
Lolich   W—Lolich
Gibson   L—Gibson

(For 1982 World Series see Appendix)

Cardinal World Series Managers

Eddie Dyer	1946
Frank Frisch	1934
Whitey Herzog	1982
Rogers Hornsby	1926
Johnny Keane	1964
Bill McKechnie	1928
Red Schoendienst	1967-1968
Billy Southworth	1942-1943-1944
Gabby Street	1930-1931

Cardinals in the World Series, Batting

Player, Years	G	AB	R	H	2B	3B	HR	RBI	BB	SO	SB	Bat Avg	Slug Avg
Elvin Adams, 1946	0	0	0	0	0	0	0	0	0	0	0	.000	.000
Sparky Adams, 1930, 31	8	25	0	4	0	0	0	1	0	5	0	.160	.160
Grover Alexander, 1926, 28	5	8	1	0	0	0	0	1	0	2	0	.000	.000
Red Barrett, 1946	3	0	0	0	0	0	0	0	0	0	0	.000	.000
John Beazley, 1942, 46	3	7	0	1	0	0	0	0	0	5	0	.143	.143
Herman Bell, 1926, 30	2	0	0	0	0	0	0	0	0	0	0	.000	.000
Les Bell, 1926	7	27	4	7	1	0	1	6	2	5	0	.259	.407
Augie Bergamo, 1944	3	6	0	0	0	0	0	1	2	3	0	.000	.000
Ray Blades, 1926, 28, 30, 31	8	12	2	1	0	0	0	0	2	5	0	.083	.083
Jim Bottomley, 1926, 28, 30, 31	24	90	8	18	5	1	1	10	7	22	0	.200	.311
Ken Boyer, 1964	7	27	5	6	1	0	2	6	1	5	0	.222	.481
Steve Braun, 1982	2	2	0	1	0	0	0	2	1	0	0	.500	.500
Glenn Brummer, 1982	1	0	0	0	0	0	0	0	0	0	0	.000	.000
Al Brazle, 1943, 46	2	5	0	0	0	0	0	0	0	1	0	.000	.000
Harry Brecheen, 1943, 44, 46	7	12	2	1	0	0	0	1	0	2	0	.083	.083
Ed Bressoud, 1967	2	0	0	0	0	0	0	0	0	0	0	.000	.000
Nelson Briles, 1967, 68	4	7	0	0	0	0	0	0	0	4	0	.000	.000
Lou Brock, 1964, 67, 68	21	87	16	34	7	2	4	13	5	10	14	.391	.655
Jim Brown, 1942	5	20	2	6	0	0	0	1	3	0	0	.300	.300
Jerry Buchek, 1964	4	1	1	1	0	0	0	0	0	0	0	.000	.000
Ken Burkhart, 1946	0	0	0	0	0	0	0	0	0	0	0	.000	.000
Bud Byerly, 1944	1	0	0	0	0	0	0	0	0	0	0	.000	.000
Tex Carleton, 1934	2	1	0	0	0	0	0	0	0	0	0	.000	.000
Steve Carlton, 1967, 68	3	1	0	0	0	0	0	0	0	0	0	.000	.000
Orlando Cepeda, 1967, 68	14	57	3	10	2	0	2	7	2	7	0	.176	.323
Ed Clough, 1926	0	0	0	0	0	0	0	0	0	0	0	.000	.000
Rip Collins, 1931	9	32	4	11	1	0	0	3	1	2	0	.183	.200
Mort Cooper, 1942, 43, 44	6	14	1	1	0	0	0	2	0	6	0	.071	.071
Walker Cooper, 1942, 43, 44	16	60	5	18	3	1	0	6	3	4	0	.300	.383
Roger Craig, 1964	2	1	0	0	0	0	0	0	0	0	0	.000	.000
Cliff Crawford, 1934	2	2	0	0	0	0	0	0	0	0	0	.000	.000
Creepy Crespi, 1942	1	0	0	0	0	0	0	0	0	0	0	.000	.000
Jeff Cross, 1946	0	0	0	0	0	0	0	0	0	0	0	.000	.000
Mike Cuellar, 1964	0	0	0	0	0	0	0	0	0	0	0	.000	.000

Player, Years	G	AB	R	H	2B	3B	HR	RBI	BB	SO	SB	Bat Avg	Slug Avg
Ron Davis, 1968	2	7	0	0	0	0	0	0	0	2	0	.000	.000
Spud Davis, 1934	2	2	0	2	0	0	0	1	0	0	0	1.000	1.000
Dizzy Dean, 1934	4	12	3	3	2	0	0	1	0	3	0	.250	.417
Paul Dean, 1934	2	6	0	1	0	0	0	2	2	1	0	.167	.167
Bill DeLancey, 1934	7	29	3	5	3	0	1	4	2	8	0	.172	.379
Frank Demaree, 1943	1	1	0	0	0	0	0	0	0	0	0	.000	.000
Paul Derringer, 1931	3	2	0	0	0	0	0	0	0	1	0	.000	.000
Murry Dickson, 1942, 43, 46	1	0	0	0	0	0	0	0	0	0	0	.000	.000
Blix Donnelly, 1944	2	1	0	0	0	0	0	0	0	1	0	.000	.000
Taylor Douthit, 1926, 28, 30	13	50	5	7	2	0	1	4	4	5	0	.140	.240
Leo Durocher, 1934	7	27	4	7	1	1	0	0	0	0	0	.259	.370
Erv Dusak, 1946	4	4	0	1	1	0	0	2	2	2	0	.250	.500
Johnny Edwards, 1968	1	1	0	0	0	0	0	0	0	1	0	.000	.000
Bill Endicott, 1946	0	0	0	0	0	0	0	0	0	0	0	.000	.000
George Fallon, 1943, 44	2	2	0	0	0	0	0	0	0	1	0	.000	.000
George Fisher, 1930	2	2	0	1	1	0	0	0	0	1	0	.500	1.000
Curt Flood, 1964, 67, 68	21	86	11	19	2	1	0	8	8	6	3	.221	.267
Jake Flowers, 1926, 31	8	14	1	1	1	0	0	0	1	1	0	.071	.143
Fred Frankhouse, 1928	0	0	0	0	0	0	0	0	0	0	0	.000	.000
Frank Frisch, 1928, 30, 31, 34	24	95	5	21	5	0	0	6	3	5	4	.226	.270
Charlie Fullis, 1934	3	5	0	0	0	0	0	0	0	0	0	.000	.000
Phil Gagliano, 1967, 68	4	4	0	0	0	0	0	0	0	3	0	.000	.000
Joe Garagiola, 1946	5	19	2	6	2	0	0	4	0	3	0	.316	.421
Debs Garms, 1943, 44	4	7	0	0	0	0	0	0	0	2	0	.000	.000
Charlie Gelbert, 1930, 31	13	40	2	12	1	1	0	5	3	7	0	.300	.375
Bob Gibson, 1964, 67, 68	9	28	4	4	0	0	2	3	2	7	0	.143	.357
Julio Gonzalez, 1982	0	0	0	0	0	0	0	0	0	0	0	.000	.000
Mike Gonzalez, 1931	0	0	0	0	0	0	0	0	0	0	0	.000	.000
Al Grabowski, 1930	0	0	0	0	0	0	0	0	0	0	0	.000	.000
Wayne Granger, 1968	1	0	0	0	0	0	0	0	0	0	0	.000	.000
David Green, 1982	7	10	3	2	1	1	0	0	1	3	0	.200	.500
Burleigh Grimes, 1930, 31	4	12	0	4	0	0	0	2	0	3	0	.333	.333
Dick Groat, 1964	7	26	3	5	1	0	0	1	4	3	0	.192	.308
John Grodzicki, 1946	0	0	0	0	0	0	0	0	0	0	0	.000	.000
Harry Gumbert, 1942, 43	2	0	0	0	0	0	0	0	0	0	0	.000	.000
Chick Hafey, 1926, 28, 30, 31	23	88	5	18	7	0	0	2	2	19	1	.205	.284

Player, Years	G	AB	R	H	2B	3B	HR	RBI	BB	SO	SB	Bat Avg	Slug Avg
Hal Haid, 1928	0	0	0	0	0	0	0	0	0	0	0	.000	.000
Jesse Haines, 1926, 28, 30, 31, 34	9	19	1	7	0	0	1	4	0	4	0	.368	.526
Bill Hallahan, 1926, 30, 31, 34	7	11	0	0	0	0	0	0	1	5	0	.000	.000
George Harper, 1928	3	9	1	1	0	0	0	0	2	2	0	.111	.111
Red Hayworth, 1944	6	17	1	2	1	0	0	1	3	1	0	.118	.176
Francis Healey, 1934	0	0	0	0	0	0	0	0	0	0	0	.000	.000
George Hendrick, 1982	7	28	5	9	0	0	0	5	2	2	0	.321	.321
Keith Hernandez, 1982	7	27	4	7	2	0	1	8	4	2	0	.259	.444
Tom Herr, 1982	7	25	2	4	2	0	0	5	3	3	0	.160	.240
Andy High, 1928, 30, 31	9	34	5	10	2	0	0	1	1	5	0	.294	.353
Joe Hoerner, 1967, 68	2	0	0	0	0	0	0	0	0	0	0	.000	.000
Wattie Holm, 1926, 28	8	22	1	3	0	0	0	2	1	3	0	.136	.136
John Hopp, 1942, 43, 44	12	48	5	8	0	0	0	0	0	10	1	.087	.087
Rogers Hornsby, 1926	7	28	2	7	1	0	0	4	2	2	0	.250	.286
Willis Hudlin, 1944	0	0	0	0	0	0	0	0	0	0	0	.000	.000
Dick Hughes, 1967, 68	3	3	0	0	0	0	0	0	0	3	0	.000	.000
Bob Humphreys, 1964	1	0	0	0	0	0	0	0	0	0	0	.000	.000
Dane Iorg, 1982	5	17	4	9	4	1	0	1	0	0	0	.529	.882
Al Jackson, 1967	3	0	0	0	0	0	0	0	0	0	0	.000	.000
Charlie James, 1964	3	3	0	0	0	0	0	0	0	1	0	.000	.000
Larry Jaster, 1967, 68	2	0	0	0	0	0	0	0	0	0	0	.000	.000
Julian Javier, 1964, 67, 68	15	52	4	18	4	0	1	7	3	10	1	.346	.485
Alex Johnson, 1967	0	0	0	0	0	0	0	0	0	0	0	.000	.000
Si Johnson, 1926, 28, 30, 31	6	2	0	0	0	0	0	0	0	2	0	.000	.000
Nippy Jones, 1946	1	1	0	0	0	0	0	0	0	1	0	.000	.000
Al Jurisich, 1944	1	0	0	0	0	0	0	0	0	0	0	.000	.000
Tony Kaufmann, 1931	0	0	0	0	0	0	0	0	0	0	0	.000	.000
Bob Keely, 1944	0	0	0	0	0	0	0	0	0	0	0	.000	.000
Vic Keen	1	0	0	0	0	0	0	0	0	0	0	.000	.000
Lou Klein, 1943	5	22	0	3	0	0	0	0	1	2	0	.136	.136
Clyde Kluttz, 1946	0	0	0	0	0	0	0	0	0	0	0	.000	.000
Howie Krist, 1942, 43, 46	1	0	0	0	0	0	0	0	0	0	0	.000	.000
Whitey Kurowski, 1942, 43, 44, 46	23	83	12	21	5	1	1	9	3	13	0	.253	.373
Jack Lamabe, 1967	3	0	0	0	0	0	0	0	0	0	0	.000	.000
Max Lanier, 1942, 43, 44	7	9	0	4	0	0	0	3	0	0	0	.444	.444
Jim Lindsey, 1930, 31	3	1	0	1	0	0	0	0	0	0	0	1.000	1.000
Danny Litwhiler, 1943, 44	10	35	2	8	2	0	1	3	4	11	0	.229	.371

Player, Years	G	AB	R	H	2B	3B	HR	RBI	BB	SO	SB	Bat Avg	Slug Avg
Gus Mancuso, 1930, 31	4	8	1	2	0	0	0	0	1	2	0	.143	.143
Rabbit Maranville, 1928	4	13	2	4	1	0	0	0	1	1	1	.308	.385
Marty Marion, 1942, 43, 44, 46	23	78	5	18	7	1	1	11	7	7	1	.231	.385
Roger Maris, 1967, 68	13	45	8	13	2	0	1	8	6	4	0	.222	.374
Pepper Martin, 1928, 31, 34, 44	15	55	14	23	7	1	1	9	5	6	7	.418	.636
Dal Maxvill, 1964, 67, 68	21	61	2	7	1	1	0	2	8	10	0	.115	.164
Tim McCarver, 1964, 67, 68	21	74	10	23	2	3	2	11	10	5	1	.311	.500
Willie McGee, 1982	7	25	6	6	0	0	2	5	1	3	2	.240	.480
Joe Medwick, 1934	7	29	4	11	0	1	1	5	1	7	0	.379	.552
Clarence Mitchell, 1928	1	2	0	0	0	0	0	0	0	0	0	.000	.000
Jim Mooney, 1934	1	0	0	0	0	0	0	0	0	0	0	.000	.000
Terry Moore, 1942, 46	12	44	3	9	1	0	0	4	4	9	0	.205	.227
Whitey Moore, 1942	0	0	0	0	0	0	0	0	0	0	0	.000	.000
George Munger, 1943, 46	1	4	0	1	0	0	0	0	0	1	0	.250	.250
Stan Musial, 1942, 43, 44, 46	23	86	12	22	7	1	1	8	12	4	1	.256	.395
Sam Narron, 1942, 43	1	1	0	0	0	0	0	0	0	0	0	.000	.000
Mel Nelson, 1968	1	0	0	0	0	0	0	0	0	0	0	.000	.000
Ken Oberkfell, 1982	7	24	4	7	1	0	0	1	2	1	2	.292	.333
Ken O'Dea, 1942, 43, 44	6	7	0	4	0	0	0	3	2	2	0	.666	.666
Bob O'Farrell, 1926	7	23	2	7	1	0	0	2	2	2	0	.304	.348
Ernie Orsatti, 1928, 30, 31, 34	13	33	4	9	1	1	0	2	4	7	0	.273	.364
Howie Pollet, 1942	1	0	0	0	0	0	0	0	0	0	0	.000	.000
Darrell Porter, 1982	7	28	1	8	2	0	1	5	1	4	0	.286	.464
George Puccinelli, 1930	1	1	0	0	0	0	0	0	0	0	0	.000	.000
Mike Ramsey, 1982	3	1	1	0	0	0	0	0	0	1	0	.000	.000
Art Reinhart, 1926, 28	1	0	0	0	0	0	0	0	0	0	0	.000	.000
Flint Rhem, 1926, 28, 30, 31	4	2	0	0	0	0	0	0	0	2	0	.000	.000
Del Rice, 1946	3	6	2	3	1	0	0	0	2	0	0	.500	.667
Gordon Richardson, 1964	2	0	0	0	0	0	0	0	0	0	0	.000	.000
Dave Ricketts, 1967, 68	4	4	0	1	0	0	0	0	0	0	0	.250	.250
Walter Roettger, 1928, 31	3	14	1	4	1	0	0	0	0	3	0	.286	.357
Jack Rothrock, 1934	7	30	3	7	3	0	0	6	1	2	0	.233	.400
Ray Sadecki, 1964	2	2	0	1	0	0	0	1	0	1	0	.500	.500
Ray Sanders, 1942, 43, 44	13	39	9	11	0	0	2	3	9	12	0	.275	.425
Fred Schmidt, 1944, 46	1	1	0	0	0	0	0	0	0	1	0	.000	.000
Red Schoendienst, 1946	7	30	3	7	1	0	0	1	0	2	1	.233	.267
Dick Schofield, 1967	2	0	0	0	0	0	0	0	0	0	0	.000	.000
Barney Schultz, 1964	4	1	0	0	0	0	0	0	0	0	0	.000	.000

Player, Years	G	AB	R	H	2B	3B	HR	RBI	BB	SO	SB	Bat Avg	Slug Avg
Walt Sessi, 1946	0	0	0	0	0	0	0	0	0	0	0	.000	.000
Mike Shannon, 1964, 67, 68	21	81	12	19	2	0	3	8	2	18	1	.235	.370
Bill Sherdel, 1926, 28	4	10	0	0	0	0	0	0	0	4	0	.000	.000
Curt Simmons, 1964	2	4	0	2	0	0	0	1	0	1	0	.500	.500
Dick Sisler, 1946	2	2	0	0	0	0	0	0	0	0	0	.000	.000
Bob Skinner, 1964	4	3	0	2	1	0	0	1	1	0	0	.667	1.000
Enos Slaughter, 1942, 46	12	44	8	13	2	1	2	4	7	5	1	.291	.517
Earl Smith, 1928	1	4	0	3	0	0	0	1	1	0	0	.750	.750
Lonnie Smith, 1982	7	28	6	9	4	1	0	1	1	5	2	.321	.536
Ozzie Smith, 1982	7	24	3	5	0	0	0	1	3	5	1	.208	.208
Al Sothoron, 1926	0	0	0	0	0	0	0	0	0	0	0	.000	.000
Billy Southworth, 1926	7	29	6	10	1	1	1	4	0	0	1	.345	.552
Ed Spiezio, 1964, 67, 68	2	2	0	1	0	0	0	0	0	0	0	.500	.500
Al Stout, 1931	0	0	0	0	0	0	0	0	0	0	0	.000	.000
Ron Taylor, 1964	2	1	0	0	0	0	0	0	0	1	0	.000	.000
Gene Tenace, 1982	5	6	0	0	0	0	0	0	1	1	0	.000	.000
Tommy Thevenow, 1926, 28	8	24	5	10	1	1	0	4	0	2	0	.417	.583
Bobby Tolan, 1967, 68	4	3	1	0	0	0	0	0	0	1	0	.000	.000
George Toporcer, 1926	1	0	0	0	0	0	0	0	0	2	0	.000	.000
Coaker Triplett, 1942	0	0	0	0	0	0	0	0	0	0	0	.000	.000
Bob Uecker, 1964	0	0	0	0	0	0	0	0	0	0	0	.000	.000
Dazzy Vance, 1934	0	0	0	0	0	0	0	0	0	0	0	.000	.000
Emil Verban, 1944	6	17	1	7	0	0	0	2	2	0	0	.412	.412
Ernie Vick, 1926	0	0	0	0	0	0	0	0	0	0	0	.000	.000
Bill Walker, 1934	2	2	0	0	0	0	0	0	0	2	0	.000	.000
Harry Walker, 1942, 43, 46	13	36	3	10	3	0	0	6	4	5	0	.278	.361
Carl Warwick, 1964	5	4	2	3	0	0	0	1	1	1	0	.750	.750
Ray Washburn, 1964, 67, 68	4	3	0	0	0	0	0	0	0	0	0	.000	.000
George Watkins, 1930, 31	9	26	6	6	1	0	2	3	3	4	1	.231	.500
Bill White, 1964	7	27	2	3	1	0	0	2	2	6	1	.111	.148
Ernie White, 1942, 43	2	2	0	0	0	0	0	0	0	0	0	.000	.000
Burgess Whitehead, 1934	1	0	0	0	0	0	0	0	0	0	0	.000	.000
Ted Wilks, 1944, 46	3	2	0	0	0	0	0	0	0	1	0	.000	.000
Howard Williamson, 1928	0	0	0	0	0	0	0	0	0	0	0	.000	.000
Ron Willis, 1967, 68	6	0	0	0	0	0	0	0	0	0	0	.000	.000
Jim Wilson, 1928, 30, 31	14	49	1	10	2	0	0	5	1	5	0	.287	.310
Hal Woodeshick, 1967	1	0	0	0	0	0	0	0	0	0	0	.000	.000

Cardinal World Series Pitching Performances

Player, Years	GP	GS	CG	IP	H	ER	BB	SO	W	L	PCT	SV	SHO	ERA
Grover Cleveland Alexander, 1926, 28	5	3	2	25.1	22	14	8	19	2	0	1.000	1	0	5.04
Joaquin Andujar, 1982	2	2	0	13⅓	10	2	1	4	2	0	1.000	0	0	1.35
Doug Bair, 1982	3	0	0	2	2	2	2	3	0	1	.000	0	0	9.00
Red Barrett, 1946	0	0	0	0	0	0	0	0	0	0	—	0	0	0.00
John Beazley, 1942, 46	3	2	2	19	18	5	3	7	2	0	1.000	0	0	2.37
Hi Bell, 1926, 30	2	0	0	3	4	2	1	1	0	0	—	0	0	6.00
Al Brazle, 1943, 46	2	1	0	14	12	7	8	8	0	2	.000	0	0	4.50
Harry Brecheen, 1943, 44, 46	7	3	3	32.2	28	3	12	18	4	1	.800	0	1	0.83
Nelson Briles, 1967, 68	4	3	0	22.1	20	9	5	11	1	1	.500	0	0	3.68
Ken Burkhart, 1946	0	0	0	0	0	0	0	0	0	0	—	0	0	0.00
Bud Byerly, 1944	1	0	0	1.1	0	0	0	1	0	0	—	0	0	0.00
Tex Carleton, 1934	2	1	0	3.2	5	3	2	2	0	0	—	0	0	7.36
Steve Carlton, 1967, 68	3	1	0	10	10	3	3	8	0	1	.000	0	0	2.70
Ed Clough, 1926	0	0	0	0	0	0	0	0	0	0	—	0	0	0.00
Mort Cooper, 1942, 43, 44	6	6	2	45	37	15	12	35	2	3	.400	0	1	3.00
Roger Craig, 1964	2	0	0	5	2	0	3	9	1	0	1.000	0	0	0.00
Mike Cuellar, 1964	0	0	0	0	0	0	0	0	0	0	—	0	0	0.00
Dizzy Dean, 1934	3	3	2	26	20	5	5	17	2	1	.667	0	1	1.73
Paul Dean, 1934	2	2	2	18	15	2	7	11	2	0	1.000	0	0	1.00
Paul Derringer, 1931	3	2	0	12.2	14	6	7	14	0	2	.000	0	0	4.26
Murry Dickson, 1942, 43, 46	3	2	0	14.2	11	6	5	7	0	0	—	0	0	3.60
Blix Donnelly, 1944	2	0	0	6	2	0	1	9	1	0	1.000	0	0	0.00
Bob Forsch, 1982	2	2	0	12⅔	18	7	3	4	0	2	.000	0	0	4.97
Fred Frankhouse, 1928	0	0	0	0	0	0	0	0	0	0	—	0	0	0.00
Bob Gibson, 1964, 67, 68	9	9	8	81	55	17	17	92	7	2	.778	0	2	1.89
Wayne Granger, 1968	1	0	0	2	0	0	1	1	0	0	—	0	0	0.00
Al Grabowski, 1930	0	0	0	0	0	0	0	0	0	0	—	0	0	0.00
Burleigh Grimes, 1930, 31	4	4	3	34.2	19	11	15	24	2	2	.500	0	0	0.00
John Grodzicki, 1946	2	0	0	0	0	0	0	0	0	0	—	0	0	0.00
Harry Gumbert, 1942, 43	2	0	0	0.2	1	0	0	0	0	0	—	0	0	0.00
Hal Haid, 1928	2	0	0	0	0	0	0	0	0	0	—	0	0	0.00
Jesse Haines, 1926, 28, 30, 31, 34	6	4	2	32.1	24	6	16	12	3	1	.750	0	1	1.67
Bill Hallahan, 1926, 30, 31, 34	7	5	3	39.2	29	6	23	27	3	1	.750	1	2	1.36
Joe Hoerner, 1967, 68	5	0	0	5.1	9	5	6	3	0	1	.000	1	0	8.44
Dick Hughes, 1967, 68	3	2	0	9.1	11	5	3	0	0	0	—	0	0	4.82

Player, Years	GP	GS	CG	IP	H	ER	BB	SO	W	L	PCT	SV	SHO	ERA
Bob Humphreys, 1964	1	0	0	1	0	0	0	1	0	0	—	0	0	0.00
Al Jackson, 1967	0	0	0	0	0	0	0	0	0	0	—	0	0	0.00
Larry Jaster, 1967, 68	2	0	0	0.1	4	3	1	0	0	0	—	0	0	81.00
Si Johnson, 1926, 28, 30, 31	7	1	0	16	18	8	5	11	0	1	.000	0	0	4.50
Al Jurisich, 1944	1	0	0	0.2	2	2	1	2	0	0	—	0	0	27.00
Jim Kaat, 1982	4	0	0	2⅓	4	1	2	2	0	0	—	0	0	3.86
Tony Kaufmann, 1931	0	0	0	0	0	0	0	0	0	0	—	0	0	0.00
Vic Keen, 1926	1	0	0	1	0	0	0	0	0	0	—	0	0	0.00
Howie Krist, 1942, 43, 46	1	0	0	0	1	0	0	0	0	0	—	0	0	0.00
Jeff Lahti, 1982	2	0	0	1⅔	4	2	1	1	0	0	—	0	0	10.80
Dave LaPoint, 1982	2	1	0	8⅓	10	3	2	3	0	1	.000	0	0	3.24
Jack Lamabe, 1967	3	0	0	2.2	5	2	0	4	0	1	.000	0	0	6.75
Max Lanier, 1942, 43, 44	7	4	0	31.2	24	6	12	25	2	1	.667	0	0	1.71
Jim Lindsey, 1930, 31	4	0	0	8	5	3	4	6	0	0	—	0	0	3.38
Clarence Mitchell, 1928	1	0	0	5.2	2	1	2	2	0	0	—	0	0	1.59
Jim Mooney, 1934	1	0	0	1	1	0	0	0	0	0	—	0	0	0.00
Whitey Moore, 1942	0	0	0	0	0	0	0	0	0	0	—	0	0	0.00
George Munger, 1943, 46	1	1	1	9	9	1	3	2	1	0	1.000	0	0	1.00
Mel Nelson, 1968	1	0	0	1	0	0	0	1	0	0	—	0	0	0.00
Howie Pollet, 1942	3	2	1	10.2	12	4	4	3	1	0	1.000	0	0	3.38
Art Reinhart, 1926, 28	1	0	0	0.1	1	3	4	0	0	1	.000	0	0	81.00
Flint Rhem, 1926, 28, 30, 31	4	2	0	10.1	15	7	4	9	0	1	.000	0	0	6.10
Gordon Richardson, 1964	2	0	0	0.2	3	3	2	0	0	1	.000	0	0	40.50
Ray Sadecki, 1964	2	2	0	6.1	12	6	5	2	1	0	1.000	0	0	8.53
Fred Schmidt, 1944, 46	2	0	0	3.1	1	0	1	1	0	0	—	0	0	0.00
Barney Schultz, 1964	4	0	0	4	9	8	3	1	0	1	.000	0	0	18.00
Bill Sherdel, 1926, 28	4	4	1	30.1	30	11	11	6	0	4	.000	0	0	3.26
Curt Simmons, 1964	2	2	0	14.1	11	4	3	8	0	0	—	0	0	2.51
Al Sothoron, 1926	0	0	0	0	0	0	0	0	0	0	—	0	0	0.00
Al Stout, 1931	0	0	0	0	0	0	0	0	0	0	—	0	0	0.00
John Stuper, 1982	2	2	1	13	10	5	5	5	1	0	1.000	0	0	3.46
Bruce Sutter, 1982	4	0	0	7⅔	6	4	3	6	1	0	1.000	2	0	4.70
Ron Taylor, 1964	2	0	0	4.2	0	0	1	2	0	0	—	1	0	0.00
Dazzy Vance, 1934	1	0	0	1.1	2	0	1	3	0	0	—	0	0	0.00
Bill Walker, 1934	2	0	0	6.1	6	5	6	2	0	2	.000	0	0	7.11
Ray Washburn, 1964, 67, 68	4	2	0	9.2	8	8	8	8	1	1	.500	0	0	7.20
Ernie White, 1942, 43	1	1	1	9	6	0	3	6	1	0	1.000	0	1	0.00
Ted Wilks, 1944, 46	3	1	0	7.1	7	4	3	7	0	1	.000	1	0	4.91
Ron Willis, 1967, 68	6	0	0	5.1	4	7	8	4	0	1	.000	0	0	11.81
Hal Woodeshick, 1967	1	0	0	1	1	0	0	0	0	0	—	0	0	0.00

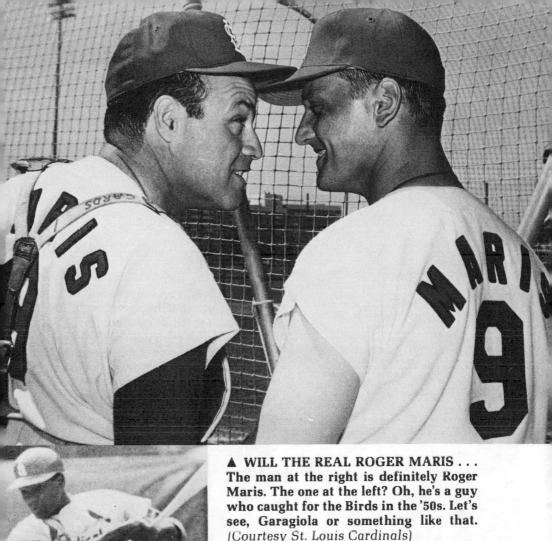

▲ WILL THE REAL ROGER MARIS . . .
The man at the right is definitely Roger
Maris. The one at the left? Oh, he's a guy
who caught for the Birds in the '50s. Let's
see, Garagiola or something like that.
(Courtesy St. Louis Cardinals)

◄ DO-IT-YOURSELF. Pitcher Bob Gib-
son lashes a Jim Lonborg pitch into the
seats in game seven of the 1967 World
Series at Boston. The Cards defeated the
Red Sox, 7–2. (Courtesy St. Louis
Cardinals)

◄ THE MAHATMA. B.R. Wesley "Branch" Rickey, the man recognized for starting the first farm system in baseball, was a player, manager, general manager, and consultant for the Cards. (Courtesy St. Louis Cardinals)

▼ 3,000 K. The scoreboard tells the story, as Bob Gibson walks off Busch Memorial Stadium mound July 17, 1974, having struck out Cincinnati outfielder Cesar Geronimo for the 3,000th strikeout of his career. (Courtesy St. Louis Cardinals)

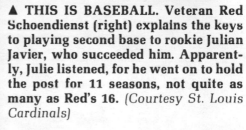

▲ THIS IS BASEBALL. Veteran Red Schoendienst (right) explains the keys to playing second base to rookie Julian Javier, who succeeded him. Apparently, Julie listened, for he went on to hold the post for 11 seasons, not quite as many as Red's 16. *(Courtesy St. Louis Cardinals)*

◀ VICTORY DANCE. Ken Boyer (left) and Bob Gibson celebrate 1964 World Series victory October 15. Gibson held on for a 7–5 game-seven victory at St. Louis. *(Courtesy St. Louis Cardinals)*

◄ **THE GODFATHER.** Joe Torre played first base, third base, and caught for the Cards from 1969 through 1974. Although he led the National League in hits (230), RBI (137), batting (.363), and total bases (352) in 1971, he wasn't enough to bring a flag to St. Louis. The Godfather-label was pinned on him during his later years with the Mets. *(Courtesy St. Louis Cardinals)*

▼ **FRIENDLIER TIMES.** Owner August A. Busch Jr. (left) is on good terms with general manager Bing Devine in this photo. Things weren't always this sweet. Gussie dumped Der Bingle August 17, 1964, rehired him December 5, 1967, and refired him October 18, 1978. *(Courtesy St. Louis Cardinals)*

ST. LOUIS' ALL-TIME ALL-STAR TEAM, gathered at Sportsman's Park, August 19, 1958. From left, Hank Severeid (c, Browns, 1915–25); Marty Marion (ss, Cards, 1940–50, Browns 1952–53); Dizzy Dean (p, Cards, 1930–37, Browns 1947); Frank Frisch (2b, Cards, 1927–37); Ken Williams (Browns, 1918–27); Rogers Hornsby (Cards, 1915–26 , 33, Browns, 1933–37); Jesse Haines (p, Cards, 1920–37); George Sisler (1b, Browns, 1915–27); John Tobin (of, Browns, 1916–25); Terry Moore (of, Cards, 1935–48); Stan Musial (of, Cards, 1941–63); Bob O'Farrell (c, Cards, 1925–28, 1933–35). *(Courtesy The Sporting News)*

JOINING THE 3,000-HIT CLUB. Lou Brock smashes career hit No. 3,000, a fourth-inning single, against the Chicago Cubs at St. Louis, August 13, 1979. Dennis Lamp was on the mound for Chicago. *(Courtesy The Sporting News)*

LEFTY MEANS DOUBLE TROUBLE. Many batters thought they were seeing double when Cardinal Lefty Steve Carlton was on the mound. Cards traded him in 1972 to Philadelphia, where he continued his winning ways. *(Courtesy St. Louis Cardinals)*

(left) THE VOICE OF THE CARDINALS. Harry Caray was behind the Cardinal microphone on radio and television for 25 years. Here, he's back from a near-crippling auto accident in 1968. *(Courtesy St. Louis Cardinals)*

(right) THE PROFESSOR. Jim Brosnan, who authored nine victories in just over a full season with the Redbirds, went on to greater fame as a writer with baseball books *The Long Season* and *Pennant Race*. *(Courtesy St. Louis Cardinals)*

▼ MR. THIRD BASEMAN. Ken Boyer won six Golden Gloves and played in 10 All-Star games as Cardinal third baseman before managing the Redbirds 1978 through 1980. *(Courtesy St. Louis Cardinals)*

▲ **A CARDINAL INSTITUTION.** Red Schoendienst played second base for the Cardinals from 1946 through 1956, and again from 1961 through 1963. He also managed the Redbirds from 1965 through 1976 and part of 1980. *(Courtesy St. Louis Cardinals)*

▼ **A NEW REDBIRD BELTER.** Keith Hernandez became a Cardinal standout at first base in the 1970s. He hit .344 in 1979 to win the National League batting title and was named Co-NLMVP of the year with Willie Stargell of the Pirates. *(Courtesy St. Louis Cardinals)*

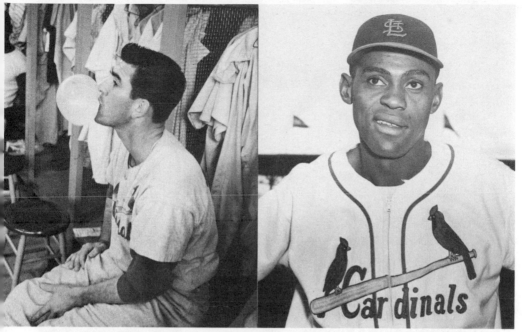

(left) DON'T BURST MY BUBBLE. Cardinal pitcher Ernie Broglio seems to be enjoying his gum in a lighter clubhouse moment as teammate Bob Gibson smiles approval. Broglio's bubble burst in 1964, as he was traded to the Chicago Cubs for Lou Brock, a deal acknowledged as one of the best in St. Louis history and one of the worst for the Bruins. (Courtesy St. Louis Cardinals)

(right) CARDINAL ICE-BREAKER. Tom Alston, the first black Cardinal, hit .244 in 91 games from 1954 through 1957. (Courtesy St. Louis Cardinals)

▲ THE CARDINAL AND THE BUNNY. Playboy Bo Belinsky spent spring training 1968 trying to make the Cardinal pitching staff. Apparently he spent too much time thinking about wife Jo Collins, a former Playboy bunny, and his comeback attempt went to the dogs. (Courtesy St. Louis Cardinals)

◀ THE BIG CAT, Johnny Mize, wore Cardinal livery from 1936 through 1941. During that time he belted 66 home runs, knocked in 546 runs, and sported a .334 batting average. He continued his cannonading with the Giants and then the Yankees for more than a decade. He was elected to the Hall of Fame in 1980. *(Courtesy The Sporting News)*

▼ THE RAJAH. Rogers Hornsby played second base for the Cardinals from 1915 through 1926, and again for a brief period in 1933. He also managed the Redbirds in 1925 and 1926, the latter team winning the first Cardinal pennant and first World Series. *(Courtesy The Sporting News)*

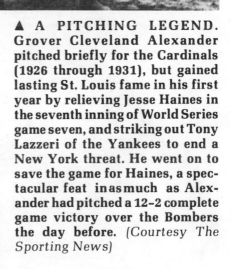

▲ A PITCHING LEGEND. Grover Cleveland Alexander pitched briefly for the Cardinals (1926 through 1931), but gained lasting St. Louis fame in his first year by relieving Jesse Haines in the seventh inning of World Series game seven, and striking out Tony Lazzeri of the Yankees to end a New York threat. He went on to save the game for Haines, a spectacular feat in as much as Alexander had pitched a 12–2 complete game victory over the Bombers the day before. *(Courtesy The Sporting News)*

◄ THE BROTHERS DEAN. Paul Dean (left) and brother Jerome, were good ol' Daffy and Dizzy to the Cardinal Faithful for the years 1934 through 1937. In that time, Dizzy won 95 games and Daffy 43, including an incredible 1934 when Daffy's 19 wins as a rookie were overshadowed by Dizzy's 30 victories. (Courtesy The Sporting News)

► DOUTHIT COULD SURELY HIT. Although he played for the Cards for nine years, Taylor Douthit is best remembered for two of them, 1929 and 1930, when he banged out 206 and 201 hits respectively for .336 and .303 batting averages. (Courtesy The Sporting News)

◄ THE BEAT OF A DIFFERENT DRUMMER. Outfielder Curt Flood always traveled to the beat of a different drummer. Upon being traded to Washington in 1970 after 12 years as a Redbird, Flood became the first to test baseball's reserve clause, his case getting as far as the Supreme Court which refused to reverse lower court decisions in baseball's favor. (Courtesy St. Louis Cardinals)

► **MANAGERS NON-PAREIL.** Connie Mack (left) meets Yankee manager Miller Huggins. Huggins piloted the Redbirds from 1913 through 1917, but gained fame as Bronx Bomber skipper from 1918 through 1929, when the Yankees won six pennants and three World Series. *(Courtesy The Sporting News)*

▼ **THE CAT.** Harry Brecheen pitched 13 years for the Redbirds, during which he won 128 and lost 79. Although he won 20 in 1948, he is most remembered for his three triumphs in the 1946 World Series, two as a starter. *(Courtesy The Sporting News)*

FIREBALLING WITH A "TOOTHPICK". Sam "Toothpick" Jones won 28 games with the Cardinals in three seasons, but is best known for having a toothpick surgically implanted in his lower lip, views *The Sporting News* at Tokyo's Imperial Hotel between games of the Redbirds' Japanese barnstorming tour in October 1958. *(Courtesy The Sporting News)*

INSTRUCTION FROM A MASTER. Veteran Cardinal shortstop Marty Marion (right) gives pointers to rookie infielder Solly Hemus. Both managed the Redbirds, Marion from 1951 through 1953, Hemus from 1959 through 1961. *(Courtesy The Sporting News)*

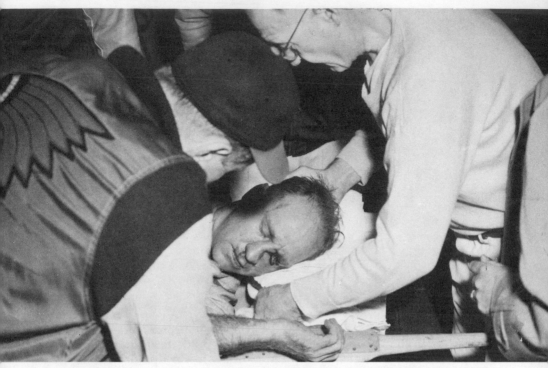

▲ OUCH! Cardinal outfielder Enos Slaughter lies on a stretcher in the dressing room after being hit by a line drive off the bat of teammate Nippy Jones vs. the Braves at Boston, September 23, 1948. Slaughter suffered a fractured nose. The Cards defeated the Braves, 8–2. *(Courtesy The Sporting News)*

◄ THE ST. LOUIS STRONG BOY. Hall of Fame outfielder Joe "Ducky" Medwick. Medwick had a lifetime batting average of .324, his best year 1937 when he led the National League with a .374 average and was named MVP. *(Courtesy The Sporting News)*

(left) THE KID. Hall of Fame pitcher Charles "Kid" Nichols, who toiled for Birds 1904 and 1905. *(Courtesy The Sporting News)*

(right) A MAN AND HIS BAT. Stan Musial and his favorite bat (Nancy?) after the 1955 All-Star game. The bat, er, Musial, won the contest on the first pitch by Frank Sullivan in the 13th inning at Milwaukee. Nationals won, 6–5. *(Courtesy The Sporting News)*

▼ **IN THE GRIP OF THE BIG CAT.** The hands and batting grip of The Big Cat, Hall of Famer Johnny Mize, who hit 359 career home runs, including 158 in Cardinal livery. *(Courtesy The Sporting News)*

▲ "WILD BILL". Wild Bill Hallaha Cardinal southpaw who started th first All-Star game in 1933. Hallaha lived up to his nickname, walking fiv and giving up three runs in tw innings pitched. He was the lose *(Courtesy The Sporting News)*

◄ THE BIG PSYCH-OUT. Al Hrabosky, the Mad Hungarian, pitched for the Redbirds from 1970 through 1977. Here, he's shown standing outside the mound area, in his psych-out routine. Hrabosky would pound his glove, stalk out to the mound, and glare at opposing batters. It worked, until the Cards got tired of his act and swapped him to Kansas City. *(Courtesy The Sporting News)*

▼ POWER-HITTER DELUXE. Chi Hafey, popular Cardinal outfield who saw service from 1924 throug 1931, before being traded to Cinci nati. He led the National League with .349 batting average in 1941, but had salary dispute with the Redbird *(Courtesy The Sporting News)*

FROM ONE CHIEF TO ANOTHER. Former Cardinal player and manager Rogers Hornsby (left) shows batting form to Mrs. Grover Cleveland Alexander and the actor who played Alexander in the 1952 film about the pitcher's life. The actor, Ronald Reagan, went on to play a more important role later in his life. *(Courtesy The Sporting News)*

TOUGH BREAK. Cardinal pitcher Bob Gibson winces in pain after being struck in the right leg by a line drive, July 15, 1967. Gibson suffered a fractured fibula on the play and was sidelined nearly two months before returning to action to pitch the pennant-clincher and World Series wins for Cards. *(Courtesy The Sporting News)*

A FAMILY BATTERY. Mort Cooper (left) and brother Walker. Cardinal battery-mates from 1940 through 1945, with Mort throwing the ball and Walker catching it. *(Courtesy The Sporting News)*

SLUGGERS TWO. Sluggers Jim Bottomley of St. Louis (left) and Babe
Ruth of the Yankees meet prior to the start of the 1928 World Series.
Each led his respective league in home runs during the regular season.
(*Courtesy The Sporting News*)

▲ BALL TWO. Two balls are in play at the same time in the fourth inning of the Cardinal-Chicago Cub contest, June 30, 1959, at Wrigley Field. Second baseman Tony Taylor (far right) leaps for the second ball, thrown by Cub catcher Sam Taylor. Cub shortstop Ernie Banks goes for the original ball, thrown by third baseman Alvin Dark who retrieved it near the backstop. A sliding Stan Musial was ruled out. Umpire is Bill Jackowski. Cards won the contest, 4–1. *(Courtesy The Sporting News)*

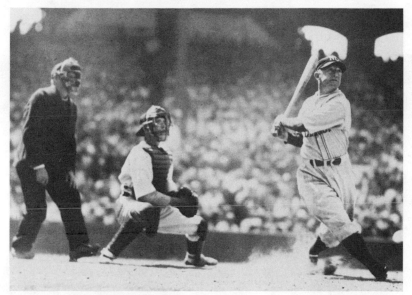

▲ THE FORDHAM FLASH. Cardinal third baseman Frank Frisch hits a sixth-inning homer in the first All-Star game at Comiskey Park, Chicago, July 7, 1933. The blast was the second in the game, Babe Ruth of the Yankees tagging one earlier. Frisch's blow didn't help, as the Americans bested the Nationals, 4–2. *(Courtesy The Sporting News)*

▲ THE SPIRIT OF ST. LOUIS. Pilot Charles A. Lindbergh, just returned from his historic New York to Paris flight in 1927 in a plane called "The Spirit of St. Louis," shakes hands with Cardinal pitching great Grover Cleveland Alexander. Observers include Commissioner Judge Kenesaw M. Landis, to Lindberg's left; Leslie O'Connor of the commissioner's office; a smiling and bow-tied umpire, Charley Moran; and Cardinal manager Bob O'Farrell. *(Courtesy The Sporting News)*

▲ A BASEBALL FAMILY. The Boyer brothers, from left, Clete, Cloyd, and Ken. Ken was with the Redbirds from 1955 through 1965 and managed from 1978 through part of 1980. Cloyd wore Cardinal togs from 1949 through 1952. (*Courtesy The Sporting News*)

105! Lou Brock breaks Maury Wills' single season stolen base record in the seventh inning of contest against Philadelphia at Busch Memorial Stadium, September 10, 1974. Larry Bowa is the Phillie shortstop. *(Courtesy The Sporting News)*

A CLASSIC STEAL. Lou Brock slides safely into second base against shortstop Bill Almon of the San Diego Padres, August 29, 1977, for his 893rd career theft, breaking Ty Cobb's major-league record. *(Courtesy The Sporting News)*

DOUBLE-NO-HIT. Gaylord Perry of San Francisco Giants (left) and Cardinal hurler Ray Washburn celebrate baseball's first back-to-back no-hitters. Perry blanked the Cards, 1–0, September 17, 1968, after which Washburn whitewashed the Giants, 2–0, less than 24 hours later. *(Courtesy The Sporting News)*

THE REAL CY YOUNG. Denton True "Cy" Young, pitcher supreme, after whom top pitching award is named. Young hurled for the Cards in 1899 and 1900. He went on to win the incredible total of 511 games and become a Hall of Famer. *(Courtesy The Sporting News)*

3,000—AND STILL GOING STRONG. Pinch-hitter Stan Musial follows the flight of two-base hit against the Chicago Cubs at Wrigley Field, May 13, 1958, for his 3,000th career base hit. The catcher is Sam Taylor and the umpire is Augie Donatelli. The hit came off Cub hurler Moe Drabowsky. *(Courtesy The Sporting News)*

A MAN FOR ALL SEASONS. Stan Musial hits a first-inning home run in the 1948 All-Star game at Sportsman's Park in St. Louis, July 13, 1948. It wasn't enough, as the American Leaguers won the contest, 5–2. *(Courtesy The Sporting News)*

A NATIVE MANAGER. St. Louis native Oliver "Patsy" Tebeau, who managed the Cardinals at the turn of the century, 1899 and 1900. (*Courtesy The Sporting News*)

► SLAUGHTER COUNTRY. Enos "Country" Slaughter, a Cardinal from 1938 through 1953, spent 1943 through 1945 in the Army Air Forces, enlisting August 28, 1942, and being discharged January 23, 1946. Slaughter was called to active duty February 25, 1943. Amazingly, Country still isn't in the Hall of Fame. (*Courtesy The Sporting News*)

LIPPY. Leo Durocher was a Cardinal shortstop from 1933 to 1937. He went on to greater fame as a manager with Brooklyn, the New York Giants and the Chicago Cubs. *(Courtesy The Sporting News)*

▲ **A BALL PARK FULL OF MEMORIES. Old Sportsman's Park, used by the Cardinals and Browns from 1920 until 1966.** *(Courtesy The Sporting News)*

▼ **FINAL GAME. Final game at old Busch Stadium, formerly Sportsman's Park, May 8, 1966.** *(Courtesy The Sporting News)*

THE GREATEST . . . The 1942 Cardinals had the most wins (106), fewest losses (48), and best winning percentage (.688) of any Redbird squad. Amazingly, only one member of the team, Stan Musial (front row, third from left), is enshrined in the Hall of Fame. St. Louis beat the Yankees, 4–1, for the World Series title. *(Courtesy The Sporting News)*

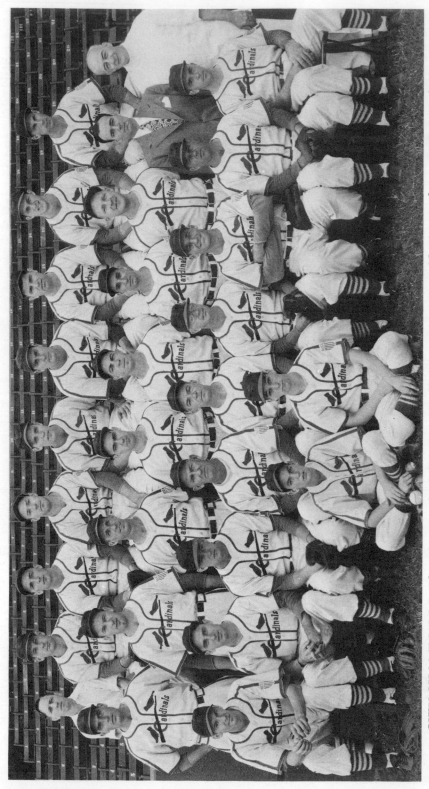

CITY CHAMPS TOO. The 1944 Cards didn't do so badly, winning 105 and losing 49 for a .682 percentage. They went on to defeat the rival Browns, 4–2, in the only city World Series St. Louis has ever seen. (*Courtesy The Sporting News*)

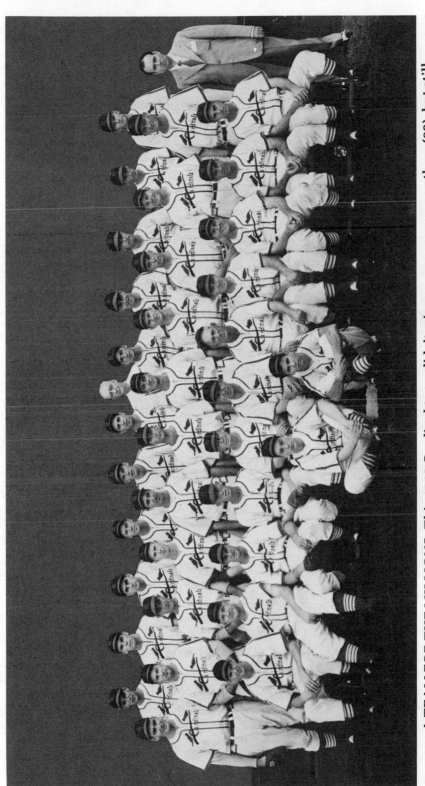

A TEAM FOR THE MILLIONS. This 1946 Cardinal team didn't win as many games as others (98), but still won the National League pennant and the World Series over Boston, 4–3. This was the first St. Louis team that played to a home audience in excess of one million—1,062,553 to be exact. The mark bettered the 1928 figure by about 300,000. (*Courtesy The Sporting News*)

TEAM PHOTO. 1967 St. Louis Cardinals. Back row, left to right: Dal Maxvill, Hal Woodeshick, Larry Jaster, Dave Ricketts, Phil Gagliano, John Romano, Eddie Bressoud, Ed Spiezio, Lou Brock, Ray Washburn. Center row: Bob Gibson, Joe Hoerner, Ron Willis, Tim McCarver, Dick Hughes, Steve Carlton, Jim Cosman, Bob Tolan, Julian Javier, Mike Shannon, Alex Johnson, trainer Bob Bauman. First row: Curt Flood, Orlando Cepeda, coach Joe Schultz, coach Billy Muffett, manager Red Schoendienst, coach Dick Sisler, coach Bob Milliken, Nelson Briles, Al Jackson, Roger Maris. Front: Batboys Don Deason and Jerry Gibson. *(John*

ALL
STARS

Cardinal All-Star Game Performances, as Cardinals Only

BATTER	Pos	G	AB	R	H	2B	3B	HR	RBI	AVG
Dick Allen	1B	1	3	0	0	0	0	0	0	.000
Don Blasingame	PH	1	1	0	0	0	0	0	0	.000
Ken Boyer	3B–PH	10	23	4	8	0	0	2	4	.348
Harry Brecheen	P	1	1	0	0	0	0	0	0	.000
Lou Brock	OH-PH	5	8	2	3	0	0	0	0	.375
Jim Brown	2B	1	2	0	0	0	0	0	0	.000
Steve Carlton	P	2	2	0	1	1	0	0	1	.500
Orlando Cepeda	1B	6	0	0	0	0	0	0	0	.000
Rip Collins	1B	2	3	0	0	0	0	0	0	.000
Mort Cooper	P	2	1	0	0	0	0	0	0	.000
Walker Cooper	C	3	8	1	4	0	0	0	1	.500
Joe Cunningham	PH	1	1	0	0	0	0	0	0	.000
Dizzy Dean	P	4	3	0	0	0	0	0	0	.000
Leo Durocher	SS	1	3	0	1	0	0	0	0	.333
Curt Flood	PR-PH	3	2	1	0	0	0	0	0	.000
Frank Frisch	2B	2	7	4	4	0	0	2	2	.571
Bob Gibson	P	6	0	0	0	0	0	0	0	.000
Dick Groat	SS	2	7	0	2	1	0	0	2	.286
Harvey Haddix	P	1	0	0	0	0	0	0	0	.000
Bill Hallahan	P	1	1	0	0	0	0	0	0	.000
George Hendrick	OF	1	2	0	1	0	0	0	1	.500
Keith Hernandez	PH-1B	2	3	0	2	0	0	0	0	.667
Ray Jablonski	3B	1	3	1	1	0	0	0	1	.333
Larry Jackson	P	3	0	0	0	0	0	0	0	.000
Julian Javier	2B	2	4	0	0	0	0	0	0	.000
Ed Kazak	3B	1	2	0	2	0	0	0	1	1.000
Whitey Kurowski	3B	3	6	0	1	1	0	0	2	.167
Marty Marion	SS	5	12	1	1	0	0	0	0	.083
Pepper Martin	3B	3	8	1	1	0	0	0	1	.125
Tim McCarver	C	2	3	0	3	1	0	0	0	1.000
Lindy McDaniel	P	1	0	0	0	0	0	0	0	.000
Lynn McGlothen	P	1	0	0	0	0	0	0	0	.000
Joe Medwick	OF	6	22	2	7	2	0	2	5	.318
Johnny Mize	1B-PH	4	11	1	1	1	0	0	0	.364
Wally Moon	PH	1	1	0	0	0	0	0	0	.000
Terry Moore	OF	4	10	0	0	0	0	0	1	.000
George Munger	P	1	0	0	0	0	0	0	0	.000
Stan Musial	OF-PH-1B	24	63	11	20	2	0	6	10	.317
Howie Pollet	P	1	0	0	0	0	0	0	0	.000
Ken Reitz	3B	1	2	0	0	0	0	0	0	.000
Rip Repulski	PH	1	1	0	0	0	0	0	0	.000
Red Schoendienst	2B-PH	8	19	1	4	0	0	1	1	.211
Ted Simmons	C	3	7	0	1	0	0	0	0	.143
Enos Slaughter	OF-PH	10	21	4	8	1	1	0	2	.381
Hal Smith	C	1	2	0	0	0	0	0	0	.000
Ozzie Smith	SS	1	0	0	0	0	0	0	0	.000
Reggie Smith	OF	2	4	2	2	0	0	1	1	.500
Garry Templeton	SS	1	1	1	1	1	0	0	0	1.000
Joe Torre	1B-3B-PH	4	10	0	1	0	0	0	0	.100

Cardinal All Star Game Performances (continued)

BATTER	Pos	G	AB	R	H	2B	3B	HR	RBI	AVG
Bill Walker	P	1	0	0	0	0	0	0	0	.000
Harry Walker	OF	1	1	0	0	0	0	0	0	.000
Wally Westlake	OF	1	0	0	0	0	0	0	0	.000
Bill White	PR-1B	6	14	1	4	1	0	0	2	.286
Burgess Whitehead	PR	1	0	0	0	0	0	0	0	.000
Jim Wilson	C	1	1	0	0	0	0	0	0	.000
Rick Wise	P	0	0	0	0	0	0	0	0	.000

Cardinal Pitching Performances, with St. Louis Only

PITCHER	GAMES	IP	H	R	ER	BB	SO	WON	LOST	PCT
Harry Brecheen	1	3	5	1	1	0	2	0	0	.000
Steve Carlton	2	4	2	2	2	1	3	1	0	1.000
Mort Cooper	2	5⅓	8	7	7	2	3	0	2	.000
Dizzy Dean	4	10	10	2	3	5	10	1	1	.500
Bob Gibson	6	11	11	4	4	5	10	0	0	.000
Harvey Haddix	1	3	3	1	1	0	2	0	0	.000
Bill Hallahan	1	2	2	3	3	5	1	0	1	.000
Larry Jackson	3	3⅔	2	0	0	3	0	0	0	.000
Lindy McDaniel	1	1	1	0	0	0	0	0	0	.000
Lynn McGlothen	1	1	0	0	0	0	1	0	0	.000
George Munger	1	1	0	0	0	1	0	0	0	.000
Howie Pollet	1	1	4	3	3	0	0	0	0	.000
Bruce Sutter	1	1	0	0	0	0	0	0	0	.000
Bill Walker	1	2	2	3	3	1	2	0	1	.000
Rick Wise	1	2	2	1	1	0	1	1	0	1.000

Sutter earned a save in 1981 game, only Cardinal to do so.

Cardinals Selected for the All-Star Game

1933 — Frank Frisch 2B, Bill Hallahan P, Pepper Martin 3B, Jim Wilson C.

1934 — Dizzy Dean P, Frank Frisch 2B, Pepper Martin 3B, Joe Medwick OF.

1935 — Frank Frisch mgr. and 2B, Rip Collins 1B, Dizzy Dean P, Pepper Martin 3B, Joe Medwick OF, Bill Walker P, Burgess Whitehead 2B.

1936 — Rip Collins 1B, Dizzy Dean P, Leo Durocher SS, Stu Martin 2B, Joe Medwick OF.

1937 — Frank Frisch coach, Jessie Haines coach, Dizzy Dean P, Pepper Martin OF, Joe Medwick OF, Johnny Mize 1B.

1938 — Frank Frisch coach, Joe Medwick OF.

1939 — Curt Davis P, Joe Medwick OF, Johnny Mize 1B, Terry Moore OF, Lon Warneke P.

1940 — Johnny Mize 1B, Terry Moore OF.

1941 — Johnny Mize 1B, Terry Moore OF, Enos Slaughter OF, Lon Warneke P.

1942 — Jim Brown 2B, Mort Cooper P, Walker Cooper C, Terry Moore OF, Enos Slaughter OF.

1943 — Billy Southworth mgr., Mike Gonzalez, coach, Mort Cooper P, Walker Cooper C, Whitey Kurowski 3B, Max Lanier P, Marty Marion SS, Stan Musial OF, Howie Pollet P, Harry Walker OF.

1944 — Billy Southworth mgr., Mike Gonzalez coach, Walker Cooper C, Whitey Kurowski 3B, Max Lanier P, Marty Marion SS, George Munger P, Stan Musial OF.

1945 — NO GAME PLAYED.
1946 — Whitey Kurowski 3B, Marty Marion SS, Stan Musial OF, Howie Pollet P, Red Schoendienst 2B, Enos Slaughter OF.
1947 — Eddie Dyer mgr., Harry Brecheen P, Whitey Kurowski 3B, Marty Marion SS, George Munger P, Stan Musial 1B, Enos Slaughter OF.
1948 — Eddie Dyer coach, Harry Brecheen P, Marty Marion SS, Stan Musial OF, Red Schoendienst 2B, Enos Slaughter OF.
1949 — Ed Kazak 3B, Marty Marion SS, George Munger P, Stan Musial OF, Howie Pollet P, Red Schoendienst 2B, Enos Slaughter OF.
1950 — Marty Marion SS, Stan Musial 1B, Red Schoendienst 2B, Enos Slaughter OF.
1951 — Eddie Stanky coach, Stan Musial OF, Red Schoendienst 2B, Enos Slaughter OF, Wally Westlake OF.
1952 — Stan Musial OF, Red Schoendienst 2B, Enos Slaughter OF, Gerry Staley P.
1953 — Harvey Haddix P, Stan Musial OF, Del Rice C, Red Schoendienst 2B, Enos Slaughter OF, Gerry Staley P.
1954 — Harvey Haddix P, Ray Jablonski 3B, Stan Musial OF, Red Schoendienst 2B.
1955 — Luis Arroyo P, Harvey Haddix P, Stan Musial 1B, Red Schoendienst 2B.
1956 — Fred Hutchinson coach, Ken Boyer 3B, Stan Musial OF, Rip Repulski OF.
1957 — Larry Jackson P, Wally Moon OF, Stan Musial 1B, Hal Smith C.
1958 — Don Blasingame 2B, Larry Jackson P, Stan Musial 1B.
1959 — (1st game) Ken Boyer 3B, Joe Cunningham OF, Vinegar Bend Mizell P, Stan Musial 1B, Hal Smith C, Bill White 1B.
(2d game) Ken Boyer 3B, Joe Cunningham OF, Vinegar Bend Mizell P, Stan Musial 1B, Hal Smith C.
1960 — (both games) Solly Hemus coach, Ken Boyer 3B, Larry Jackson P, Lindy McDaniel P, Stan Musial OF, Bill White 1B.
1961 — (both games) Ken Boyer 3B, Stan Musial OF, Bill White 1B.
1962 — (both games) Johnny Keane coach, Ken Boyer 3B, Bob Gibson P, Stan Musial OF.
1963 — Ken Boyer 3B, Dick Groat SS, Julian Javier 2B, Stan Musial OF, Bill White 1B.
1964 — Ken Boyer 3B, Curt Flood OF, Dick Groat SS, Bill White 1B.
1965 — Bob Gibson P.
1966 — Curt Flood OF, Bob Gibson P, Tim McCarver C.
1967 — Lou Brock OF, Orlando Cepeda 1B, Bob Gibson P, Tim McCarver C.
1968 — Red Schoendienst mgr., Steve Carlton P, Curt Flood OF, Bob Gibson P, Julian Javier 2B.
1969 — Red Schoendienst mgr., Steve Carlton P, Bob Gibson P.
1970 — Richie Allen 1B, Bob Gibson P, Joe Torre c.
1971 — Joe Torre 3B, Steve Carlton P, Lou Brock OF.
1972 — Bob Gibson P, Lou Brock OF, Joe Torre 3B, Ted Simmons C, Red Schoendienst coach.
1973 — Ted Simmons C, Joe Torre 3B, Rick Wise P.
1974 — Red Schoendienst coach, Lou Brock OF, Lynn McGlothen P, Ted Simmons C, Reggie Smith OF.
1975 — Red Schoendienst coach, Lou Brock OF, Reggie Smith OF.
1976 — Bake McBride OF.
1977 — Ted Simmons C, Garry Templeton SS.
1978 — Ted Simmons C.
1979 — Dave Ricketts coach, Keith Hernandez 1B, Lou Brock OF, Ted Simmons C, Garry Templeton SS.
1980 — George Hendrick OF, Keith Hernandez 1B, Ken Reitz 3B.
1981 — Bruce Sutter P.
1982 — Ozzie Smith SS.

Cardinals Selected For The All-Star Games (continued)

NOTES: 1943 Pollet replaced by Ace Adams, P, New York; 1944 Lanier and Munger replaced by Jim Tobin, P, Boston, and Bill Voiselle, P, New York; 1947 Kurowski replaced Bob Elliott, 3B, Boston; 1948 Marion replaced by John Kerr, SS, New York; 1953 Rice replaced by Wes Westrum, C, New York; 1954 Haddix replaced by Jim Wilson, P, Milwaukee; 1959 Mizell replaced by Don Elston, P, Chicago; 1963 Javier replaced Bill Mazeroski, 2B, Pittsburgh; 1966 Gibson replaced by Phil Regan, P, Los Angeles; 1979 Hernandez replaced Dave Kingman, OF, Chicago, Simmons replaced by Johnny Bench, C, Cincinnati, who was replaced by John Stearns, C, New York.

Cardinal Players on Gillette All-Star Ballots

1970			1975	
Richie Allen	1B		Ted Sizemore	2B
Julian Javier	2B		Ted Simmons	C
Mike Shannon	3B		Lou Brock	OF
Joe Torre	C		Bake McBride	OF
Lou Brock	OF		Reggie Smith	OF
1971			1976	
Julian Javier	2B		Don Kessinger	SS
Dal Maxvill	SS		Ted Simmons	C
Joe Torre	3B		Lou Brock	OF
Matty Alou	OF		Bake McBride	OF
Lou Brock	OF		Reggie Smith	OF
1972			1977	
Ted Sizemore	2B		Mike Tyson	2B
Dal Maxvill	SS		Garry Templeton	SS
Joe Torre	3B		Lou Brock	OF
Ted Simmons	C		Bake McBride	OF
Matty Alou	OF			
Lou Brock	OF		1978	
			Keith Hernandez	1B
1973			Mike Tyson	2B
Ted Sizemore	2B		Garry Templeton	SS
Joe Torre	3B		Ken Reitz	3B
Ted Simmons	C		Ted Simmons	C
Tommie Agee	OF		Lou Brock	OF
Lou Brock	OF		George Hendrick	OF
			Jerry Morales	OF
1974				
Joe Torre	1B		1979	
Ted Simmons	C		Keith Hernandez	1B
Lou Brock	OF		Mike Tyson	2B
Reggie Smith	OF		Garry Templeton	SS
			Ted Simmons	C
			George Hendrick	OF

1980		1982	
Keith Hernandez	1B	Keith Hernandez	1B
Ken Oberkfell	2B	Tom Herr	2B
Garry Templeton	SS	Ozzie Smith	SS
Ken Reitz	3B	Ken Oberkfell	3B
Ted Simmons	C	Darrell Porter	C
Bobby Bonds	OF	George Hendrick	OF
George Hendrick	OF	Lonnie Smith	OF

1981	
Keith Hernandez	1B
Garry Templeton	SS
Ken Oberkfell	3B
George Hendrick	OF
Sixto Lezcano	OF

AWARDS, HONORS

Sporting News MVP Cardinals

1934 — Dizzy Dean
1937 — Joe Medwick
1942 — Mort Cooper
1943 — Stan Musial
1944 — Marty Marion
   In 1948, Sporting News selected player, pitcher in each league.
1948 — Stan Musial, OF-1B
1949 — Enos Slaughter, OF
        Howie Pollet, P
1951 — Stan Musial, OF
1957 — Stan Musial, 1B
1964 — Ken Boyer, 3B
1967 — Orlando Cepeda, 1B
1968 — Bob Gibson, P
1970 — Bob Gibson, P
1971 — Joe Torre, 3B
1974 — Lou Brock, OF
1979 — Keith Hernandez, 1B

Fireman of the Year (Sporting News)

1960 — Lindy McDaniel
1975 — Al Hrabosk
1981 — Bruce Sutter

Sporting News Player of the Year

1944 — Marty Marion
1946 — Stan Musial
1951 — Stan Musial
1964 — Ken Boyer
1971 — Joe Torre
1974 — Lou Brock

Awards, Honors (continued)

Sporting News Rookie of the Year

1954 — Wally Moon
1955 — Bill Virdon
1967 — Dick Hughes
1971 — Reggie Cleveland

Sporting News Major League Executive of the Year

1936 — Branch Rickey
1942 — Branch Rickey
1957 — Frank Lane
1963 — Bing Devine
1964 — Bing Devine

Sporting News Major League Manager of the Year

1941 — Billy Southworth
1942 — Billy Southworth
1944 — Luke Sewell
1946 — Eddie Dyer
1952 — Eddie Stanky
1957 — Fred Hutchinson
1964 — Johnny Keane
1982 — Whitey Herzog

Cardinals on Sporting News Major League All-Star Team

1925 — Jim Bottomley 1B, Rogers Hornsby 2B.
1926 — Rogers Hornsby 2B, Bob O'Farrell C, Grover Cleveland Alexander P.
1930 — Frank Frisch 2B.
1931 — Frank Frisch 2B.
1934 — Dizzy Dean P.
1935 — Pepper Martin 3B, Joe Medwick OF, Dizzy Dean P.
1936 — Joe Medwick OF, Dizzy Dean P.
1937 — Joe Medwick OF.
1938 — Joe Medwick OF.
1939 — Joe Medwick OF.
1942 — Enos Slaughter OF, Mort Cooper P.
1943 — Stan Musial OF, Walker Cooper C, Mort Cooper P.
1944 — Ray Sanders 1B, Marty Marion SS, Stan Musial OF, Walker Cooper C,
Mort Cooper P.
1945 — Marty Marion SS, Whitey Kurowski 3B.
1946 — Stan Musial 1B, Enos Slaughter OF.
1948 — Stan Musial OF, Harry Brecheen P.
1949 — Stan Musial OF.
1950 — Stan Musial OF.
1951 — Stan Musial OF.
1952 — Stan Musial OF.
1953 — Red Schoendienst 2B, Stan Musial OF.
1954 — Stan Musial OF.
1956 — Ken Boyer 3B.
1957 — Stan Musial 1B.

1958 — Stan Musial 1B.
1960 — Ernie Broglio P.
   Starting in 1961, Sporting News selected team in each league.
1961 — Ken Boyer 3B.
1962 — Ken Boyer 3B.
1963 — Bill White 1B, Dick Groat SS, Ken Boyer 3B.
1964 — Bill White 1B, Dick Groat SS, Ken Boyer 3B.
1967 — Orlando Cepeda 1B, Tim McCarver C.
1968 — Curt Flood OF, Bob Gibson P.
1969 — Steve Carlton LHP.
1970 — Bob Gibson RHP.
1971 — Joe Torre 3B, Steve Carlton LHP.
1974 — Lou Brock OF.
1977 — Garry Templeton SS, Ted Simmons C.
1978 — Ted Simmons C.
1979 — Keith Hernandez 1B, Garry Templeton SS, Ted Simmons C.
1980 — Keith Hernandez 1B, Garry Templeton SS, George Hendrick RF.

Cardinals on Sporting News Silver Slugger Teams

1980	**National League**
1B	Keith Hernandez
SS	Garry Templeton
OF	George Hendrick
C	Ted Simmons
P	Bob Forsch

1981	**National League**
1B	Keith Hernandez

NO-HITTERS

No-Hitters by Cardinal Pitchers

DATE	PITCHER	OPPONENT	SITE	SCORE
July 15, 1876	George Bradley	Hartford	St. Louis	2-0
September 24, 1906	Grant McGlynn	Brooklyn	Brooklyn	1-1 (2d game) (7 innings)
August 11, 1907	Ed Karger	Boston	St. Louis	4-0 (2d game) (7 perfect innings)
August 6, 1908	John Lush	Brooklyn	Brooklyn	2-0 (6 innings)
July 17, 1917	Jesse Haines	Boston	St. Louis	5-0
September 21, 1934	Paul Dean	Brooklyn	Brooklyn	3-0 (2d game)
August 30, 1941	Lon Warneke	Cincinnati	Cincinnati	2-0
September 18, 1968	Ray Washburn	San Francisco	San Francisco	2-0
August 14, 1971	Bob Gibson	Pittsburgh	Pittsburgh	11-0
April 16, 1978	Bob Forsch	Philadelphia	St. Louis	5-0

No-Hitters Against St. Louis Cardinals

July 15, 1901	Christy Mathewson	New York	St. Louis	5-0
September 14, 1903	Red Ames	New York	St. Louis	5-0 (5 innings) (2d game)
July 29, 1906	Mal Eason	Brooklyn	St. Louis	2-0
July 31, 1910	Leonard Cole	Chicago	Chicago	4-0 (2d game) (7 innings)
May 11, 1919	Hod Eller	Cincinnati	Cincinnati	6-0
May 15, 1960	Don Cardwell	Chicago	Chicago	4-0 (2d game)
September 17, 1968	Gaylord Perry	San Francisco	San Francisco	1-0
June 16, 1978	Tom Seaver	Cincinnati	Cincinnati	4-0

Cardinal League Leaders
Batting

Runs Scored

1901	Jesse Burkett	139
1921	Rogers Hornsby	131
1922	Rogers Hornsby	141
1924	Rogers Hornsby	121
1933	Pepper Martin	122
1937	Joe Medwick	111
1946	Stan Musial	124
1948	Stan Musial	135
1952	Stan Musial-Solly Hemus	105
1967	Lou Brock	113
1971	Lou Brock	126
1979	Keith Hernandez	116
1980	Keith Hernandez	111

Singles

1901	Jesse Burkett	180
1906	Bill Shannon	141
1920	Milt Stock	170
1942	Enos Slaughter	127
1946	Stan Musial	142
1949	Red Schoendienst	160
1959	Don Blasingame	144
1963	Curt Flood	152
1964	Curt Flood	178
1968	Curt Flood	160
1972	Lou Brock	156
1977	Garry Templeton	155

Doubles

1911	Ed Konetchy	38
1920	Rogers Hornsby	44
1921	Rogers Hornsby	44
1922	Rogers Hornsby	46
1924	Rogers Hornsby	43
1925	Jim Bottomley	44
1926	Jim Bottomley	40
1931	Sparky Adams	46
1936	Joe Medwick	64
1937	Joe Medwick	56
1938	Joe Medwick	47
1939	Enos Slaughter	52
1941	Johnny Mize	39
1942	Marty Marion	38
1943	Stan Musial	48
1944	Stan Musial	51
1946	Stan Musial	50

1948	Stan Musial	46
1949	Stan Musial	41
1950	Red Schoendienst	43
1952	Stan Musial	42
1953	Stan Musial	53
1954	Stan Musial	41
1963	Dick Groat	43
1968	Lou Brock	46
1979	George Hendrick	48

Triples

1893	Perry Werden	33
1915	Tom Long	25
1917	Rogers Hornsby	17
1921	Rogers Hornsby	18
1928	Jim Bottomley	20
1934	Joe Medwick	18
1938	Johnny Mize	16
1942	Enos Slaughter	17
1943	Stan Musial	20
1946	Stan Musial	20
1947	Harry Walker	16
1948	Stan Musial	18
1949	Stan Musial-Enos Slaughter	13
1951	Stan Musial	12
1966	Tim McCarver	13
1968	Lou Brock	14
1977	Garry Templeton	18
1978	Garry Templeton	13
1979	Garry Templeton	19

Total Bases

1901	Jesse Burkett	314
1917	Rogers Hornsby	253
1920	Rogers Hornsby	329
1921	Rogers Hornsby	378
1922	Rogers Hornsby	450
1924	Rogers Hornsby	373
1925	Rogers Hornsby	381
1926	Jim Bottomley	305
1928	Jim Bottomley	362
1934	Rip Collins	369
1935	Joe Medwick	365
1936	Joe Medwick	367
1937	Joe Medwick	406
1938	Johnny Mize	326
1939	Johnny Mize	353
1940	Johnny Mize	368
1942	Enos Slaughter	292
1943	Stan Musial	347
1946	Stan Musial	366
1948	Stan Musial	429
1949	Stan Musial	383
1951	Stan Musial	355
1952	Stan Musial	311
1971	Joe Torre	352

Base on Balls

1910	Miller Huggins	116
1914	Miller Huggins	105
1924	Rogers Hornsby	89
1953	Stan Musial	105

Strikeouts

1953	Steve Bilko	125

Stolen Bases

1927	Frank Frisch	48
1931	Frank Frisch	28
1933	Pepper Martin	26
1934	Pepper Martin	23
1936	Pepper Martin	23
1945	Red Schoendienst	26
1966	Lou Brock	74
1967	Lou Brock	52
1968	Lou Brock	62
1969	Lou Brock	53
1971	Lou Brock	64
1972	Lou Brock	63
1973	Lou Brock	70
1974	Lou Brock	118

Slugging Percentage

1917	Rogers Hornsby	.484
1920	Rogers Hornsby	.359
1921	Rogers Hornsby	.659
1922	Rogers Hornsby	.722
1923	Rogers Hornsby	.627
1924	Rogers Hornsby	.696
1925	Rogers Hornsby	.756
1927	Chick Hafey	.590
1934	Rip Collins	.615
1937	Joe Medwick	.641
1938	Johnny Mize	.614
1939	Johnny Mize	.626
1940	Johnny Mize	.636
1943	Stan Musial	.562
1944	Stan Musial	.549
1946	Stan Musial	.587
1948	Stan Musial	.702
1950	Stan Musial	.596
1952	Stan Musial	.538

Pitching

Winning Percentage

		W L	PCT
1921	Bill Doak	15–6	.714
1925	Bill Sherdel	15–6	.714
1931	Paul Derringer	18–8	.692
1934	Dizzy Dean	30–7	.811
1943	Mort Cooper	21–8	.724
1944	Ted Wilks	17–4	.810
1945	Harry Brecheen	15–4	.789
1946	Murry Dickson	15–6	.714
1948	Harry Brecheen	20–7	.714
1960	Ernie Broglio	21–9	.700
1967	Dick Hughes	16–6	.727
1970	Bob Gibson	23–7	.767

Strikeouts

1906	Fred Beebe	171
1930	Bill Hallahan	177
1931	Bill Hallahan	159
1932	Dizzy Dean	191
1933	Dizzy Dean	199
1934	Dizzy Dean	195
1935	Dizzy Dean	182
1948	Harry Brecheen	149
1958	Sam Jones	225
1968	Bob Gibson	268

Earned Run Average

		Games	Innings	ERA
1914	Bill Doak	36	256	1.72
1921	Bill Doak	32	209	2.58
1942	Mort Cooper	37	279	1.77
1943	Howie Pollet	16	118	1.75
1946	Howie Pollet	40	266	2.10
1948	Harry Brecheen	33	233	2.24
1950	Jim Hearn	22	134	2.49
1968	Bob Gibson	34	305	1.12
1976	John Denny	30	207	2.52

Shutouts

1900	Cy Young	4
1921	Jesse Haines	3
1924	Al Sothoron	4
1927	Jesse Haines	6
1932	Dizzy Dean	4
1934	Dizzy Dean	7
1942	Mort Cooper	10
1944	Mort Cooper	7
1948	Harry Brecheen	7
1949	Howie Pollet	5
1953	Harvey Haddix	6
1962	Bob Gibson	5
1966	Bob Gibson	5
1966	Larry Jaster	5
1968	Bob Gibson	13
1971	Bob Gibson	5

Cardinal Yearly Batting Leaders

SEASON	BATTING AVERAGE	HOME RUNS	RUNS BATTED IN
1876	Pike .323	Pike-Mack 1	Pike 50
1877	Clapp .318	Battin 1	Clapp 34
1885	McKinnon .294	Dunlap 2	McKinnon 44
1886	Glasscock .325	Denny 9	McKinnon 72
1892	Caruthers .277	Werden 8	Werden 84
1893	Cooley .346	Brodie 2	Werden 94
1894	Miller .339	Ely 12	Ely 89
1895	Cooley .339	Connor 8	Connor 77
1896	Cooley .307	Connor 11	Connor 72
1897	Douglas .329	Grady 7	Hartman 67
1898	Cross .317	Cross-Clements 3	Cross 79
1899	Burkett .396	Wallace 12	Wallace 108
1900	Burkett .363	Donlin 10	Keister 72
1901	Burkett .376	Burkett 10	Wallace 91
1902	Donovan .315	Smoot-Barclay 3	Barclay 53
1903	Donovan .329	Smoot 4	Brain 60
1904	Beckley .325	Brain 7	Brain 72
1905	Smoot .311	Smoot-Grady 4	Smoot 58
1906	Himes .271	Grady 3	Beckley 44
1907	Murray .262	Murray 7	Murray 46
1908	Murray .282	Murray 7	Murray 62
1910	Konetchy .286	Konetchy 4	Konetchy 80
1911	Konetchy .302	Ellis 4	Konetchy 78
1911	Evans .294	Konetchy 6	Konetchy 88
1912	Konetchy .314	Konetchy 8	Konetchy 82
1913	Oakes .291	Konetchy 7	Konetchy 68
1914	Wingo .300	Wilson 9	Miller 88
1915	Snyde .298	Bescher 4	Miller 72
1916	Hornsby .313	Hornsby-Smith-Bescher 6	Hornsby 65
1917	Hornsby .327	Hornsby 8	Hornsby 66
1918	Fisher .317	Cruise 6	Hornsby 60
1919	Hornsby .318	Hornsby 8	Hornsby 71
1920	Hornsby .370	McHenry 10	Hornsby 94
1921	Hornsby .397	Hornsby 21	Hornsby 126
1922	Hornsby .401	Hornsby 42	Hornsby 152
1923	Hornsby .384	Hornsby 17	Stock 96
1924	Hornsby .424	Hornsby 25	Bottomley 111
1925	Hornsby .403	Hornsby 39	Hornsby 143
1926	Bell .325	Bottomley 19	Bottomley 120
1927	Frisch .337	Bottomley 19	Bottomley 124
1928	Roettger .341	Bottomley 31	Bottomley 136
1929	Smith .345	Bottomley-Hafey 29	Bottomley 137
1930	Blades .396	Hafey 26	Frisch 114
1931	Hafey .349	Hafey 16	Hafey 95
1932	Orsatti .336	Collins 21	Collins 91
1933	Hornsby .325	Medwick 18	Medwick 98
1934	Collins .333	Collins 35	Collins 128
1935	Medwick .353	Collins-Medwick 23	Medwick 126
1936	Medwick .351	Mize 19	Medwick 138
1937	Medwick .374	Medwick 31	Medwick 154
1938	Mize .337	Mize 27	Medwick 122

SEASON	BATTING AVERAGE	HOME RUNS	RUNS BATTED IN
1939	Mize .349	Mize 28	Medwick 117
1940	Martin .316	Mize 43	Mize 137
1941	Crabtree .341	Mize 16	Mize 100
1942	Slaughter .318	Slaughter 13	Slaughter 98
1943	Musial .357	Musial-Kurowski 13	Musial-W. Cooper 81
1944	Musial .347	Kurowski 20	Sanders 102
1945	Kurowski .323	Kurowski 21	Kurowski 102
1946	Musial .365	Slaughter 18	Slaughter 130
1947	Musial .312	Kurowski 27	Kurowski 104
1948	Musial .376	Musial 39	Musial 131
1949	Musial .338	Musial 36	Musial 123
1950	Musial .346	Musial 28	Musial 109
1951	Musial .355	Musial 32	Musial 108
1952	Musial .336	Musial 21	Slaughter 101
1953	Schoendienst .342	Musial 30	Musial 113
1954	Musial .330	Musial 35	Musial 126
1955	Musial .319	Musial 33	Musial 108
1956	Musial .310	Musial 27	Musial 109
1957	Musial .351	Musial 29	Ennis 105
1958	Musial .337	Boyer 23	Boyer 90
1959	Cunningham .345	Boyer 28	Boyer 94
1960	Boyer .304	Boyer 32	Boyer 97
1961	Boyer .329	Boyer 24	Boyer 95
1962	Musial .330	Boyer 24	White 102
1963	Groat .319	White 27	Boyer 111
1964	Flood .311	Boyer 24	Boyer 119
1965	Flood .310	White 24	Flood 83
1966	Cepeda .303	Cepeda 17	Flood 78
1967	Flood .335	Cepeda 25	Cepeda 111
1968	Flood .301	Cepeda 16	Shannon 79
1969	Brock .298	Torre 18	Torre 101
1970	Torre .325	Allen 34	Allen 101
1971	Torre .363	Torre 24	Torre 137
1972	Brock .311	Simmons 16	Simmons 96
1973	Simmons .310	Simmons-Torre 13	Simmons 91
1974	McBride-Smith .309	Smith 23	Simmons 103
1975	Simmons .332	Smith 19	Simmons 100
1976	Crawford .304	Cruz 13	Simmons 75
1977	Templeton .322	Simmons 21	Simmons 95
1978	Simmons .287	Simmons 22	Simmons 80
1979	Hernandez .344	Simmons 26	Hernandez 105
1980	Hernandez .321	Hendrick 25	Hernandez 109
1981	Hernandez .306	Hendrick 18	Hendrick 61
1982	L. Smith .307	Hendrick 19	Hendrick 104

Cardinal Yearly Pitching Leaders

SEASON	GAMES PITCHED	WINS	EARNED RUN AVG
1876	Bradley 64	Bradley 45	Bradley 1.23
1877	Nichols 42	Nichols 18	Nichols 2.60
1885	Boyle 42	Boyle 16	Boyle 2.75
1886	Healy 42	Healy 17	Boyle 2.24
1892	Gleason 46	Gleason 20	Hawley 3.19
1893	Breitenstein-Gleason 48	Breitenstein 24	Breitenstein 3.18

SEASON	GAMES PITCHED	WINS	EARNED RUN AVG
1894	Breitenstein 56	Breitenstein 27	Breitenstein 4.79
1895	Breitenstein 54	Breitenstein 19	Breitenstein 4.44
1896	Breitenstein 44	Breitenstein 18	Breitenstein 4.48
1897	Donahue 46	Donahue 10	Carsey 6.00
1898	Taylor 50	Taylor 15	Taylor 3.90
1899	Powell 48	Young 26	Young 2.58
1900	Young 41	Young 19	Young 3.00
1901	Powell 45	Harper 23	Sudhoff 3.52
1902	Yerkes 39	O'Neill 17	Currie 2.75
1903	McFarland 28	McFarland-Brown 9	Brown 2.60
1904	Taylor 41	Nichols 21	Nichols 2.02
1905	Taylor 37	Taylor-Theilman 15	Taylor 3.44
1906	Brown 32	Beebe 9	Taylor 2.15
1907	McGlynn 45	McGlynn-Karger 14	Karger 2.03
1908	Raymond 48	Raymond 14	Raymond 2.03
1909	Beebe 44	Beebe 15	Sallee 2.42
1910	Harmon 43	Lush 14	Bachman 3.03
1911	Harmon 51	Harmon 23	Harmon 3.13
1912	Sallee 48	Harmon 18	Sallee 2.60
1913	Johnson 44	Johnson 14	Ames 2.88
1914	Sallee 46	Doak 20	Doak 1.72
1915	Sallee 46	Doak 16	Doak 2.64
1916	Meadows 51	Meadows 13	Meadows 2.58
1917	Doak 44	Doak 16	Ames 2.71
1918	Doak 31	Packard 12	Ames 2.31
1919	Tuero 45	Doak 13	Goodwin 2.51
1920	Haines 47	Doak 20	Doak 2.53
1921	North 40	Haines 18	Doak 2.59
1922	North 53	Pfeffer 19	Pfeffer 3.58
1923	Sherdel 39	Haines 20	Haines 3.11
1924	Sherdel-Haines 35	Sothoron 10	Dickerman 2.41
1925	Sherdel 32	Sherdel 15	Reinhart 3.05
1926	Rhem-Sherdel 34	Rhem 20	Alexander 2.91
1927	Haines 38	Haines 24	Alexander 2.52
1928	Sherdel 38	Sherdel 21	Sherdel 2.86
1929	Johnson 42	Johnson-Haines 13	Johnson 3.60
1930	Bell-Lindsey 39	Hallahan 15	Grimes 3.01
1931	Hallahan 37	Hallahan 19	Lindsey 2.77
1932	Dean 46	Dean 18	Hallahan 3.11
1933	Dean 48	Dean 20	Haines 2.50
1934	Dean 50	Dean 30	Dean 2.66
1935	Dean 50	Dean 28	Dean 3.11
1936	Dean 51	Dean 24	Dean 3.17
1937	Weiland 41	Warneke 18	Dean 2.69
1938	McGee 47	Weiland 16	McGee 3.31
1939	Shoun 53	Davis 22	Bowman 2.60
1940	Shoun 54	Warneke-McGee 16	Warneke 3.14
1941	Warneke-Krist 37	Warneke-White 17	White 2.40
1942	Beazley 43	M. Cooper 22	M. Cooper 1.78
1943	M. Cooper 37	M. Cooper 21	Pollet 1.75
1944	Schmidt 37	M. Cooper 22	Munger 1.34
1945	Burkhart 42	Barrett 21	Brecheen 2.52
1946	Dickson 47	Pollet 21	Pollet 2.10
1947	Dickson 47	Munger-Brecheen 16	Brazle 2.84
1948	Wilks 57	Brecheen 20	Brecheen 2.24

300

SEASON	GAMES PITCHED	WINS	EARNED RUN AVG
1949	Wilks 59	Pollet 20	Staley 2.73
1950	Brazle 46	Pollet 14	Lanier 3.13
1951	Brazle 56	Staley 19	Brazle 3.09
1952	Yuhas 54	Staley 17	Brazle-Yuhas 2.72
1953	Brazle 60	Haddix 20	White 2.98
1954	Brazle 58	Haddix 18	Poholsky 3.06
1955	LaPalme 56	Haddix 12	LaPalme 2.75
1956	Jackson 51	Mizell 14	Dickson 3.07
1957	Merritt 44	Jackson-McDaniel 15	Muffett 2.25
1958	Jackson 49	Jones 14	Jones 2.88
1959	McDaniel 62	Jackson-McDaniel 14	Jackson 3.30
1960	McDaniel 65	Broglio 21	McDaniel 2.09
1961	McDaniel 55	Sadecki-Jackson 14	Simmons 3.13
1962	McDaniel 55	Jackson 16	Shantz 2.18
1963	Shantz 55	Gibson-Broglio 18	Simmons 2.48
1964	Taylor 63	Sadecki 20	Schultz 1.64
1965	Woodeshick 51	Gibson 20	Woodeshick 1.81
1966	Hoerner 57	Gibson 21	Hoerner 1.54
1967	Willis 65	Hughes 16	Hoerner 2.59
1968	Hoerner 49	Gibson 22	Gibson 1.12
1969	Hoerner 45	Gibson 20	Carlton 2.17
1970	Taylor 56	Gibson 23	Taylor-Gibson 3.12
1971	Drabowsky 51	Gibson 16	Gibson 3.04
1972	Wise 35	Gibson 19	Gibson 2.46
1973	Segui 65	Wise 16	Hrabosky 2.09
1974	Hrabosky 65	McGlothen 16	Pena 2.60
1975	Hrabosky 65	Forsch-McGlothen 15	Hrabosky 1.67
1976	Hrabosky 68	McGlothen 13	Denny 2.54
1977	Metzger 58	Forsch 20	Schultz 2.33
1978	Littell 72	Denny 14	Vuckovich 2.55
1979	Littell 63	Martinez-Vuckovich 15	Martinez 3.26
1980	Littlefield 52	Vuckovich 12	Frazier 2.74
1981	Sutter 48	Forsch 10	Sutter 2.63
1982	Sutter 70	Andujar—Forsch 15	Andujar 2.47

Cardinals Batting Records

Most years, league, except pitchers	22	Stan Musial
Most games, season	162	Bill White, 1963
		Ken Boyer, 1964
		Curt Flood, 1964
Most games, league	3,026	Stan Musial
Most at-bats, season	689	Lou Brock, 159 games, 1967
Most at-bats, league	10,972	Stan Musial
Most runs, season	141	Rogers Hornsby, 154 games, 1922
Most runs, league	1,949	Stan Musial
Most hits, season	250	Rogers Hornsby, 154 games, 1922
Most hits, league	3,630	Stan Musial
Most singles, season	180	Jesse Burkett, 142 games, 1901
Most singles, league	2,253	Stan Musial
Most doubles, season	64	Joe Medwick, 155 games, 1936
Most doubles, league	725	Stan Musial
Most triples, season	33	Perry Werden, 124 games, 1893
Most triples, season, since 1900	25	Tom Long, 140 games, 1915
Most triples, league	177	Stan Musial

Cardinals Batting Records (continued)

Most homers, lefthanded batter, season	43	Johnny Mize, 155 games, 1940
Most homers, righthanded batter, season	42	Rogers Hornsby, 154 games, 1922
Most homers, season, at home	25	Johnny Mize, 1940
Most homers, season, on the road	23	Stan Musial, 1948
Most homers, one month	12	Whitey Kurowski, August, 1947
Most homers, rookie season	21	Ray Jablonski, 157 games, 1953
Most homers, league, lefthanded batter	475	Stan Musial
Most homers, league, righthanded batter	255	Ken Boyer
Most homers with bases filled, season	3	Jim Bottomley, 153 games, 1925
		Keith Hernandez, 161 games, 1977
Most homers with bases filled, league	9	Stan Musial
Most total bases, season	450	Rogers Hornsby, 154 games, 1922
Most total bases, league	6,134	Stan Musial
Most long hits, righthanded batter, season	102	Rogers Hornsby, 154 games, 1922
Most long hits, lefthanded batter, season	102	Stan Musial, 155 games, 1948
Most long hits, league	1,377	Stan Musial
Most extra bases on long hits, season	200	Rogers Hornsby, 154 games, 1922
Most extra bases on long hits, league	1,377	Stan Musial
Most stolen bases, season	118	Lou Brock, 153 games, 1974
Most stolen bases, league	888	Lou Brock
Most times caught stealing, season	36	Miller Huggins, 148 games, 1914
Most sacrifices (sacrifice hits and sacrifice flies), season	37	Taylor Douthit, 139 games, 1926
Most sacrifice hits, season	36	Harry Walker, 148 games, 1943
Most sacrifice flies, season	14	George Hendrick, 162 games, 1982
Most base on balls, season	116	Miller Huggins, 151 games, 1910
Most base on balls, league	1,599	Stan Musial
Most intentional base on balls, season	26	Stan Musial, 135 games, 1958
Most strikeouts, season	134	Lou Brock, 156 games, 1966
Most strikeouts, league	1,469	Lou Brock
Fewest strikeouts, season	10	Frank Frisch, 153 games, 1927
Most times hit by pitch, season	31	Lou Evans, 151 games, 1910
Most runs batted in, season	154	Joe Medwick, 156 games, 1937
Most runs batted in, league	1,951	Stan Musial
Most game-winning RBI	21	Keith Hernandez, 162 games, 1982
Most consecutive games, one or more runs batted in	10	Bill White, (15 RBI), 1961
Highest batting average, season	.424	Rogers Hornsby, 153 games, 1924
Highest batting average, league	.359	Rogers Hornsby
Highest slugging percentage, righthanded batter, season	.756	Rogers Hornsby, 138 games, 1925
Highest slugging percentage, lefthanded batter, season	.702	Stan Musial, 155 games, 1948

Most consecutive games hit safely,
season   33   Rogers Hornsby, 1922
Most times grounded into double play,
season   29   Ted Simmons, 161 games, 1973
Fewest times grounded into double
play, season   2   Lou Brock, 155 games, 1965

Cardinal Pitching Records

Most years	18	Jesse Haines
Most games, righthander, season	72	Mark Littell, 1978
Most games, lefthander, season	68	Al Hrabosky, 1976
Most games, league	554	Jesse Haines
Most games started, season	39	Jack Taylor, 1904
Most games started, league	482	Bob Gibson
Most complete games, season	39	Jack Taylor, 1904
Most complete games, league	255	Bob Gibson
Most games finished, righthander	51	Mark Littell, 1978
Most games finished, lefthander	45	Al Hrabosky, 1976
Most innings, season	352	Grant McGlynn, 1907
Most innings, league	3,885	Bob Gibson
Most games won, season	30	Dizzy Dean, 1934
Most games won, league	251	Bob Gibson
Most years winning 20 or more games	5	Bob Gibson
Most games lost, season	25	Grant McGlynn, 1907; Art Raymond, 1908
Most games lost, league	174	Bob Gibson
Highest percentage games won, season	.811	Dizzy Dean (30-7 in 1934)
Most consecutive games won, season	15	Bob Gibson, 1968
Most consecutive games lost, season	9	Bill McGee, 1938; Tom Poholsky, 1951; Bob Forsch, 1978
Most saves, season	36	Bruce Sutter, 1982
Most base on balls, season	181	Bob Harmon, 1911
Most base on balls, league	1,336	Bob Gibson
Most strikeouts, season	274	Bob Gibson, 1970
Most strikeouts, nine-inning game	19	Steve Carlton, September 15, 1969
Most strikeouts, league	3,117	Bob Gibson
Most shutouts, season	13	Bob Gibson, 1968
Most shutouts, league	56	Bob Gibson
Most 1-0 shutouts won	4	Bob Gibson, 1968
Most 1-0 shutouts lost	4	Lee Meadows, 1916
Most shutouts lost, season	11	Art Raymond, 1908
Most at-bats, season	1,352	Jack Taylor, 1904
Most runs, season	162	Grant McGlynn, 1907
Most earned runs, season	129	Bill Sherdel, 1929
Most hits, season	337	Cy Young, 1900
Most hit batsmen, season	17	Gerry Staley, 1953
Most wild pitches, season	15	Fred Beebe, 1907 and 1909
Most home runs, season	39	Murry Dickson, 1948
Most sacrifice hits, season	16	Ray Sadecki, 1964; Lynn McGlothen, 1974

Cardinals Pitching Records (continued)

Most sacrifice flies	13	Bob Forsch, 1980
Lowest earned run average	1.12	Bob Gibson, 305 innings, 1968

Cardinal All-Time to Ten in Batting Departments

GAMES
Musial	3,026
Brock	2,289
Slaughter	1,820
Schoendienst	1,795
Flood	1,738
K. Boyer	1,667
Hornsby	1,580
Javier	1,578
Simmons	1,564
Marion	1,502

AT-BATS
Musial	10,972
Brock	9,125
Schoendienst	6,841
Slaughter	6,775
K. Boyer	6,334
Flood	6,318
Hornsby	5,881
Simmons	5,725
Javier	5,631
Bottomley	5,314

RUNS
Musial	1,949
Brock	1,427
Hornsby	1,089
Slaughter	1,071
Schoendienst	1,025
K. Boyer	988
Bottomley	921
Flood	845
Frisch	831
Medwick	811

HITS
Musial	3,630
Brock	2,713
Hornsby	2,110
Slaughter	2,064
Schoendienst	1,980
K. Boyer	1,855
Flood	1,853
Bottomley	1,727
Simmons	1,704
Medwick	1,590

DOUBLES
Musial	725
Brock	434
Medwick	377
Hornsby	367
Slaughter	366
Schoendienst	352
Bottomley	344
Simmons	332
Frisch	286
Flood	271

TRIPLES
Musial	177
Hornsby	143
Slaughter	135
Brock	121
Bottomley	119
Konetchy	93
Medwick	81
J. Martin	75
Templeton	69
Mize	66

HOME RUNS
Musial	475
K. Boyer	255
Hornsby	193
Bottomley	181
Simmons	172
Mize	158
Medwick	152
Slaughter	146
White	140
Brock	129
Hafey	127

TOTAL BASES
Musial	6,134
Brock	3,776
Hornsby	3,342
Slaughter	3,138
K. Boyer	3,011
Bottomley	2,852
Schoendienst	2,657
Simmons	2,626
Medwick	2,585
Flood	2,464

RUNS BATTED IN		BATTING PCT.	
Musial	1,951	Hornsby	.359
Slaughter	1,148	Mize	.336
Bottomley	1,105	Medwick	.335
Hornsby	1,067	Musial	.331
K. Boyer	1,001	Hafey	.326
Simmons	929	Bottomley	.325
Medwick	923	Frisch	.312
Brock	814	Watkins	.309
Frisch	720	Torre	.308
Mize	653	J. Collins	.307

EXTRA BASE HITS		STOLEN BASES	
Musial	1,377	Brock	888
Hornsby	703	Frisch	195
Brock	684	J. Smith	192
Slaughter	647	Huggins	174
Bottomley	644	Konetchy	151
Medwick	610	Martin	146
K. Boyer	585	Templeton	138
Simmons	541	Javier	134
Schoendienst	482	Donovan	132
Mize	442	Hornsby	117

Cardinals' All-Time Home Run Leaders

SEASON — BY POSITION

Catcher — Ted Simmons	26 — 1979
First Base — Johnny Mize	43 — 1940
Second Base — Rogers Hornsby	42 — 1922
Shortstop — Solly Hemus	15 — 1952
Third Base — Ken Boyer	32 — 1960
Left Field — Stan Musial	32 — 1951
Center Field — Stan Musial	21 — 1952
Right Field — Stan Musial	39 — 1948

Cardinals' All-Time Runs-Batted-In Leaders

SEASON — BY POSITION

*Catcher — Ted Simmons	96 — 1972
First Base — Jim Bottomley	137 — 1929
Johnny Mize	137 — 1940
Second Base — Rogers Hornsby	152 — 1922
Shortstop — Doc Lavan	82 — 1921
Third Base — Joe Torre	137 — 1971
Left Field — Joe Medwick	154 — 1937
Center Field — Buster Adams	101 — 1945
Right Field — Stan Musial	131 — 1948

*Simmons had 103 RBI in 1974, but drove in only 95 while catching.
Simmons had 100 RBI in 1975, but drove in only 95 while catching.

Cardinals Who Have 200 or More Hits in a Season

Year	Player	Hits	Year	Player	Hits
1899	Jesse Burkett	228	1939	Joe Medwick	201
1900	Jesse Burkett	202	1943	Stan Musial	220
1901	Jesse Burkett	228	1946	Stan Musial	228
1920	Rogers Hornsby	218	1948	Stan Musial	230
	Milt Stock	204	1949	Stan Musial	207
1921	Rogers Hornsby	235	1951	Stan Musial	205
	Austin McHenry	201	1953	Stan Musial	200
1922	Rogers Hornsby	250	1963	Dick Groat	201
1924	Rogers Hornsby	227		Bill White	200
1925	Jim Bottomley	227		Curt Flood	200
	Rogers Hornsby	203	1964	Curt Flood	211
1927	Frankie Frisch	208		Lou Brock	200
1929	Taylor Douthit	206	1967	Lou Brock	206
1930	Taylor Douthit	201	1970	Joe Torre	203
1934	Rip Collins	200		Lou Brock	202
1935	Joe Medwick	224	1971	Joe Torre	230
1936	Joe Medwick	223		Lou Brock	200
1937	Joe Medwick	237	1977	Garry Templeton	200
	Johnny Mize	204	1979	Garry Templeton	211
				Keith Hernandez	210

Cardinals Who Have Hit 30 or More Home Runs in a Season

Year	Player		Year	Player	
1940	Johnny Mize	43	1970	Dick Allen	34
1922	Rogers Hornsby	42	1955	Stan Musial	33
1925	Rogers Hornsby	39	1951	Stan Musial	32
1948	Stan Musial	39	1960	Ken Boyer	32
1949	Stan Musial	36	1928	Jim Bottomley	31
1934	Rip Collins	35	1937	Joe Medwick	31
1954	Stan Musial	35	1953	Stan Musial	30

Cardinals Who Hit in 25 or More Consecutive Games

Year	Player	Games	Year	Player	Games
1922	Rogers Hornsby	33	1959	Ken Boyer	29
1950	Stan Musial	30	1935	Joe Medwick	28
1943	Harry Walker	29	1954	Red Schoendienst	28
			1971	Lou Brock	26

Cardinals Who Hit .400 in a Season

Year	Player	Avg.	Year	Player	Avg.
1899	Jesse Burkett	.402	1924	Rogers Hornsby	.424
1922	Rogers Hornsby	.401	1925	Rogers Hornsby	.403

Cardinals Who Had 350 or More Total Bases in a Season

1922	Rogers Hornsby	450	1936	Joe Medwick	367
1948	Stan Musial	429	1946	Stan Musial	366
1937	Joe Medwick	406	1935	Joe Medwick	365

1949	Stan Musial	382
1925	Rogers Hornsby	381
1921	Rogers Hornsby	378
1924	Rogers Hornsby	373
1934	Rip Collins	369
1940	Johnny Mize	368
1928	Jim Bottomley	362
1953	Stan Musial	361
1954	Stan Musial	359
1925	Jim Bottomley	358
1951	Stan Musial	355
1939	Johnny Mize	353
1971	Joe Torre	352

Cardinals Who Were 20-Game Winners

Year	Pitcher	W	L
1876	George Bradley	45	19
1892	Kid Gleason	20	24
1894	Ted Breitenstein	27	22
1895	Ted Breitenstein	20	29
1899	Cy Young	26	15
	Jack Powell	23	21
1900	Cy Young	20	18
1901	Jack Harper	20	12
1904	Kid Nichols	21	13
	Jack Taylor	20	19
1911	Bob Harmon	23	16
1920	Bill Doak	20	12
1923	Jesse Haines	20	13
1926	Flint Rhem	20	7
1927	Jesse Haines	24	10
	Grover Alexander	21	10
1928	Bill Sherdel	21	10
	Jesse Haines	20	8
1933	Dizzy Dean	20	18
1934	Dizzy Dean	30	7
1935	Dizzy Dean	28	12
1936	Dizzy Dean	24	13

Year	Pitcher	W	L
1939	Curt Davis	22	16
1942	Mort Cooper	22	7
	Johnny Beazley	21	6
1943	Mort Cooper	21	8
1944	Mort Cooper	22	7
1945	Red Barrett		
	(2-3 Boston)		
	(21-9 St. Louis)	23	12
1946	Howie Pollet	21	10
1948	Harry Brecheen	20	7
1949	Howie Pollet	20	9
1953	Harvey Haddix	20	9
1960	Ernie Broglio	21	9
1964	Ray Sadecki	20	11
1965	Bob Gibson	20	12
1966	Bob Gibson	21	12
1968	Bob Gibson	22	9
1969	Bob Gibson	20	13
1970	Bob Gibson	23	7
1971	Steve Carlton	20	9
1977	Bob Forsch	20	7

The Last Time It Happened Through 1981

STEAL HOME — 4 times in 1981 — Mike Ramsey vs. New York on May 23 at home. Keith Hernandez vs. Montreal, on September 17, on the road. Tom Herr vs. Philadelphia on the road, August 11. Tom Herr vs. Pittsburgh on September 27 at home.

OPPONENT STEALS HOME — Andrew Dawson of Montreal Expos, August 4, 1977, pitcher was Eric Rasmussen.

CARDINAL HIT INSIDE-THE-PARK HOME RUN — George Hendrick vs. Los Angeles at home, 1st inning with one man on, June 11, 1981 off of Fernando Valenzuela. Cardinals won the game 2-1.

OPPONENT HIT INSIDE-THE-PARK HOME RUN — Gary Carter, Montreal Expos, 6th inning, May 31, 1980.

NO-HITTER — Bob Forsch vs. Philadelphia (at St. Louis) April 16, 1978, 5-0.

NO-HITTER VS. CARDINALS — Tom Seaver (Cincinnati Reds) vs. Cards, at Cincinnati on June 16, 1978, 4-0.

The Last Time It Happened (continued)

TRIPLE PLAY — Garry Templeton-Darrell Porter-Keith Hernandez-Tom Herr-Ken Oberkfell vs. Philadelphia, 8th inning, April 11, 1981. Gary Matthews hit into it. Jim Otten was pitching.

TRIPLE PLAY VS. CARDINALS — Montreal Expos, August 12, 1969 at St. Louis, 4th inning, Larry Parrish to Rodney Scott to Warren Cromartie (George Hendrick hit into it).

CARDINAL HIT FOR CYCLE — Lou Brock vs. San Diego at San Diego on May 27, 1975.

CARDINAL HIT 3 HOME RUNS IN A GAME — Reggie Smith at Philadelphia, May 22, 1976.

OPPONENT HIT 3 HOME RUNS IN A GAME — Larry Parrish, Montreal at St. Louis, May 29, 1977.

PINCH HIT GRAND SLAM HOME RUN — Roger Freed (off Joe Sambito) at St. Louis, 11th inning, May 1, 1979.

HOME RUN BY CARDINAL PITCHER — Jim Kaat, August 26, 1980 vs. Houston at St. Louis (Joe Niekro).

Cardinal Players Who Hit for the Cycle

Lou Brock	May 27, 1975	Stan Musial	July 24, 1949
Joe Torre	June 27, 1973	Johnny Mize	July 13, 1940, 1st game
Ken Boyer	June 16, 1964	Joe Medwick	June 29, 1935
Ken Boyer	September 14, 1961, 2nd game	Pepper Martin	May 5, 1933
		Chick Hafey	August 21, 1930
Bill White	August 14, 1960, 1st game	Jim Bottomley	July 15, 1927
		Cliff Heathcote	July 13, 1918

MISCELLANY

St. Louis Cardinal Ballparks

Grand Avenue Grounds	1876–77
Union Park	1885–86, 92–97
League Park	1898
Robison Field	1899–1920
Sportsman's Park	1920–52
Busch Stadium	1953–66
Busch Memorial Stadium	1966–82

Cardinals Retired Uniform Numbers

6	Stan Musial
17	Dizzy Dean
20	Lou Brock
45	Bob Gibson

Modern Day Cardinal Attendance Records

At Sportsman's Park
Day game: 41,284 vs. New York 9-15-35
Doubleheader: 45,770 vs. Chicago 7-12-31
Night: 33,323 vs. Brooklyn 8-25-42
Twi-Night: NONE PLAYED
Opener: 26,246 vs. Chicago 4-15-62 (night)
Season high: 1,430,676   1949
Season low: 256,171   1933

At Busch Memorial Stadium
Day game: 48,085 vs. Los Angeles 7-31-66
Doubleheader: 49,743 vs. Atlanta 6-23-68
Night: 49,093 vs. San Francisco 8-13-67
Twi-Night: 46,550 vs. San Francisco 9-6-68
Opener: 45,960 vs. New York 4-10-70
Season High: 2,090,145   1967
Season Low: 1,010,247   1981

All Time St. Louis All-Star Team

NAMED BY ST. LOUIS CHAPTER OF BASEBALL WRITERS ASSOCIATION
JANUARY 20, 1958 AT HOTEL SHERATON-JEFFERSON

1st base	George Sisler	Browns 1915-1927
2nd base	Rogers Hornsby	Cardinals 1915-26, 1933, Browns 1933-37
shortstop	Marty Marion	Cardinals 1940-50, Browns 1952-53
3rd base	Frank Frisch	Cardinals 1927-37
utility infield	Red Schoendienst	Cardinals 1945-56, 1961-63
left field	Ken Williams	Browns 1918-1927
center field	Terry Moore	Cardinals 1935-1948
right field	Stan Musial	Cardinals 1941-1963
utility outfield	John Tobin	Browns 1916-25
catchers	Hank Severeid	Browns 1915-25
	Bob O'Farrell	Cardinals 1925-28, 1933, 1935
pitchers	Dizzy Dean	Cardinals 1930-37, Browns 1947
	Jesse Haines	Cardinals 1920-1937
	Urban Shocker	Browns 1918-24
	Grover Cleveland Alexander	Cardinals 1926-29

All Time St. Louis Team Voted by Fan Ballot
ANNOUNCED JULY 21, 1969

1st base	George Sisler	Browns 1915–1927
2nd base	Rogers Hornsby	Cardinals 1915–26, 1933, Browns 1933–37
shortstop	Marty Marion	Cardinals 1940–50, Browns 1952–53
3rd base	Ken Boyer	Cardinals 1956–1965
left field	Joe Medwick	Cardinals 1930–1940
center field	Curt Flood	Cardinals 1958–1969
right field	Stan Musial	Cardinals 1941–1963
catcher	Walker Cooper	Cardinals 1940–1945
pitchers	Bob Gibson	Cardinals 1959–1975
	Dizzy Dean	Cardinals 1930–37, Browns 1947

Greatest St. Louis Player: STAN MUSIAL

Rogers Hornsby also made the "Greatest Team Ever" at 2nd base, while George Sisler and Stan Musial tied at 1st base on the "Greatest Living Team."

Cardinals Who Lost Time in World War II

PLAYER	POSITION	BRANCH OF SERVICE
John Beazley	pitcher	U.S. Army Air Force
Al Brazle	pitcher	U.S. Army
Jimmy Brown	infield	U.S. Army
Walker Cooper	catcher	U.S. Navy
Creepy Crespi	infield	U.S. Army
Jeff Cross	infield	U.S. Navy
Murry Dickson	pitcher	U.S. Army
Erv Dusak	outfield	U.S. Army
Bill Endicott	outfield	U.S. Army
John Grodzicki	pitcher	U.S. Army
Nippy Jones	outfield-1st base	U.S. Marines
Lou Klein	infield	U.S. Coast Guard
Howie Krist	pitcher	U.S. Army
Danny Litwhiler	infield	U.S. Army
Fred Martin	pitcher	U.S. Army
Terry Moore	outfield	U.S. Army
George Munger	pitcher	U.S. Army
Stan Musial	outfield	U.S. Navy
Howie Pollet	pitcher	U.S. Army Air Force
Red Schoendienst	infield	U.S. Army
Walter Sessi	outfield	U.S. Army
Enos Slaughter	outfield	U.S. Army Air Force
Max Surkont	pitcher	U.S. Navy
Harry Walker	outfield	U.S. Army
Ernie White	pitcher	U.S. Army
Johnny Wyrostek	outfield	U.S. Army

Cardinal Selections in Re-Entry Draft

NOVEMBER 4, 1976

Sal Bando	3B
Bill Campbell	P
Rollie Fingers	P
Bobby Grich	IF
Don Gullett	P
Joe Rudi	OF

NOVEMBER 4, 1977

Rich Gossage	P
Ross Grimsley	P
Tom Hausman	P
Larry Hisle	OF
Mike Jorgensen	1B
Dave Kingman	OF
Jerry Terrell	IF
Mike Torrez	P
Richie Zisk	OF

NOVEMBER 3, 1978

Bernie Carbo	OF
Larry Gura	P
Tommy John	P
Darold Knowles	P
Mike Marshall	P
Pete Rose	IF
Jim Slaton	P

NOVEMBER 2, 1979

John Curtis	P
Dave Goltz	P
Don Hood	P
Al Hrabosky	P
Bruce Kison	P
Skip Lockwood	P
Rudy May	P
Fred Norman	P
Nolan Ryan	P
Don Stanhouse	P

NOVEMBER 13, 1980

Darrell Porter	C
Dave Winfield	OF

NOVEMBER 13, 1981

Joaquin Andujar	P
Mark Belanger	SS
Dave Chalk	IF
Dave Collins	OF
John Denny	P
Ron Guidry	P
Joe Rudi	OF
Mike Vail	OF

Cardinal Spring Training Sites 1901-1982

1901–02	St. Louis, Missouri
1903	Dallas, Texas
1904	Houston, Texas
1905	Marlin Springs, Texas
1906–08	Houston, Texas
1909–10	Little Rock, Arkansas
1911	West Baden, Indiana
1912	Jackson, Mississippi
1913	Columbus, Georgia
1914	St. Augustine, Florida
1915–17	Hot Wells, Texas
1918	San Antonio, Texas
1919	St. Louis, Missouri
1920	Brownsville, Texas
1921–22	Orange, Texas
1923–24	Bradenton, Florida
1925	Stockton, California
1926	San Antonio, Texas
1927–29	Avon Park, Florida
1930–36	Bradenton, Florida
1937	Daytona Beach, Florida
1938–42	St. Petersburg, Florida
1943–45	Cairo, Illinois
1946–Present	St. Petersburg, Florida

Recap of the Early Years

1903
In 1903, the Cardinals and St. Louis Browns played a spring and fall exhibition series. In the spring series, four games were played with each club winning two. In the fall series, seven games were played with the Browns winning 5, the Cardinals 2.

1904
The Cardinals and St. Louis Browns played a spring and fall series of games in 1904. In the spring series, seven games were played with the Cardinals winning 4, the Browns 3. In the fall series, the Browns and Cardinals each won three games.

1905
The Cardinals and St. Louis Browns played a spring and fall city championship series in 1905. In the spring series, seven games were played with the Browns winning 4, the Cardinals 3. In the fall series, again the Browns won, 4 games to 3.

1906
The Cardinals and St. Louis Browns played a spring and a fall series for the city championship in 1906. In the spring series the Browns won, 6 games to 1. In the fall series, the Browns won, 4 games to 1.

1907

THE ST. LOUIS CITY SERIES

Spring Training Series
March 30 — Browns 6, Cardinals 2
March 31 — Cardinals 5, Browns 4
April 2 — Cardinals 6, Browns 2
April 4 — Browns 1, Cardinals 0 (13 innings)
April 5 — Cardinals 5, Browns 4
April 6 — Browns 4, Cardinals 2
April 9 — Cardinals 9, Browns 1
    Cardinals win spring series, 4 games to 3

Fall Series
In October, 1907, another seven-game series was played between the Cardinals and the Browns in St. Louis with the Cardinals winning the series, 5 games to 2.

1908
In the spring of 1908, the Cardinals and the St. Louis Browns played a five-game series to determine the City Championship. The Browns won 3 games, the Cardinals two. No fall series was played between the two clubs that year.

1909-1910
In 1910, as in 1909, no series was played between the Cardinals and the St. Louis Browns to determine the City Championship.

1911
In the first game of the series between the National League and American League St. Louis clubs for the City Championship, the teams played nine innings

without either side making a run. Darkness put an end to the contest. It was the closest and in some respects the best played game of the series.

The better batting of the American League players proved to be the strong point. After the first contest they had little trouble in hitting the opposing pitchers safely, and game-by-game wore the National League team down. In one afternoon the teams undertook to play a doubleheader at Robison Field. The first game was completed with the full nine innings played, but the second had to be called at the end of the fifth inning, with the American League club so far in front that there was no question as to the probable outcome of the contest if it had gone for the full nine innings.

First game, Oct. 11, at Sportsman's Park: Cardinals 0, Browns 0
Second game, Oct. 12, at Robison Field: Browns 3, Cardinals 2
Third game, Oct. 14, at Sportsman's Park: Browns 10, Cardinals 2
Fourth game, Oct. 15, at Robison Field: Browns 6, Cardinals 2
Fifth game, Oct. 15, at Robison Field: Browns 10, Cardinals 8 (5 innings)
Sixth game, Oct. 16, at Sportsman's Park: Browns 5, Cardinals 1

Browns won the series 5 games to 0 (1 tie).

1912
Owing to the fact that a tie game took place between the St. Louis clubs, it was necessary to play eight contests in the fall of 1912 before the City Championship was decided. The National League team won the eighth game and the series. By doing so, the Cardinals had the distinction of winning the only autumn series for the National League, as the Giants, Cubs, and Phillies lost their city championship series. (No game dates were found in reference materials.)

First game, at Sportsman's Park: Cardinals 7, Browns 6
Second game, at Sportsman's Park: Cardinals 3, Browns 2
Third game, at Sportsman's Park: Browns 4, Cardinals 0
Fourth game, at Sportsman's Park: Browns 2, Cardinals 2 (Tie)
Fifth game, at Sportsman's Park: Cardinals 10, Browns 4
Sixth game, at Sportsman's Park: Browns 3, Cardinals 1
Seventh Game, at Robison Field: Browns 2, Cardinals 0
Eighth game, at Sportsman's Park: Cardinals 6, Browns 1

Cardinals won the series, 4 games to 3 (one tie).

1913
The rival clubs of St. Louis, the American League Browns and the National League Cardinals, played a post-season series in the fall of 1913 for the local championship. The series was not played under National Commission auspices, and the result was that discipline did not prevail and the series terminated abruptly after the sixth game, owing to a fight between the players upon the diamond. This fight caused such bad feeling between the players and the fans that the two club managements decided to call the series off with honors even, each club having won three games. The players of each club received less than $1,700 to divide any way they desired. The average per Brown player was $77.22. The pot was split 24 ways, although some players received more than others. Crossin, Taylor, Wares, Bisland, and Sloan, recruits who joined the club after Sept. 1, each came in for half a share. The Browns gave a share to George Stovall, former manager, and a share to Manager Branch Rickey, although Rickey told the players that he did not want the money because he believed he had not been with the club long enough.

The series came to an abrupt end on Monday, Oct. 13, called off by the two clubs owing to a row between players. In the first game Derril Pratt, the Browns' first baseman, insisted that a batted ball which hit him in the eye was foul, and when Umpire Hildebrand called it fair he rushed to the plate to argue with the arbiter. While he was talking to the umpire, a player on the Cardinals' bench, Pratt says, called him an abusive name. Pratt rushed to the bench and clinched with utility player Beck. The players finally separated the fighters, and Pratt resumed his argument with Hildebrand, and was banished. The remainder of the game went on in peace with the Cardinals winning, 1 to 0.

When the Cardinals took the field for the second game they objected to Pratt playing. Manager Rickey, of the Browns, said Hildebrand promised to permit Pratt to play, and he would not let his team take the field until the regular first baseman was at his position. After arguing with Manager Huggins without result, Rickey appealed to the umpires to settle the dispute. The arbiters ruled Pratt out, but the American leader continued to argue until the umpires left the field and went to their dressing rooms. Both umpires announced they were through. Later Brennan and Hildebrand returned, however, with Pratt not playing. The game went four innings before darkness ended it.

First game, Oct. 9, at Sportsman's Park: Cardinals 1, Browns 0
Second game, Oct. 10, at Sportsman's Park: Cardinals 4, Browns 1
Third game, Oct. 11, at Sportsman's Park: Browns 8, Cardinals 5
Fourth game, Oct. 11, at Sportsman's Park: Browns 2, Cardinals 2 (tie) six innings, called because of darkness.
Fifth game, Oct. 12, at Robison Field: Browns 7, Cardinals 6
Sixth game, Oct. 12, at Robison Field: Browns 6, Cardinals 2 (six innings, called because of darkness)
Seventh game, Oct. 13, at Sportsman's Park: Cardinals 5, Browns 2
Eighth game, Oct. 13, at Sportsman's Park: Cardinals 1, Browns 1 (called after 5 innings because of players' fight)

1914

Five games and an exhibition game were played by the St. Louis clubs in the annual fall series. The attendance was fair and the Browns won the city championship in the first five games played, as the Cardinals succeeded in capturing but one contest from their rivals. That was the fourth, which lasted but five innings and was the last half of a doubleheader. It was asserted that the playing of the National League players was affected by the fact that some of them were about to desert their club for others outside of organized baseball and did not make any great effort to play because of that fact.

One remarkable feature of these games was the closeness of the contests. In the first the score was 2-1, and in the second 7-4 in favor of the Browns, the latter being the highest score which was made during the series. In the third the Browns won 2-0 and they lost the fourth 2-0. The fifth was won by the Browns 2-0. The last game which was seven innings long, the second part of a doubleheader and called at the end of the seventh inning, was 2-2.

The series was a fair success financially and the players did better by it than they did in the postseason series of 1913. In the second game C. Walker made a home run drive over the left field wall of the Browns' park, which was one of the longest hits ever made on the field. On the whole, the pitchers for the American League club did better than their rivals. The National League batters were unable to hit very effectively. The scores of the games are as follows:

First game, at Robison Field: Browns 2, Cardinals 1
Second game, at Robison Field: Browns 7, Cardinals 4
Third game, at Robison Field: Browns 2, Cardinals 0

Fourth game, at Sportsman's Park: Cardinals 2, Browns 0
Fifth game, at Robison Park: Browns 2, Cardinals 0
Sixth game, at Sportsman's Park: Browns 2, Cardinals 2 (tie in 7 innings)

Browns won the series 4 games to 1 (1 tie).
In the 1914 spring series between the two clubs, the Cardinals won, 5 games to 1.

1915
The 1915 fall series for the organized ball championship of St. Louis, between the St. Louis Browns of the American League and the St. Louis Cardinals of the National League, resulted in a hollow victory for the Browns, who made almost a sweep with four victories in six games played, one game being an extra-inning tie game.

The opening game of the Browns-Cardinals fall series for the championship of St. Louis (not counting the St. Louis Federals, who finished higher than either the Cardinals or Browns) was played on Oct. 5, and was won by the Browns. In the third inning Pratt scored for the Americans on Walker's single; in the fifth inning Shotton scored on Sisler's sacrifice, and the final tally for the Americans was made in the seventh, when Shotton made home on an infield hit by Sisler. The score: Browns 3, Cardinals 2.

The second game was played on Oct. 6, and was called on account of darkness at the end of the twelfth inning, with the score at 3–3. Miserable fielding prevented the Cardinals from winning. They held the lead three times and always erred to give the Browns a chance to tie the score. The Cardinals had the game in the ninth, 2 to 1, with Austin on second and two out when Howard singled, tying the score. In the seventh they were in front again, when Jacobson's single counted Pratt when there were two out. McCabe fanned 10 Cardinals. The score: Browns 3, Cardinals 3 (tie).

The game scheduled for Thursday, Oct. 7, was prevented by rain, and no game was played on Friday, Oct. 8. The series was resumed on Saturday, Oct. 9, two games being played. In the first game of the doubleheader, the Browns won with ease, Sallee being hit hard in the first inning and until the seventh, when Niehaus relieved him. The score: Browns 5, Cardinals 1.

Lee Meadows was manager Miller Huggins' pitching selection in the sunset tilt. The Durham boy twirled fine ball for five innings, but in the sixth he made an ascension. Three runs were scored in this session, and the Browns added another counter in each of the seventh and eighth stanzas. Chester Huff, the Ossining portsider, relieved Ernie Koob, who was removed in favor of a pinch-hitter in the fifth. Chet did not allow a hit in the five innings he toiled. The score: Browns 6, Cardinals 2.

The series came to an end on Sunday, Oct. 10, when the Browns won the second game of a doubleheader. Hamilton and Koob were trounced by the Nationals in the opener, the Cardinals landing on their delivery for 17 healthy swats. Bill Doak, on the other hand, held the Browns to two hits. The score: Cardinals 7, Browns 2.

Tim McCabe, who came to the Browns from the Three I League only a few months earlier, won the postseason championship for his team by shutting out the Cardinals. The score: Browns 5, Cardinals 0.

1916
In the annual fall city series between the St. Louis clubs of the rival major leagues, the National League representatives won but one game. The series was much more interesting than that in Chicago, but the players of the St. Louis National League club were outbatted a trifle. Their fielding was, in a way, as good as that of their rivals, although their errors were more costly. The Cardinals carried one game into extra innings and were outgeneraled in that contest.

First game, Oct. 4, at Robison Field: Browns 5, Cardinals 3
Second game, Oct. 5, at Robison Field: Browns 4, Cardinals 3
Third game, Oct. 7, at Sportsman's Park: Cardinals 5, Browns 4
Fourth game, Oct. 8, at Robison Field: Browns 3, Cardinals 2
Fifth game, Oct. 8, at Robison Field: Browns 4, Cardinals 1 (stopped by darkness
    after 8 innings)

Browns won the series, 4 games to 1.
In the 1916 spring series between the two clubs, the Cardinals won 4 games, the
Browns 2.

1917
Although seven games were played in the annual fall series of the St. Louis clubs
in 1917, six decided that the St. Louis National League team earned the honor of
the local championship for the year. The seventh game, also the sixth of the series,
was the second of a doubleheader played to a 0-0 tie on the American League
grounds Sunday, Oct. 7, in nine innings. On the following day the teams again met
on the American League club grounds and the Cardinals won the decisive game by
brisk batting.
In the main the contests were interesting. In one or two the fielding was quite
poor. In almost all there was enough batting to maintain interest.
The series was under the jurisdiction of the National Commission, but with
slight modification in the rules. The players, by reason of the agreement which
they had with their clubs, were permitted to share in the receipts of all of the
games. The players' share of the receipts was $3,700, divided on the usual basis of
60 and 40 percent, with twenty-one eligible on the Cardinal team, the winners, and
twenty-four eligible on the American League team.

First game, Oct. 3, at Robison Field: Cardinals 3, Browns 2
Second game, Oct. 4, at Sportsman's Park: Cardinals 3, Browns 1
Third game, Oct. 6, at Robison Field: Browns 5, Cardinals 4
Fourth game, Oct. 6, at Robison Field: Cardinals 6, Browns 1 (5 innings)
Fifth game, Oct. 7, at Sportsman's Park: Browns 2, Cardinals 0
Sixth game, Oct. 7, at Sportsman's Park: Browns 0, Cardinals 0
Seventh game, Oct. 8, at Sportsman's Park: Cardinals 6, Browns 1

Cardinals won the series, 4 games to 2 (one tie).
In the 1917 spring series between the two clubs, the Cardinals won three games,
the Browns none.

1918
In the annual spring series between the Cardinals and St. Louis Browns, the
Browns won four games, the Cardinals none; there were three tie games.

1919
In 1919, the Cardinals and St. Louis Browns played a spring and a fall series to
determine the City Championship. In the spring series, the Browns won 4 games,
the Cardinals 2 and there was one tie game. In the fall series, the Cardinals won 2
games, the Browns none.

1920
In 1920, the Cardinals and St. Louis Browns played a spring series to determine
the City Championship. In the spring series, the Browns won 4 games, the Cardinals 2, and there was one tie game.

1921
In the spring of 1921, the Cardinals and St. Louis Browns played seven games with the Browns winning 4, the Cardinals 3.

1922
In the spring of 1922, the Cardinals and St. Louis Browns played a five-game series. The Browns won 3, the Cardinals 1, and there was one tie game.

1923
In the spring of 1923, the Cardinals and Browns played a two-game series with the Browns winning both games.

CITY SERIES

Fall City Series Recap 1903-1917
(DISCONTINUED ON ACCOUNT OF WORLD WAR I)

Series Played	12	Games Played	80
Won by Browns	7	Won by Browns	41
Won by Cards	3	Won by Cards	29
Series Tied	2	Games Tied	10
Postponed	0		
Not Scheduled	4	(1902, 08-09-10)	

Spring City Series Recap 1903-1953

Series Played	48	Games Played	178
Won by Browns	19	Won by Browns	95
Won by Cards	10	Won by Cards	83
Series Tied	19	Games Tied	0
Postponed	1	(1952, rain)	
Not Scheduled	3	(1902, 09-10)	

Composite City Series Totals 1903-1953

Series Played	60	Games Played	258
Won by Browns	26	Won by Browns	136
Won by Cards	13	Won by Cards	112
Series Tied	21	Games Tied	10
Postponed	1	(1952, rain)	
Not Scheduled	7	(1902, 08-09-10)	

July 10, 1945 War Fund Exhibition
Browns 3–Cards 0

RESULT—BROWNS CITY CHAMPIONS

Players Who Played for Both Cardinals and Browns

PLAYER	POSITION	WITH CARDS	WITH BROWNS
Ethan Allen	outfield	1933	1937–38
Bill Bailey	pitcher	1921–22	1907–12
Jim Bottomley	infield	1922–32	1936–37
Harry Brecheen	pitcher	1940, 43–52	1953
Herman Bronkie	infield	1918	1919, 22
Frank Buelow	catcher	1899–1901	1902–04
Jesse Burkett	outfield	1899–1901	1902–04
Verne Clemons	catcher	1919–24	1916
Bill Cox	pitcher	1936	1938–40
Doc Crandell	pitcher	1913	1916
Lou Criger	catcher	1899–1900	1912
Dizzy Dean	pitcher	1930, 32–37	1947
Paul Dean	pitcher	1934–39	1943
Frank Demaree	outfield	1943	1944
Red Donahue	pitcher	1895–97	1902–03
Hal Epps	outfield	1938–40	1943–44
Showboat Fisher	outfield	1930	1932
Debs Garms	outfield	1943–45	1932–35
Don Gutteridge	infield	1936–40	1942–45
Bob Habenicht	pitcher	1951	1953
Hal Haid	pitcher	1928–30	1919
John Heidrick	outfield	1899–1901	1902–04, 08
Charlie Hemphill	outfield	1899	1902–04, 06–07
Rogers Hornsby	infield	1915, 26–33	1933–37
Frank Huelsman	outfield	1897	1904
Pat Hynes	pitcher	1903	1904
Darrell Johnson	catcher	1960	1952
Ellis Kinder	pitcher	1956	1946–47
Clyde Kluttz	catcher	1946	1951
Lyn Lary	infield	1939	1935–36, 40
Doc Lavan	outfield	1919–24	1913–17
Dick Littlefield	pitcher	1956	1952–53
Grover Lowdermilk	pitcher	1909, 11	1915, 17–19
Marty Marion	infield	1940–50	1953
Ed Mickelson	infield	1950	1953
Buster Mills	outfield	1934	1938
Gene Moore	outfield	1933–35	1944–45
Bob Nieman	outfield	1960–61	1951–52
Jack O'Connor	catcher	1899–1900	1904–07, 10
Dick Padden	infield	1901	1902–05
Al Papai	pitcher	1948, 50	1949
Gene Paulette	infield	1917–19	1916–17
Ray Pepper	outfield	1932–33	1934–36
Jeff Pfeffer	pitcher	1921–24	1911
J.W. Porter	utility	1959	1952
Nels Potter	pitcher	1936	1943–48
Red Powell	pitcher	1899–1901	1902–03, 05–19
George Puccinelli	outfield	1903–32	1934
Stan Rojek	infield	1951	1952
John Schulte	catcher	1927	1923, 32
Charlie Shields	pitcher	1907	1902

PLAYER	POSITION	WITH CARDS	WITH BROWNS
Burt Shotton	outfield	1919-23	1909, 11-17
Willie Sudhoff	pitcher	1897-1901	1902-05
Joe Sugden	catcher	1898	1902-05
Bill Trotter	pitcher	1944	1937-42
Bobby Wallace	infield	1899-1901, 17-18	1902-16
Art Weaver	catcher	1902-03	1905
Bob Weiland	pitcher	1937-40	1935
Hal White	pitcher	1953-54	1953
Joe Willis	pitcher	1911-13	1911
Bobby Young	infield	1948	1951-53

Rogers Hornsby holds the distinction of being the only man to manage both the Cardinals and the Browns. He piloted the Cards in 1925 and 1926, serving as player-manager both years, and the Browns 1933 through 1937 as player-manager, and again in 1952 as manager.

Cardinal Farm Club Success

YEAR	AFFILIATED CLUBS	PLAYERS	1ST PLACE FINISHES
1925	8	182	0
1926	8	209	0
1927	7	172	1
1928	8	196	2
1929	9	240	1
1930	11	295	3
1931	10	298	3
1932	8	210	2
1933	8	206	3
1934	10	285	3
1935	14	379	6
1936	19	451	5
1937	24	552	8
1938	25	577	3
1939	22	638	8
1940	22	632	5
1941	23	677	8
1942	21	631	2
1943	7	255	1
1944	8	234	2
1945	8	339	0
1946	17	649	1
1947	19	494	3
1948	21	507	6
1949	20	468	4
1950	21	501	6
1951	16	423	2
1952	15	347	3
1953	18	622	6
1954	22	837	1
1955	19	631	3
1956	15	489	3
1957	12	378	4

YEAR	AFFILIATED CLUBS	PLAYERS	1ST PLACE FINISHES
1958	14	334	1
1959	12	399	2
1960	9	298	1
1961	8	289	0
1962	6	207	1
1963	5	237	0
1964	6	239	2
1965	6	217	2
1966	7	242	4
1967	7	207	2
1968	7	262	2
1969	7	295	0
1970	7	295	2
1971	7	250	1
1972	7	265	1
1973	7	262	2
1974	5	212	1
1975	5	168	2
1976	5	183	1
1977	6	197	2
1978	6	180	2
1979	5	160	2
1980	5	125	4
1981	6	150	1

THREE GREATS

Louis (Lou) Clark Brock

Outfielder   Ht: 5-11   Wt: 170
Bats: Left   Throws: Left
Born: 6-18-39 at El Dorado, Arkansas

BROCK—COMPLETE RECORD

Year	Club	AVG.	G	AB	R	H	2B	3B	HR	RBI	BB	SO	SB
1961	St. Cloud	.361	128	501	117	181	33	6	14	82	51	105	38
	Chicago	.091	4	11	1	1	0	0	0	0	1	3	0
1962	Chicago	.263	123	434	73	114	24	7	9	35	35	96	16
1963	Chicago	.258	148	547	79	141	19	11	9	37	31	122	24
1964	Chicago	.251	52	215	30	54	9	2	2	14	13	40	10
	St. Louis	.348	103	419	81	146	21	9	12	44	27	87	33
1965	St. Louis	.288	155	631	107	182	35	8	16	69	45	116	63
1966	St. Louis	.285	156	643	94	183	24	12	15	46	31	134	74
1967	St. Louis	.299	159	689	113	206	32	12	21	76	24	109	52
1968	St. Louis	.279	159	660	92	184	46	14	6	51	46	124	62
1969	St. Louis	.298	157	655	97	195	33	10	12	47	50	115	53
1970	St. Louis	.304	155	664	114	202	29	5	13	57	60	99	51
1971	St. Louis	.313	157	640	126	200	37	7	7	61	76	107	64
1972	St. Louis	.311	153	621	81	193	26	8	3	42	47	93	63
1973	St. Louis	.297	160	650	110	193	29	8	7	63	71	112	70
1974	St. Louis	.306	153	635	105	194	25	7	3	48	61	88	118
1975	St. Louis	.309	136	528	78	163	27	6	3	47	38	64	56
1976	St. Louis	.301	133	498	73	150	24	5	4	67	35	75	56
1977	St. Louis	.272	141	489	69	133	22	6	2	46	30	74	35
1978	St. Louis	.221	92	298	31	66	9	0	0	12	17	29	17
1979	St. Louis	.304	120	405	56	123	15	4	5	38	23	43	21
MAJOR TOTALS		.293	2616	10332	1610	3023	486	141	149	900	761	1730	938

BROCK—WORLD SERIES RECORD

Year	Club	AVG.	G	AB	R	H	2B	3B	HR	RBI	BB	SO	SB
1964	St. Louis	.300	7	30	2	9	2	0	1	5	0	3	0
1967	St. Louis	.414	7	29	8	12	2	1	1	3	2	3	7
1968	St. Louis	.464	7	28	6	13	3	1	2	5	3	4	7
SERIES TOTALS		.391	21	87	16	23	7	2	4	13	5	10	14

BROCK—ALL-STAR GAME RECORD

Year	Club	AVG.	AB	R	H	2B	3B	HR	RBI	BB	SO	SB
1967	National	.000	0	0	0	0	0	0	0	0	0	0
1971	National	.000	1	0	0	0	0	0	0	0	0	0
1972	National				DID NOT APPEAR							
1974	National	1.000	1	1	1	0	0	0	0	0	0	1
1975	National	.333	3	1	1	0	0	0	0	0	0	1
1979	National	1.000	1	0	1	0	0	0	0	0	0	0
ALL-STAR TOTALS		.375	8	0	3	0	0	0	0	0	0	2

TEAM	SB	CS	PCT.
San Diego	62	12	.838
New York	97	26	.789
San Francisco	88	25	.779
Houston	105	31	.772
Cincinnati	64	19	.771
Chicago	97	29	.770
Pittsburgh	97	31	.758
Philadelphia	101	35	.743
St. Louis	5	2	.714
Milw-Atlanta	87	37	.702
Los Angeles	67	29	.698
Montreal	68	31	.687
CAREER TOTALS	938	307	.760

2 Stolen Bases in Game — 135 times
3 Stolen Bases in Game — 19 times (last accomplished — August 17, 1976 vs. San Diego)
4 Stolen Bases in Game — 3 times
    August 29, 1969 vs. Pittsburgh
    September 6, 1971 vs. Philadelphia
    September 1, 1974 vs. San Francisco

MAJOR LEAGUE ALL-TIME STOLEN BASE LEADERS*

1. LOU BROCK (1961–1979) 938
2. Ty Cobb (1905–1928) 892
3. Eddie Collins (1906–1930) 743
4. Max Carey (1910–1929) 738
5. Honus Wagner (1898–1917) 696

*List compiled for stolen bases since 1898. Prior to 1898 a runner was credited with a stolen base for each extra base advanced on another player's hit. In 1898 the rule was changed to the one used today. William (Sliding Billy) Hamilton had 937 stolen bases. His career spanned from 1888–1901.

BROCK'S MILESTONE THEFTS

Number	Date	Inning	Base	Opponent
600	7-30-73	1st	2nd	at Chicago
700	7-29-74	1st	2nd	at Chicago
739 (104 of '74)	9-10-74	1st	2nd	vs. Philadelphia
740	9-10-74	7th	2nd	vs. Philadelphia
892	8-29-77	1st	2nd	at San Diego
893	8-29-77	7th	2nd	at San Diego
900	9-30-77	8th	2nd	vs. New York
917	8-29-78	8th	2nd	at Houston
937	9-22-79 (1G)	4th	2nd	at New York
938	9-23-79	5th	2nd	at New York

Theft-by-Theft with Larcenous Lou

SB. No.	Game No.	Date	Opponent	Place	SB. No.	Game No.	Date	Opponent	Place
1	7	Apr. 13	Pittsburgh	Away	60	95	July 21	Houston	Home
2	7	13	Pittsburgh	Away	61	97	25†	New York	Home
3	9	14†	Pittsburgh	Away	62	98	26	New York	Home
4	10	15	Philadelphia	Away	63	98	26	New York	Home
5	11	16	Philadelphia	Away	64	99	27	Chicago	Away
6	12	17	Philadelphia	Away	65	101	29	Chicago	Away
7	16	21	Montreal	Home	66	104	Aug. 1	Pittsburgh	Away
8	16	21	Montreal	Home	67	106	3	Philadelphia	Home
9	17	23	Houston	Home	68	106	3	Philadelphia	Home
10	17	23	Houston	Home	69	107	4*	Philadelphia	Home
11	17	23	Houston	Home	70	108	4†	Philadelphia	Home
12	19	26	Cincinnati	Home	71	108	4†	Philadelphia	Home
13	22	30	Atlanta	Home	72	108	4†	Philadelphia	Home
14	23	May 1	Atlanta	Home	73	109	5	Philadelphia	Home
15	24	3	Houston	Away	74	109	5	Philadelphia	Home
16	24	3	Houston	Away	75	110	6*	Montreal	Away
17	25	4	Houston	Away	76	115	10	Los Angeles	Home
18	26	5	Houston	Away	77	116	11	Los Angeles	Home
19	27	7	Cincinnati	Away	78	117	12	San Diego	Home
20	27	7	Cincinnati	Away	79	117	12	San Diego	Home
21	29	10	Montreal	Away	80	118	13	San Diego	Home
22	29	10	Montreal	Away	81	120	16	San Francisco	Home
23	32	15	New York	Home	82	121	17	San Francisco	Home
24	34	17	Chicago	Home	83	123	19	Atlanta	Away
25	35	18	Chicago	Home	84	123	19	Atlanta	Away
26	36	19	Chicago	Home	85	124	20	Atlanta	Away
27	36	19	Chicago	Home	86	125	21	Atlanta	Away
28	38	21	Philadelphia	Home	87	126	23	Los Angeles	Away
29	40	24	Chicago	Away	88	127	24	Los Angeles	Away
30	41	25	Chicago	Away	89	129	27	San Diego	Away
31	48	June 2	San Diego	Home	90	130	28	San Diego	Away
32	48	2	San Diego	Home	91	130	28	San Diego	Away
33	50	5	San Francisco	Away	92	131	29	San Diego	Away
34	50	5	San Francisco	Away	93	131	29	San Diego	Away
35	51	6	San Francisco	Away	94	133	31	San Francisco	Away
36	52	7	San Diego	Away	95	134	Sept. 1	San Francisco	Away
37	52	7	San Diego	Away	96	134	1	San Francisco	Away
38	53	8	San Diego	Away	97	134	1	San Francisco	Away
39	55	10	Los Angeles	Away	98	134	1	San Francisco	Away
40	56	11	Los Angeles	Away	99	136	3†	Montreal	Home
41	62	18	San Francisco	Home	100	138	6	New York	Home
42	62	18	San Francisco	Home	101	138	6	New York	Home
43	66	23	Montreal	Home	102	140	8	New York	Home
44	66	23	Montreal	Home	103	140	8	New York	Home
45	68	24†	Pittsburgh	Home	104	142	10	Philadelphia	Home
46	69	25	Pittsburgh	Home	105	142	10	Philadelphia	Home
47	69	25	Pittsburgh	Home	106	145	13	Philadelphia	Away
48	74	30†	New York	Away	107	146	14	Philadelphia	Away
49	75	July 2	Chicago	Home	108	148	17	Pittsburgh	Away
50	76	3	Chicago	Home	109	148	17	Pittsburgh	Away
51	82	8	Houston	Away	110	149	18	Pittsburgh	Away
52	83	9	Houston	Away	111	150	19	Pittsburgh	Away
53	84	10	Houston	Away	112	152	21	Chicago	Home
54	86	12†	Atlanta	Home	113	153	22	Chicago	Home
55	87	13	Atlanta	Home	114	153	22	Chicago	Home
56	88	14	Atlanta	Home	115	154	23	Pittsburgh	Home
57	92	18	Houston	Home	116	155	24	Pittsburgh	Home
58	92	18	Houston	Home	117	157	27	Chicago	Away
59	95	21	Houston	Home	118	159	29	Chicago	Away

*First game of doubleheader.

†Second game of doubleheader.

	SB	CS		SB	CS
In April	13	1	3rd Base	6	2
In May	17	1	Home	0	1
In June	18	4	vs. Chicago	15	0
In July	17	7	vs. Montreal	8	2
In August	29	12	vs. New York	9	4
In September	24	8	vs. Philadelphia	16	5
Before All-Star Game	60	13	vs. Pittsburgh	13	5
After All-Star Game	58	20	vs. Eastern Division	61	16
Home	62	20	vs. Atlanta	9	3
Away	56	13	vs. Cincinnati	3	2
Day	40	3	vs. Houston	14	3
Night	78	30	vs. Los Angeles	6	4
Vs. Left-handers	34	12	vs. San Diego	13	3
Vs. Right-handers	84	21	vs. San Francisco	12	2
2nd Base	112	30	vs. Western Division	57	17

Stan Musial

COMPLETE RECORD

Year	Club	G	AB	R	H	2B	3B	HR	RBI	BA	PO	A	E	FA
1938	Williamson	26	62	5	16	3	0	1	6	.258	7	22	6	.829
1939	Williamson	23	71	10	25	3	3	1	9	.352	5	19	3	.889
1940	Daytona Beach	113	405	55	126	17	10	1	70	.311	183	69	11	.958
1941	Springfield, Mo.	87	348	100	132	27	10	26	94	.379	185	7	3	.985
	Rochester	54	221	43	72	10	4	3	21	.326	102	5	1	.991
	St. Louis	12	47	8	20	4	0	1	7	.426	20	1	0	1.000
1942	St. Louis	140	467	87	147	32	10	10	72	.315	296	6	5	.984
1943	St. Louis	157	617	108	220	48	20	13	81	.357	376	15	7	.982
1944	St. Louis	146	568	112	197	51	14	12	94	.347	353	16	5	.987
1945					(Military Service)									
1946	St. Louis	156	624	124	228	50	20	16	103	.365	1166	69	15	.988
1947	St. Louis	149	587	113	183	30	13	19	95	.312	1360	77	8	.994
1948	St. Louis	155	611	135	230	46	18	39	131	.376	354	11	8	.981
1949	St. Louis	157	612	128	207	41	13	36	123	.338	337	11	3	.991
1950	St. Louis	146	555	105	192	41	7	28	109	.346	760	39	8	.990
1951	St. Louis	152	578	124	205	30	12	32	108	.355	816	45	10	.989
1952	St. Louis	154	578	105	194	42	6	21	91	.336	502	18	5	.990
1953	St. Louis	157	593	127	200	53	9	30	113	.337	294	9	5	.984
1954	St. Louis	153	591	120	195	41	9	35	126	.330	307	15	5	.985
1955	St. Louis	154	562	97	179	30	5	33	108	.319	1000	94	9	.992
1956	St. Louis	156	594	87	184	33	6	27	109	.310	954	95	8	.992
1957	St. Louis	134	502	82	176	38	3	29	102	.351	1167	99	10	.992
1958	St. Louis	135	472	64	159	35	2	17	62	.337	1019	100	13	.989
1959	St. Louis	115	341	37	87	13	2	14	44	.255	624	63	7	.990
1960	St. Louis	116	331	49	91	17	1	17	63	.275	97	2	1	.990
1961	St. Louis	123	372	46	107	22	4	15	70	.288	149	9	1	.994
1962	St. Louis	135	433	57	143	18	1	19	82	.330	164	6	4	.977
1963	St. Louis	124	337	34	86	10	2	12	58	.255	121	1	4	.968
MAJOR TOTALS		3026	10972	1949	3630	725	177	475	1951	.331	12236	801	140	.989

BATTING RECORD OF STAN MUSIAL BY MONTHS

MONTH	AB	R	H	AVG.
October	48	13	21	.438
September	1824	319	627	.344
June	1951	350	652	.334
July	2173	378	712	.3276
August	2128	376	697	.3275
April	887	346	288	.325
May	1961	367	633	.323
Totals	10972	1949	3620	.331

		HIS APRIL RECORD					HIS MAY RECORD		
YEAR	AB	R	H	AVG.	YEAR	AB	R	H	AVG.
1941	0	0	0	.000	1941	0	0	0	.000
1942	51	10	14	.275	1942	76	23	24	.316
1943	27	4	9	.333	1943	115	24	40	.348
1944	38	8	17	.447	1944	102	19	34	.333
1946	54	10	20	.370	1946	93	18	30	.322
1947	41	5	6	.146	1947	85	12	19	.224
1948	35	6	14	.400	1948	110	28	43	.391
1949	37	8	9	.243	1949	99	19	28	.283
1950	29	6	13	.448	1950	101	24	41	.406
1951	31	5	10	.323	1951	101	27	39	.386
1952	48	7	15	.313	1952	94	14	32	.340
1953	41	6	13	.317	1953	114	19	28	.246
1954	48	8	16	.333	1954	123	37	48	.390
1955	50	12	12	.240	1955	102	12	34	.333
1956	35	7	9	.257	1956	105	18	34	.324
1957	42	5	20	.476	1957	117	19	36	.308
1958	53	13	28	.528	1958	91	9	34	.374
1959	57	3	14	.245	1959	70	9	16	.229
1960	40	9	12	.300	1960	54	7	11	.204
1961	44	2	9	.205	1961	53	8	20	.377
1962	48	10	19	.396	1962	68	8	18	.279
1963	38	2	9	.237	1963	88	13	24	.273
Totals	887	146	288	.325		1961	367	633	.323

		HIS JUNE RECORD					HIS JULY RECORD		
YEAR	AB	R	H	AVG.	YEAR	AB	R	II	AVG.
1941	0	0	0	.000	1941	0	0	0	.000
1942	51	7	20	.392	1942	103	16	32	.311
1943	108	13	30	.278	1943	131	23	49	.374
1944	103	23	41	.398	1944	133	24	43	.323
1946	116	20	45	.388	1946	117	26	42	.359
1947	105	30	35	.333	1947	125	19	40	.320
1948	102	22	42	.412	1948	120	26	44	.367
1949	115	24	39	.339	1949	125	19	37	.296
1950	97	17	26	.268	1950	117	22	43	.368
1951	109	20	40	.367	1951	113	26	43	.381
1952	114	26	39	.342	1952	109	23	35	.321
1953	111	23	37	.333	1953	105	25	38	.362
1954	100	19	27	.270	1954	113	22	38	.336
1955	111	21	36	.324	1955	115	22	31	.270
1956	110	14	35	.318	1956	110	17	39	.355
1957	113	18	39	.345	1957	111	19	31	.279
1958	93	15	24	.258	1958	95	9	28	.295
1959	60	9	19	.317	1959	62	5	17	.234
1960	27	1	9	.333	1960	71	13	25	.352
1961	81	13	26	.321	1961	70	6	17	.243
1962	80	11	29	.363	1962	68	11	27	.397
1963	45	4	14	.311	1963	60	5	13	.217
Totals	1951	350	652	.334	Totals	2173	378	712	.3276

	HIS AUGUST RECORD					HIS SEPTEMBER RECORD			
YEAR	AB	R	H	AVG.	YEAR	AB	R	H	AVG.
1941	0	0	0	.000	1941	47	8	20	.426
1942	96	19	29	.302	1942	90	12	28	.311
1943	129	23	51	.395	1943	103	20	39	.379
1944	107	23	35	.327	1944	76	11	21	.276
1946	119	25	48	.403	1946	117	22	43	.350
1947	129	32	41	.318	1947	102	15	42	.411
1948	138	31	48	.348	1948	95	20	35	.368
1949	121	27	46	.380	1949	105	29	43	.410
1950	109	18	39	.358	1950	99	17	29	.293
1951	108	22	34	.315	1951	116	24	39	.336
1952	116	17	39	.336	1952	97	18	34	.351
1953	109	27	36	.330	1953	113	27	48	.425
1954	117	23	43	.368	1954	90	11	23	.256
1955	104	16	33	.317	1955	80	14	33	.413
1956	132	14	36	.273	1956	102	17	31	.304
1957	85	14	33	.388	1957	34	7	17	.500
1958	96	15	32	.333	1958	44	3	13	.295
1959	64	5	15	.234	1959	28	6	6	.214
1960	75	11	19	.253	1960	62	8	14	.226
1961	59	8	14	.237	1961	64	9	21	.323
1962	76	5	20	.263	1962	93	12	30	.323
1963	39	1	6	.154	1963	67	9	20	.299
Totals	2128	376	697	.3275		1824	319	627	.344

	HIS OCTOBER RECORD			
YEAR	AB	R	H	AVG.
1943	4	1	2	.500
1944	9	4	6	.667
1946	8	3	2	.250
1948	11	2	4	.364
1949	10	2	5	.500
1950	3	1	1	.333
1960	2	0	1	.500
1961	1	0	0	.000
Totals	48	13	21	.438

BATTING RECORD, STAN MUSIAL, IN DAY AND NIGHT GAMES
(Twilight games are considered night games)

YEAR	MUSIAL BY DAY					MUSIAL AT NIGHT					SEASON RECORD				
	G	AB	R	H	AVG.	G	AB	R	H	AVG.	G	AB	R	H	AVG.
1941	12	47	8	20	.426	—	—	—	—	—	12	47	8	20	.426
1942	119	401	80	125	.312	21	66	7	22	.333	140	467	87	147	.315
1943	133	525	98	196	.373	24	92	10	24	.261	157	617	108	220	.357
1944	99	384	82	131	.341	17	184	30	66	.359	146	568	112	197	.347
1946	102	412	83	161	.391	54	212	41	67	.316	156	624	124	228	.365
1947	89	361	66	107	.296	60	226	47	76	.336	149	587	113	183	.312
1948	92	373	76	135	.362	63	238	59	95	.399	155	611	135	230	.376
1949	86	337	73	108	.320	71	275	55	99	.360	157	612	128	207	.338
1950	73	285	60	108	.379	73	270	45	84	.311	146	555	105	192	.346
1951	74	286	66	113	.395	78	292	58	92	.315	152	578	124	205	.355
1952	70	260	44	93	.358	84	318	61	101	.318	154	578	105	194	.336
1953	70	268	58	95	.354	87	325	69	105	.323	157	593	127	200	.337
1954	71	272	66	89	.327	82	319	54	106	.332	153	591	120	195	.330
1955	70	264	44	82	.311	84	298	53	97	.326	154	562	97	179	.319
1956	80	313	53	97	.310	76	281	34	87	.310	156	594	87	184	.310
1957	65	252	46	91	.361	69	250	36	85	.340	134	502	82	176	.351
1958	64	216	39	70	.324	71	256	25	89	.348	135	472	64	159	.337
1959	51	152	17	44	.289	64	189	20	43	.227	115	341	37	87	.255
1960	45	111	15	29	.261	71	220	34	62	.282	116	331	49	91	.275
1961	52	143	11	38	.266	71	229	35	69	.301	123	372	46	107	.288
1962	53	172	34	65	.376	82	261	23	78	.299	135	433	57	143	.330
1963	64	167	13	14	.246	60	170	21	45	.265	124	337	34	86	.255
Totals	1634	6001	1132	2038	.340	1392	4971	817	1592	.320	3026	10972	1949	3630	.331

BATTING RECORD OF STAN MUSIAL AGAINST EACH OPPONENT

OPPONENT	G	AB	R	H	AVG.
Boston	217	830	160	293	.353
New York	349	1266	245	442	.349
Brooklyn	330	1233	266	424	.344
Pittsburgh	425	1544	274	525	.340
Philadelphia	417	1549	297	523	.338
Los Angeles	102	298	34	98	.329
Cincinnati	427	1570	274	499	.318
Chicago	424	1554	253	493	.317
San Francisco	99	311	42	95	.305
Milwaukee	209	738	97	221	.299
Houston	27	79	7	17	.215
Totals	3026	10972	1949	3630	.331

BATTING RECORD OF STAN MUSIAL AT HOME

OPPONENT	G	AB	R	H	AVG.
Boston	109	392	79	141	.360
Philadelphia	208	741	150	266	.359
New York	178	636	112	226	.355
Pittsburgh	210	744	145	254	.341
Brooklyn	165	604	124	200	.331
Chicago	220	794	145	259	.326
Cincinnati	215	781	137	251	.323
Milwaukee	105	367	54	114	.311
Los Angeles	52	135	20	43	.311
San Francisco	50	167	26	51	.305
Houston	12	41	4	10	.244
Totals	1524	5402	999	1815	.336

BATTING RECORD OF STAN MUSIAL ON ROAD

OPPONENT	G	AB	R	H	AVG.
Brooklyn	165	629	142	224	.356
Boston	108	438	81	152	.347
New York	171	630	133	216	.343
Pittsburgh	215	800	129	271	.339
Los Angeles	50	163	14	55	.337
Philadelphia	209	808	147	257	.318
Cincinnati	212	789	137	248	.314
Chicago	204	760	108	234	.308
San Francisco	49	144	16	44	.306
Milwaukee	104	371	40	107	.288
Houston	15	38	3	7	.184
Totals	1502	5570	950	1815	.326

NOTE: Through a fantastic coincidence, Musial, in his entire career, made exactly as many hits, 1,815, at home as he did on the road.

BATTING RECORD OF STAN MUSIAL AT VARIOUS PLAYING POSITIONS

Before making a detailed breakdown, consider the batting work of Musial as an outfielder, first baseman and pinch-hitter.

POSITION	G	AB	R	H	AVG.
Outfield	1905	7125	1295	2392	.336
First Base	982	3733	649	1208	.324
Pinch-hitter	139	114	5	30	.263
Totals	3026	10972	1949	3630	.331

It is immediately apparent that the decision to move Musial to first base at the height of his career cost him numerous points of batting percentage.

Here are some detailed statistics pertaining to his batting while playing the three outfield positions:

POSITION	G	AB	R	H	AVG.
Left field	907	3332	583	1098	.330
Center field	299	1155	227	399	.345
Right field	699	2638	485	895	.339
Totals	1905	7125	1295	2392	.336

The above figures include games in which Musial played more than one outfield position. Since the shifts in those games, which were few, occurred usually in the late innings, he is shown at the position at which he started the game.

Here is his complete breakdown by positions, and the first position listed is the one at which he started the game:

POSITION	G	AB	R	H	AVG.
1B-CF	1	5	3	3	.600
1B-LF	1	2	0	1	.500
RF-LF	14	47	13	22	.468
RF-CF	16	66	18	31	.467
PH-1B	6	7	3	3	.429
CF-RF	77	310	82	127	.410
LF-RF	11	43	11	17	.396
CF-1B	4	17	2	6	.353
RF	648	2458	447	828	.337
CF-P	1	3	0	1	.333
LF	877	3224	566	1063	.330
CF	207	784	136	253	.323
LF-CF	13	51	6	16	.314
CF-LF	10	41	7	12	.293
PH	139	114	5	30	.263
RF-1B	16	62	7	14	.226
1B-RF	4	18	1	4	.222
PH-LF	10	15	0	2	.133
LF-1B	1	4	0	0	.000
Totals	3026	10972	1949	3630	.331

BATTING RECORD OF STAN MUSIAL UNDER EACH OF HIS MANAGERS

MANAGER	G	AB	R	H	AVG.
Marion, Martin W. 1951	152	578	124	205	.355
Dyer, Edwin H. 1946–50	763	2989	605	1040	.348
Southworth, Wm. H. 1941–44	455	1699	315	584	.344
Stanky, Edward R. 1952–55	500	1900	374	631	.332
Hutchinson, Fred C. 1956–58	418	1540	231	510	.331
Walker, Harry W. 1955	118	424	75	137	.323
Hack, Stanley C. 1958	7	28	2	9	.321
Keane, John J. 1961–63	321	950	112	278	.293
Hemus, Solomon J. 1959–61	292	864	111	236	.273
Totals	3026	10972	1949	3630	.331

Bob Gibson

BOB GIBSON—CAREER RECORD

YEAR	CLUB	W	L	ERA	G	GS	CG	IP	H	R	ER	BB	SO
1957	Omaha	2	1	4.29	10	4	0	42	46	26	20	27	25
	Columbus	4	3	3.77	8	8	2	43	36	26	18	34	24
1958	Omaha	3	4	3.51	13	11	2	87	79	45	32	39	47
	Rochester	5	5	2.45	20	11	7	103	88	35	28	54	75
1959	Omaha	9	9	3.07	24	18	10	135	128	59	46	46	98
	St. Louis	3	5	3.22	13	9	2	76	77	35	28	39	48
1960	Rochester	2	3	2.85	6	6	3	41	33	15	13	17	36
	St. Louis	3	6	5.39	27	6	2	87	97	61	54	48	69
1961	St. Louis	13	12	3.24	35	27	10	211	186	91	76	119	166
1962	St. Louis	15	13	2.85	32	30	15	234	174	84	74	95	208
1963	St. Louis	18	9	3.39	36	33	14	255	224	110	96	96	204
1964	St. Louis	19	12	3.01	40	36	17	287	250	106	96	86	245
1965	St. Louis	20	12	3.07	38	36	20	299	243	110	102	103	270
1966	St. Louis	21	12	2.44	35	35	20	280	210	90	76	78	225
1967	St. Louis	13	7	2.98	24	24	10	175	151	62	58	40	147
1968	St. Louis	22	9	1.12	34	34	28	305	198	49	38	62	268
1969	St. Louis	20	13	2.18	35	35	28	314	251	84	76	95	269
1970	St. Louis	23	7	3.12	34	34	23	294	262	111	102	88	274
1971	St. Louis	16	13	3.04	31	31	20	246	215	96	83	76	185
1972	St. Louis	19	11	2.46	34	34	23	278	226	83	76	88	208
1973	St. Louis	12	10	2.77	25	25	13	195	159	71	60	57	142
1974	St. Louis	11	13	3.83	33	33	9	240	236	111	102	104	129
1975	St. Louis	3	10	5.04	22	14	1	109	120	66	61	62	60
MAJOR TOTALS		251	174	2.92	528	482	255	3884	3279	1420	1258	1336	3117

GIBSON—WORLD SERIES RECORD

YEAR	CLUB	W	L	ERA	G	GS	CG	IP	H	R	ER	BB	SO
1964	St. Louis	2	1	3.00	3	3	2	27	23	11	9	8	31
1967	St. Louis	3	0	1.00	3	3	3	27	14	3	3	5	26
1968	St. Louis	2	1	1.67	3	3	3	27	18	5	5	4	35
SERIES TOTALS		7	2	1.89	9	9	8	81	55	19	17	17	92

YEAR	CLUB	W	L	ERA	IP	H	R	ER	BB	SO
1962	National (2nd game)	0	0	4.50	2	1	1	1	2	1
1965	National	0	0	0.00	2	2	0	0	1	3
1967	National	0	0	0.00	2	2	0	0	0	2
1969	National	0	0	9.00	1	2	1	1	1	2
1970	National	0	0	9.00	2	3	2	2	1	2
1972	National	0	0	0.00	2	1	0	0	0	0
ALL-STAR TOTALS		0	0	3.27	11	11	4	4	5	10

GIBSON AS A HITTER

YEAR	AVG.	AB	R	H	2B	3B	HR	RBI	BB	SO	SB
1959	.115	26	1	3	2	0	0	1	0	10	0
1960	.179	28	4	5	1	0	0	1	0	7	0
1961	.197	66	4	13	5	0	1	10	3	23	0
1962	.263	76	11	20	0	0	2	5	4	28	0
1963	.207	87	12	18	3	1	3	20	8	35	0
1964	.156	96	8	15	3	1	0	4	3	38	0
1965	.240	104	14	25	2	0	5	19	3	26	2
1966	.200	100	11	20	4	0	1	8	3	35	3
1967	.133	60	7	8	0	0	0	3	8	26	0
1968	.170	94	3	16	5	0	0	6	7	32	1
1969	.246	118	11	29	6	0	1	8	3	36	5
1970	.303	109	14	33	3	1	2	19	8	25	0
1971	.172	87	5	15	0	1	2	10	3	24	1
1972	.194	103	12	20	6	0	5	12	1	25	0
1973	.185	65	8	12	0	0	2	8	3	17	1
1974	.210	81	6	17	4	1	0	6	3	19	0
1975	.179	28	1	5	0	0	0	4	3	9	0
Totals	.206	1328	132	274	44	5	24	144	63	415	13

GIBSON'S MAJOR LEAGUE AND NATIONAL LEAGUE RECORDS

MAJOR LEAGUE RECORDS HELD:

Lowest earned run average, 300 or more innings, season—1.12, 1968.

Lowest earned run average, 300 or more innings, right-handed pitcher—1.12, 1968.

Most clubs shut out (won or tied), one season (10-club league)—8, 1968.

Most years 200 or more strikeouts—9.

Most consecutive starting assignments—303, 8/31/65 thru 5/31/75.

MAJOR LEAGUE RECORDS SHARED:

Most strikeouts, inning—4, 1966.

Three strikeouts, inning, on 9 pitched balls.

Most consecutive strikeouts, start of game (Since 1900)—5, 1967.

NATIONAL LEAGUE RECORDS HELD:

Lowest earned run average, 200 or more innings, season—1.12, 1968.

NATIONAL LEAGUE RECORD SHARED:

Most shutout games won or tied, one month—5, 1968.

TEN OR MORE STRIKEOUT GAMES (72 times):

10 K's — 26 times	14 K's — twice
11 K's — 18 times	15 K's — twice
12 K's — 13 times	*16 K's — once
13 K's — 10 times	*Regular season high vs. Philadelphia 5/23/71

LOW HIT COMPLETE GAMES (3 hits or less):
1 no-hitter
2 one-hitters
8 two-hitters
24 three-hitters

THE WILD RACE — 1964

	CARDINALS Result	GB	REDLEGS Result	GB	PHILLIES Result	GB
Sept.						
21	No Game	6	W (Phils, 1–0)	5½	L (Reds, 1–0	—
22	W (Mets, 2–1)	5	W (Phils, 9–2)	4½	L (Reds, 9–2)	—
23	L (Mets, 2–1)	5	W (Phils, 6–4)	3½	L (Reds, 6–4)	—
24	W (Pir. 4–2)	4	No Game		L Braves, 5–3)	—
	W (Pir. 4–0)	3½				
25	W (Pir. 5–3)	2½	W (Mets, 3–0)	2	L (Braves, 7–5)	—
			W (Mets, 4–1)	1½		
26	W (Pir. 6–3)	1½	W (Mets, 6–1)	½	L (Braves, 6–4)	—
27	W (Pir. 5–0)	1½	W (Mets, 4–1)	—	L (Braves, 14–8)	1
			W (Mets, 3–1)	—		
28	W (Phils, 5–1)	1	No Game	—	L (Cards, 5–1)	1½
29	W (Phils, 4–2)	—	L (Pir. 2–0)	—	L (Cards, 4–2)	1½
30	W (Phils, 8–5)	—	L (Pir. 1–0)	1	L (Cards, 8–5)	2½
Oct.						
1	No Game		W (Pir. 5–4)	½	No Game	2½
2	L (Mets, 1–0)	—	L (Phils, 4–3)	½	W (Reds, 4–3)	1½
3	L (Mets, 15–5)	—	No Game	—	No Game	1
4	W (Mets, 11–5)	—	L (Phils, 10–0)	1	W (Reds, 10–0)	1

A day-by-day account of the hectic last two weeks, including the standing at the close of each day's activity, follows:

Sept. 21 Phillies' Art Mahaffey dropped 1–0 duel to John Tsitouris   Phila. 90–61
and Reds on Chico Ruiz' theft of home in sixth inning.   Cincy. 84–66
Cardinals were enjoying an open date in their schedule.   St. L. 83–66
Giants bowed to four-hitter by Colts' Ken Johnson, 3–1.   San F. 83–68

Sept. 22 Jumping on Chris Short for four runs in third inning,   Phila. 90–62
Reds whipped Phillies, 9–2, behind lefty Jim O'Toole.   Cincy. 85–66
Cardinals edged Mets, 2–1, on Curt Simmons' six-hitter.   St. L. 84–66
Giants' Dick Estelle gained first triumph, 7–1, over Colts. San F. 84–68

Sept. 23 Vada Pinson walloped two homers, good for four runs, as Phila. 90–63
Reds completed three-game sweep over Phillies, 6–4.   Cincy. 86–66
Cards muffed chance when Mets beat ex-mate Craig, 2–1. St. L. 84–67
Marichal won No. 20 as Giants breezed, 3–1, at Houston. San F. 85–68

Sept. 24 Braves beat Jim Bunning, 5–3, as Joe Torre had three RBIs. Phila. 90–64
While Reds and Giants had day off, Cards swept twin-bill Cincy. 86–66
at Pittsburgh, 4–2 and 4–0, behind Bob Gibson and Ray St. L. 86–67
Sadecki, but were still 3½ back with only 9 games left. San F. 85–68

Sept. 25 Phillies dropped fifth in row, 7–5 in 12 innings to Braves. Phila. 90–65
Maloney and Purkey led Reds to 3–0, 4–1 wins in New York. Cincy. 88–66
Although held to four hits, Cards edged Pittsburgh, 5–3. St. L. 87–67
Giants won at Chicago, 3–1, on Jim Perry's three-hitter. San F. 86–68

Sept. 26 Braves edged Phils, 6–4, on Carty's three-run triple in ninth. Phila. 90–66
Reds only half game out after Tsitouris downed Mets, 6–1. Cincy. 89–66
Simmons pitched Cardinals to 6–3 victory at Pittsburgh. St. L. 88–67
Giants' contest at Chicago was postponed due to rain. San F. 86–68

Sept. 27 Reds gained lead when O'Toole and Jay beat Mets, 4–1, 3–1. Cincy. 91–66
Despite Callison's three homers, Phils lost to Braves, 13–8. Phila. 90–67
Craig completed Cards' five-game sweep at Pittsburgh, 5–0. St. L. 89–67
Giants' hopes dipped when Cubs won twin-bill, 4–1, 4–2. San F. 86–70

Sept. 28 While Reds and Giants enjoyed a day off, Phillies opened Cincy. 91–66
series in St. Louis, where Bob Gibson outpitched Chris St. L. 90–67
Short, 5–1. Victory marked Cardinals' sixth in a row, Phila. 90–68
while defeat was eighth straight for Philadelphians. San F. 86–70

Sept. 29 Cardinals tied Reds for first place when Ray Sadecki de- St. L. 91–67
feated Phillies, 4–2, while Pirates' Bob Friend bested Cincy. 91–67
Bill McCool with 11-hit shutout, 2–0, to halt Red spurt. Phila. 90–69
Giants beat Colts, 5–4, on Matty Alou's homer in eleventh. San F. 87–70

Sept. 30 Cards capped sweep of Phil series behind Simmons, 8–5. St. L. 92–67
Stranding 18 batters, Reds lost 16-inning thriller to Pirates, Cincy. 91–68
1–0; squeeze bunt by rookie Jerry May scored lone run. Phila. 90–70
Giants stayed in race by nipping Colts in 11 innings, 2–1. San F. 88–70

Oct. 1 With Cardinals and Phillies both idle, Reds galloped to St. L. 92–67
within half game of lead by edging Pirates, 5–4, as Cincy. 92–68
sub catcher Jim Coker rapped homer, double and single. Phila. 90–70
Marichal kept Giant hopes alive by whipping Colts, 6–3. San F. 89–70

Oct. 2 Mets halted Cardinals' eight-game winning streak when Al St. L. 92–68
Jackson tossed five-hit sparkler to best Bob Gibson, 1–0. Cincy. 92–69
Phils ended ten-game losing skein by edging Reds, 4–3. Phila. 91–70
Giants whipped Cubs, 9–0, behind Bob Bolin's three-hitter. San F. 90–70

Oct. 3 Cincinnati, enjoying day off, tied Cardinals for first place St. L. 92–69
when Mets unloaded 17 hits to wallop Redbirds, 15–5; Cincy. 92–69
idle Phillies still had a chance at three-way pennant tie. Phila. 91–70
Cubs knocked Giants from race by winning 10–7 slugfest. San F. 90–71

Oct. 4 Cardinals rebounded to trim Mets, 11–5, and win pennant St. L. 93–69
when Phils wrecked Reds' hopes by whipping them, 10–0, Cincy. 92–70
behind Jim Bunning's pitching, Richie Allen's slugging. Phila. 92–70
Giants dropped season finale to Cubs' Larry Jackson, 9–2. San F. 90–72

DID YOU KNOW
THAT?

Did You Know . . .

That Mickey Owen (C, 1937–40) married a 17-year-old beauty queen of Southern California, Florence Taylor, December 24, 1937?

That Jersey Joe Stripp (3B, 1938) believed that he could end a batting slump by sticking a wad of chewing gum on the bottom of his cap?

That Lon Warneke (P, 1937–42) umpired in the National League from 1949 through 1955?

That in 1953, Card pitcher Clyde Shoun pitched in 53 ball games, two of them starts, and didn't have a complete game to his credit?

That Ethan Allen (OF, 1933) wrote two books, *Major League Baseball* in 1938 and *Winning Baseball,* in addition to creating the popular "All-Star Baseball" game, based on lifetime records, a game that is still popular today?

That the 1965 Cardinals, dwellers of seventh place, were the first club in major-league history to fall so low after being World Champions the previous year?

That the St. Louis National League team officially became the Cardinals in 1899 when *St. Louis Republic* sportswriter William McHale referred to them by the nickname because they had changed striping on their uniforms from Brown to Cardinal Red?

That Johnny Hopp's daughter, Terrill, was born on the day he played his first major-league game and got a hit in his first at-bat against Brooklyn pitcher Luke Hamlin in 1939?

That Pete Whisenant was the first major-leaguer to pinch-hit twice for Stan Musial, in 1955?

That the Cardinals held their first Ladies Day during the 1917 season, the sixth major-league club to adopt the practice?

That George Toporcer (1921–1928) was the first major-league infielder to wear glasses?

That pitcher Al Jurisich was the first Cardinal to return to baseball after serving in the Armed Forces, gaining an honorable discharge in 1943?

That the Cardinals were the first major-league club to utilize a farm system, started in the 1920s?

That the Cardinals began wearing numbers on their sleeves in 1924?

That pitcher Les Meadows was the second player in the major leagues to wear glasses (1915)?

That first baseman Rip Collins, a member in good standing of the Gashouse Gang, never threw away broken bats, always bringing them home and later converting them to a fence for the front of his home?

That the Cards were the first team to fly, winging from Boston to Chicago in 1938?

That Giant pitcher Phil Douglas was one of the first players banned from baseball for gambling? In 1922, the young right-hander, who enjoyed drinking, was chewed out by manager John McGraw one day in front of the entire ball club following one of his binges. Still in a muddled frame of mind, Douglas wrote a letter to Les Mann of the Cards, suggesting that he could "go fishing for the rest of the season" if the price was right. That would have made it easier for the Cards to capture their first pennant (they didn't anyway). Later, in command of his faculties, Douglas phoned Mann and asked that the letter be destroyed. Unfortunately for Douglas, Mann had shown the letter to manager Branch Rickey, who notified Judge Kenesaw Mountain Landis, commissioner of baseball. Confronted with the evidence, Douglas confessed, and was banished from the game for life.

That in 1933 and 1934, infielder Charlie Gelbert was on the voluntarily retired list, because of a leg injury incurred by accidentally shooting himself while hunting?

That one man, Harrison "Doc" Weaver acted as Cardinal trainer from 1927 to 1955, a 29-season span?

That Leo Ward was traveling secretary for 35 years, from 1937 through 1971?

That Morris "Butch" Yatkeman, who began as a batboy in 1924 and became full-time clubhouse man in 1932 is still on the job, giving him 59 seasons with the Cardinals, through 1982?

That Ed Kazak is the only Cardinal in history whose name is the same spelled backwards: KAZAK?

That the first Cardinal captain, in 1876, was first baseman Harmon Dehlman?

That in St. Louis' first year in the majors, 1876, it had a 45–19 record, the same as its top pitcher, George Washington Bradley, who won 45 and lost 19?

That the name Schoendienst means "Beautiful servant," translated from German to English?

CARDINALS IN THE HALL OF FAME

Grover Cleveland Alexander	Elected 1938, Baseball Writers Assn.
Jake Beckley	Named 1971, Committee on Veterans
Jim Bottomley	Named 1974, Committee on Veterans
Roger Bresnahan	Named 1945, Old Timers Committee
Mordecai Brown	Named 1949, Old Timers Committee
Jesse Burkett	Named 1948, Old Timers Committee
Roger Connor	Named 1976, Committee on Veterans
Dizzy Dean	Elected 1953, Baseball Writers Assn.
Frank Frisch	Elected 1947, Baseball Writers Assn.
Pud Galvin	Named 1965, Committee on Veterans
Bob Gibson	Elected 1981, Baseball Writers Assn.
Burleigh Grimes	Named 1964, Committee on Veterans
Chick Hafey	Named 1971, Committee on Veterans
Jesse Haines	Named 1970, Committee on Veterans
Rogers Hornsby	Elected 1942, Baseball Writers Assn.
Miller Huggins	Named 1964, Committee on Veterans
Rabbit Maranville	Elected 1954, Baseball Writers Assn.
John McGraw	Named 1937, Centennial Commission
Bill McKechnie	Named 1962, Committee on Veterans
Joe Medwick	Elected 1968, Baseball Writers Assn.
Johnny Mize	Named 1981, Committee on Veterans
Stan Musial	Elected 1969, Baseball Writers Assn.

Kid Nichols	Named 1949, Old Timers Committee
Branch Rickey	Named 1967, Committee on Veterans
Wilbert Robinson	Named 1945, Old Timers Committee
Dazzy Vance	Elected 1955, Baseball Writers Assn.
Cy Young	Elected 1937, Baseball Writers Assn.

AND TWO WHO SHOULD BE:

Lou Brock and Enos Slaughter

Grover Cleveland Alexander, Pitcher, 1926-1929

When the Cardinals acquired the 39-year-old right-hander from the Chicago Cubs on waivers June 22, 1926, many of the so-called experts felt the deal was a waste of good money. After all, they reasoned, his best days were behind him. And besides, he couldn't even win the biggest fight—over alcohol. What made him think he could win?

The critics were silenced in Pete's first start as a Cardinal, a four-hit, 3-2 decision over the Cubs in 10 innings June 27, 1926. He finished the season with 12 victories, and went on to post 21 wins in 1927, 16 in 1928, and nine in 1929.

Alex's biggest contribution to the Cardinals came in the seventh and deciding game of the 1928 World Series. Relieving Jesse Haines in the seventh inning with the bases loaded and two out, he struck out Yankee shortstop Tony Lazzeri on four pitches and didn't allow a hit the rest of the way, earning a save as the Cards won their first World Series in their first try. Alex also pitched in two contests in the 1928 Series, one the Yankees took 4-0.

The Cards traded Alex to Philadelphia December 11, 1929, with catcher Harry McCurdy for outfielder Homer Peel and pitcher Bob McGraw.

Alexander was elected to the Hall of Fame in 1938, with a lifetime record of 373-208. He was named to the all-time St. Louis team by the St. Louis chapter of the Baseball Writers Association in 1958. He died in poverty at St. Paul, Mn., his birthplace, November 4, 1950, at age 63.

Jake Beckley, First Baseman, 1904-1907

St. Louis was the last stop for the great first baseman, who began his career with Pittsburgh in 1888. The Cardinals purchased him from Cincinnati in 1904.

At the time of his trade, Beckley was one of only three players (Monte Cross of the Athletics and John Titus of the Phillies were the others) to still sport a handlebar mustache.

In his four years with St. Louis, Beckley hit .280.

He died June 25, 1918 in his birthplace of Hannibal, Mo. He was named to the Hall of Fame in 1971.

Jim Bottomley, First Baseman, 1922-1932

Sunny Jim was one of the first products of the Cardinal farm system, recalled from Syracuse in the International League near the end of the 1922 season.

Bottomley's best year with the Redbirds came in 1925, when he hit .367, and led the National League in hits with 227 and doubles with 44. In 1928, he had his best all-around year, leading the league with 20 triples and 136 RBI, and hitting 31 homers to share the title with Hack Wilson of the Cubs, while batting .325. The year earned him Most Valuable Player honors.

His greatest single game performance came September 26, 1924 against Brooklyn as he got six hits and a record 12 RBI.

With Rip Collins ready to take over the first base chores, Jim was sent to Cincinnati for pitcher Owen Carroll and outfielder Estel Crabtree December 17, 1932.

337

Bottomley died December 11, 1959 of a heart attack in a parking lot in St. Louis. He was named to the Hall of Fame in 1974.

Roger Bresnahan, Catcher, Manager, 1909–1912

Another player the Cardinals got in the twilight of his career, Roger was obtained in December 1908 from the New York Giants for pitcher Bugs Raymond, outfielder John Murray, and catcher George Schlei. The Cards got Schlei from Cincinnati for pitchers Art Fromme and Eddie Karger.

The Cards used him as combination catcher-manager from 1908 to 1912, when they sold him to the Chicago Cubs after a long contract squabble.

Bresnahan died in his hometown Toledo December 4, 1944. He was named to the Hall of Fame a year later.

Mordecai Brown, Pitcher, 1903

Three-Finger Brown was 9–13 in his first major-league year with the Cardinals in 1903. They traded him to Chicago with catcher Jack O'Neill for pitcher Jack Taylor following that year. All he did was win 199 more games in the majors.

Called Three-Finger because an accident with a corn chopper at age seven chopped off half of his right index finger and left his thumb and middle finger badly mauled. The injury and grip on a baseball caused Brown's pitches to sink naturally.

He died in Terre Haute, Ind., February 14, 1948 and was named to the Hall of Fame a year later.

Jesse Burkett, Outfielder, 1899–1901

Jesse came to St. Louis in 1899, when the Cleveland Spiders folded. He hit .402 his first year with the team, the third time he bettered the magic mark, and .361 and .382 the next two years, the latter a National League-leading total.

He jumped to the St. Louis Browns in 1902, with whom he spent three of his last four years in baseball.

The Crab died in Worcester, Mass., May 27, 1953. He was named to the Hall of Fame in 1946 and commented, "It took them long enough, and I thought they weren't going to pick me because everybody forgot about me."

Roger Connor, First Baseman, 1894–1897

Connor came to the then Browns in 1894 at the advanced age of 37 and finished his career in a St. Louis uniform.

His biggest day as a Cardinal came June 1, 1895 against the New York Giant team that traded him. He went six for six with two doubles and a triple in a 23–8 rout.

He died January 4, 1931 in his hometown Waterbury, Ct. He was named to the Hall of Fame in 1976.

Dizzy Dean, Pitcher, 1930, 1932–1937

Christened Jay Hanna Dean on January 16, 1911, he changed his name to Jerome Herman some years later out of respect for the son of a neighbor who had died. No matter, he was Dizzy to St. Louisans and the rest of the baseball world.

A member in good standing in the Cardinals Gashouse Gang, Dizzy lived up to his nickname off the field. On it, he made opposing batters dizzy.

He won 20 or more games in four of his seven Cardinal campaigns, including an unbelievable 30–7 in 1934, the year brother Paul, or Daffy as he was known, broke into the big show with the Redbirds. Paul won an amazing 19 games that year, giving the Brothers Dean a 49–18 combined mark.

The only honor to elude Dizzy was a no-hitter, a feat brother Paul got September 21 of his rookie year in the second game of a twin bill against Brooklyn. Brother Dizzy, who posted a three-hitter in the opener, said, "If I'd have known Paul was gonna do it, I would have, too."

Prior to the 1934 Series against Detroit, Dizzy predicted that he and Paul would each win two games to lead the Cardinals to the crown. They did just that, Dizzy taking games one and seven, brother Paul games three and six.

He was traded to the Cubs in 1938, and remained in baseball until 1941. He came back for another try with the Browns in 1947, and pitched four shutout innings in his appearance. He went on to become a popular broadcaster, and was elected to the Hall of Fame in 1963. He died of a heart attack in Reno, Nev., July 17, 1974.

Frank Frisch, Infielder, Manager, 1927–1937

If there was a captain of the Gashouse Gang Cardinal teams of the 1930s, it was the colorful Fordham Flash.

Obtained with pitcher Jimmy Ring for second baseman Rogers Hornsby from New York December 20, 1926, he went on to miss the National League Most Valuable Player Award by just one vote in his initial Redbird campaign.

He hit the first two homers in All-Star game history for the National League in 1933 and 1934.

In the first year of Most Valuable Player Award voting by the Baseball Writers' Association in 1931, Frisch copped the prize.

He managed the Cards from 1933 through 1938, winning a league pennant and subsequent World Series in 1942.

He was elected to the Hall of Fame in 1947, while serving as a New York Giant radio announcer.

Frisch was badly injured in an auto accident February 8, 1973 and died March 12 in Wilmington, Del.

James "Pud" Galvin, Pitcher, 1892

"Pud" spent the final season of his illustrious career with St. Louis in 1892. Although he was a disappointing 5–6 for the Redbirds, he ended with a career mark of 361–309.

He died in poverty in Pittsburgh March 7, 1902. He was named to the Hall of Fame in 1965.

Bob Gibson, Pitcher, 1959–1975

There have been few pitchers in history that have left their mark like Bob Gibson. But in the beginning, it wasn't that easy.

After appearing in Cardinal livery for the first time in 1959, Gibby finally found a pitching groove in 1961. From then on, he won 20 games five times and captured Cy Young honors in 1968 and 1970. His 1.12 ERA led the majors in 1968.

His greatest career accomplishment was career 3,117 strikeouts, one of the top five figures in baseball history.

Gibby was also a fair country hitter, belting 24 regular season home runs in a 17-year career, and hitting home runs in the 1967 and 1968 World Series.

In the 1967 classic, Gibby returned after suffering a broken leg July 15 to win three complete games against Boston, en route to the championship.

He won the Most Valuable Player Award in the 1964 and 1967 World Series.

A dismal 3–10 year in 1975 prompted his retirement. He was elected to the Hall of Fame in 1981.

Burleigh Grimes, Pitcher, 1930-1931, 1933-1934

Old Stubblebeard averaged 10 wins per season in his four with St. Louis, ending his career with a 270-212 record in the majors.

His most memorable moment as a Cardinal came in 1931, when he played the final seven weeks of the season and the World Series with an ice pack taped to his stomach, refusing to give in to an inflamed appendix.

He was traded to the Cubs for Hack Wilson and Art Teachout the following December.

Burleigh was named to the Hall of Fame in 1964.

Chick Hafey, Outfielder, 1924-1931

Chick made the Cardinals on a tryout in spring training 1923, when he showed up as a pitcher. Branch Rickey noticed his batting prowess, and converted him to the outfield.

He was constantly having contract disputes with Rickey later in his Card career; the biggest involved a lengthy holdout in 1931. He finally signed a contract 10 days before the season began.

Hafey was constantly feuding with Rickey that year, but it didn't affect his play. He was in a three-way race for the National League batting title with Bill Terry and his roommate and best friend, Jim Bottomley. Hafey wound up with a .3489 mark, besting Terry's .3486, and Bottomley's .3482.

Another contract hassle followed, and Rickey traded the star outfielder to Cincinnati April 11, 1932 for infielder Harvey Hendrick, pitcher Benny Frey, and cash.

Chick was named to the Hall of Fame in 1971, and died in Calistoga, Cal., July 2, 1973 at age 70.

Jesse Haines, Pitcher, 1920-1937

It took $10,000 in borrowed money to get Pops in 1920. But the funds were well spent, as he went on to 210 victories in regular season competition, three in four World Series.

Prior to his Redbird connection, Haines played but one contest in the big leagues, that in 1918 with Cincinnati. Red manager Christy Mathewson, himself a former pitcher, didn't think Haines was big-league material, and dispatched him to the minors the same year.

One of the finest games in Haines' career was a 17-inning loss to Chicago's Grover Cleveland Alexander 3-2. In that game, Haines pitched 10 hitless innings before being removed.

Pops eventually pitched and won a no-hitter, July 7, 1924 against the Braves 5-0. Unfortunately, his record that year was a dismal 8-19.

His greatest claim to fame came in the 1926 World Series against the Yankees. He relieved Bill Sherdel in the first game and went on to a 2-1 victory, and shut out the Bronx Bombers 4-0 with a five-hitter in Game Three. He also hit a homer in that contest, one of only four in his entire major-league career.

In the late 1930s, Pops became a reliever with a 3-3 record in 1937 prompting him to retire at age 44. He was named to the Hall of Fame in 1970, and died at Dayton, Ohio, August 5, 1978.

Rogers Hornsby, Infielder, Manager, 1915-1926, 1933

One of the greatest hitters of all time, The Rajah gained batting championships in six consecutive years with the Cards, 1920 through 1925. It was the first time

On December 20, 1926, Hornsby's first tenure as a Redbird came to an end when he was dispatched to the New York Giants for Frank Frisch and pitcher Jimmy Ring.

He returned as a free agent in 1933, playing a mere 46 games and hitting .325 before he was named manager of the Browns July 27. He stayed in that position until July 20, 1937, when the Browns let him go.

Elected to the Hall of Fame in 1942, Rogers died in Chicago on January 5, 1963, only two months after an operation for cataracts.

Miller Huggins, Second Baseman, Manager, 1910-1916

Remembered primarily as manager of the great New York Yankee teams of the late 1920s, Huggins came to the Redbirds in February 1910 from the Cincinnati Reds. He finished his career in St. Louis as a player-manager 1913 through 1916, and a final year as skipper in 1917 before the lure of the Yankees offered more than he could get with the Redbirds.

Known as The Rabbit during his Cardinal playing days, Huggins was the personal choice as manager of Mrs. Helene Britton.

When Mrs. Britton was to sell the team in 1916, she offered the little manager an opportunity to buy it. but she reneged on the deal while Huggins was away in Cincinnati raising money.

Huggins managed the Bronx Bombers from 1918 until his death September 25, 1929. He was named to the Hall of Fame in 1964.

James "Rabbit" Maranville, Shortstop, 1927-1928

One of the greatest infielders in National League history, Rabbit made his mark with Boston, Pittsburgh, Chicago, and Brooklyn prior to coming to the Cardinals in 1927 as a replacement for shortstop Tommy Thevenow, who was out with a fractured leg.

His greatest moment as a Redbird came in 1928, when he helped St. Louis into the World Series. He batted .308 in the October classic, but the Cards lost to the mighty Yankees.

St. Louis sold Rabbit to the Braves, his first major-league team, December 8, 1928. He went on to play six seasons, retiring at age 42.

Maranville died of a heart attack January 5, 1954 in Woodside, N.Y. Ironically, he was elected to the Hall of Fame in the same month.

John McGraw, Third Baseman, 1900

Sold to St. Louis by Baltimore in 1899, McGraw batted .337 in 98 games. He jumped to the Baltimore Orioles following his only St. Louis season.

McGraw made his mark in Major League baseball as a manager, piloting the Giants to nine National League flags and three World Championships.

McGraw died at New Rochelle, N.Y., February 25, 1934. He was named to the Hall of Fame in 1937.

Bill McKechnie, Manager, 1928-1929

Although he made most of his headlines elsewhere, Deacon Bill had one year of glory with the Redbirds in 1928.

Cardinal General Manager Branch Rickey named McKechnie skipper for the 1928 campaign, and the Birds posted a 95-59 mark, capturing the National League pennant. The Cards lost the Series to the Yankees in four games, a fact that incensed owner Sam Breadon so much that he banished the quiet McKechnie to

such a feat was accomplished in the National League, and no one has since come close.

His .424 average in 1924 is the highest recorded in the major leagues in modern times.

The Cardinals named Rogers player-manager on June 1, 1925, the team having a 13–25 record at the time. They went on to win 64 and lose 51. For his efforts, Hornsby was named Most Valuable Player, the first Cardinal to receive such honors since the awards were instituted in 1911.

Hornsby guided the Cardinals into their first World Series in 1926, a year they defeated the Yankees. Although he was successful, a disagreement with owner Sam Breadon over an exhibition game led to his being offered only a one-year pact by the club, as opposed to the three-year deal he had sought.

Rochester of the International League, replacing him with Billy Southworth. Eighty-eight games into the 1929 campaign, Breadon reversed the switch.

McKechnie left for the Boston Braves following the 1929 campaign, although he could have stayed in St. Louis.

He was named to the Hall of Fame in 1962, and died in Bradenton, Fla., October 29, 1965.

Joe Medwick, Outfielder, 1932-1940, 1947-1948

Everything was indeed Ducky with the Redbirds of the 1930s, in no small part because of Joe Medwick's contribution.

Medwick was a perfect example of the Gas House Gang style of play, always aggressive, always colorful.

Medwick was probably the only player in baseball history to be removed from a contest by the commissioner. The incident happened in the final game of the 1934 World Series at Detroit, when Tiger fans began throwing bottles at Ducky following a hard, spikes-high slide he took against Tiger third baseman Marv Owen. Commissioner Kenesaw Mountain Landis, who was in the stands, elected to remove Medwick for the outfielder's safety.

Muscles' finest season came in 1937, when he led the Senior Circuit in games, at-bats, runs, hits, doubles, batting average, and runs batted in. He also tied Mel Ott for the league lead in homers with 31, and would have won that honor had a game in which he belted a round-tripper not been forfeited. Medwick led the league outfielders in fielding percentage the same year. For his efforts, Ducky was awarded the Most Valuable Player honors.

Just before the trading deadline in 1940, Ducky was dealt to the Brooklyn Dodgers. He remained there until he was dealt to the rival Giants in 1943, spent 1945 with the Boston Braves, went back to Brooklyn in 1946, and wound up his big-league career with the Cardinals in 1947 and 1948.

Medwick returned to the Cardinals as a minor-league hitting instructor in 1966, and was assisting young Redbirds in training camp when he died of a heart attack March 21, 1975 at age 63. He was elected to the Hall of Fame in 1968, overcoming the unpopularity he had with many baseball people because of his fiery nature.

Johnny Mize, First Baseman-Outfielder, 1936-1941

It took a while, but Big Jawn Mize was finally named to the Baseball Hall of Fame in 1981. The Cardinals were his first big-league club in 1936, but they traded him to the Giants five years later. There, he reaffirmed that he was indeed one of the best-hitting first basemen in National League history.

From a rookie year .329 batting average, Mize hit above .300 each year through 1948, despite spending three seasons in the Navy.

Mize won the National League batting title in 1939 as a Card with a .349 average,

342

took the home run leadership with 28, and missed winning the triple crown by falling 20 RBI short of Frank McCormick of Cincinnati who had 128.

Mize ended his career with the Yankees, competing in the World Series in each of his five years in the Bronx.

Stan Musial, First Baseman-Outfielder, 1941-1963

When you think of the Cardinals, the first name that usually pops into your head is Stan Musial.

A pitcher in the minor leagues, Stan was converted to the outfield by Dickie Kerr while at Daytona Beach in the Florida State League. The transition paid hefty dividends for the Redbirds, who had The Man up at the tail end of the 1941 campaign.

Musial became a regular in 1942 and played a starting role until his retirement in 1963, except for a year in military service.

Stan owned better than 50 National League records at retirement, among them most games played, at-bats, runs scored, hits, and runs batted in. His 475 major-league home runs are still among the tops in baseball history.

Musial also owns most All-Star Game records, playing in 24 such contests. He was named Player of the Decade by *The Sporting News* in 1956, and captured league MVP honors in 1943, 1946, and 1948.

One of his more impressive records was the 895 consecutive games played from April 15, 1952, through August 22, 1957.

In 1962, the 41-year-old grandfather batted .330, good for third place in the National League race.

He announced his retirement during the 1963 campaign, and was one of the few players ever accorded "Day" honors in opposing ball parks. The Cardinals' lasting tribute was a bronze statue outside Busch Memorial Stadium.

Musial stayed in baseball as vice-president of the Cardinals, and he was general manager of the 1967 pennant winners.

He was elected to the Hall of Fame in 1969.

Kid Nichols, Pitcher, 1904-1905

Although Kid pitched only a little over a full season with St. Louis, he left his mark with a 21-13 record in 1904.

Nichols came back for another year as player-manager in 1905, but managed a dismal 1-5 record. In fact, he was replaced as manager in mid-June.

An attack of pleurisy, a sub-par season, and not seeing eye-to-eye with St. Louis management led to his release in July.

With Philadelphia, Kid was 10-6 in 17 games to round out a rather dismal season. And at age 36 in 1906, he pitched his final major-league game for Philadelphia. He ended up with a career won-lost record of 361-208.

He was named to the Hall of Fame in 1949, and died in Kansas City, April 11, 1953 following a severe neck ailment.

Branch Rickey, Manager, Vice-President, Business Manager 1917-1942, 1963-1965

Best known for establishing baseball's first farm system, The Mahatma moved to the Cardinals from the Browns following the 1916 campaign.

He continued with the Redbirds the many innovations, such as Knothole Gangs and Ladies Days that he started with the Browns. Others were batting cages, blackboard teaching, and authorization of the first radio broadcasts of major-league games.

343

He went on to gain greater fame with the Dodgers, being the single person most responsible for breaking baseball's color line with the recall of infielder Jackie Robinson in 1947.

Rickey returned to the Redbirds in a surprise move by owner Busch in 1963 as advisor to Gussie. He resigned the post in October, 1964.

He died December 9, 1965 in Columbia, Mo., and was named to the Hall of Fame in 1967.

Wilbert Robinson, Catcher, 1900

Perhaps best known for his managerial prowess with the Brooklyn Dodgers from 1914 through 1931, Uncle Robbie appeared in a mere 56 games for the 1900 edition of the Cardinals, sporting a .255 average.

He jumped to the Baltimore American League franchise after his year in St. Louis.

He died August 8, 1934 and was named to the Hall of Fame in 1945.

Dazzy Vance, Pitcher, 1933–1934

Although he pitched for the Redbirds a mere two seasons, A.C. Dazzy Vance realized the one ambition he kept missing in his 19-year big-league career, playing in a World Series.

Dazzy pitched one-and-one-third innings of relief in the 1934 classic, striking out three Detroit Tigers, including catcher Mickey Cochrane.

Traded to the Reds in 1934, he ended his career as a relief pitcher.

He was elected to the Hall of Fame in 1955, and died of a heart attack at Homosassa Springs, Fla., February 16, 1961.

Cy Young, Pitcher, 1899–1900

The winningest pitcher of all time, Denton True Young won 46 games in his two seasons with the Cards, 26 in 1899.

Young was signed by the Boston Red Sox of the new American League in 1901. He went on pitching until 1911 at age 44.

Young was elected to the Hall of Fame in 1936, and passed away near Peoli, Ohio, November 4, 1955 at age 88. A year after his death, Commissioner Ford Frick announced that an award bearing Cy Young's name would be presented to the pitcher of the year from then on.

and two who should be:

Lou Brock, Outfielder, 1964–1979

Safe!

Lou Brock heard that word 938 times during his 19-year major-league career, more than any man in history. Brock stole that many bases in his illustrious career, one which began with the Chicago Cubs in 1961.

Brock was obtained by the Cards June 15, 1964 with pitchers Jack Spring and Paul Toth for pitchers Ernie Broglio and Bobby Shantz, and outfielder Doug Clemens. The trade is acknowledged as the best in Cardinal history, the worst for Chicago.

It was no coincidence that the Redbirds won the National League pennant and World Series in Lou's maiden season with them. They also captured pennants in 1967 and 1968, winning the Series in 1967.

In his 16 years in a Cardinal uniform, Brock led the majors in stolen bases six times, the National League eight.

He also established the major-league single-season stolen base record in 1974 with 118. He got his 3,000th career hit August 13, 1979 against the Cubs at St. Louis.

Brock became the first player to have a National League award named after him, a prize given to the top base stealer annually. Frank Taveras won the first Lou Brock Award in 1970.

Lou was named the most memorable personality in Cardinal history in a 1975 fan vote, while stolen base No. 105 of 1974, which broke Maury Wills' single-season record, was judged the most memorable moment.

Retired following the 1979 season, Lou was then named the Fred Hutchinson Award winner, symbolic of the comeback of the year player.

The Hall of Fame doors in Cooperstown will be ready to open in 1985, Lou's first year of eligibility.

Enos Slaughter, Outfielder, 1938–1942, 1946–1953

If ever a man deserved to be in the Hall of Fame, it's Enos Slaughter. The man known as Country batted over .300 in 10 of his 19 major-league seasons, hit 169 career homers, had 1,304 RBI, and played key roles not only for the Cards, but also for the New York Yankees in the twilight of his career.

Slaughter is probably best remembered for two things, his superb defensive play and his "Mad Dash" in the 1946 World Series.

It was game seven at St. Louis and the Cards and Boston Red Sox were tied at three in the bottom of the eighth. Ol' Country led off with a single against Red Sox reliever Bob Klinger and remained on first as Whitey Kurowski popped out and Del Rice flied to left.

Harry Walker hit a line drive over shortstop Johnny Pesky's head into center and Pesky hesitated with Leon Culberson's throw long enough to allow Slaughter to circle the bases with what proved to be the Series winning run.

Slaughter had seven more productive years with the Redbirds before they shipped him to the Yankees April 11, 1954. When informed of the swap at Sportsman's Park, Country broke down and cried. He loved St. Louis and never quite got over the trauma, although he had some fine years in the American League.

His major-league career ended with Milwaukee in 1959, but he played in the minor leagues two more seasons before officially retiring at age 45.

Since that time, Enos has waited for the doors of Cooperstown to open for him.

If ever a man deserved to be in the Hall of Fame, it's Enos Slaughter.

Where They Finished, 1876–1982, As Members of the National League

Year	Position	Won	Lost	Pct.	Attendance	Manager
1876	2	45	19	.703	—	S. Mason Graffen
1877	4	28	32	.467	—	John Lucas, George McManus
1885	8	36	72	.333	—	Henry Lucas
1886	6	43	79	.352	—	Gus Schmelz
1892	11	56	94	.373	—	Chris Von derAhe
1893	10	57	75	.432	—	Bill Watkins
1894	9	56	76	.424	—	George Miller
1895	11	39	92	.298	—	Al Buckenberger, Joe Quinn, Lew Phelan, Chris Von derAhe
1896	11	40	90	.308	—	Chris Von derAhe, Harry Diddledock, Arlie Latham, Roger Connor, Tommy Dowd
1897	12	29	102	.221	—	Chris Von derAhe Tommy Dowd, Hugh Nicol, Bill Hallman
1898	12	39	111	.260	—	Tim Hurst
1899	5	84	67	.556	—	Oliver Tebeau
1900	5+	65	75	.464	—	Oliver Tebeau & Louis Heilbroner
1901	4	76	64	.543	379,988	Patsy Donovan
1902	6	56	78	.418	226,417	Patsy Donovan
1903	8	43	94	.314	263,538	Patsy Donovan
1904	5	75	79	.487	386,750	Charles "Kid" Nichols
1905	6	58	96	.377	292,800	Nichols, Jimmy Burke, Matthew Robison
1906	7	52	98	.347	283,770	John J. McCloskey
1907	8	52	101	.340	185,377	John J. McCloskey
1908	8	49	105	.318	205,129	John J. McCloskey
1909	7	54	98	.355	299,982	Roger Bresnahan
1910	7	63	90	.412	363,624	Roger Bresnahan
1911	5	75	74	.503	447,768	Roger Bresnahan
1912	6	63	90	.412	241,759	Roger Bresnahan
1913	8	51	99	.340	203,531	Miller Huggins
1914	3	81	72	.529	346,025	Miller Huggins
1915	6	72	81	.471	252,657	Miller Huggins
1916	7+	60	93	.392	224,308	Miller Huggins
1917	3	82	70	.539	301,948	Miller Huggins
1918	8	51	78	.395	110,596	Jack Hendricks
1919	7	54	83	.394	173,604	Branch Rickey
1920	5	75	79	.487	325,845	Branch Rickey
1921	3	87	66	.569	384,790	Branch Rickey
1922	3+	85	69	.552	536,343	Branch Rickey
1923	5	79	74	.516	338,548	Branch Rickey
1924	6	65	89	.422	272,884	Branch Rickey

Where They Finished, 1876–1982 (Cont.)

Year	Position	Won	Lost	Pct.	Attendance	Manager
1925	4	77	76	.503	405,297	Rickey & Rogers Hornsby
1926	1*	89	65	.578	681,575	Rogers Hornsby
1927	2	92	61	.601	763,615	Bob O'Farrell
1928	1	95	59	.617	778,147	Bill McKechnie
1929	4	78	74	.513	410,921	McKechnie & Billy Southworth
1930	1	92	62	.597	519,647	Gabby Street
1931	1*	101	53	.656	623,960	Gabby Street
1932	6+	72	82	.468	290,370	Gabby Street
1933	5	82	71	.536	268,404	Street & Frank Frisch
1934	1*	95	58	.621	334,863	Frank Frisch
1935	2	96	58	.623	517,805	Frank Frisch
1936	2+	87	67	.565	457,925	Frank Frisch
1937	4	81	73	.526	443,039	Frank Frisch
1938	6	71	80	.470	295,229	Frisch & Mike Gonzales
1939	2	92	61	.601	410,778	Ray Blades
1940	3	84	69	.549	331,899	Blades, Gonzales & Billy Southworth
1941	2	97	56	.634	642,496	Billy Southworth
1942	1*	106	48	.688	571,626	Billy Southworth
1943	1	105	49	.682	535,014	Billy Southworth
1944	1*	105	49	.682	486,751	Billy Southworth
1945	2	95	59	.617	594,180	Billy Southworth
1946	1*	98	58	.628	1,062,553	Eddie Dyer
1947	2	89	65	.578	1,248,013	Eddie Dyer
1948	2	85	69	.552	1,111,454	Eddie Dyer
1949	2	96	58	.623	1,430,676	Eddie Dyer
1950	5	78	75	.519	1,093,199	Eddie Dyer
1951	3	81	73	.526	1,013,429	Marty Marion
1952	3	88	66	.571	913,113	Eddie Stanky
1953	3+	83	71	.539	880,242	Eddie Stanky
1954	6	72	82	.468	1,039,698	Eddie Stanky
1955	7	68	86	.442	849,130	Stanky & Harry Walker
1956	4	76	78	.494	1,029,773	Fred Hutchinson
1957	2	87	67	.565	1,183,575	Fred Hutchinson
1958	5+	72	82	.468	1,063,730	Hutchinson & Stan Hack
1959	7	71	83	.461	929,953	Solly Hemus
1960	3	86	68	.558	1,096,632	Solly Hemus
1961	5	80	74	.519	855,305	Hemus & Johnny Keane
1962	6	84	78	.519	953,895	Johnny Keane
1963	2	93	69	.574	1,170,546	Johnny Keane
1964	1*	93	69	.574	1,143,294	Johnny Keane
1965	7	80	81	.497	1,241,195	Albert Schoendienst
1966	6	83	79	.512	1,712,980	Albert Schoendienst
1967	1*	101	60	.627	2,090,145	Albert Schoendienst

347

Year	Position	Won	Lost	Pct.	Attendance	Manager
1968	1	97	65	.598	2,011,177	Albert Schoendienst
1969	4**	87	75	.537	1,682,583	Albert Schoendienst
1970	4	76	86	.469	1,628,729	Albert Schoendienst
1971	2	90	72	.556	1,604,671	Albert Schoendienst
1972	4	75	81	.481	1,196,894	Albert Schoendienst
1973	2	81	81	.500	1,574,012	Albert Schoendienst
1974	2	86	75	.535	1,838,413	Albert Schoendienst
1975	3★	82	80	.506	1,695,394	Albert Schoendienst
1976	5	72	90	.445	1,207,036	Albert Schoendienst
1977	3	83	79	.512	1,659,287	Vernon Rapp
1978	5	69	93	.426	1,278,175	Rapp, Jack Krol & Ken Boyer
1979	3	86	76	.531	1,627,256	Ken Boyer
1980	4	74	88	.457	1,385,147	Boyer, Jack Krol, Whitey Herzog, Albert Schoendienst
1981***	1	59	43	.578	1,010,247	Whitey Herzog
1982	1*	92	70	.568	2,111,906	Whitey Herzog
Totals		7,120	7,079	.501	66,034,979	

★ — Tied for Position   * — World Champions   ** — Start of Divisional Play

World Champions—1926, 1931, 1934, 1942, 1944, 1946, 1964, 1967, 1982.

Finished first 13 times, second 14 times, third 12 times, fourth 9 times, fifth 11 times, sixth 10 times, seventh 8 times, eighth 5 times.

*** — Split season due to players' strike. Cardinals finished second in each half, but had best over-all record in Eastern Division.

APPENDIX

1982 NATIONAL LEAGUE AND WORLD SERIES CHAMPIONSHIPS

Cardinals in National League Championship Series Play

Year	Opponent	Won	Lost	Pct.	Manager	Result
1982	Atlanta	3	0	1.000	Whitey Herzog	National League Champions

1982 National League Championship Series

St. Louis, Eastern Division 3, Atlanta, Western Division 0

Batting	Pos	G	AB	R	H	2B	3B	HR	RBI	BB	SO	SB	BA	Slug %
Keith Hernandez	1B	3	12	3	4	0	0	0	1	2	3	0	.333	.333
Tom Herr	2B	3	13	1	3	1	0	0	0	1	2	0	.231	.308
Ozzie Smith	SS	3	9	0	5	0	0	0	3	3	0	1	.556	.556
Ken Oberkfell	3B	3	15	1	3	0	0	0	2	0	0	0	.200	.200
Lonnie Smith	LF	3	11	1	3	0	0	0	1	0	1	0	.273	.273
Willie McGee	CF	3	13	4	4	0	2	1	5	0	5	0	.308	.846
George Hendrick	RF	3	13	2	4	0	0	0	2	1	2	0	.308	.308
Darrell Porter	C	3	9	3	5	3	0	0	1	5	2	0	.556	.889
Steve Braun	PH	1	1	0	0	0	0	0	0	0	0	0	.000	.000
David Green	LF	2	1	1	1	0	0	0	0	0	0	0	1.000	1.000
Bob Forsch	P	1	3	1	2	0	0	0	1	0	0	0	.666	.666
Joaquin Andujar	P	1	1	0	0	0	0	0	0	0	0	0	.000	.000
Doug Bair	P	1	0	0	0	0	0	0	0	0	0	0	.000	.000
John Stuper	P	1	1	0	0	0	0	0	0	0	0	0	.000	.000
Bruce Sutter	P	2	2	0	0	0	0	0	0	0	0	0	.000	.000
Dane Iorg	Did not play													
Gene Tenace	Did not play													
Mike Ramsey	Did not play													
Glenn Brummer	Did not play													
Julio Gonzalez	Did not play													
Jim Kaat	Did not play													
Jeff Lahti	Did not play													
Dave LaPoint	Did not play													
John Martin	Did not play													
Steve Mura	Did not play													
Team Totals		3	103	17	34	4	2	1	16	12	16	1	.330	.437

Double Plays — 3   Left on Bases — 31

LINESCORES:

FIRST GAME (Oct. 7, at St. Louis)
ATLANTA .... 0 0 0 0 0 0 0 0 0—0 3 0
ST. LOUIS .... 0 0 1 0 0 5 0 1 x—7 13 1
Perez, Bedrosian (6th), Moore (6th), Walk (8th)   W—Forsch
Forsch   L—Perez

SECOND GAME (Oct. 9, at St. Louis)
ATLANTA .... 0 0 2 0 1 0 0 0 0—3 6 0
ST. LOUIS .... 1 0 0 0 0 1 0 1 1—4 9 1
Niekro, Garber (8th)   W—Sutter
Stuper, Bair (7th), Sutter (8th)   L—Garber

THIRD GAME (Oct. 10, at Atlanta)
ST. LOUIS .... 0 4 0 0 1 0 0 0 1—6 12 0
ATLANTA .... 0 0 0 0 0 0 2 0 0—2 6 0
Andujar, Sutter (7th)   W—Andujar
Camp, Perez (2d), Moore (4th), Mahler (6th), Bedrosian   L—Camp
(8th), Garber (9th)

349

At 10:17 P.M., C.D.T. on October 20, 1982, all hell broke loose in St. Louis' Busch Memorial Stadium.

Cardinal pitcher Bruce Sutter had just struck out Milwaukee Brewer power hitter Gorman Thomas to give St. Louis its first World Series triumph since 1967. The celebration was on.

Thousands swarmed the field, despite warnings, police attack dogs, and mounted police. They stole the bases. They ripped the Astro Turf. They tried to take their heroes' clothing and, in some cases heads, as fall-classic memorabilia.

The Gateway City euphoria was indeed just. In fact, when Redbird patriarch August Busch, Jr. was told about the ripping of the infield carpet, he said in graveled tones "Who cares?"

The Cardinals won the Series in seven games, having come back from a three-games-to-two deficit. And they used the same method with which they captured the National League East Division title and later defeated the Atlanta Braves for the Senior Circuit title: Whitey Ball.

Named after manager Whitey Herzog, the game was hit and run, with lots of speed, speed, speed. The formula gave the Cards the division title on September 27, when they defeated the Montreal Expos 4–2 in Olympic Stadium. It gave them the League title October 10, when they won the final best-of-five game against the Braves, 6–2 in Atlanta.

In the Series, the Cards lost the first, fourth and fifth games, but came back. They did it with the bat of Series and League Championship Series MVP Darrell Porter; the pitching of Joaquin Andujar, whose status was doubtful after being hit on the right knee in game three, beat the Brew Crew in game seven, John Stuper and Bruce Sutter; the surprising fielding and hitting of rookie outfielder Willie McGee; the resurgence in games six and seven in St. Louis of the silent bats of Keith Hernandez and George Hendrick; and the sheer speed of Lonnie and Ozzie Smith.

The Series victory was St. Louis' ninth, more than any team except the New York Yankees.

1982
World Series

St. Louis N.L. 4, Milwaukee A.L. 3

Batting	Pos	G	AB	R	H	2B	3B	HR	RBI	BB	SO	SB	BA
St. Louis													
Keith Hernandez	1B	7	27	4	7	2	0	1	8	4	2	0	.259
Tom Herr	2B	7	25	2	4	2	0	0	5	3	3	0	.160
Ozzie Smith	SS	7	24	3	5	0	0	0	1	3	0	1	.208
Ken Oberkfell	3B	7	24	4	7	1	0	0	1	2	1	2	.292
Lonnie Smith	LF	7	28	6	9	4	1	0	1	1	5	2	.321
Willie McGee	CF	6	25	6	6	0	0	2	5	1	3	2	.240
George Hendrick	RF	7	28	5	9	0	0	0	5	2	2	0	.321
Darrell Porter	C	7	28	1	8	2	0	1	5	1	4	0	.286
Dane Iorg	DH	5	17	4	9	4	1	0	1	0	0	0	.529
Gene Tenace	DH-PH	5	6	0	0	0	0	0	0	1	2	0	.000
Steve Braun	DH-PH	2	2	0	1	0	0	0	2	1	0	0	.500
David Green	CF-PR-PH	7	10	3	2	1	1	0	0	1	3	0	.200
Mike Ramsey	PR-3B	3	1	1	0	0	0	0	0	0	1	0	.000
Glenn Brummer	C	1	0	0	0	0	0	0	0	0	0	0	.000
Julio Gonzalez	Did not play												
Team Total		7	245	39	67	16	3	4	34	20	26	7	.273

Double Plays—9   Left on Bases—49

Batting	Pos	G	AB	R	H	2B	3B	HR	RBI	BB	SO	SB	BA
Milwaukee													
Cecil Cooper	1B	7	28	3	8	1	0	1	6	1	1	0	.286
Jim Gantner	2B	7	24	5	8	4	1	0	4	1	1	0	.333
Robin Yount	SS	7	29	6	12	3	0	1	6	2	2	0	.414
Paul Molitor	3B	7	31	5	11	0	0	0	3	2	4	1	.355
Ben Oglivie	LF	7	27	4	6	0	1	1	1	2	4	0	.222
Gorman Thomas	CF	7	26	0	3	0	0	0	3	2	7	0	.115
Charlie Moore	RF	7	26	3	9	3	0	0	2	1	0	0	.346
Ted Simmons	C	7	23	2	4	0	0	2	3	5	3	0	.174
Roy Howell	DH	4	11	1	0	0	0	0	0	0	3	0	.000
Don Money	DH	5	13	4	3	1	0	0	1	2	3	0	.231
Marshall Edwards	PR-CF	1	0	0	0	0	0	0	0	0	0	0	.000
Ned Yost	C	1	0	0	0	0	0	0	0	1	0	0	.000
Rob Picciolo	Did not play												
Ed Romero	Did not play												
Mark Brouhard	Did not play												
Team Total		7	238	33	64	12	2	5	29	19	28	1	.269

Double Plays—3   Left on Bases—44

Pitching	G	GS	CG	IP	H	R	ER	BB	SO	W	L	SV	ERA
St. Louis													
Joaquin Andujar	2	2	0	13⅓	10	3	2	1	4	2	0	0	1.35
Doug Bair	3	0	0	2	2	2	2	2	3	0	1	0	9.00
Bob Forsch	2	2	0	12⅔	18	10	7	3	4	0	2	0	4.97
Jim Kaat	4	0	0	2⅓	4	1	1	2	2	0	0	0	3.86
Jeff Lahti	2	0	0	1⅔	4	2	2	1	1	0	0	0	10.80
Dave LaPoint	2	1	0	8⅓	10	6	3	2	3	0	0	0	3.24
John Stuper	2	2	1	13	10	5	5	5	5	1	0	0	3.46
Bruce Sutter	4	0	0	7⅔	6	4	4	3	6	1	0	2	4.70
John Martin	Did not play												
Steve Mura	Did not play												
Team Total	7	7	1	61	64	33	23	19	28	4	3	2	3.39

Pitching	G	GS	CG	IP	H	R	ER	BB	SO	W	L	SV	ERA
Milwaukee													
Dwight Bernard	1	0	0	1	0	0	0	0	1	0	0	0	0.00
Mike Caldwell	3	2	1	17⅔	19	4	4	3	6	2	0	0	2.04
Moose Haas	2	1	0	7⅓	8	7	6	3	4	0	0	0	7.36
Peter Ladd	1	0	0	⅔	1	0	0	2	0	0	0	0	0.00
Bob McClure	5	0	0	4⅓	5	2	2	3	5	0	2	2	4.15
Doc Medich	1	0	0	2	5	6	4	1	0	0	0	0	18.00
Jim Slaton	2	0	0	2⅔	1	0	0	2	1	1	0	0	0.00
Don Sutton	2	2	0	10⅓	12	11	9	1	5	0	1	0	7.84
Pete Vuckovich	2	2	0	14	16	9	7	5	4	0	1	0	4.50
Rollie Fingers	Did not play												
Team Totals	7	7	1	60	67	39	32	20	26	3	4	2	4.80

Total Attendance—384,570. Average Attendance—54,930. Club Share—$895,034.19.

LINESCORES:

FIRST GAME (Oct. 12, at St. Louis)
MILWAUKEE _____ 2 0 0 1 1 2 0 0 4—10 17 0
ST. LOUIS _____ 0 0 0 0 0 0 0 0 0— 0 3 1
Forsch, Kaat (6th), LaPoint (8th), Lahti (9th)   W—Caldwell
Caldwell   L—Forsch

SECOND GAME (Oct. 13, at St. Louis)
MILWAUKEE _____ 0 1 2 0 1 0 0 0 0—4 10 1
ST. LOUIS _____ 0 0 2 0 0 2 0 1 x—5 8 0
Sutton, McClure (7th), Ladd (8th)   W—Sutter
Stuper, Kaat (5th), Bair (5th), Sutter (7th)   L—McClure

THIRD GAME (Oct. 15, at Milwaukee)
ST. LOUIS _____ 0 0 0 0 3 0 2 0 1—6 6 1
MILWAUKEE _____ 0 0 0 0 0 0 0 2 0—2 5 3
Andujar, Kaat (7th), Bair (7th), Sutter (7th)   W—Andujar
Vuckovich, McClure (9th)   L—Vuckovich

352

FOURTH GAME (Oct. 16, at Milwaukee)
ST. LOUIS _____ 1 3 0   0 0 1   0 0 0—5 8 1
MILWAUKEE _____ 0 0 0   0 1 0   0 0 x—7 10 2
LaPoint, Bair (7th), Kaat (7th), Lahti (7th)   W—Slaton
Haas, Slaton (6th), McClure (8th)   L—Bair

FIFTH GAME (Oct. 17, at Milwaukee)
ST. LOUIS _____ 0 0 1   0 0 0   1 0 2—4 15 2
MILWAUKEE _____ 1 0 1   0 1 0   1 2 x—6 11 1
Forsch, Sutter (8th)   W—Caldwell
Caldwell, McClure (9th)   L—Forsch

SIXTH GAME (Oct. 19, at St. Louis)
MILWAUKEE _____ 0 0 0   0 0 0   0 0 1— 1 4 4
ST. LOUIS _____ 0 2 0   3 2 6   0 0 x—13 12 1
Sutton, Slaton (5th), Medich (6th), Bernard (8th)   W—Stuper
Stuper   L—Sutton

SEVENTH GAME (Oct. 20, at St. Louis)
MILWAUKEE .... 0 0 0   0 1 2   0 0 0—3 7 0
ST. LOUIS .... 0 0 0   1 0 3   0 2 x—6 15 1
Vuckovich, McClure (6th), Haas (6th), Caldwell (8th) W—Andujar
Andujar, Sutter (8th)   L—McClure

National League Championship Series Most Valuable Player

1982   Darrell Porter

Sport Magazine World Series Most Valuable Player

1964   Bob Gibson
1967   Bob Gibson
1982   Darrell Porter